The Landscape of Family Business

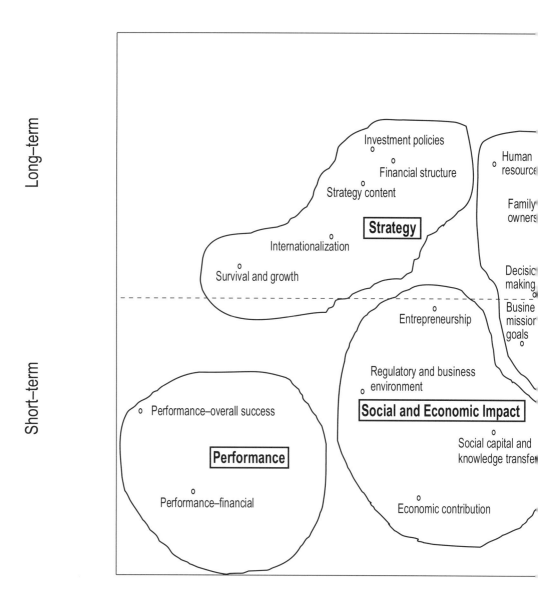

Source: adapted from Yu, Lumpkin, Sorenson, & Brigham, 2012.

Figure P.1   A Map of the Landscape of Family Business

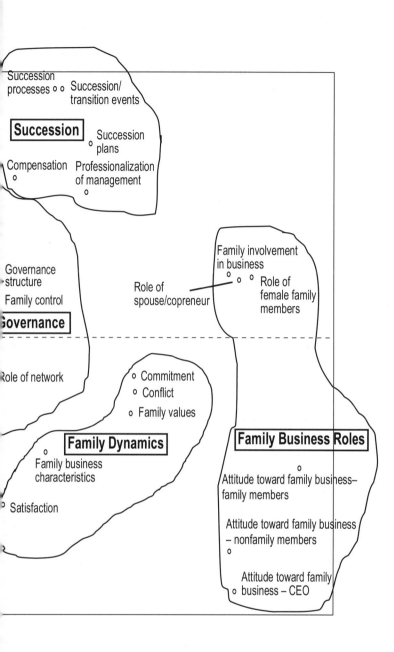

Succession
processes o o Succession/
transition events

Succession   o Succession
plans

Compensation   Professionalization
o   of management
  o

Family involvement
in business
o
o o Role of
Role of   female family
spouse/copreneur   members

Governance
structure

Family control

Governance

Role of network

o Commitment
o Conflict
o Family values

Family Dynamics

o
Family business
characteristics

Satisfaction

Family Business Roles

o
Attitude toward family business–
family members

Attitude toward family business
– nonfamily members
o

Attitude toward family
o business – CEO

Family

Cluster Heading		Outcome Categories by Chapter								
	Category Heading	Chapter 1	Chapter 2	Chapter 3	Chapter 4	Chapter 5	Chapter 6	Chapter 7	Chapter 8	Chapter 9
Family/Business — Governance	Business mission/goals		•	•			•			
	Decision making	•	•	•				•		•
	Family control	•	•	•		•	•	•		
	Family ownership	•	•	•			•	•		
	Governance structure	•	•	•		•	•	•	•	•
	Human resources	•	•	•		•		•		
	Role of the network		•					•		
Business — Performance	Performance-financial	•	•	•			•		•	•
	Performance-overall success	•	•	•			•		•	•
Business — Social and Economic Impact	Entrepreneurship	•			•	•				•
	Economic contribution	•			•				•	•
	Regulatory and business environment	•		•	•		•	•		
	Social capital and knowledge transfer	•			•				•	
Business — Strategy	Financial structure	•		•	•	•		•		
	Internationalization					•				
	Investment policies			•		•				•
	Strategy content				•	•	•		•	
	Survival and growth		•			•		•	•	•

Cluster Heading		Category Heading	Outcome Categories by Chapter								
			Chapter 1	Chapter 2	Chapter 3	Chapter 4	Chapter 5	Chapter 6	Chapter 7	Chapter 8	Chapter 9
Family	Family Business Roles	Attitude toward family business- CEO	•					•			
		Attitude toward family business- family members	•		•			•		•	
		Attitude toward family business and non-family members			•			•			•
		Family involvement in business	•		•			•	•	•	•
		Role of the spouse/ copreneur	•					•	•		
		Role of female family members						•	•	•	
	Family Dynamics	Commitment						•	•	•	•
		Conflict		•	•			•	•	•	•
		Family business characteristics	•		•			•	•		•
		Family values	•	•		•	•	•	•	•	
		Satisfaction	•		•			•	•		•
	Succession	Compensation	•								
		Profession-alization of management	•		•			•	•	•	
		Succession processes	•		•			•	•	•	•
		Succession plans	•	•				•		•	
		Succession transition event	•					•	•	•	

The Landscape of Family Business

Edited by

Ritch L. Sorenson
University of St. Thomas, USA

Andy Yu
University of Wisconsin-Whitewater, USA

Keith H. Brigham
Texas Tech University, USA

G.T. Lumpkin
Syracuse University, USA

Edward Elgar
Cheltenham, UK • Northampton, MA, USA

Published by
Edward Elgar Publishing Limited
The Lypiatts
15 Lansdown Road
Cheltenham
Glos GL50 2JA
UK

Edward Elgar Publishing, Inc.
William Pratt House
9 Dewey Court
Northampton
Massachusetts 01060
USA

A catalogue record for this book
is available from the British Library

Library of Congress Control Number: 2013938071

This book is available electronically in the ElgarOnline.com
Business Subject Collection, E-ISBN 978 1 78254 754 9

ISBN 978 1 78254 753 2 (cased)

Typeset by Servis Filmsetting Ltd, Stockport, Cheshire
Printed and bound in Great Britain by T.J. International Ltd, Padstow

Contents

Figures

Tables

Contributors

Massimo Baù

Massimo is a Research Fellow at the Centre for Family Enterprise and Ownership, at Jönköping International Business School. His research topics are related with the entrepreneurial process and their relationship to three main research areas: First, family dynamics and the influence of family members on the actor's decisions, and the entry and exit in the entrepreneurial process through the embeddedness perspective; second, academic entrepreneurship and factors enabling new venture startup and technology transfer; third, the firm's growth paths through collaborative agreements and inter-firms networks.

Keith H. Brigham

Keith H. Brigham is an Associate Professor of Entrepreneurship and the Director of Entrepreneurship Programs at the Rawls College of Business at Texas Tech University. His primary research interests are in entrepreneurship, entrepreneurial cognition and decision-making, and family business. His research has been published in a number of journals such as the *Journal of Business Venturing, Entrepreneurship Theory & Practice, Family Business Review, Organizational Research Methods, Business Ethics Quarterly*, and *The Leadership Quarterly*. He currently serves on the editorial review board of *Family Business Review*.

Mary Schmid Daugherty

Mary is an Associate Professor of Finance at the University of St. Thomas. Mary teaches corporate finance and investment related topics at the undergraduate, graduate and executive level. In addition to her teaching duties, Mary is the lead faculty member for the Aristotle Fund, a student-managed portfolio responsible for approximately $3 million dollars of the university's endowment. Mary co-authored the fourth edition of the book, *Family Business*, with Ernesto Poza. Mary also consults family business owners on financial education and family/board governance issues to help enhance the value of their business. Mary has held a variety of leadership positions in the Association for Investment Management and Research, served as President of the Chartered Financial Analyst Society of Minnesota, and serves on a number of private business and public boards. Mary is a proud owner and board member of a third-generation family business.

Gregory G. Dess

Greg is the Andrew R. Cecil Endowed Chair in Management, at the University of Texas at Dallas. Greg's primary research interests are in strategic management, entrepreneurship, and knowledge management. He has published articles in leading academic and practitioner journals such as *Academy of Management Journal, Strategic Management Journal, Academy of Management Review, Strategic Management Journal*, and *Administrative Science Quarterly*. He presently serves on several editorial boards including *Strategic Entrepreneurship Journal* and *Journal of Business Venturing*. In 2000, he was inducted as one of 33 charter members of the Academy of Management Journals' Hall of Fame. He has also co-authored several books, including *Strategic Management: Text and Cases* (2012) as well as two books targeted at the practitioner market: *Beyond Productivity* (1999), and *Mission Critical* (1997).

Prior to joining the University of Texas at Dallas in 2002, he spent six years as the Gatton Endowed Chair at the University of Kentucky and has served on the faculties of the University of Texas at Arlington, Florida State University, and the University of South Carolina. Greg received his bachelor's degree from Georgia Tech (1971), his MBA from Georgia State University (1976) and his PhD from the University of Washington (1980).

Karin Hellerstedt

Karin is an Assistant Professor at Jönköping International Business School. She has conducted research on entrepreneurship and knowledge intensive industries, and on how firms and entrepreneurial teams are formed and develop over time. She has been involved in several research projects dealing with aspects of entrepreneurship such as, academic, rural and knowledge-intensive entrepreneurship. Karin has written and published various research reports and also published in international peer-review journals. Her current research is centered on ownership transitions and the succession of privately held businesses, and the short- and long-term effects that firm failure may have on its' owners and their family members.

Frank Hoy

Frank is the Paul R. Beswick Professor of Innovation & Entrepreneurship at Worcester Polytechnic Institute. Recently, he and co-author, Pramodita Sharma, published the book *Entrepreneurial Family Firms* (Pearson, 2010). Frank serves as president of the Family Enterprise Research Conference. He is a member of the global board of directors of the Successful Transgenerational Entrepreneurship Practices (STEP) project. Frank is a Fellow of the Family Firm Institute and the International Family Enterprise Research Academy. From 1988 to 1991, he held the Carl R. Zwerner Professorship of Family-Owned Businesses at Georgia State University and from 1991 to 2001 was Dean of the College of Business Administration at the University of Texas at El Paso.

Franz W. Kellermanns

Franz is a Professor of Management in the College of Business at the University of Tennessee. He holds a joint appointment with the INTES Center at the WHU–Otto Beisheim School of Management (Germany). He received his PhD from the University of Connecticut. His research interests include strategy process and entrepreneurship with a focus on family business research. He is an associate editor of *Family Business Review* and has published in journals such as *Organization Science, Journal of Management, Journal of Management Studies, Journal of Organizational Behavior, Journal of Business Venturing, Entrepreneurship Theory and Practice, Academy of Management Learning and Education*, etc. He serves on the editorial boards of *Entrepreneurship Theory and Practice, Journal of Business Venturing, Journal of Management, Journal of Management Studies, Journal of Family Business Strategy and Strategic Entrepreneurship Journal*.

G.T. Lumpkin

Tom is the Witting Chair of Entrepreneurship and head of the Department of Entrepreneurship and Emerging Enterprises at the Whitman School of Management at Syracuse University in New York. Tom's primary research interests include entrepreneurial orientation, social entrepreneurship, opportunity recognition, family business, and strategy-making processes. Tom is a globally recognized scholar publishing and serving on editorial boards of several premier journals such as *Academy of Management Journal, Academy of Management Review, Entrepreneurship Theory and Practice, Journal of Business Venturing, Strategic Entrepreneurship Journal, and Family Business Review*. He currently serves as co-editor of *Strategic Entrepreneurship Journal*. In 2009, Tom received the IDEA Awards' Foundational Paper award from the Academy of Management for the paper, "Clarifying the Entrepreneurial Orientation Construct and Linking it to Performance" (1996). Recently, Tom and co-authors, Greg Dess, Alan Eisner, and Gerry McNamara published the sixth edition of the textbook, *Strategic Management: Creating Competitive Advantages*. Tom received his PhD in Business Administration from the University of Texas in Arlington and his MBA from the University of Southern California.

Mattias Nordqvist

Mattias is the Hamrin International Professor of Family Business and co-director of the Center for Family Enterprise and Ownership at Jönköping International Business School in Sweden. He is on the faculty of the Department of Entrepreneurship, Strategy, Organization and Leadership where he also has served as the associate dean for doctoral programs. Mattias is a former co-director of the global Successful Transgenerational Entrepreneurship Practices (STEP) project and a visiting scholar at Babson College, USA, the University of Alberta, Canada, and Bocconi University, Italy. He was selected as a "Family Owned Business Institute Scholar" twice; 2007–2008 and 2011–2012 by the Seidman College of Business at Grand Valley State University in Grand Rapids, Michigan, and won the Family Firm Institute's award for the "Best Unpublished Research Paper" in 2005 and again in 2011. Mattias also received the "Young Entrepreneurship Researcher" award in 2006 from the Swedish Entrepreneurship Forum and the Swedish Agency for Economic and Regional Growth.

Kirby Rosplock

Kirby is Director of Research and Development at GenSpring Family Offices. Kirby has extensively researched family wealth and the family office and is a published author and speaker on the topics. Kirby also conducted research on women and wealth and men and wealth as well as the intersections of entrepreneurship in family businesses and family offices. Kirby is the editor of GenSpring's *A Thought Leader's Guide to Family Wealth* (2009), comprised of insights from leading family wealth experts and created in celebration of the firm's 20th anniversary. Kirby is a fifth-generation family member of a separate family enterprise. Kirby directs and co-researches with notable scholars in the field including, Dr. Dianne H.B. Welsh, from the University of North Carolina – Greensboro, and Dr. Juan Roure and Juan Luis Segurado, from the IESE Business School at the University of Navarra.

Pramodita Sharma

Dita is the Sanders Professor for Family Business at the School of Business Administration at the University of Vermont. Prior to this appointment, she was the CIBC Distinguished Professor of Family Business at the John Molson School of Business, Concordia University in Montreal. Her research on the succession, governance, innovation, and the unique dynamics underlying family firms has been honored with several international awards including the NFIB "Best Dissertation" award from the Academy of Management. In 2011, Dita was presented with the Family Firm Institute's prestigious Barbara Hollander award. Dita has co-authored two books and published approximately 50 scholarly articles and book chapters on family business. Dita is active in leadership and advisory roles in several professional associations including her role as editor-in-chief of the *Family Business Review* and as a co-founder of the *Family Enterprise Research Conference*. Dita is a frequent speaker at gatherings of family business leaders and her research remains focused on issues of significant importance to the family business community. Dita's experiences as a member of a family enterprise prepare her understanding of the complexity and dynamics of family business.

Ritch L. Sorenson

Ritch is a Full Professor and teaches a graduate and undergraduate class on family business management at the University of St. Thomas. Ritch was an early pioneer in establishing family business education. He continues to develop new courses and an academic concentration in family business at St. Thomas. Ritch is an associate editor for *Family Business Review*, the premier journal in family business, and publishes research in top management journals. In addition to his journal publications, Ritch recently co-authored and edited the book *Family Business and Social Capital* (2011). In 2008, Ritch led the development of a unique series of family business conferences at the University of St. Thomas on family capital. In addition to his duties at Saint Thomas, he is an active participant in many professional organizations including the Family Firm Institute, the United States Association for Small Business and Entrepreneurship, and the Academy of Management.

Laura J. Stanley

Laura is an Assistant Professor of Management in the College of Business at East Carolina University. She received her PhD in Management from the University of Georgia. She holds an MS in accounting and a BS in business administration from UNC-Chapel Hill. Her primary research interests include organizational commitment and emotions. Her work has appeared in such journals as *Entrepreneurship Theory and Practice*, *Journal of Vocational Behavior*, *Journal of Occupational and Organizational Psychology*, and *Human Performance*. She currently serves on the editorial board of *Journal of Vocational Behavior*. Outside of her university related activities, Laura worked as a human resource consultant for Aon Consulting and Arthur Andersen, LLP.

Karl Wennberg

Karl is an Assistant Professor at the Stockholm School of Economics and vice-President at the Ratio Institute. His research investigates the interaction between social influences and economic performance for entrepreneurial action. He has published in, among other journals, *Strategic Entrepreneurship Journal*, *Journal of Business Venturing*, *Management*

Science, Research Policy, and authored the book *The Birth, Growth and Demise of Entrepreneurial Firms* (Edward Elgar, 2010). His research earned best paper awards at Babson College Entrepreneurship Research Conference (2006) and the Academy of Management's Entrepreneurship Division (2008), and best dissertation award from the Academy of Management's Entrepreneurship Division (2010).

Andy Yu

Andy is an Assistant Professor of Management at the University of Wisconsin – Whitewater. He earned a doctorate in management and an MBA in marketing from Texas Tech University and received a BS in management information systems from National Chengchi University in Taiwan. He not only teaches entrepreneurship, strategy, and family business, but also had hands-on experience in new venture creation and family firms. He currently serves on the editorial review board of *Family Business Review* and has received several awards including "Best Paper" and the "Distinguished Reviewer" from the Entrepreneurship Division of Academy of Management, Family Business Review's "Outstanding Reviewer," and honorable mentions from the United States Association for Small Business and Entrepreneurship (USASBE). His research has appeared in *Family Business Review, Journal of Management Policy and Practice, and Advances in Entrepreneurship*, and *Firm Emergence and Growth: Entrepreneurship and Family Business*.

Foreword

Harry G. (Paddy) McNeely, III

About three years ago, Ritch Sorenson introduced me to the focus of this book, "A Map of the Landscape of Family Business," and indicated that it was a summary of 12 years of research about important outcomes in family business.* Because of my background, which includes 20 years of family business studies and working in our family-owned company, I was intrigued by the Landscape Map. The map depicts the key elements and processes that I have found at work in our family and business systems, and I was impressed that years of my family's learning, work, and trial and error were captured on one page.

In the late 1980's my father became committed to providing an opportunity for education about family business to my five siblings, myself, and our spouses. In 1990 my family enrolled in a family business program at Wharton. For several years we travelled quarterly to Philadelphia to learn from the early advisors in the family business field and to interact with other families enrolled in the program. We continued our learning experience at the newly formed Family Business Center at the University of St. Thomas. In addition, as a family group we spent many days working privately with impactful consultants who had a significant influence on our evolution as a business owning family.

Eventually, all of the education, theory, and trial by fire took hold and we began to develop formal and informal processes that led our business and family to become far more successful than we would have been otherwise.

The number one motivation for my interest in the Landscape Map is that *governance* is its central feature. Our family is focused on multi-generational ownership of the business. What success we've had in this regard is largely due to a strong commitment to effective governance. Our respect for strong governance has greatly improved the performance of the business and made the family more disciplined, thorough, and accountable to each other and the business.

More than 20 years ago my father created a very talented, committed, and independent board of directors. The board has had an invaluable impact on our business. A decade ago the board and management developed an Annual Business and Strategic Planning Calendar that is used to regularly examine our business strategy and the impact of social and economic trends, which are significant areas on the Landscape Map. Not unexpectedly, this has substantially improved our family and business performance.

In addition to the board, the family – including shareholders and spouses – has a significant role in the governance functions on the Landscape Map. In our case, family governance is continuing to evolve, and as the ownership has become multi-generational,

---

* To better understand this discussion of the Landscape Map, it would be useful to first look at "A Map of the Landscape of Family Business" located inside the front cover of this book.

we see the need for more formality and structure to heighten transparency, inclusiveness and participation.

With the goal of becoming a multi-generational entity, *succession* was a paramount task. Succession of ownership and leadership in the business and family are pivotal events. As the Landscape Map illustrates, succession is closely linked to governance, but it is also dependent on the development of *family roles* and the recognition of the importance of *family dynamics*. We had many occasions in seminars and working with experts in the field that were focused on strengthening our familial relationships and developing the qualities of individual family members. Success in these areas is just as essential as success in business.

In addition, I was impressed with another aspect of the Landscape Map's layout: the issues for both the business and family systems that arise with greater frequency are found on the bottom of the map, and those of lesser frequency, but which may have a more significant impact, are found on the top. This reflects what I have learned about family business – family and business skills, and unity are built over time.

After Ritch presented the Landscape Map, I thought it would be interesting to populate the map with our family and business practices. Ritch provided me an electronic copy and, using my own labels, I added our practices to each of the key areas of the map. In essence, this was a summary of 20 years work by the family, board, and management team. Mapping our family business activities was largely an intuitive task, and through creating our family business map, I became more impressed with the practical value and the research behind the Landscape Map.

When I showed my version of the map to Ritch, he invited me to present it to his Family Business class. Since then, I have presented our family business map to family business owners at the University of St. Thomas and the University of Pittsburgh. In addition, I participated in a conference where owners, advisors, and researchers gathered to discuss the Landscape Map. At Ritch's request, I have included my version of the Landscape Map in Appendix A of this book.

After using the map and discussing it with family business stakeholders, its value is clear to me. The Landscape Map provides owners a way to summarize and assess important outcomes within their family businesses; it provides advisors a way to help owners balance and navigate the complexities of family business ownership; and it provides scholars a way to link the research with application. Based on my own experience and application, I endorse "A Map of the Landscape of Family Business" as a helpful tool owners may use to understand their family business.

Paddy McNeely is the Chairman and CEO of Meritex, based in Minneapolis, MN. Paddy's family has been recognized as Family Business of the Year by the State of Minnesota. Paddy serves as the Chair of the Advisory Board for the Family Business Center at the University of St. Thomas, where he frequently speaks about family business.

Acknowledgements

The publication of this book represents the labors of many people, but primarily Andy Yu working closely with his dissertation chair, Tom Lumpkin, to develop the research design and carry out the four studies included in the paper entitled "The landscape of family business outcomes: A summary and numerical taxonomy of dependent variables." Ritch Sorenson and Keith Brigham actively participated in that research effort and joined Andy and Tom in developing the paper.

We were encouraged when this original landscape paper received a "best paper" award at the 2009 Academy of Management Conference. So, we continued to develop the paper and ultimately submitted it to the 25th Anniversary Edition of *Family Business Review*. Pramodita Sharma, James Chrisman, and Kelin Gersick, editors for 25th anniversary edition, provided especially helpful developmental feedback.

Other scholars who provided evaluation and feedback that ultimately produced the Landscape Map included Elaine Allen, Ray Bagby, Isabel Botero, Sharon Danes. Alan Carsrud, Gibb Dyer, Tomasz Fediuk, Frank Hoy, Franz Kellermanns, Michael Lubatkin, Jeffrey Pollack, Ernesto Poza, Carol Sánchez, William Schulze, Tom Schwartz, Manisha Singal, David Sirmon, Alex Stewart, Karen Vinton and John Ward.

We appreciate the insights provided by the family business owners, advisors, and scholars at a conference dedicated to the Landscape Map. The names of those participants are listed in Appendix C. The conference was sponsored by the Family Business Center at the University of St. Thomas in Minneapolis. We acknowledge the help of Sara McGinley, Director of the Family Business Center at St. Thomas, in managing the conference. Others who provided support for the conference were Kathy Sauro, Daniel Vevang, and Trina Smith.

We also acknowledge Grace Noyes who provided editorial feedback for manuscripts. Later, Joseph Grodahl Biever helped to prepare the final manuscript for submission to the publisher.

We express special appreciation to Jackie Milbrandt, Managing Editor for the book. Jackie has a Master's Degree in Teaching English and that, together with experience in supporting family business research for over three years, uniquely prepared her for the role. As a Managing Editor, Jackie corresponded with authors, organized and arranged content, obtained and edited biographies, consulted with the editors about the organization development of this book, and reviewed articles for content to develop the Outcome Categories by Chapter Table. Jackie's academic training enabled her to provide editorial and developmental feedback, organize content, and prepare the manuscript for the publisher. She has worked tirelessly on the book and deserves much credit for its completion.

Finally, we express special appreciation to the authors, listed in the table of contents, who have contributed chapters to this book. Many hours of writing and revising are represented in their writing. Their reward will be moving forward our understanding of family business.

Introduction: The landscape of family business

Ritch L. Sorenson, Andy Yu, Keith H. Brigham and G.T. Lumpkin

What are the important outcomes in family business? What are the relationships among those outcomes? And, what does an overall pattern of outcome relationships reveal about family business? The editors of this book, Ritch Sorenson, Andy Yu, Keith Brigham, and Tom Lumpkin, engaged in a literature review and additional research to answer these questions. The primary results of the study (Yu, Lumpkin, Sorenson, & Brigham, 2012) were an article that summarized 12 years of research on important family business outcomes and a figure that portrays these outcomes as a visual map.[1]

In this book, we refer to the research as "The Landscape of Family Business Outcomes" and to the figure as, "A Map of the Landscape of Family Business" or "Landscape Map."[2] Our purpose for publishing this book, *The Landscape of Family Business*, is to increase awareness about family business, encourage researchers to further explore family business outcomes, and invite owning families to use the Landscape Map as a tool to examine and improve their family businesses. As a visual representation of the current family business research, the Landscape Map will, undoubtedly, need to be updated as researchers uncover more about the family business landscape. Although the research (Yu et al., 2012) revealed much about the landscape of family business, research about family business is rapidly expanding.

This introduction combined with material included just inside the front cover of the book enable readers to get the most out of the book. For easy reference, readers will find "A Map of the Landscape of Family Business" just inside the book's front cover. This Landscape Map will help readers place specific outcomes within the context of the overall landscape of family business. The remainder of this introduction provides a description of the background and purpose of the book. And finally, this introduction also provides a brief summary of each chapter. To begin with, we provide an overview of the Landscape Map.

The landscape map

We believe that readers may gain many insights about family businesses by studying the Landscape Map that is located inside the front cover of the book. The Landscape Map provides a comprehensive visual aid that reflects the scope of family business outcomes and helps define their relationship to one another. Below, we provide a description of how the Landscape Map was developed, its features – dimensions, clusters, and categories.

As described in greater detail in Chapter 1 of this book, we (Sorenson, Yu, Brigham and Lumpkin) conducted a series of studies to identify and categorize family business outcomes (Yu et al., 2012). In addition, we obtained expert ratings of similarities among outcome categories and used a statistical procedure to create a visual representation of the relationships among family business outcomes. The figure originally titled, "Landscape of Family Business Outcomes," is referred to here as "A Map of the Landscape of Family Business."

The Landscape Map was the result of cluster analyses that plotted categories of family business outcomes in two dimensions. The two dimensions of the Landscape Map represent a conceptual framework of the potential outcomes in family businesses. It includes a systems dimension (family/business) on the horizontal axis and a temporal dimension (short-term/long-term) on the vertical axis. The combination of family and business systems makes family businesses unique. Family involvement in business is related to a concern about long-term outcomes. Thus, multi-generational family businesses attend to both family and long-term outcomes.

In addition to the visual depiction of family business outcomes on the systems and temporal dimensions, the Landscape Map also provides us with seven outcome clusters within the family business landscape: 1) Performance, 2) Strategy, 3) Social and Economic Impact, 4) Family Dynamics, 5) Family Business Roles, 6) Succession, and 7) Governance (see Landscape Map). Each cluster represents conceptually related outcome categories. For example, within the Performance cluster are the outcome categories are "performance – overall success," and "performance – financial."

The clusters represent categorizations of outcomes used in family business research. As is reported in Yu et al. (2012) and in Chapter 1, we examined 12 years of studies published in nine journals and identified 327 outcome variables studied in family business research. Based on similarities among these outcomes, we grouped them into 34 outcome categories.[3] It is important to note that these were the outcomes identified in the family business research literature and hence capture the empirical outcomes reported in those journals between 1998 and 2009. The articles that were used to obtain the outcome variables are summarized in Appendix B.

Then, using a Delphi technique, researchers categorized the outcome variables, resulting in 34 categories. Next, to expand beyond the categories and understand how they were conceptually related, family business experts engaged in a judgment task designed to create an overall classification. That is, these experts were asked to sort the 34 categories into groupings based on similarity. Based on the expert assessment of similarities among categories, we used a statistical procedure to create a visual summary of relationships among categories, which produced the seven clusters that can be seen in "A Map of the Landscape of Family Business" (See Chapter 1 and Yu et al., 2012 for a more detailed description of the research). Note that while the clusters are represented as distinct groupings, there are conceptual overlaps and linkages among the outcomes and clusters.

As was mentioned above, each chapter in the book focuses on one of the seven clusters. However, because of the overlap that naturally occurs when discussing the complexities of family businesses, the authors for each chapter also made comments about outcomes from other clusters. For example, the cluster focus in Chapter 3 is Performance, yet the outcome category "conflict," represented in the Family Dynamics cluster, is also discussed.

Background and purpose for book

After the Landscape Map was developed, the editors of this book spent time contemplating the overall utility of the figure. During those discussions, we realized that the Landscape Map helped us to better visualize the content and understand the nature of family business. While the applications for the research community were apparent, we wondered if practitioners would feel the same way if they examined the Landscape Map. So, as he had done previously, in the fall of 2010, Ritch Sorenson sponsored a multi-stakeholder family business conference at the University of St. Thomas in Minneapolis.[4] Family business owners and advisors were invited to join family business researchers in a dialogue about the "Landscape of Family Business Outcomes" research and figure.

At the Landscape conference, Andy Yu gave a presentation summarizing the Landscape research and presenting the map. Then, papers were presented about different clusters with the map: Mary Daugherty presented a paper on family business performance, Tom Lumpkin and Greg Dess presented on strategy, Keith Brigham presented on the social and economic impact of family business, and Ritch Sorenson presented on governance.[5] Following the presentations, conference participants engaged in dialogue about the presentations and added their insights and perspectives.

Because conference participants were unfamiliar with Landscape research, at first they were curious about the Landscape Map, but uncertain of its applications. However, as the conference progressed and dialogue about the Landscape continued, both practitioners and researchers gained insights about family business. Everyone, including practitioners, suggested potential applications for the Landscape Map. Family business owners made the following comments.

> *When you are in a family business that is actually active and functioning there are a lot of pieces that are scattered all over the place. This makes your family grow tired and your business grow tired, and any tools that we can have as a family to pull all those pieces together is very exciting. (University of St. Thomas, Landscape Conference, 2010)*

> *Where I'm coming from is that somewhere along the line I've got to implement it and to me the implementation is more important than the diagram, but I believe the diagram is a road map to get me to the implementation. (University of St. Thomas, Landscape Conference, 2010)*

Some practitioners were very enthusiastic about the Landscape Map and the opportunity to use it. One family business advisor made the following comment:

> *So what I see from this is perhaps a checklist of questions that might help unearth what they [family business owners] want; what they're thinking about; and how to go to the next generation to try and build a consensus among the different groups. (University of St. Thomas, Landscape Conference, 2010)*

The final presentation of the conference was given by Franz Kellermanns,[6] a well-known family business scholar who attended the conference. In his presentation, he provided a review and synthesis for the overall Landscape, suggesting how researchers might conceptualize the Landscape Map and outcomes research for further study.

Immediately following the conference, we, the editors for this book, met to discuss our impressions of the conference. We were pleased by the positive reception to the

Landscape research. And, given the insights gained from discussing the map, we were encouraged to 1) move forward in preparing a paper for publication summarizing the Landscape research, and 2) further develop the conference papers into a book.

Consistent with our determination, the four studies that comprised the original research about family business outcomes were published in the 25th Anniversary Edition of *Family Business Review* under the title, "The Landscape of Family Business Outcomes: A Summary and Numerical Taxonomy of Dependent Variables" (Yu et al., 2012). While the research paper was prepared for publication, we also worked to develop the conference papers for this book. Using the seven clusters revealed in the Landscape Map as the organizing framework, we asked the scholars who presented at the conference to further develop their papers by incorporating relevant research about family business and insights gained from the conference. Though all seven clusters were discussed during the conference, only four clusters were represented as conference papers. So, we invited additional family business scholars to read our initial research paper (Yu et al., 2012) and write chapters about the three remaining clusters. The following scholars graciously agreed to write chapters for this book: Pramodita Sharma and Frank Hoy wrote a paper about family business roles; Kirby Rosplock authored a paper about family dynamics; and, Massimo Baù, Karin Hellerstedt, Mattias Nordqvist, and Karl Wennberg wrote a paper about succession. Based on their review and analysis, the authors for each of the chapters also provide thoughtful suggestions for further research and practical applications of the Landscape. Below, we provide an overview summary of each of the chapters in the book.

Chapter summaries

The book is organized so that the first and last chapters provide an introduction and final commentary about the Landscape Map. Chapter 1, written by Andy Yu, provides an overview of the original research that produced "A Map of the Landscape of Family Business," and adds details about the clusters and categories within the map. Chapter 9, written by Franz Kellermanns and Laura Stanley, provides a conceptual framework for organizing the outcome clusters. Chapter 2 through Chapter 8 each focus on one of the seven clusters in the Landscape Map. Based on their review of the Yu et al. (2012) research, authors for each chapter describe implications for researchers and practical recommendations for practitioners.

As noted earlier, the Landscape Map has two dimensions – a business/family dimension and short-term/long-term dimension. Thus, the Landscape Map can be divided into quadrants: 1) a short-term business, 2) a long-term business, 3) a short-term family, and 4) a long-term family (see Landscape Map). Because of the relational implication of these quadrants, we will comment on the position of the clusters within the overall Landscape Map as we introduce each chapter.

Chapter 1:   Understanding the landscape of family business

This chapter, by Andy Yu, provides an overview and introduction to the *Landscape of Family Business*. Yu reviews the four studies that developed and validated the "Landscape of Family Business Outcomes" (Yu et al., 2012). Then, he discusses the rationale for selecting the two dimensions underlying the Landscape Map and the process of deriving the seven clusters in the Landscape Map. In addition, Yu includes tables that provide more complete detail than were included in Yu et al. (2012). One table briefly summarizes all dependent variables included in each outcome category. Another table lists experts' views of outcome variables that were either missing or underrepresented in family business research.

Chapter 2:   Governance within the two dimensions of family business

The Governance cluster spans into all four quadrants, but is located primarily in the long-term quadrants, suggesting that governance primarily has a long-term focus (see Landscape Map). Ritch Sorenson discusses the dimensions of the Landscape and the central position of governance in steering the family enterprise to obtain desired outcomes in part or all of the Landscape. He notes that decision-making is at the center of the overall Landscape. Sorenson then discusses how the following influence decisions: approaches to decision-making; structures and dispersion of family ownership; family control of ownership and the board, including board make up; family and non-family networks; family business mission and goals; and family resource policies.

Chapter 3:   Performance in family business: Financial and socio-emotional outcomes

This chapter examines the Performance cluster, which is found in the short-term business quadrant of the Landscape Map. This is the cluster that family business owners give most, if not all, of their attention. To survive and thrive, family businesses must deliver positive business outcomes. Mary Daugherty – a scholar, family business owner, and advisor – begins by describing how the addition of family makes business a unique structure. Then, she reviews literature about financial and socio-emotional outcomes and discusses the importance of these outcomes to family firms.

Chapter 4:   Social and economic impact of family business

In addition to the Performance cluster, the Social and Economic Impact cluster is found in the short-term business quadrant of the Landscape Map. Keith Brigham notes that outcomes in this category have received little research attention. This cluster focuses on how family businesses influence, and are influenced by, the economic, legal, and social environments. Brigham suggests that to survive family firms need to monitor their competition and foster an entrepreneurial mindset. He notes that family business social capital is unique because family business owners can retain social capital within communities and industries across generations through mentoring and educating family members to maintain relationships. Brigham also reviews research about the economic impact of family business and discusses the regulatory and business environment. Then, he suggests an integrating framework for the seemingly disparate outcome categories in this cluster.

Chapter 5:   Strategy in family business: Recent findings and future challenges

The Strategy cluster lies in the long-term business quadrant of the Landscape Map. Tom Lumpkin and Greg Dess indicate that although little research has been conducted about strategy in family business, family ownership influences strategy and can provide a strategic advantage. They discuss unique family business applications of business level strategies, namely: "familiness," family-based branding, internationalization, financial structure, and investment policies. To promote strategic growth in family business, Lumpkin and Dess review the concept of "entrepreneurial orientation," and apply it to family businesses including discussion of outcomes such as innovativeness, risk taking, pro-activeness, competitive aggressiveness, and autonomy.

Chapter 6:   Family business roles

The Family Business Roles cluster is on the extreme family side of the Landscape Map but extends into both the short-and long-term term quadrants (see the Landscape Map). Outcome categories of attitude toward family business including family members, non-family members, and CEOs who work in the family business are in the short-term quadrant. And outcome categories related to family involvement and roles of family members in the business are in the long-term quadrant. In this chapter, Pramodita Sharma and Frank Hoy indicate that very little research has been conducted about family business roles, and then, they provide an extensive discussion of the topic.

   The chapter begins by exploring the question, "What is a family?" Sharma and Hoy then discuss family involvement as well as outsider and insider attitudes toward the family business enterprise. Using the three-circle model to frame a discussion of the roles of family and non-family members in a family business enterprise, Chapter 6 covers the roles of incumbents, next-generation family members, gender, in-laws, family, as well as non-family owners and employees.

Chapter 7:   Family dynamics in the family business

Together with the "attitude" portion of Family Business Roles cluster, the Family Dynamics cluster lies in the short-term family quadrant of the Landscape Map. Kirby Rosplock writes from the perspective of a family business scholar, owner, and advisor. She begins by reviewing the potential advantages inherent in family businesses, including family values, brand, identity, patient capital, and "familiness." Rosplock then discusses issues that can produce conflict and disrupt family dynamics such as sibling rivalry, nepotism, gender bias, and the "shirtsleeves-to-shirtsleeves" cycle in family businesses. She also provides insights about managing conflict and developing family satisfaction and commitment.

Chapter 8:   Succession in family firms

The Succession cluster together with the roles characteristics in the Family Business Roles cluster make up the long-term family quadrant in the Landscape Map. Massimo Baù, Karin Hellerstedt, Mattias Nordqvist, and Karl Wennberg provide a comprehensive academic review of the literature on family business succession covering 15 years. These authors used a cluster analysis to group studies. They reviewed studies about the external environment, the firm, and individual/interpersonal issues. In Chapter 8, the authors summarize research about *pre-succession* participant attitudes and relationships; *planning for succession*, including managing contingencies and the effects of planning on relationships; *managing succession* in terms of family relationships, internal and external succession, co-habitation of predecessors and successors; and *post-succession*. They also summarize multilevel studies and make recommendations for future research including a focus on ownership transition, examining the succession context, and considering the impact of succession on the firm and on economic development.

Chapter 9: A second look and commentary on the landscape of family business

Franz Kellermanns and Laura Stanley provide an overview and commentary about the outcome clusters in the Landscape Map. First, they refer to the "macro outcomes" within the family business Performance and Succession clusters and suggest that without posi- tive outcomes in these clusters, the family business would be jeopardized. Second, they refer to the Governance, Strategy, and Social and Economic Impact clusters as "inter- mediate business-related outcomes," which either facilitate or hinder the aforementioned macro-level outcomes. Finally, they label the Family Business Roles and the Family Dynamics clusters as "softer outcomes." Finally, Kellermanns and Stanley discuss the nature, interdependence, and mutual influence of these three cluster groups.

Summary

While we believe readers will obtain many insights by reading the individual chapters, none of the authors in this book limited their discussion exclusively to their own cluster. To make sense of their assigned cluster within the context of the Landscape, the authors discuss how the outcomes within their cluster relate to each other and to other clusters' outcomes in the Landscape Map.

Thus, we invite readers to reflect on the overall Landscape and the interconnections of outcomes across the entire Landscape Map. For example, the Performance, Strategy, Succession, and Family Business Roles clusters appear to anchor the boundaries of family business. As Kellermans and Stanley suggest, owners need performance and suc- cession to survive as a family business. Although Kellermanns and Stanley provide one perspective that seems to have merit, there are likely other meaningful interpretations. The editors of this book would add that survival as a family business also requires good strategy and family member participation, which may not be limited to ownership, but often, involves many more roles in governance, family, and the business.

If the Performance, Strategy, Succession, and Family Business Roles clusters are the anchors for family business, then the remaining three clusters perform mediating roles in maintaining the anchors. The Governance cluster, which falls in the heart of the Landscape Map, oversees and guides the overall enterprise to obtain desired outcomes and unify the four anchor clusters. The Family Dynamics cluster helps families to iden- tify common values, engage in communication, and manage conflict so as to maintain the satisfaction and commitment needed to perform in the Family Business Roles cluster. And, the Social and Economic Impact cluster enables family business owners to maintain social and entrepreneurial connections with the larger community and industry which contributes to the business' ability to maintain performance.

In a broad sense, this book provides a visual representation of the important outcomes in family business. Like a painting hanging in a gallery, the interpretation of the work will vary across individuals. Through their own unique lenses and perspectives, the individual authors of each chapter have offered their interpretation and extension of the Landscape Map. We invite readers to reflect on these and other possible interpretations of the Landscape Map, applying their own theoretical lenses and practical perspectives.

Notes

1. The original research published by Yu, Lumpkin, Sorenson and Brigham (2012) in the 25th Anniversary edition of *Family Business Review* was titled, "The landscape of family business outcomes: A summary and numerical taxonomy of dependent variables."
2. The figure, "A Map of the Landscape of Family Business" was originally titled, "The Landscape of Family Business Outcomes."
3. See Appendix 1 in Yu, Chapter 1.
4. Previous multi-stakeholder conferences held at the University of St Thomas (Minneapolis) addressed family capital (2008) and family social capital (2009). The papers from the family capital conference were published in 2009 in *Family Business Review*, 22, issues 3 and 4. The papers for the family social capital conference were published in, Sorenson, R.L. (Ed.) (2011). *Family business and social capital*. Cheltenham, UK, and Northampton, MA, USA: Edward Elgar Publishing.
5. Short biographies for all paper authors are provided following this introduction.
6. Laura Stanley joined Franz Kellermanns in writing a chapter in this book that comments on the Landscape of Family Business Outcomes.

1. Understanding the landscape of family business

Andy Yu

Introduction

Yu, Lumpkin, Sorenson, and Brigham (2012) recently published a paper titled, "The landscape of family business outcomes: A summary and numerical taxonomy of dependent variables." One purpose of that paper was to summarize outcomes (dependent measures) used in empirical family business research, and another was to identify areas for future research. As a result of Yu et al.'s (2012) research, a new visual framework for understanding family business was developed.* The figure, titled the "Landscape of Family Business Outcomes," was created to help family business scholars and owners understand the importance and impact of family business outcomes. Understanding these outcomes is critical for both family business owners and researchers; it confirms what we know about family businesses and what we need to know in the future to create more positive outcomes.

To achieve their goals and identify the outcome measures being used in family business research and identify future areas of study, Yu et al. (2012) asked three questions: "(a) What dependent variables are currently used in family business research and which ones are unique to the domain? (b) What are the relationships among those dependent variables? (c) What dependent variables are missing from family business research or deserve more attention?"(p. 34).

The importance of outcome research and its impact in the field of family business is explained by Yu et al. (2012) in the following excerpt:

> Indeed, dependent variables help define a domain's boundaries. For example, financial performance is one of the defining outcome variables in strategic management (e.g., Ketchen, Thomas, & McDaniel, 1996; Nag, Hambrick, & Chen, 2007), and opportunity recognition is regarded as a core outcome in entrepreneurship (e.g., Busenitz et al., 2003; Short, Ketchen, Shook, & Ireland, 2010). By looking at its critical dependent variables, scholars in the family business discipline can gain a deeper understanding of the scope and distinctiveness of the field. (p. 34)

By obtaining such an overview of outcome measures, we can enhance our understanding of how outcomes impact family businesses and how owners and scholars may benefit from this knowledge.

---

* "A Map of the Landscape of Family Business" (also referred to as the Landscape Map) can be found on the page just inside the cover of this book and in the Yu, Lumpkin, Sorenson, and Brigham (2012) article published in *Family Business Review*. Following the Landscape Map, the "Outcome Categories by Chapter Table" (also referred to as the Outcome Categories Table) is provided. This table shows all chapters that contain content about the outcome categories that appear in this chapter.

One way family business owners can benefit from this research is in the depth of their understanding of the outcomes associated with family business. If family business owners understand how outcomes are important to family businesses and how they differ from those found in non-family businesses, it may help them accept these differences as well as adopt appropriate actions (e.g., systematic development of a family successor's business knowledge and social capital for positive succession outcomes). Once family business owners begin to understand how family firms are unique they can then clarify their family business identity, define outcomes important to that identity, and make informed decisions about how to obtain desired results. Thus, the research reported in Yu et al. (2012) may help family business owners further define and enhance their businesses.

One way scholars benefit from this research is in the advancement of the theories and knowledge within the field of family business (Chua, Chrisman, & Steier, 2003). Identifying dependent variables helps to establish the boundaries and uniqueness of the family business domain. As Sekaran (2002) pointed out, "the dependent variable is the variable of primary interest to the researcher" (p. 92). Thus, the Yu et al. (2012) article is important to scholars in that it provides a framework indicating outcomes specific to family businesses for prospective scholars to compare with outcomes associated with other types of businesses.

In this chapter, I will provide a brief overview of the research related to "The landscape of family business outcomes: A summary and numerical taxonomy of dependent variables" (Yu et al., 2012). In addition, I will introduce the Landscape Map and discuss its details. Furthermore, I will add to the Yu et al. (2012) article by contributing two appendices showing the complete data used in the research, an analysis of the appendices content, and a rationale for the developing the Landscape Map which includes possible implications of the research for practitioners as well.

Outcome research in the field of family business

Yu et al. (2012) conducted four studies to complete their project. They followed Priem, Love, and Shaffer's (2002) procedure for developing a numerical taxonomy: First, Yu et al. (2012) identified a comprehensive set of 327 outcome *variables*, next they condensed them into 34 outcome *categories*, and finally grouped the categories into seven *clusters*. Yu et al. (2012) completed the procedure with a figure to help practitioners and family owners visualize research results.

In Study 1, Yu et al. (2012) gathered and categorized a comprehensive set of dependent variables, collected from published, empirical studies in nine major journals between 1998 and 2009. During this 12-year period, 257 articles including 327 dependent/outcome variables in published studies were identified and then the outcome variables were organized into 34 dependent variable categories. All the dependent/outcome variables and categories are summarized in Appendix 1. This appendix is a more complete description of outcome variables than was included in Yu et al. (2012). Study 1 summarizes the contribution researchers have made to the field that may help identify important outcomes for research and practice.

In Study 2, Yu et al. (2012) invited family business scholars to judge similarities and differences among the 34 outcome categories that were identified in Study 1. With statistical procedures to analyze the data, the 34 categories were grouped into seven clusters and plotted on a two-dimensional grid. The grid dimensions consist of a systems dimension (family vesus business) and a temporal dimension (short-term versus long-term). The findings were validated by another group of international scholars. The final result was a numerical taxonomy (McKelvey, 1982), which is what Yu et al. (2012) called the "Landscape of Family Business Outcomes." All the initial labels and dimensions of the Landscape Map were named at this stage.

In Study 3, Yu et al. (2012) further refined and validated the labels for the outcome categories and clusters. In this study, the authors met with a multi-stakeholder group (family business owners, advisors, and scholars) in a conference to discuss how to more accurately reflect the outcomes represented. Through this collaboration, every label in the Landscape Map is the result of a mutual creation among family business owners, scholars, and advisors.

In this final study, Yu et al. (2012) summarized questionnaire data gathered in Study 2 from the two panels of family business researchers. From this data, Yu et al. (2012) confirmed the uniqueness of the 34 outcome categories and identified important dependent variables missing in current research and/or those that deserve more attention. Appendix 2, included in this chapter, is a more complete list than previously published (Yu et al., 2012) which offers specific information on the missing variables as well as a summary of the variables that may deserve more attention.

Defining the landscape of family business outcomes[1]

In Study 2 (Yu et al., 2012), two important dimensions underlying the 34 categories were identified in the empirical literature: a systems dimension (business versus family) and a temporal dimension (short-term versus long-term). The business versus family dimension, which represents both of the sub-systems within family business, was placed on the horizontal axis. While 16 of the outcome categories are highly related to business issues, such as internationalization and investment policies, the other 18 categories refer to family themes, such as family values and the role of female family members. The label for the business versus family dimension is appropriate and easily understood. The other dimension, short-term versus long-term, used to label the vertical axis, is related to temporal issues within family firms.

Yu et al. (2012) found that over time, in a family business, issues may become increasingly complex. Issues have their own temporal property and require different levels of attention at different life-cycle stages in the development of a family firm. For instance, the lower half of the Landscape Map, which covers short-term outcomes, contains the category called performance-financial which often needs immediate attention and is reviewed in short intervals (i.e., annually). However, the upper half of the Landscape Map includes long-term themes, such as succession plans which require long-range consideration and planning over extended periods of time (i.e., multiple years or decades).

Accordingly, the two dimensions form quadrants within the Landscape Map: short-term family, long-term family, short-term business, and long-term business. Using statistical procedures, Yu et al. (2012) found that the 34 outcome categories were organized into seven outcome clusters plotted along the two-dimensional space. In the short-term family quadrant, the outcome categories (conflict, commitment, family values, family business characteristics, and satisfaction) formed a cluster Yu et al. (2012) labeled *Family Dynamics* because the categories relate to the owning family's relationships and defining characteristics. The same quadrant also contained most of the *Family Business Roles* cluster (attitude toward family business-family members, attitude toward family business-non-family members, and attitude toward family business-CEO). These outcome categories are instantly concerned about the attitudes of family and non-family members as well as attitudes toward family roles within the business. Because attitude impacts the daily operations and the decision-making process, which can change quickly, much of the Family Business Roles cluster resides within the short-term family quadrant.

In the long-term family quadrant are the remaining portion of the Family Business Roles cluster (role of female family members, role of spouse/copreneur, and family involvement in business) and the Succession cluster. The outcome categories within long-term family quadrant that are grouped in Family Business Roles are concerned with the long-term nature of developing and preparing family members for involvement in the business. If a family owner reflects on how she/he will prepare family members for different roles at different stages of the family business life cycle, it may help define the potential roles family members hold within and outside the business. For example, an in-law without ownership or involvement in business could become an employee, shareholder, CEO, or even the owner-manager of a family firm over time. In addition, all family members need to understand and learn their roles over time because roles are the primary mechanism to define the structure of the family business and the relationship among family members (e.g., a father CEO and a daughter manager). It takes time to clarify the roles and respective duties.

Likewise, the *Succession* cluster occupies the upper-most position on the landscape making the cluster the most prominent long-term issue in family businesses. Because succession is not an urgent, short-term issue few owners consider it an immediate issue, which may result in the delay or absence of succession planning; recognizing succession planning as a potentially neglected outcome can be vital for family businesses to plan successful transitions to next generations.

The short-term business quadrant includes the *Social and Economic Impact* cluster and the *Performance* cluster. These two clusters contain critical variables which immediately relate to family business survival and ways that family enterprises can contribute to social and economic welfare or can be influenced by the social and economic environments. While performance is the lifeblood of the business and thus becomes an immediate outcome that is always of concern, the family firm's social and economic impact is relevant to its embeddedness within the larger socio-economic environments, and its contribution to the economy.

In the long-term business quadrant is the *Strategy* cluster. Strategy issurrounded by the Performance, Social and Economic Impact, and Governance clusters. The literature shows that family-owned ventures have advantages over non-family businesses (e.g., Anderson & Reeb, 2003) and these advantages are usually embedded in their strategy-making process to guide the behavior of the firms. Therefore, the performance outcomes follow the implementation of a firm's strategy. Compared with performance in the short-term business quadrant, strategy issues are critical for the family firm to survive and thrive in the long run. In addition, family firms are embedded in a larger socio-economic system. The interaction between family firms and the entire social and economic system emerges from the firm's business policies and strategies, the interaction which surely is under the control of a firm's heart – governance.

Interestingly, the *Governance* cluster is at the core of the entire Landscape Map and is concerned with both short-term and long-term issues and the business and family systems. This is an important finding because it is different from the conceptual map that Gersick, Davis, Hampton, and Lansberg (1997) suggested which placed ownership at the center of the overlapping systems. In the Landscape Map, ownership is one of the outcome categories within the Governance cluster, but the cluster includes several other outcome categories that act as a bridge between the family and the business. For example, this cluster includes decision-making and human resources – outcomes that typically involve both family and business. Furthermore, when comparing the Landscape Map to the Gersick et al. (1997) conceptual map, an advantage of the Landscape Map is that the Governance cluster can be subdivided into separate components, which offers a more refined framework for scholars and owners trying to understand how specific outcomes impact family business.

In general, the distribution of these seven clusters on the two outcome dimensions summarizes the researched outcomes in the domain of family business. The Landscape Map implies that a family business should maintain a balanced view of development, including both business and family. Owners, managers, and board members in a family firm may use governance to help coordinate the needs and development of both the family and the business. Future research should provide more information on the effective use of governance to enhance the effectiveness of the entire family business enterprise.

By looking more closely at the contents of the seven clusters in the Landscape Map, scholars and family business owners may deepen their understanding of family businesses. In the following sections, I elaborate on the content and significance of the outcome categories within each of the seven clusters; then I turn to Yu et al.'s (2012) findings from Study 4 and discuss their implications; and finally, I summarize ways that the clusters and their outcome categories provide meaningful and practical implications for family business owners and advisors.

Performance

Performance is defined as the effectiveness of the family business system. The Performance cluster in the Landscape Map includes *performance-overall success* and *performance-financial*. The primary difference between these two outcomes is how researchers measure performance. In the family business literature, some researchers used general questions to collect data from managers' perceived firm performance, other researchers adopted objective measures of firm performance. In their analysis of the past research, Yu et al. (2012) did find these two outcomes had been studied frequently to help owner-managers understand what factors significantly influence business performance. In terms of frequency, the performance-financial outcome was ranked as the first among the 34 categories. Why was this cluster studied so often between 1998 and 2009? The answer could be that performance has played a critical and immediate role in business sustainability and that there is an ease of measuring perceived performance.

However, performance should not be limited to economic growth or wealth creation

(Basco & Rodríguez, 2009; Dyer & Dyer, 2009). In the one-page survey, experts answered two open-ended questions that attempted to capture missing outcomes in family business research. Yu et al. (2012) asked, 1) "In your opinion, were any dependent/outcome variable categories unaccounted for in our set? In other words what, if anything, is missing?" (p. 43) and, 2) "In general, what outcome variables deserve more attention in future family business research? Why?" (pp. 43–44). A brief summary of the answers to these questions were included in Yu et al. (2012). However, a more complete summary of the answers included at the end of this chapter (Table 1A.2) identify missing variables and variables that deserve more attention.

Those surveyed emphasized the importance of understanding non-economic outcomes. As found in Table 1A.2, one expert wrote, "non-economic goals – influence relative behavior and performance of family firms." Another expert responded, "soft performance – socio-emotional wealth," and another indicated the "functional integrity of family system; family patterns during times of change and disruption; investigate/ include more than financial or objective indicators of business success." These responses of family business experts suggest that the current research merely captures a partial meaning of family business performance, and that we need to apply a more holistic view to measure firm performance than we needed before. Non-economic and soft outcomes of a family firm deserve more attention. As scholars, we need to take a closer look at how the research measures performance by asking essential questions about performance. What is performance? What types of performance matter to a family enterprise? How do we measure, predict, and evaluate a family firm's performance? Through these inquiries, we may develop a more comprehensive view to help the success of a family firm.

Furthermore, Dyer and Dyer (2009) and Basco and Rodríguez (2009) indicate that owner-managers and researchers should understand holistically when and why the outcomes from family and business systems will be in conflict or be in harmony. Should the needs of family outweigh those of the business or the other way around? Because expectations may differ among both the family and business stakeholders – especially at distinct stages of the business life cycle, certain levels of dispersed ownership, and during times when strategic directions are being decided – finding the answer to this question may help family business. If outcomes are carefully and holistically considered, family ventures can evaluate gain and loss in business performance while they determine how aspects such as timing, business and ownership needs, and other decisions will affect the entire enterprise.

Also, because the Landscape Map identifies governance as the primary coordinating mechanism aligning the overall effort and creating a potential competitive advantage in a family enterprise (Carney, 2005) questions related to governance-performance may interest researchers as well. For example, what governance structures, such as a board of directors, help to balance performance of both family and business? Likewise, questions related to conflicting or harmonious performance outcomes may be another direction to pursue.

Strategy

Strategy is defined as policies and plans enacted by the family business. This cluster contains *strategy content, investment policies, financial structure, internationalization,* and *survival and growth*. These themes are more relevant to long-term issues and to the business sub-system in a family venture. Yu et al. (2012) found that like the Performance cluster, the Strategy cluster was not considered unique to family business by the 22 experts surveyed, but was considered critical to sustain a family business for generations. This finding agrees with the cluster position on the Landscape Map. The Strategy cluster on the far-left end of the Landscape Map is surrounded by the Performance, Social and Economic Impact, Governance, and Succession clusters, thus showing strategy as the approach, process, and mechanism to sustain a business. Going beyond this "wall" of clusters are the Family Dynamics and Family Business Roles. Neither of these two clusters have direct contact with strategy, implying that they indirectly drive the strategic direction of the family firm; which is to say that the family steers the family business behind the scenes.

While most scholars in Yu et al.'s study did not think strategy is that unique for the domain of family business, some still considered a few specific dependent variables within the outcome categories worth further investigation (see Table 1A.1). For example, one scholar pointed out that the variable "family intermingling of resources" (Table 1A.2) should be studied more. I consider the exchanges of assets and resources between the household and business for mutual support an important and unique characteristic of family firms that may help a family firm's survival and growth over the long run. Other comments on what's missing from the experts included were, "family resources available to the business," "anticipated growth (sales/revenue)," and "employee growth" (see Table 1A.2). Variables identified by surveyed participants as those deserving more attention included:

- "strategy, formal structure;"
- "strategic decision-making – is it any different in family firms?" "Size of family firms is a very important variable – even larger size family firms retain the 'family' flavor;"
- "performance-survival because it's more about the issue of combining economic and non-economic goals to generate survival as a family business – even though the business can remain, the role of the family may diminish so the familiness may be lost;" and
- "you might want to dig more into the RBV. Networking and associations seem to have an impact on family business success." (see Table 1A.2)

Hopefully, sharing these thoughts may spur more discussion and research beneficial to family businesses.

In addition to the survey insights, we can look at the trend of how strategy-related variables are used to further our understanding of how outcomes impact family businesses. Often, these variables are used as independent or control variables (e.g., outsider/family funding, debt/equity financing) to predict performance of family businesses. However, it would be also interesting and may have a greater potential impact to use these variables as dependent variables and variables specific to family businesses as independent variables to form inquiries that further establish the uniqueness of this domain. For example inquiries might include such questions as: 1) How do family members on boards influence dividend policies, debt/equity financing strategies? 2) What family characteristics impede or facilitate the strategies of internationalization? and 3) How do the generational differences influence investment policies or firm growth? Discovering answers to these relational questions may not only help build theories and create new knowledge in the domain of family business, but would also add knowledge to the strategy discipline.

Social and economic impact

Social and economic impact refers to the reciprocal exchanges between the family business and its business environments. This cluster includes *economic contribution, entrepreneurship, social capital and knowledge transfer*, as well as *regulatory and business environment*. Within the Landscape Map, the Social and Economic Impact cluster is encircled by the Performance, Strategy, Governance, and Family Dynamics clusters, thus implying its central role to the impact and economic and social characteristics of family enterprises. Current research widely reflects the importance of family businesses in today's economy. For example, Astrachan and Shanker (2003) conducted an empirical research and found that family business contributed to 29–64 percent of Gross Domestic Product (GDP) in the US and hired 27–62 percent of workforce in the year of 2000. Using the data between 1992 and 1999, Anderson and Reeb (2003) found that over 35 percent of Standard & Poor's 500 firms were family businesses. In Netherlands, family enterprises generated 40–60 percent of GDP and approximately hired 29–46 percent of workers (Flören, 1998). These examples illustrate the prevalent economic contribution of family business.

Within this cluster, it is worth noting that the business conditions or environments that impact a firm can be internal or external. For example, Steier (2001) developed a model describing how to manage social capital by passing the business to the next generation's entrepreneurs. García-Élvarez, López-Sintas, and Gonzalvo (2002) analyzed the socialization patterns of successors from the first to the second generation. These are exemplar studies relevant to managing social capital and knowledge transfer within and outside of a family enterprise, which refers to the social impact of the business. It is also understandable that a family firm needs to be entrepreneurial to become trans-generational. To illustrate, Bergfeld and Weber (2011) found that the innovative behavior of German family firms across several generations depends on routines to make strategic changes.

Another study, by Salvato, Chirico, and Sharma (2010), indicated that persistence blocked entrepreneurship for an Italian family enterprise because the family was afraid to lose its institutional identity and make changes. However, the institutional identity may be renewed and enhanced by shifting the focus on the past success to the focus of further entrepreneurial effort. And experts in Yu et al.'s (2012) investigation also reflected on the importance of entrepreneurship for a family venture with the following remarks: "entrepreneurial behavior – the family's unique ability to start new ventures and innovate over time seems critical to all themes – performance, longevity, etc." (see Table 1A.2).

Generally, compared with the other six, the Social and Economic Impact cluster was the least researched and unique in the domain of family business. We still need more research to update our knowledge and understanding about the social and economic impact of family business. Areas of future research as indicated by Yu et al.'s (2012) survey suggested high interest in the theme of entrepreneurship. Also, several comments from the survey indicated that understudied topics were, "entrepreneurial behavior," "corporate entrepreneurship/entrepreneurial orientation," "new product success," and "innovation/innovativeness" (see Table 1A.2). Research inquiries could be: What family business resources, structures, routines, procedures, and characteristics promote or impede entrepreneurship, new product success, innovation, and opportunity recognition? Is there any entrepreneurial conflict between long-term orientation of family firms and the immediate short-term profit? Under what types of circumstances, entrepreneurial orientation would benefit the effectiveness of a family firm (i.e., enhancing both economic and non-economic outcomes)?

Although Yu et al. (2012) covered several important outcome variables in this cluster, there are other critical outcomes that still need attention. For instance, experts noted there is a big research gap in "community responsibility – sustainability," and "corporate or environmental responsibility" (see Table 1A.2). According to Yu et al.'s (2012) review, there were only two empirical studies (Dyer & Whetten, 2006; Niehm, Swinney, & Miller, 2008) which used corporate social responsibility as the dependent variable. Practitioners may be eager to know how being socially responsible to communities and natural environments enhances a family business' effectiveness. Another theme noted in the survey, "job creation," has become a particularly popular topic since the economic tsunami we suffered in 2008." Given that entrepreneurial and small family firms are claimed to be the engine of economic development in the US, the impact of family firms on job creation and on GDP is very salient. The consequence, for policy-makers, is that they must have urgency in seeking ways to facilitate the birth, growth, exit, and/or transition of family firms. These intriguing research opportunities may not only benefit family businesses, but help the communities in which family businesses reside as well.

Succession

Succession refers to the success and sustainability of a family business over the long run. This cluster consists of themes including *succession processes, succession plans, succession/transition events, professionalization of management*, and *compensation*. Given that there have been so many studies covering succession before 1998, Yu et al. (2012) found different kinds of succession fit into different conceptual categories. Similar to different types of performance, succession was sub-divided into three areas: processes, events, or plans.

For measuring diversified concepts on succession, researchers employed different units of analysis or measures to achieve their goals. Sharma, Chrisman, and Chua (1996) researched 226 family business articles among 32 journals and found that the most dominant topic in this family business field was succession. However, in Yu et al.'s (2012) research, the frequency the category of succession/transition events was studied ranked seventh among the 34 categories, approximately 4.38 percent of research used it as the outcome variable. Furthermore, the frequency in which the succession process category was studied ranked 15th and the succession plans category ranked 25th. The statistics show succession research was saturated during 1998–2009. This fact can also be observed in the relatively small amount of survey testimony Yu el al. (2012) received on succession. Only two commented on succession research. One participant mentioned the importance of studying succession stating that, "next generation issues [are missing]' – what do they

want to be attracted to stay/join family firm – the world/opportunity from their eyes"
(see Table 1A.2). Another survey participant commented on the potential research area
related to succession stating: "I trust 'compensation' would include 'exit strategies' for
family members" (see Table 1A.2). Considering research on transitions out of ownership
and how the execution may impact family business owners is an exciting area of opportunity for future research.

In summary, because succession is a critical mechanism to keep a family involved in
the business, and it is one of the most frequent and practical issues facing a family firm,
it is not surprising that researchers and consultants are greatly interested in it. In the
Landscape Map, we can see that the two outcome categories, compensation and professionalization of management, are located in the Succession cluster, but are close to the
human resources category within the Governance cluster. One interpretation about what
this indicates could be that the family enterprise should develop a formalized system to
supervise its management practice (i.e., professionalization of management), develop
incentives to retain and reward its managers (i.e., compensation), and align the interests
between the principal (e.g., family shareholders) and agents (e.g., non-family CEO/
managers) to reduce agency costs.

The Succession cluster within the Landscape Map helps us learn at least two key
things. First, although Sharma et al. (1996) found that succession was the most dominant topic about two decades ago, the number of succession studies did not increase
between 1998 and 2009. It seems that traditional succession research is so saturated that
the research paradigm has shifted from succession to other outcomes or clusters, such as
family dynamics, to further the understanding of how the interactions and aspirations
from the family influence the business. Second, Yu et al.'s (2012) review of literature
showed that succession, measured as an event, consumed about 50 percent of the past
succession studies whereas succession, measured as processes and plans took up the other
50 percent. While the greatest part of the existing research contributes to our knowledge
of the factors that affect succession as an event, and some contributes to the processes or
plans, there is a need for future research to focus on models that more effectively predict
successful transitions of family firms. I encourage further research to focus on succession
processes or plans to help to do this. Equally important to succession research are the
outcome two categories professionalization of management and compensation. These
areas should be considered over the succession process to enhance the effectiveness of
succession. Whether the successors are family members or not, research or textbooks
(e.g., Carlock & Ward, 2001; Poza, 2007) view a well-established, professional system as
the key contributing to the longevity of a family enterprise.

Family business roles

Family business roles are defined as roles and attitudes of family business members and
related non-members. This cluster is located at the far right end of the Landscape Map
and includes *role of spouse/copreneur*, *role of female family members*, *family involvement
in business*, and *attitude toward family business* from three types of stakeholders: family
members, non-family members, and the CEO. The cluster is recognized by family business experts as a unique characteristic of this field. For example, family involvement

in business within this cluster distinguishes the domain of family business from other close disciplines, such as small business domain defined by "the size of businesses" and entrepreneurship characterized by "opportunity recognition." In Yu et al.'s (2012) study, all 22 family business scholars agreed that "family involvement in business" is the most distinctive dependent variable category. Furthermore, the category "attitude toward family business – family members," received 19 votes out of 22 for its uniqueness. In the Landscape Map, three types of stakeholders' attitude toward family business (family members, non-family members, and CEO) are plotted within the short-term family quadrant; in contrast, family involvement in business, role of female family members, and role of spouse/copreneur are in the long-term/family quadrant. The placement of these outcomes within the Landscape Map quadrants is significant and informative to family business research.

While role and attitude reciprocally influence and shape each other, roles fundamentally define the structure of a family and of a business. Thus, roles act as an important mechanism to involve family in the business and control the firm in the long run. Because "humanness is socio-culturally variable" attitude is usually learned by a person to adjust oneself to the expectation of the role (Berger & Luckmann, 1966, p. 49). This could be the explanation why within the Landscape Map attitude is located in the short-term dimension. Regarding roles in the long-term dimension, Berger and Luckmann (1966) elucidate the relationship between institution (e.g., habitualized actions, symbols, ceremonies, etc.) and roles assumed by actors stating, "All institutionalized conduct involves roles. Thus, roles share in the controlling character of institutionalization. . .The roles make it possible for institutions to exist" (pp. 74–75). If we consider Berger and Luckmann's (1966) role concept along with Taguiri and Davis' (1992) three-circle model (i.e., ownership, family, and business), it would follow that over time an individual, (e.g., a family member finally becomes the owner-manager) could be in any of the following seven positions within the Taguiri and Davis Venn diagram playing different roles:

1) a family member without ownership and business involvement,
2) a non-family employee without ownership,
3) an outside shareholder,
4) a family shareholder without business involvement,
5) a non-family employee with ownership,
6) a family-member employee without ownership, and
7) a family owner-manager.

These various roles would assume different duties/expectations (e.g., an owner-manager is a business coach and parent to the next generation), define the structure or authority order among people (e.g., mother-daughter; owner-employee), and control the entire family business (e.g., an owner-manager assigns/removes an employee to/from the position of middle manager). As the owner-manager passing the baton to the next generation, the institutionalized roles are kept to ensure the successful operations of the firm.

Since roles are so important and could last for generations in a family business, what could be done to ensure the effectiveness of the family firm? First, family members should clearly understand the role boundaries in a family business (Santiago, 2011) to avoid possible conflict and assume appropriate duties. Too often, an owner-manager brings business pressure to home or tries to play the conflicting roles at the same time, such as a parent and a coach to the next generation. Frustration is no surprise. Second, a well-developed family business structure and intermittent review of the roles in a family firm are necessary. To adapt to the ever-changing environments (e.g., external business environments, internal family expansion/shrinking) or the life-cycles of a business, the roles/structure of a family firm should be defined, reviewed, and modified to ensure the firm is on the right track. For example, should in-laws be considered in the business involvement (Santiago, 2011)? If yes, under what conditions? If not, what roles should in-laws play in a family? Last but not least, roles should be appropriately designed and used as a mechanism to get family involved in the business. For example, family owner-manager may trust a senior employee to be the business coach of the possible successors, rather than playing the two conflicting roles (i.e., a parent and coach).

In terms of research, the two topics on the role of spouse/copreneur and of female family members remain understudied and are still missing in family business education (Sorenson, Yu, & Brigham, 2010). In Yu et al.'s (2012) survey, one expert described these themes missing in family business research stating, "affinal ties – that is, role of in-laws and relatives by marriage; comparative kinship systems; legal issues. . .situating businesses in the wider kinship systems and not assuming we know what is meant by 'family'" (see Table 1A.2). Another commented "I think the cluster of family member roles is very interesting for future research. A typology of roles played, more on how to clarify set roles, the relationships between roles in family firms, etc." (see Table 1A.2). Understanding more about the role of spouse/copreneur and the role of female members will enhance the effectiveness of a family firm (Sorenson, Folker, & Brigham, 2008) and better promote entrepreneurship.

Because of the shortage of research on family business roles, family business educators do not yet have a good framework to teach professionals or students how to adjust to various roles over the different stages of firm development. There is also little research in how the roles of family members/non-members influence the attitudes toward the family business. Conversely, in Yu et al.'s (2012) research, family involvement in business continues to attract more and more attention and has generated some initial findings to help family business education. Research about the cluster of family business roles is important because it is the only dependent variable category that the family business experts unanimously considered unique in this discipline. I hope that calling attention to this area will promote future research and subsequently help practitioners, policy-makers, and family business owners adjust family business roles to achieve the best possible results.

Family dynamics

Family dynamics refers to the interactions and aspirations of family members. This cluster, like the Family Business Roles cluster, is unique within the family business field, and is composed of five outcome categories: *family values, family business characteristics, conflict, commitment*, and *satisfaction*. Of the 257 articles Yu et al. (2012) identified during the span of 12 years, this cluster was the second most frequently studied among the seven clusters and one of the most unique clusters (i.e., family values and family business characteristics). This tells us that over the past decade the research has gradually shifted from succession and business performance to family dynamics, which captures more of the uniqueness of the family business domain. In response to Yu et al.'s (2012) question about what outcomes deserve more attention in family enterprise research, one expert said, "family outcomes and socio-emotional wealth" (see Table 1A.2). In addition, another expert explained:

> In my opinion, all outcome variables in which the family dimension is explicit deserve more attention (e.g., satisfaction, commitment, conflicts, family values and concerns, attitude toward family business). The reason is adopting this type of variables may help unveil the actual role played by the family in affecting outcomes. In too many "family-business studies" the "family" dimension is a simple demographic variable, but the actual family-related mechanisms that should make these firms so special are too often black-boxed. (see Table 1A.2)

Hence, related research inquiries mentioned here may help us shed light on the family impact and interaction in business and move the entire field forward. Another expert shared his/her insight on relevant missing topics listing "management of family; family satisfaction with and commitment to the business; effect of business on family life style. . ." and further explained that "commitment of family members to the family business and family business decisions. This DV will reveal processes that can help explain family management processes (governance) that contribute to both family and firm success" (see Table 1A.2). It seems that researchers may not only think about family in business, but consider business in family as well. In this two-way interaction process we may discover other missing variables related to family dynamics; those mentioned in the survey were:

- "family unity and decreased or increased family ties in adulthood (in extended family),"
- "cultural impacts,"
- "family values,"
- "ethical behavior; productivity; employee/family development; family/personal success," "altruism,"
- "longevity,"
- "trust; change,"
- "functional integrity of family system; family patterns during times of change and disruption," "family outcomes,"
- "family harmony,"
- "non-family advisors/involvement/family structures and systems/communication/ quality of relationships," and
- "emotional profitability." (see Table 1A.2)

I consider these issues relevant to family dynamics and think they may generate interesting research. However, these *soft* themes may pose an instant challenge and opportunity for researchers on the definition and measurement of these outcomes. One of the survey participants commented on the challenges of this cluster stating, "Commitment, conflict and softer issues as these are more difficult to assess in terms of the impact on the business (and the family)."

While this may be true, I urge professionals to re-think the definition of effectiveness for a family business. As Yu et al. (2012) emphasized in the performance cluster, a business should seriously consider the needs or goals of its family, not just those of business. Without a balanced view to guide the development of both family and business, a family firm collapsing on one side may have a seriously negative impact on the other (Dyer & Dyer, 2009). While the literature has begun to address the issues in this cluster, too much remains unknown and only scratches the surface of the knowledge we need to understand how outcomes in family dynamics impact family businesses.

Governance

Governance refers to decision processes and control mechanisms that balance the needs of the family and the business systems and oversees succession. This cluster includes themes on *human resources* (e.g., employee training programs), *business mission/goals*, *role of network* (e.g., inter-firm cooperation capability in the context of networking family firms), *decision-making* (e.g., allocation of financial resources), *governance structure* (e.g., board of directors), *family control* (e.g., types of family relationships in top management teams), and *family ownership*. Perhaps, the most interesting property of this cluster is that it lies at the center of the Landscape Map. The centrality of the Governance cluster within the Landscape Map implies its role within the family business domain and helps to distinguish the Landscape Map from other family business conceptual maps (Gersick et al., 1997; Taguiri & Davis, 1992); Yu et al.'s (2012) data revealed that governance, which includes ownership and management outcomes, also includes additional, specific outcomes that coordinate and integrate the family and business systems, and short-term and long-term issues that family businesses face.

Among all the clusters, Governance was the most researched in Yu et al.'s (2012) investigation of the literature between 1998 and 2009. Although this cluster comprises about 20 percent of the past studies, Yu et al. (2012) found little empirical research focusing on a governance system that simultaneously focuses on both family and business, and long- and short-term issues and outcomes. What mechanism within the governance could be developed to help the effectiveness of the entire family enterprise? How do governance structures effectively coordinate to obtain desired outcomes from both family and business systems? Do we need more or fewer family board members to enhance the effectiveness of business and of family? What configurations would be best?

I believe this cluster may be the most salient and have greatest potential in helping a family venture to achieve balanced, positive outcomes. Experts shared their opinions about missing research stating:

- "ownership dispersion, management practices – HR/OB/Planning,"
- "role of network,"
- "Incentive system (different from compensation) for family and non-family employees; distributive and procedural justice for family and non-family employees,"
- "HR aspects/processes in FOB,"
- "family values, ownership because most research still is done from the business context/business circle instead of ownership or family circle," and
- "what about generational control? Is it the founding generation or subsequent gen-

erations? Additional areas may include family versus non-family management and the intent of the founder: i.e., was the firm started as an entrepreneurial venture and evolved into a family firm, or did it start as a family venture?" (see Table 1A.2).

Researchers could link any of these variables to business performance or soft family outcomes and get insights on their relationship. Often, researchers used one of the categories in governance as control or independent variables, such as family directors, family control, and ownership, to link with performance. I encourage future research projects creatively employ these variables as dependent variables or contingencies to help this field accumulate more knowledge on effective designs of governance structure, or reasonable family control/ownership. Take Lambrecht and Lievens' study (2008) as an example. With 17 cases, they found that simplicity in family ownership, governance, and business management is a good structure to obtain both business performance and family harmony. The knowledge advancement of governance can be extremely beneficial to family business owners, advisors, and scholars in the effort to design appropriate structures that help guide and sustain a family venture.

Implications for practice

The Landscape Map not only benefits researchers, but also helps family business practice in at least four possible ways. First, family business owners and consultants are able to use the Landscape Map as a framework to assess the extent to which attention is given to the dimensions (i.e., business versus family; short-term versus long-term) and all clusters of family business. Overlooking any of the clusters or dimensions may result in poor outcome performance in those areas. So the landscape could be divided into four quadrants for an assessment: short-term business outcomes, short-term family outcomes, long-term business outcomes, and long-term family outcomes; in each quadrant, issues could be captured to facilitate a discussion. Questions to identify such issues may include: What are the outcomes desired most at this point? Are there any conflicts among these outcomes? And, is there any way to resolve the possible conflicts between family/business and short-/long-term issues? To achieve a balanced, healthy development of family business, the assessment should be brought to the table for open discussion among the family members and/or critical non-family stakeholders. Because the family and the business have their own life cycles, an intermittent review of and reconsideration of outcomes are necessary to adjust a family firm to the changes of environments.

Second, the seven clusters provide more specific ideas for further discussion between the advisors and family business owners. If owners and advisors find that attention is not being given to a cluster, they can use the outcome categories within the clusters to examine and identify areas they wish to work on. For example, family values may be a core concern as an owner passes the baton to the next generation. If this is the case, then the outcome categories contained in the Landscape Map can be used to generate critical discussion questions: Do the successor, family members, and/or key stakeholders share and understand the family values? Does the family have regular meetings or retreats to promote family values? Should these values be included in the vision/mission statements or any family agreements? What mechanisms should be adopted to re-evaluate the viability of these values in order to adjust the family and business to changing environments? Using the Landscape Map to stimulate these types of questions can help further a family business owner's ability to balance the complexities of family business.

Third, the Landscape Map also helps owners and advisors to examine the extent to which decision-makers represent all dimensions in the Landscape Map. To illustrate: family members from next generations may not be included in decisions. Thus, the family owners may be overlooking family dynamics, family business roles, and succession issues. Advisors and owners could develop solutions to fix or prevent problems emerging from the three categories.

Last but not least, the entire Landscape Map could be developed into *scorecards* to review the entire family business system and identify its critical problems. Based on the 34 categories, advisors could develop cards with questions related to each outcome category. For example, questions regarding the performance-overall category could be: How do you define success for your family business? What factors may not be in your imagination of success? To what degree does your business achieve your definition of success?

However, not all the seven clusters or 34 outcome categories have the same weight in analyzing a family firm. From the research, we know that the contingencies (e.g., industries, ownership, generations, family vision, values, etc.) and life-cycle stages within family businesses produce different outcome concerns. At some point, one cluster may be more imperative than other clusters, or a specific outcome more important than others within that cluster. For example, professionalization of management may be more important than compensation or a succession event because of its high relevance to the qualification of possible successors involved in the family firm operations. Using these type of scorecards could give family businesses the appropriate tool to break down and identify problems and goals, strategize priorities, and develop plans to better their business.

Conclusion

Taking stock of 12 years (1998–2009) of research findings on dependent/outcome variables, Yu et al. (2012) identified and categorized recent research on family business outcomes to form "A Map of the Landscape of Family Outcomes." The Landscape Map offers practitioners, scholars, and family business owners a visual representation of the research findings in an attempt to illustrate what we know and further our understanding about the domain of family business. The two dimensions (business versus family; short-term versus long-term) and seven clusters (performance, strategy, economic and social impact, governance, succession, family business roles, and family dynamics) can help family business scholars identify and investigate unique, missing, and under-researched outcome variables in future research. Using the Landscape Map owners and practitioners can identify and investigate outcome variables that may help achieve more positive outcomes in the areas of their businesses greatest concern.

Evidence shown in Yu et al.'s (2012) survey confirms that family business succession, family dynamics, and family business roles are unique clusters within the family business domain, and non-economic performance and family-specific topics deserve more attention. Governance, at the core of the Landscape Map, may become a unique mechanism to integrate these concerns from both family and business systems. Hence, Yu et al.'s

(2012) research shares the view of Dyer and Dyer (2009) and of Basco and Rodríguez (2009) that researchers should adopt a holistic view in evaluating the family business effectiveness and the Landscape Map provides a conceptual framework and tool to do this.

Different from Yu et al.'s (2012) contribution to the domain of family business, this chapter goes beyond the implications of the research and begins to elaborate on how practitioners can use the Landscape Map. I hope the Landscape Map will be a helpful tool to visualize the domain of family business, and that it generates a pedagogical framework that owners, practitioners, and scholars can use to understand family businesses and develop more positive outcomes.

Note

1.　All the labels shown in this article for the Landscape Map were refined and validated in Study 3.

References

Anderson, R.C., & Reeb, D.M. (2003). Founding-family ownership and firm performance: Evidence from the S&P 500. *Journal of Finance*, *58*(3), 1301–28.

Astrachan, J.H., & Shanker, M.C. (2003). Family businesses' contribution to the U.S. economy: A closer look. *Family Business Review*, *16*(3), 211–19.

Basco, R., & Rodríguez, M.J.P. (2009). Studying the family enterprise holistically: Evidence for integrated family and business systems. *Family Business Review*, *22*(1), 82–95.

Berger, P.L., & Luckmann, T. (1966). *The social construction of reality*. Garden City, NY: Doubleday.

Bergfeld, M.M.H., & Weber, F.M. (2011). Dynasties of innovation: Highly performing German family firms and the owners' role for innovation. *International Journal of Entrepreneurship and Innovation Management*, *13*(1), 80–94.

Busenitz, L.W., West, G.P., III, Shepherd, D., Nelson, T., Chandler, G.N., & Zacharakis, A. (2003). Entrepreneurship research in emergence: Past trends and future directions. *Journal of Management*, *29*(3), 285–308.

Carlock, R.S., & Ward, J.L. (2001). *Strategic planning for the family business: Parallel planning to unify the family and business*. New York: Palgrave.

Carney, M. (2005). Corporate governance and competitive advantage in family-controlled firms. *Entrepreneurship Theory and Practice*, *29*(3), 249–65.

Chua, J.H., Chrisman, J.J., & Steier, L.P. (2003). Extending the theoretical horizons of family business research. *Entrepreneurship Theory and Practice*, *27*(4), 331–8.

Dyer, W.G., Jr., & Dyer, W.J. (2009). Putting the family into family business research. *Family Business Review*, *22*(3), 216–19.

Dyer, W.G., Jr., & Whetten, D.A. (2006). Family firms and social responsibility: Preliminary evidence from the S&P 500. *Entrepreneurship Theory and Practice*, *30*(6), 785–802.

Flören, R.H. (1998). The significance of family business in the Netherlands. *Family Business Review*, *11*(2), 121–34.

García-Álvarez, E., López-Sintas, J., & Gonzalvo, P.S. (2002). Socialization patterns of successors in first- to second-generation family businesses. *Family Business Review*, *15*(3), 189–203.

Gersick, K.E., Davis, J.A., Hampton, M.M., & Lansberg, I. (1997). *Generation to generation: Life cycles of the family business*. Boston, MA: Harvard Business School Press.

Ketchen, D., Jr., Tomas, J.B., & McDaniel, R., Jr. (1996). Process, content, and context: Synergistic effects on organizational performance. *Journal of Management*, *22*(2), 231–57.

Lambrecht, J., & Lievens, J. (2008). Pruning the family tree: An unexplored path to family business continuity and family harmony. *Family Business Review*, *21*(4), 295–313.

McKelvey, B. (1982). *Organizational systematics: Taxonomy, evolution, classification*. Berkeley, CA: University of California Press.

Nag, R., Hambrick, D.C., & Chen, M.J. (2007). What is strategic management, really? Inductive derivation of a consensus definition of the field. *Strategic Management Journal*, *28*(9), 935–55.

Niehm, L.S., Swinney, J., & Miller, N.J. (2008). Community social responsibility and its consequences for family business performance. *Journal of Small Business Management*, *46*(3), 331–50.

Poza, E.J. (2007). *Family business*. Mason, OH: Thomson South-Western.

Priem, R.L., Love, L.G., & Shaffer, M.A. (2002). Executives' perceptions of uncertainty sources: A numerical taxonomy and underlying dimensions. *Journal of Management*, *28*(6), 725–46.

Salvato, C., Chirico, F., & Sharma, P. (2010). A farewell to the business: Championing entrepreneurial exit in family firms. *Entrepreneurship and Regional Development: An International Journal*, *22*(3–4), 321–48.

Santiago, A.L. (2011). The family in family business: Case of the in-laws in Philippine businesses. *Family Business Review*, *24*(4), 343–61.

Sekaran, U. (2002). *Research methods for business: A skill-building approach* (4th ed.). New York, NY: Wiley.

Sharma, P., Chrisman, J.J., & Chua, J.H. (1996). *A review and annotated bibliography of family business studies*. London, UK: Kluwer Academic Publishers.

Short, J.C., Ketchen, D.J., Jr., Shook, C.L., & Ireland, R.D. (2010). The concept of "opportunity" in entrepreneurship research: Past accomplishments and future challenges. *Journal of Management*, *36*(1), 40–65.

Sorenson, R.L., Folker, C.A., & Brigham, H.K. (2008). The collaborative network orientation: Achieving business success through collaborative relationships. *Entrepreneurship Theory and Practice*, *32*(4), 615–34.

Sorenson, R.L., Yu, A., & Brigham, K.H. (2010). Taking stock of one decade of research: An outcome-based framework for teaching family business. In A. Stewart, G.T. Lumpkin & J.A. Katz (Eds.), *Advances in entrepreneurship, firm emergence, and growth: Entrepreneurship and family business* (pp. 367–75). Bingley, UK: Emerald Group Publishing.

Steier, L. (2001). Next-generation entrepreneurs and succession: An exploratory study of modes and means of managing social capital. *Family Business Review*, *14*(3), 259–76.

Taguiri, R., & Davis, J.A. (1992). On the goals of successful family companies. *Family Business Review*, *5*(1), 43–62.

Yu, A., Lumpkin, G.T., Sorenson, R.L., & Brigham, H.K. (2012). The landscape of family business outcomes: A summary and numerical taxonomy of dependent variables. *Family Business Review*, *25*(1), 33–57.

Appendix

Table 1A.1   Table of seven clusters, 34 dependent variable categories, and dependent variables[a]

Cluster	Category	Dependent Variable
Family Dynamics	Commitment	Successor commitment; Decision commitment; Attitude of the second generation; Shareholder organizational commitment; Employee commitment
	Conflict	Conflict; Substantive conflict; Types of family relationships in top management team; Intention/behavior of the family; Challenges in the succession process for females; Family business interaction; Generational differences among family businesses; Anxiety; Work-family conflict; Family business success; Emotional well-being; Overcoming limits to the growth; Issues about family relationships during the succession process; Tensions; Characteristics and key success factors; Cognitive conflict; Relationship conflict
	Family business characteristics	F-PEC (2); Family business definition (2); Family Climate Scale; Family business development; Family Orientation Index; Born or made; Family business interaction; Inheritance; Financial logic; Differences between family businesses and non-family businesses at start-up and critical operational phase (2); Family business domains; Characteristics, attributes, and family forces on entrepreneurship; Family business values (2); Patterns in serial business families; Family change; Key success factors; Family Business Index; Stewardship; Stagnation
	Family values	Family values (3); Family business characteristics (3); Corporate social responsibility; Intention/behavior of the family; Family business' response to merger or takeover process (2); Company objectives; Fair process; The most important issues; Culture; Family business interaction; Family cohesion; Family business concerns; Socialization processes and patterns; Family outcomes (3); Key success factors; Trust; Ethics violations; Continuity; Family performance; Stewardship; Stagnation; Perceived community social responsibility
	Satisfaction	Satisfaction with the succession process (3); The process of management buy-out or buy-in; Satisfaction with the deal; Attitude of the second generation; Employee satisfaction; Opportunism; Niche marginalization; Family harmony

Table 1A.1   (continued)

Cluster	Category	Dependent Variable
Family Business Roles	Attitude toward family business – CEO	Owner-manager's attitude to family and business issues; Successful non-family CEO; Professional management (cultural competence and formal competence)
	Attitude toward family business – family members	Attitude to the family and the business; Reasons for children not joining the business; Owner-manager's attitude to family and business issues; The future leader's perception of the business; Attitude of the second generation; Professional management (cultural competence and formal competence)
	Attitude toward family business – non-family members	Successful non-family CEO; Family business concerns; Professional management (cultural competence and formal competence)
	Family involvement in business	Reasons for children not joining the business (3); Board composition; Predecessor's roles during or after instatement of the successor; Family business self-efficacy scale in succession; Family business' response to merger or takeover process; Familiness; Born or made; Culture; Family business interaction; Generational difference among family businesses; Inheritance (2); Family business concerns; Partial retirement; Socialization processes and patterns; Financial intermingling (2); Managers' adjustment strategies; Family business practices; Continued involvement and knowledge transfer; Amount of perceived benefits for the next generation (educational and relational); Existence of board of director; Percentage of family members in the top management team
	Role of spouse/ copreneur	Successful coprenurial relationships after divorce; The continuum of coprenuerial couples' business relationships; Copreneur versus non-copreneur; Spousal role types; Wives' contribution and employment to family economic well-being
	Role of female family members	The visibility of heiresses; Challenges in the succession process for females; Generational differences among family businesses; Wives' contribution and employment to family economic well-being; Women's pathways to participation and leadership
Succession	Compensation	CEO compensation (3); Corporate governance structures; Employee compensation; Stewardship; Stagnation
	Professionalization of management	Professionalization of management; Management strategies; Intention/behavior of the family; Planning; Familiness; Generational differences among family businesses; Strategic responses to emerging economies; Family business practices; Professional management (cultural competence and formal competence)

Table 1A.1   (continued)

Cluster	Category	Dependent Variable
Succession	Succession processes	Succession transition process (5); The extensiveness of the succession planning process; Predecessor roles during and after instatement of the successor; Challenges in the succession process for females; The perceived success of the succession process; Issues about family relationship during the succession process; Satisfaction with the succession process; Successor leadership
	Succession plans	Succession plan (3); Planning; Generational differences among family businesses; Family business concerns; Management and ownership; Characteristics and key success factors
	Succession/ transition events	Management transfer (4); Growth transitions; Transfer and management of social capital; Intention/behavior of the family; Intention to join the family business (3); Dependence on a single decision-maker; Family business interaction; Partial retirement; Socialization processes and patterns; Succession outcome; Successor attributes (2); Family business practices; Challenges in family business growth; Superior organizational performance; The selection of internal or external successor
Governance	Business mission/ goals	Business practices/goals (5); Company objectives; Culture; Merger and acquisition; Continuity
	Decision-making	Strategic investment decisions; Start-up decision; Allocation of financial resources; The future leader's perception of the business; Intention to join the family business (5); Dependence on a single decision-maker; Internalization process; Management transfer; Fair process; Familiness; Generational differences among family businesses; Succession planning activities (2); Merger and acquisition; Decision quality and decision commitment; Management and ownership; The intermingling of family and business finance (3); The purchase of child care service; Women's pathways to participation and leadership; Foreign direct investment behavior; Probability of new venture start-up
	Family control	Family control (2); Control sales; Types of family relationships in top management team; Intention/ behavior of the family; Organizational flexibility; Market; Bureaucratic and clan control in organizational life-cycle stages; Existence of board of director; Percentage of family members in the top management team

Table 1A.1   (continued)

Cluster	Category	Dependent Variable
Governance	Family ownership	Ownership (7); Corporate governance structure (2); Allocation of financial resources; Intention/behavior of the family; Control sales; Management (2); Perceived control; Fair process; Piercing the corporate veil; Issues about family relationship during the succession process; Characteristics and key success factors; Continuity; Equity financing; Interest rate premium; Business collateral and personal collateral
	Governance structure	Corporate governance structure (4); Informal cooperation; Management and ownership; Executive tenure (3); Agency costs; Transaction costs; Types of family relationships in top management team; Board composition (2); Family business structure; Issues about family relationship during the succession process; Continuity; Existence of board of director; Percentage of family members in the top management team
	Human resources	Employee training programs; Professional human resource management practices; Strategic human resource; Fair process; Flexibility; The purchase of child care service; Mentoring in family businesses; Human capital; Opportunism; Group cohesion; Amount of perceived benefits for the next generation (educational and relational); Stewardship; Stagnation
	Role of network	Network composition; Interfirm cooperation capability in the context of networking family firms; Business group formation; Group membership; Family business' response to merger or takeover process; Survival strategies in a hostile environment; Establishment and growth of an entrepreneurial family business; Congruity between business and family
Performance	Performance–financial	Firm performance (28); Business group performance; Allocation of financial resources; Sales growth performance (4); Short-term financial performance; Long-term stock performance; Firm value (2); Operating efficiency (2); Production function for sales; Succession performance; Cost of equity capital; Financial behavior; Family business development; Familiness; Long-term IPO (2); Equity routes; Financial logic; The growth and development of family business (3); Growth transitions; Overcoming limits to the growth (2); Compensation to performance; Business outcomes (3); Profitability (2); Growth characteristics; Financing; Sustainability; Likelihood of first sale and resources

Table 1A.1   (continued)

Cluster	Category	Dependent Variable
Performance	Performance–overall success	Familiness qualities (2); Performance; Successful non-family CEO; Success (3); Firm performance; The perceived success of succession process (3); The growth and development of family businesses; Business outcomes (2); Characteristics and key success factors; Sustainability; Perceived success; Perceived community social responsibility
Strategy	Financial structure	Debt; Leverage; Financial structure (3); Generational differences among family businesses; Financial logic; The role of going public; Characteristics, attributes, and family forces on entrepreneurship; Venture capital; Financial management techniques; Intermingling (6); Financial policies; Equity financing (2); Family funding versus outsider funding; Interest rate premium; Business collateral and personal collateral; Earning management (profitability, leverage, and R&D capitalization)
	Internationalization	Internationalization process; Internationalization (5); International involvement; Organizational flexibility; Foreign direct investment behavior; International commitment
	Investment policies	Investment policies (3); Strategic investment decisions; Allocation of financial resources; Differences between family angels and other informal investors; Venture capital; Family funding versus outsider funding; R&D ratio
	Strategy content	Strategic persistence; Strategic responses to emerging economies; Strategy; Customer relationship management; Innovation; Service quality; Survival strategies in a hostile environment; The strengths and weaknesses of industrial family businesses; Continuity; Product diversification; Strategic flexibility; Entrepreneurial orientation; Turnaround strategies; Dynamic family-controlled business strategic adaptation; Competitive improvement
	Survival and growth	Length of organization survival (4); Organizational failure (2); Target performance; Performance variance; The survival of low value-added firms; Succession performance; The growth and development of family businesses (2); Organizational performance (sales growth); Establishment and growth of an entrepreneurial family business; Business expansion; Longevity; Turnaround strategies; Employment growth
Social and Economic Impact	Entrepreneurship	Entrepreneurial orientation (2); Strategic persistence; Corporate entrepreneurship (3); The future leader's perception of the business; Innovation

Table 1A.1 (continued)

Cluster	Category	Dependent Variable
Social and Economic Impact		(3); Entrepreneurial risk-taking; Familiness; Characteristics, attributes, and family forces on entrepreneurship; Family funding versus outsider funding; Establishment and growth of a entrepreneurial family business; Prevalence of family firms; Start-up decisions; Probability of new venture start-up; R&D ratio; Value creation across generations; Competitive improvement
	Economic contribution	US economy; Dutch economy; Family business domain; Business group formation; Family business prevalence (2)
	Regulatory and business environment	Perceptions of pre-venture entrepreneurs toward environments; The most important issues facing private family businesses; Survival strategies in a hostile environment; Family businesses domination (2); The prevalence of family businesses; Dutch economy; Establishment and growth of an entrepreneurial family business
	Social capital and knowledge transfer	Mentoring in family businesses; Predecessor roles during and after instatement of the successor; Family business self-efficacy scale in succession; Internationalization process; Interfirm cooperation capability in the context of networking family businesses; Socialization processes and patterns; Transfer and management of social capital; Continued involvement and knowledge transfer; Amount of perceived benefits for the next generation (educational and relational)

Note: [a] I merged some referents and showed their frequency in the parentheses as they had the same or very similar terms or were operationalized by similar measures.

Table 1A.2   Table of quotations about missing and understudied DV/outcome variable categories[a]

Subject	Question 2: In your opinion, were any dependent variable/outcome variable categories unaccounted for in our set? In other words what, if anything, is missing?	Question 3: In general, what outcome variables (either in the above list or otherwise) deserve more attention in future family business research? Why?
#1	Management of family; family satisfaction with and commitment to the business; effect of business on family life style; family resources available to the business.	Commitment of family members to the family business and family business decisions. This DV will reveal processes that can help explain family management processes (governance) that contribute to both family and firm success.
#2	Affinal ties – that is, role of in-laws and relatives by marriage; comparative kinship systems; legal issues.	Situating businesses in the wider kinship systems and not assuming we know what is meant by "family."
#3	Family unity and decreased or increased family ties in adulthood (in extended families); job creation; community responsibility-sustainability.	All of the above (34 DV categories) because as a result of the lack of sufficient data from private companies, we have only scratched the surface of knowledge.
#5	Cultural impacts.	Family values.
#9	Non-economic goals; succession intentions; family vision; altruism (could be dependent or independent variable).	1. Non-economic goals – influence relative behavior and performance of family firms; 2. Altruism – we've only scratched the surface on that topic.
#11 [b]	"Soft performance" – socio-emotional wealth, see Astrachan et al. 2008 in FBR, also Gómez-Mejía ASQ, also family firm ??	Please see above → non-financial performance, as a DV that explains FF behavior, e.g., long-term orientation.
#12	Not on the DV side – lots of IVs are missing but DVs are OK.	Strategy, formal structure, ownership dispersion, management practices – HR/OB/Planning.
#13	Next generation issues – what do they want to be attracted to stay/join family firm – the world/opportunity from their eyes.	Satisfaction, conflict, entrepreneurial behavior, role of network, learning.
#14	Seems quite complete. I trust "compensation" would include "exit strategies" for family members.	Performance: what is it? How it is perceived/understood.
#15	Social responsibility; ethical behavior; productivity; employee/family development; family/personal success.	Performance of family firm (financial or otherwise). To better understand how family ownership affects performance.
#16	Longevity; family goals and outcomes.	Entrepreneurial behavior – the family's unique ability to start new ventures and innovate over time seems critical to all themes – performance, longevity, etc.
#19		I believe the ones checked above deserve more attention, although all listed have some aspects that distinguish family from non-family businesses.

Table 1A.2   (continued)

Subject	Question 2: In your opinion, were any dependent variable/outcome variable categories unaccounted for in our set? In other words what, if anything, is missing?	Question 3: In general, what outcome variables (either in the above list or otherwise) deserve more attention in future family business research? Why?
#20	Incentive system (different from compensation) for family and non-family employees; distributive and procedural justice for family and non-family employees.	Sales growth – given that many of these firms are privately owned – tax implications associate with being private.
#22	Trust; change/tradition; emotional asset; industry situation.	
#26[c]	Not that I can think of.	HR aspects/processes in FOB; comparisons of consumer attitudes toward products from FOB vs. non-FOB.
#27		Stakeholder relations with family businesses. They are critical in the business environment. Perceptions of these relationships would be of interest.
#28	Ethical focus; anticipated growth (sales/ revenue); employee growth.	Ethical focus.
#29		Strategic decision-making – is it any different in family firms? Size of family firms is a very important variable – even larger-size family firms retain the "family" flavor.
#30	Family and business goals; generations in business; culture of family; functional integrity of the family system; family intermingling of resources; family patterns during times of change and disruption.	Functional integrity of family system; family patterns during times of change and disruption; investigate/include more than financial or objective indicators of business success.
#31	Nothing missing in my view.	Corporate entrepreneurship/ entrepreneurial orientation/ internationalization/family goals.
#32		Entrepreneurial orientation.
#33	Can't think of any.	Family values, ownership because most research still is done from the business context/business circle instead of ownership or family circle.
#34	Socio-emotional wealth.	Family outcomes and socio-emotional wealth.
#35	In my opinion, the EMOTIONAL BENEFIT of owning and managing a business is under-represented. It may fall within the "Satisfaction" or "Commitment" variables, but I believe it should have an autonomous role. Please, refer to Zellweger and Astrachan (2008) "On the emotional	In my opinion, all outcome variables in which the "family" dimension is explicit deserve more attention (e.g., Satisfaction, Commitment, Conflicts, Family values and concerns, Attitude of family members towards business). The reason is adopting this type of variables

Table 1A.2   (continued)

Subject	Question 2: In your opinion, were any dependent variable/outcome variable categories unaccounted for in our set? In other words what, if anything, is missing?	Question 3: In general, what outcome variables (either in the above list or otherwise) deserve more attention in future family business research? Why?
#35	value of owning a firm", FBR 21(4): 347–363. I would also consider "Exit" (e.g., from the founder's business, or from one of the traditional lines of products) as an outcome variable. You may here want to consider DeTienne, D.R. (2008). "Entrepreneurial exit as a critical component of the entrepreneurial process: Theoretical development," in the *Journal of Business Venturing* (for the conceptual case of Exit as an outcome variable), and Salvato, Chirico, and Sharma (forthcoming) for an empirical case.	may help unveil the actual role played by the family in affecting outcomes. In too many "family-business studies" the "family" dimension is a simple demographic variable, but the actual family-related mechanisms that should make these firms so special are too often blackboxed.
#36		I thought that cluster 3 was one of the most interesting, but also felt that it was the least cohesive. Entrepreneurial behavior did not seem to fit with the prevalence of family firms in the economy for instance. I would see this fitting better with a performance cluster. I think the cluster of family member roles is very interesting for future research. A typology of roles played, more on how to clarify set roles, the relationships between roles in family firms, etc.
#38	New product success; corporate or environmental responsibility.	
#39	Innovation.	
#40	No.	Family harmony (on the family side)/ business profitability (on the business side).
#43	The explicit usage of innovation/innovativeness seems to have been missing.	Innovation/innovativeness.
#44	Don't think so.	Non-economic outcome variables.
#45		1. Performance-survival because it's more about the issue of combining economic and non-economic goals to generate survival as a family business – even though the business can remain, the role of the family may diminish so the familiness may be lost; 2. family involvement – something beyond the F-PEC.

Table 1A.2   (continued)

Subject	Question 2: In your opinion, were any dependent variable/outcome variable categories unaccounted for in our set? In other words what, if anything, is missing?	Question 3: In general, what outcome variables (either in the above list or otherwise) deserve more attention in future family business research? Why?
#47		I think a diversity is preferable to uniformity. There are lots of research questions worth asking, so probably lots of possible perspectives on outcomes. Also, different stakeholders (family members of different generations, non-family employees, economic development officials etc.) are likely to be interested in different types of outcomes.
#48	Ethical values or norms in the family business.	Ethical behavior.
#49	Non-family advisors/involvement/family structures and systems/communication/ quality of relationships.	
#52	I cannot think of any other variables.	Both financial and non-financial variables listed above deserve attention. Family businesses cannot survive without financial success. At the same time, financial success is not the only goal of most family businesses.
#54		Emotional profitability.
#55		Strategy/intergenerational differences
#56		Commitment, conflict and softer issues as these are more difficult to asses in terms of the impact on the business (and the family).
#60		Definition of family business, successful succession.
#61	What about generational control? Is it the founding generation or subsequent generations? Additional areas may include family versus non-family management and the intent of the founder: i.e., was the firm started as an entrepreneurial venture and evolved into a family firm, or did it start as a family venture?	You might want to dig more into the RBV. Networking and associations seem to have an impact on family business success. I didn't really see this here.

Notes:
[a] The information provided by subjects #1 to #30 was from the 22 experts doing the card-sorting activity in Study 2; the remainder was from the 52 international scholar validating the taxonomy in Study 2 (Yu et al., 2012).
[b] In subject #11's answer, I could not recognize the last word and put "??" to express this missing word. FF represents family firms.
[c] In subject #26's answer, FOB means family-owned businesses.

2. Owning family governance within the two dimensions of the family business

Ritch L. Sorenson

Introduction

The word governance is derived from a Greek term that means "to steer." For family firms, the purpose of governance is to steer the entire enterprise toward desired outcomes, which often include outcomes beyond financial performance. Current governance research focuses primarily on traditional corporate governance and on business profitability as *the* measure of performance. However, family owned businesses include family governance structures beyond those traditionally examined, and outcomes important to the owning family that are typically not measured. In effect, current family business research overlays the governance structures and outcome measures used in non-family business research. And yet, this research does not fully account for the range of structures and outcomes preferred by business owning families.

Based on a summary of 12 years of research, Yu, Lumpkin, Sorenson, and Brigham (2012) depict the overall landscape of family business with governance holding the central position in the family enterprise. Unlike previous research that focuses on some individual elements of governance and associated outcomes, particularly financial performance, the Yu et al. research summarizes the components of governance and the overall family business landscape in which it resides, referred to in this book as "A Map of the Landscape of Family Business"* or Landscape Map. The Landscape Map summarizes the major outcomes, potential reach, and central role of governance.

The Landscape Map, provided just inside the front cover of this book, shows that governance is centrally located within an array of family and business, and short- and long-term outcomes. The Landscape Map is a generalized depiction. It summarizes, organizes, and shows relationships among potential outcomes – not all of these outcomes are important to individual family businesses. The central location of governance suggests that those who govern, steer the family enterprise toward desired outcomes and coordinate the overall enterprise, both family and business, to obtain those outcomes.

From a governance perspective, the Landscape Map has applications for both researchers and practitioners. The bulk of this chapter reviews selected literature about

---

* "A Map of the Landscape of Family Business" (also referred to as the Landscape Map) can be found on the page just inside the cover of this book and in the Yu, Lumpkin, Sorenson, and Brigham (2012) article published in *Family Business Review*. Following the Landscape Map, the "Outcome Categories by Chapter Table" (also referred to as the Outcomes Categories Table) is provided. This table shows all chapters that contain content about the outcome categories that appear in this chapter.

each of the elements in Governance. I begin by providing an overview of family business outcomes and the dimensions that underlie them as described by Yu et al. (2012). Then I discuss research related to the elements that make up governance, followed by a brief summary. Finally, at the end of the chapter, I discuss potential research opportunities and practitioner applications.

The Landscape dimensions and clusters

The Landscape Map was the result of a study designed to discover, organize, and summarize relationships of outcome variables used in family business research. The research was accomplished in four steps. First, Yu et al. (2012) reviewed 12 years of research in major journals to identity outcome variables used in that research. Second, they used a Delphi technique to categorize outcome variables (see Yu et al., 2012, and Chapter 1 for details). Third, they asked family business experts to use a card-sorting procedure to capture similarities among outcome categories. Finally, similarity scores were entered into multi-dimensional scaling and cluster analyses producing a two-dimensional grid that provides a visual representation of relationships among outcome categories.

After examining the content of the Landscape Map, Yu et al. (2012) labeled the clusters that emerged from analyses as *Performance, Social and Economic Impact, Strategy, Family Business Roles, Family Dynamics, Succession*, and *Governance*. Yu and his colleagues (2012) also examined the content and location of the clusters in the Landscape Map and labeled the two dimensions on which the outcomes were plotted. Observing the horizontal axis, Yu et al. found that the clusters on the left side – Performance, Strategy, and Social and Economic Impact – were all business-related; and the clusters on the right side – Family Business Roles, Family Dynamics, and Succession – were family-related. So this dimension was labeled *Business/Family*. In the vertical axis, Yu et al. found that the clusters at the top of the Landscape Map – Strategy, Succession, Governance, and the family roles portion of Family Business Roles – have a relatively long-term focus. And clusters at the bottom of the Landscape Map – Performance, Social and Economic Impact, Family Dynamics, and the attitudes portion of Family Business Roles – have a relatively short-term focus. So this dimension was labeled *Short-Term/Long-Term*.

Using the lateral and horizontal axes as dividing lines, the Landscape Map can be divided into four quadrants. The short-term/business quadrant includes relatively immediate, short-term business issues and performance outcomes. The short-term/family quadrant includes family dynamics and attitudes toward the CEO and the family business. The cluster in the long-term/business quadrant is family business strategy. The long-term/family quadrant includes succession and family business roles.

Governance

Governance is the focus for the remainder of this chapter. The central positioning of Governance in family business is shown in the Landscape Map. The Governance cluster

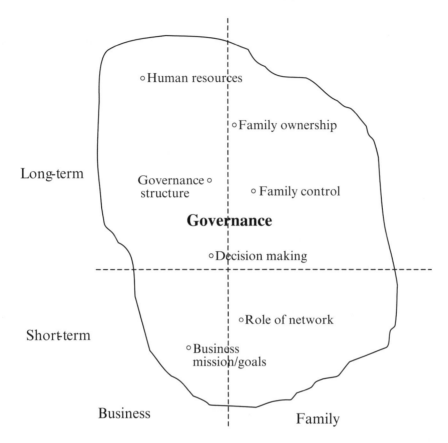

Figure 2.1   Elements of governance within the two dimensions of family business

spans into all four quadrants of the map, suggesting that those who govern, steer and coordinate the entire family enterprise toward desired outcomes. The outcome categories within Governance are *decision-making, family ownership, family control, governance structure, role of network, business mission/goals,* and *human resources.* For the reader's convenience, Figure 2.1 shows the Governance cluster and the outcome categories within it. Below, I discuss each of these outcome categories.

The study of family business is growing, but it is relatively new. The primary dependent variable in general business research is business performance. Easy access to financial performance data from public records has resulted in much research about public corporations. However, limiting research to outcomes only derived from public corporations also limits our understanding of family business. The majority of family businesses are privately owned, and yet most of the family business research focuses on public firms and short-term business performance, which neglects family and long-term outcomes depicted in the Landscape Map.

In addition, firms that are controlled by both family and non-family owners, as is the case in public firms, may significantly limit the focus on long-term and family outcomes that family owners often prefer. For example, a study of small family businesses associated with the National Federation of Independent Business (NFIB) in the US (Fiegener, 2010) found that owning families have significantly less influence when non-family owners had 60 percent or more ownership in the business.

Thus, this chapter will focus primarily on studies about businesses in which owning families have total or controlling ownership. A family business is defined here as one in which the family has controlling ownership and that seeks both short- and long-term business and family outcomes. Furthermore, a hyphen is added in *family-business* throughout the remainder of this chapter to illustrate that business and family cooperate to obtain the business *and* family outcomes desired by the owning family (see Eddleston, 2011).

Researchers are currently in the process of defining the primary dependent variables in family-business, which include financial (see Yu et al., 2012) and, more recently, socio-emotional outcomes (Gómez-Mejía, Takács, Núñez-Nickel, Jacobson & Moyano-Fuentes, 2007). In addition to business outcomes, Yu et al. (2012) have identified other promising long-term and family outcome variables that might be particularly useful in governance research. For example, their Landscape Map includes the following outcome clusters that might be used as indicators of long-term and family outcomes: 1) strategy as an indicator of long-term business outcomes, 2) succession and family business roles as indicators of long-term family outcomes, and 3) family attitudes and family dynamics as indicators of short-term family outcomes. When relevant, I will make reference to these outcomes when discussing governance.

Of the principle elements included in the Governance cluster, decision-making is closest to the intersection of the four quadrants in the Landscape Map, visually suggesting that decision-making is at the heart of Governance (see Figure 2.1). Therefore, I begin the discussion of governance with decision-making.

Decision-making

From a governance perspective, decision-making includes choosing desired outcomes, identifying decision participants, and making decisions. In Chapter 1, Yu summarizes the outcomes measures included in the decision-making category.[1]

When framing their approach to decision-making, owners of family businesses make two fundamental decisions. The first decision is, *Will theirs be a family business?* Put differently, do owners intend to keep business ownership and control in the family? The second decision is, *Do owners seek to retain the business into the next generation?* When owners answer yes to these two questions, theirs might be considered a multi-generational family business. And family stakeholders become important to developing a strategy that will sustain the business for the long-term and to preparing family members for succession.

Mustakallio, Autio & Zahra (2002) explored governance decisions in a sample of medium-sized businesses in Spain. They suggested that within the business, a *contractual* form of governance is used. Within the family, a *relational* form of governance is used. Mustakallio et al. found significant positive relationships (as indicated by arrows below) among measures of family relational governance.

Multiple family institutions ———→ Social interaction ———→ Shared vision
———→ Stragetic decision quality and commitment

Multiple family institutions were defined as informal and formal family meetings, family councils, and family plans. These family governance institutions were positively related to social interaction that in turn was positively associated with a shared vision. And shared vision, together with counsel from the board of directors, was positively related to high-quality strategic decisions and commitment to those strategic decisions.

The Mustakallio et al. (2002) study informs us about the nature of governance decisions in family-business. Decision-making participants and processes are different within the governance of the family and the business, and boards help to integrate decision-making that includes the owning family and the business.

In a study of small- and medium-size enterprisess (SMEs), Perry & Ring (2013) asked family-business owners who their most trusted advisors are. They found that for family socio-emotional outcomes (e.g., Gómez-Mejía, Haynes, Núñez-Nickel, Jacobson, & Moyano-Fuentes, 2007), the most trusted advisor is the family, primarily the owner's spouse. For financial outcomes, the most trusted advisor is an accountant. A study by Danes, Zuiker, Kean, & Arbuthnot (1999) sheds light on why the spouse is a trusted advisor. Danes et al. indicate that in small family businesses, there is typically a business manager and a household manager. Both managers need to cooperate to accomplish desired business and family outcomes. Thus, when family outcomes are important, owners rely on family advice.

In a study of 5,500 small, private firms, Fiegener, Brown, Dreux, & Dennis (2000) found that when planning for intra-family firm succession – a long-term and family outcome – family directors were added to the board. This study reveals the importance of including family in governance decisions regarding long-term family outcomes.

In a study of 732 medium-sized family businesses, Basco & Rodriquez (2009) found that 26 percent of those businesses emphasized business outcomes (e.g., business performance and growth) but not family outcomes. These businesses used external and professional advisors for advice in decision-making. Another 46 percent of the businesses in the Basco & Rodriquez study emphasized both business and family outcomes (e.g., development of family skills, family unity, and family opportunities). Governing owners in these businesses included family members on boards to enable owners to more easily integrate family perspectives into governance decisions. Both business and family desires were considered in decisions about strategy, human resources, and succession. Business outcomes for the two types of businesses were similar. However, family outcomes were significantly better in businesses that integrated family members into governance decision-making.

Smaller family businesses often do not have formal governance structures that help mediate between business and family. So owners of family firms use decision processes that help to integrate business and family outcomes. In studies of SMEs, Sorenson (1999, 2000) found that when owners used collaborative and participative decision processes, both business and family outcomes were significantly better than when other decision approaches were used. Measures of family outcomes included family satisfaction and independence, tight-knit family, respect in community, and child and business development. Collaboration was measured by the tendency to "work with one another for a proper understanding of the problem," "exchange accurate information to solve the problem," and "bring all concerns out into the open so that issues can be resolved in the best possible way" (Rahim, 1983).

Similarly, in another study of SMEs, Eddleston & Kellermanns (2007) found that an altruistic stewardship perspective that emphasized family bonds was significantly and positively related to participative decision-making. And participative decision-making was positively and significantly related to firm performance.

Summary.

Owners who commit to making theirs a multi-generation family business are motivated to include family stakeholders in governance, which help to integrate long-term and family issues into decisions. Research suggests that family members are often included in governance decisions regarding socio-emotional outcomes, strategy, and succession. Owners of smaller family businesses rely on collaborative and participative decision-making, which results in significantly stronger business and family outcomes. Owners of larger family businesses use a relational approach to governance that includes institutions designed to help family owners agree on a variety of issues, including mission. And they use a contractual approach to governance in forming and managing business agreements.

Family ownership

Ownership in family business refers to the right of business possession, control, and decision-making. The nature of ownership in family firm differs significantly from non-family controlled, public firms. In public firms, the shareholders hold only one outcome in common – financial returns on their investment. In contrast, family owners have more values in common and, therefore, can agree to pursue a broader range of outcomes than can occur in publically traded firms. And, owners of family businesses likely exert more decision authority to achieve desired outcomes than do the shareholders in publically traded firms. Thus, the assumptions that guide research about governance in public corporations only partially fit family owned and controlled firms. In the eyes of owning families, even when their financial profits are relatively low, family owners may be very satisfied because in addition to receiving financial returns, they seek other long-term and family outcomes.

In Chapter 1,[2] Yu reports the outcome measures that were summarized in Yu et al.'s (2012) research about ownership. Researchers have explored the role of owners in managing financial resources such as reinvesting in the business, allocating profits as dividends or distributions, using business equity and personal collateral, and monitoring interest paid for financing. Ownership research has also addressed relationships between family ownership and ownership control, and issues of fairness, process, and openness. In addition, researchers have examined continuity of ownership, ownership succession, and the structure of ownership in the next generation.

Below, I provide an overview of the variety of different forms of ownership and discuss the relationships of sole and family ownership to governance decisions.

Structure of ownership.

A variety of ownership structures exist in family firms. For example, a study of family firms in the Chicago area revealed that within 134 owner-managed firms,

- 36 percent were sole-owned,
- 18 percent were jointly owned by husbands and wives,
- 38 percent had parent(s) as majority owner(s) and successor(s) as minority owner(s), and
- 8 percent had successors as majority owners and parents as minority owners. (Ward & Dolan, 1998)

And within 55 sibling partnerships, 75 percent had relatively equal ownership distributed among two or more siblings, and 25 percent had one member with controlling ownership. Only 7 percent of the firms were cousin collaborations. Another study (Corbetta & Montemerlo, 1999) similarly found a variety of ownership structures. Discussing all of these forms of ownership is beyond the scope of this paper. Therefore, I focus my discussion on sole and family ownership.

Sole ownership.

Estimates suggest that very high percentages of businesses are family firms. For example, 73 percent of Australian firms (Smyrnios & Walker, 2003) and 80–90 percent of US firms (Astrachan & Shanker, 2003) are estimated to be family firms. However, some observers have questioned that all sole-owned firms should be classified as family firms (see Uhlanner, 2013). For example, a ten-country study found that 47 percent of new firms and 52 percent of established firms are owned and managed by one person (Reynolds et al., 2002). Are all these sole-owned businesses *family* firms?

Perhaps one rationale for categorizing sole-owned businesses as family firms may be that they provide income for the family. However, the extent to which sole-owners intend to make theirs a multi-generational family business is unknown. For example, Beckhard & Dyer (1983) observed that only a third of family firms make it to the second generation and that the average life expectancy of family firms is 24 years, which is also the average tenure of firm founders. Beyond obtaining income, do owners seek other family and long-term outcomes? If they do, they would likely seek family input.

Research indicates that sole-owners make most decisions themselves. In a national study of medium-sized Canadian businesses, Feltham, Feltham, & Barnett (2005) found that 75 percent of owners felt that their businesses were totally or highly dependent on them, 65 percent of owner-managers made all major business decisions, and 57 percent had two or fewer key managers. And importantly, like most other business owners (e.g., see Kertesz & Atalaya, 1999), 62 percent of the businesses studied by Feltham et al. (2005) had not chosen a successor nor engaged in succession planning, indicating lack of attention to long-term family outcomes.

We need to know much more about the motivations and profile of sole-owners in relation to long-term and family issues. For example, it would be helpful to know whether sole owners intend to make theirs a multi-generational family business, when in the life-cycle of the business the decision is made, and what motivates the decision.

One method for determining whether sole-owned firms will become family firms is to assess the extent of family influence in governance decisions. Research indicates that compared to firms owned by multiple family members, sole-proprietors and owner-managers seek significantly less input from the family (Fiegener, 2010). Without family influence, many firms may not be concerned about long-term and family outcomes. One approach to assessing family influence might be to determine whether, in addition to the owner, other family members work in the business.

Another approach for determining family influence would be to assess the nature of spousal influence. For example, when seeking advice about family socio-emotional outcomes (e.g., Gómez-Mejía, et al., 2007), Perry and Ring found that for sole-owners the most trusted advisor is the spouse (Perry & Ring, 2013). Another study found that spouses provide owners a variety of input, including about family and socio-economic outcomes (Poza & Messer, 2004).

Research suggests that including spouses in conversations about the business may shift the focus to family and the long-term concerns. Danes, Haberman, & McTavish (2005) compared the discourse of women and men who were owners of small family businesses. They found that men's language had more focus on the here and now, consistent with a short-term business orientation. Women more frequently used the term "we," which the authors interpreted as relationship building and pliable adhesiveness that hold business and family together. Moreover, women's language had more focus on the future and on change, consistent with long-term and entrepreneurial orientation.

Family ownership.
Compared to sole-owned firms, businesses owned by multiple family members have significantly more input from family members (Fiegener, 2010), and CEOs have a role in family oversight and monitoring (Livingston, 2007). However, the extent and nature of input depends on relational dynamics among owners. For example, a national representative US sample of small family businesses (Danes, Rueter, Kwon, & Doherty, 2002) found that some owning couples do not seek input, influence, and participation from one another in decision-making. Those who include one another have more collaboration and less conflict about financial decisions. Another study (Danes et al., 1999) found that when tensions were high, neither business nor household managers were able to achieve business or family goals.

Using data from public firms, Miller, Le Breton-Miller, & Lester (2011) found that sole-owned (majority owner) firms sought aggressive growth-oriented strategies, while family-owned firms sought conservative growth, higher dividends, reduced financial leverage, and reduced investment in research, development, and advertising. Based on these findings, Miller et al. (2011) suggested that different logics dominate decision-making: Lone owners seek reinvestment for immediate growth in the short-term. Family owners seek more conservative strategies to sustain the business for the long-term.

Another study of small, privately owned firms found that, compared to sole-owned firms, when more than one family member has a financial stake in the business, there is a significantly stronger tendency to emphasize a long-term stewardship perspective that included investment of products for the future, development of employees, and investment in customer relationships (Miller, Le Breton-Miller, & Scholnick, 2008).

Summary.

More research is needed about the relationship between the types of ownership and the tendency to seek business/family and short-/long-term outcomes. Research indicates that lone owners, who control business decisions, tend to focus on business performance and growth. However, they also trust the advice of spouses and other family members with regard to socio-emotional outcomes. Little is known about the nature of this family input and its influence on emphasizing long-term and family outcomes. Firms owned by multiple family members, on the other hand, seem to obtain family influence that results in a focus on family and long-term family outcomes.

Family control

Control refers to the authority to guide, regulate, and influence the family enterprise. The summary of outcome measures provided by Yu in Chapter 1[3] indicates that researchers have studied how families exert controlling influence through bureaucratic or clan control, the expression of family desires, and personal relationships with the top management team and the board of directors. Below, I discuss family control of ownership and of the board.

Family control of ownership.

Studies suggest that a predominant pattern in family businesses is that family owners maintain control through concentrated family ownership (see Bammens, Voordeckers, & van Gils, 2011; Uhlaner, 2013). For example, one study of 472 privately owned businesses in the UK found that, compared to a sample of non-family businesses, family business shareholders held a significantly higher percentage of stock (Westhead, Cowling, & Howorth, 2001).

In addition, family firms tend to avoid financing that could result in giving up control. A study of Canadian SMEs suggests that to maintain control, family firms prefer not to obtain equity financing, and when they do, they prefer private to public financing (Wu, Chua, & Chrisman, 2007).

One outcome of family control is that when making governance decisions family owners can maximize the outcomes they prefer. For owning families, socio-economic or other desired outcomes the family may be more important than profitability and business growth. For example, one study of 1,854 family firms (Mahto, Davis, Pearce, & Robinson, 2010) revealed that family interaction and family identity and commitment to the business were more highly related to family owner satisfaction than sales growth.

Because they control the firm, family owners can pursue a range of family objectives including reinvesting profits, minimizing risks, stimulating community employment, engaging in philanthropy, supporting new family ventures, or providing dividends. For example, one study of family businesses in Hong Kong revealed that when ownership and managerial control are both held by the family, shareholders receive relatively high levels of dividends, retain relatively high levels of liquidity, and make less capital investment in the business (Carney & Gedajlovic, 2002).

Alternatively, a study of family controlled olive oil mills in Spain (Gómez-Mejía et al., 2007) found that family firms make decisions that risk business performance to maintain family socio-emotional wealth (e.g., family values, identity, belonging, social capital, status, obligation to family). Another study found that even when a family firm is part of a merger or takeover, family members strive to maintain involvement and influence to help maintain the family legacy (Steen & Welch, 2006).

Family control of the board.

Owners of family businesses tend to develop boards that correspond with their ownership structure and that facilitate decision-making to achieve a variety of business, family, and long-term objectives. For example, a study of 211 SME family firms (Voordeckers, Van Gils, & Van den Heuvel, 2007) found that owning families are more likely to have insider family boards when 1) the CEO is also chairman, 2) the family is in the second generation, 3) owners are highly focused on family objectives, and 4) the business is focused on growth. Family firms are more likely to have boards that include outside advisors/directors when 1) the business approaches succession, 2) the focus is profit maximization, 3) the firm is in the third generation and beyond, and 4) the firm is large.

In Fiegener et al.'s (2000) study of over 5,500 small private firms associated with the NFIB in the US, researchers found that the percentage of CEO ownership is negatively associated with board size. In addition, CEO controlling ownership is positively associated with an increased number of family, inside, and affiliate directors, and a decreased number of outside owner-directors. Fiegener et al. suggested that *non-family directors who are owners* may threaten family control of the business. However, *non-owning directors* may add value without threatening family control.

Furthermore, a higher percentage of family ownership is negatively associated with board size and independent director ratio, and positively associated with a dependent director ratio, which reduces threats to family control (Fiegener et al., 2000). Finally, to include representation of family interests, boards include more family directors when families are planning intra-family firm succession.

A study of firms listed on the Australian stock exchange found that family firms have substantially different corporate governance structures than non-family firms (Bartholomeusz & Tanewski, 2006). Family firms have a lower percentage of outside ownership, a higher percentage of family directors, and a greater percentage of CEOs who also chair the board. In addition, family firm CEOs tend to receive less remuneration than non-family firm CEOs. While the authors argue that family firms could benefit from the discipline and transparency that comes from having external directors, they also suggest that non-family directors should not be owners because such ownership is related to higher levels of conflict and suboptimal firm performance. These researchers suggest that family boards would benefit from reducing the number of shares held by non-family directors and redistributing those shares to the CEO.

Somewhat consistent with the studies reported above, a study of Spanish non-listed family firms (Arosa, Iturralde, & Amaia, 2010) found that independent directors on a board significantly improve firm performance only in the first generation. In the second generation and beyond, affiliated directors who have an enduring and vested interest, who are more familiar with the business, and who are concerned with stewardship of the business significantly improve firm performance.

Finally, there seems to be a growing consensus that the role of independent directors is different for family and non-family businesses (see Uhlaner, 2013). For example, Anderson & Reeb (2004), in a study of S&P 500 firms, found that the presence of independent directors on a board improved family business performance. However, consistent with some of the studies cited above, Klein, Astrachan, & Smyrnios, (2005) found in a sample of 263 Canadian firms that the presence of independent directors had a negative impact on firm performance. Neither of these studies assessed long-term or family outcomes.

Summary.
Family owners almost universally prefer to keep decision control within the owning family. Such control enables families to obtain desired outcomes, including socio-emotional, family, and long-term outcomes. Smaller family firms tend to include family members on the board and to change board membership to achieve family objectives such as insider succession. In general, because family owners seek outcomes unique to the family, family business boards have less conflict when independent directors are not owners. For family firms in the second generation and beyond, there is some evidence that affiliated directors positively impact firm performance.

Governance structure

Governance structure refers to the composition of individuals and institutions within formal and informal systems that cooperate to make decisions that guide the family enterprise. In Chapter 1, Yu identifies outcomes assessed in relation to Governance structure.[4] Corporate governance has been the subject of most governance structure research (for a review, see Uhlaner, 2013). Because of concentrated ownership and family owner involvement in governance, the governance structure of family firms differs, sometimes dramatically, from that of non-family firms (e.g., Bartholomeusz & Tanewski, 2006; Martin-Reyna & Duran-Encalada, 2012).

The unique characteristic of family business is the inclusion and accommodation of the owning family in governance. Both current and potential family owners may have influence. Initially, a sole-owned family business is governed by the founding owner with family governance influence most likely coming from a spouse (Perry & Ring, 2013). In other small businesses, multiple family members may have a financial stake in the business (Miller et al., 2008). As the business grows and numbers of owners increase across generations, formal business and family governance structures such as family councils or assemblies are added. For example, Astrachan & Kolenko (1994) found that formal business plans, regular board meetings, and regular family meetings were significantly related to firm survival across generations. For larger, older businesses, governance structures can become quite complex.

> A family that owns a business, or substantial investments, is at the intersection of several complex systems and serves a multitude of masters, purposes, and constituencies. . . .in order to thrive, the family must develop a clear infrastructure to manage the interrelationships of people, business, and investment. . . .As a family enters the third generation, it has become a complex structure with several family branches, diverse interests and stakeholders, and challenges to sustain collaboration and effectiveness. (Jaffe & Lane, 2004, p. 81)

Thus, governance in family business is unlike non-family businesses due to family influence and additional institutions that accommodate family involvement in governance.

Consistent with Yu (Chapter 1), family firm governance includes family involvement in firm ownership, management, and boards.

An empirically validated classification identifies three organization types based on variables such as ownership, and family and non-family involvement (Salvato, 2002). The three types are (1) the founder-centered family firm; (2) the sibling or cousin consortium, which is still fully owned and managed by the family(ies); and (3) the open family firm, in which both ownership and control are partially shared with non-family shareholders and professional managers. These firms differ in the role that the founder and/or owner families play in governance (Corbetta & Salvato, 2004).

Corbetta and Salvato (2004) indicate that the three types of organizations differ in terms of agency costs. Agency costs occur when non-owner managers require monitoring to ensure they act in the best interest of the owners (e.g., Anderson & Reeb, 2003; Daily & Dollinger, 1992; Gómez-Mejía, Núñez-Nickel, & Gutierrez et al., 2001; Jensen & Meckling, 1976; La Porta, Lopez-de-Silanes, & Shleifer, 1999; Schulze, Lubatkin, & Dino, 2003a, 2003b; Morck & Yeung, 2003). For example, resources are required to monitor non-family business managers or to coordinate business direction with non-family owners.

Corbetta and Salvato (2004) indicate that agency costs are higher when non-family owners or managers have significant influence in the business. In the majority of small, private family firms, family members serve on the board and in top management, which tends to reduce agency costs because members readily understand one another and can make business decisions that are consistent with family values (e.g., see Bartholomeusz & Tanewski, 2006).

Additional institutions required for family governance in large family businesses also increase transaction costs. Transaction costs refer to resources required to exchange information, and to form and maintain agreements within the owning family and between the owning family and the business. For example, communication demands increase when increased numbers of family members and generations are included in governance (Ling & Kellermanns, 2010), or when family councils or assemblies are developed to enable families to participate in governance decisions (e.g., Mustakallio et al., 2002).

Agency and transaction costs are economic concepts that focus on business efficiency. In Corbetta and Salvato's (2004) framework, the agency costs arguments may best apply to open family firms that share ownership and control with non-family owners and managers. In these businesses, the least common denominator is business performance. In such firms, family involvement in governance is likely viewed as a cost, especially when the family seeks long-term family outcomes.

However, family-owned and controlled businesses are in a unique position. In governance decisions, their least common denominator can be expanded beyond business performance. Each family may define those outcomes differently. But fundamentally, according to the Yu et al. (2012) study, family owners will likely seek desired long-term and family outcomes in addition to short-term outcomes.

Instead of a focus on agency costs, owning families may focus on stewardship (Corbetta & Salvato, 2004; Miller & Le Breton-Miller, 2006; Zahra, Hayton, Neubaum, Dibrell, & Craig, 2008) that seeks a common purpose that is defined by the family. Instead of viewing family participation in governance as a cost, family owners see family involvement as an important element of stewardship that helps to obtain desired long-term family outcomes (Corbetta & Salvato, 2004). Family governance institutions give families a common purpose, structure, and social interaction that help to maintain family relationships (Mustakallio et al., 2002). And participation in family governance helps to unite the family around a common mission, culture, identity, and legacy (e.g., Eddleston, 2011; Eddeston & Kellermanns, 2007; Mustakallio et al., 2002).

Research indicates that family-controlled businesses tend to focus on stewardship more than agency (Davis, Allen, & Hayes, 2010), on maximizing performance more than minimizing costs, and on productive involvement of family owners (Eddleston & Kellermanns, 2007) and the achievement of long-term and family outcomes (Miller et al., 2008; Zahra et al., 2008) more than short-term profits.

Summary.
In family business, the simplest and most efficient governance structure that can address both business and family outcomes is that of a sole owner; the most common structures for SMEs with multiple owners is frequent family owner meetings or a board that represents both business and family interests; and the most complex structures are large cousin consortiums that include multiple family governance structures. To adequately assess the impact of governance on long-term and family outcomes, researchers need measures of different forms of family governance. Moreover, researchers might consider the nature and goals of owning families as they consider research frameworks. An agency framework may work well for firms that have both family and non-family owners. A stewardship framework may work best for firms that are wholly owned by a family.

Role of network

Networks refer to cooperative interconnections among individuals or entities. The outcome variables associated with "role of network" include external networks of cooperation with other business-related entities and internal networks that help develop congruity between business leaders and family owners (see Yu, Chapter 1).[5] Below, I provide an overview of research related to family and non-family networks.

Family network.
Anderson, Jack, and Dodd (2005) indicate that business owners have three kinds of network relationships with family members: 1) "family out" – family members who have no social connections with the owning family; 2) "family in" – family members formally involved in the family firm; and 3) "jugglers" – family members not formally involved with the family firm but who have social ties with the owning family.

The "family in" networks are family members who are included in formal gatherings and informal networks. The communication patterns and norms in formal and informal social gatherings sustain cultural beliefs, values, and norms within the family, and help to establish and sustain consistent values across the family and the business (see Mustakallio et al., 2002; Sorenson, 2011). This network includes spouses and other family members who may become owners (Fiegener, 2010).

According to Anderson et al. (2005), "jugglers" are family members not formally associated with the business but who make up about a quarter of the external network ties to a family business. Anderson et al. suggest that when relationships of trust exist, external family members can provide expertise, perspective, contacts, temporary business support, a sounding board, and problem solving. Moreover, Anderson et al. suggest that external family linkages can provide these resources without the hazards of managing potentially negative relationships with family members who are employees.

Other authors suggest that external linkages might be profitably increased by maintaining social network contacts with distant kin (Karra, Tracey, & Phillips, 2006). Family networks provide a potentially valuable resource for family firms. It would be helpful to know more about how both internal and external family networks are cultivated, maintained, and employed to benefit family firms.

Non-family network.

Several studies have found that non-family networks external to the business are important to family business survival and growth. For example, a longitudinal study of family firms in Australia found that linkages between established firms that exchange timely and business-relevant information help promote innovation, especially for early-stage firms (Craig & Moores, 2006). Another study of family businesses in Lithuania suggested that family firms stay viable in a hostile environment when they cultivate social networks to gain favor with local authorities, customers, and suppliers, and use family networks to gain access to human and financial resources (Dyer & Mortensen, 2005).

In addition, researchers found that the most trusted advisors outside the family are accountants, followed by lawyers and business peers (Perry & Ring, 2013). Family owners benefit from establishing collaborative networks with customers (Sorenson, Folker, & Brigham, 2008) and other external stakeholders such as contacts in industry associations (Hatum & Pettigrew, 2004). Researchers have also found that SMEs that establish collaborative networks with employees, customers and family members improve firm performance (Sorenson, 1999; Sorenson et al., 2008).

However, one study indicated that family firms could benefit from being circumspect about how they adapt within their networks to avoid losing their independence. A study family-business connections to industry associations Hatum and Pettigrew (2004) found that that instead of relying exclusively on industry associations for guidance, family firms can adapt and grow by being less formal and centralized in general, formalizing strategic decision-making, hiring high-level managers to bring in new ideas, maintaining strong relationships with customers and suppliers, formalizing environmental scanning, and retaining core values across generations. In other words, adaptive organizations can succeed by building around family values and strategy, and by not being overly influenced by industry norms (see also Zahra et al., 2008).

Summary.

Networks are an important element in governance. Maintaining both formal and informal social network develops congruence between family owners and business leaders. In addition, family owners who retain ties with family members not formally involved in the business have access to low-cost resources that may help their businesses and owning families survive and prosper. Maintaining networks with non-family, business-related entities combined with judicious use of input enables family businesses to adapt, survive, and grow.

Family business mission and goals

The family-business mission and goals category is centrally located in the Landscape Map but within the Short-term business quadrant, suggesting that this category may help to align Short-term business outcomes with Family and Long-term outcomes (see Figure 2.1). Business practices, goals, and culture are included in the research related to mission and goals (see Yu, Chapter 1).[6]

Families and businesses are very different kinds of social institutions. The purpose of business is to provide a product or service that yields income for owners and employees. The purpose of family is to nurture, support, develop, and sustain family members. Relationships in business tend to be temporary and contractual, whereas relationships in families tend to be enduring and personal (Mustakallio et al., 2002). As social institutions, businesses and families accomplish common objectives through cooperative efforts. Below, I will discuss how common mission, goals, and culture help to develop unity between business and family institutions.

Mission and goals.

The central position of mission and goals in the overall Landscape Map suggests that common mission and goals help to align Short-term business outcomes with desired outcomes in the other three quadrants (see Figure 2.1). Consistent with this assumption, studies of privately held SMEs have found that mission statements help to align purpose so as to improve business performance (e.g., Alavi & Karami, 2009; Nam & Herbert, 1999). A study identifying best management practices used by top managers worldwide revealed that formal mission statements were consistently the top-rated management practice (Bain et al., 1996). And studies suggest that when the entire enterprise – family, employees, and the board – participate in developing mission and goals, businesses have higher levels of performance. A study among some of the largest businesses in North America (Bart, Bontis, & Taggar, 2001) found that employee performance increased when there was 1) commitment to a mission and 2) alignment of internal structure, policies, and procedures with the mission.

One study (Mustakallio et al., 2002) found that family agreement about mission is positively related to strategic decision quality and commitment. Another study (Alavi & Karami, 2009) found that firms perform significantly better when employees are involved in developing the firm's mission statement. Thus, stakeholder involvement in developing mission and goals is important. Collaboration and collaborative networks provide an infrastructure that helps family businesses agree on mission and goals (Sorenson, 1999; Sorenson et al., 2008).

For example, Danes et al. (1999) found that in each small family business, there is typically a business manager and a household manager. Both managers need to cooperate to obtain desired business and family outcomes. Danes and her colleagues (1999) found that owning families are more successful in achieving their goals when they maintain good communication and decision practices that enable business and household managers to commit to common goals.

In larger business families, collaboration in setting common goals becomes a challenge. Mustakallio et al. (2002) found a significant negative relationship between family size and family agreement about family vision, goals, and long-term objectives. One way to help larger families agree is developing family institutions such as reunions, family councils, and assemblies. Such structures help owning families agree on mission and goals (Mustakallio et al., 2002, Sorenson, 1999). However, Mustakallio et al. report than only 27 percent of the families in their study held formal family meetings, which raises questions about the extent to which family institutions are used to govern.

Culture.

In addition to agreement about family-business mission and goals, developing a common culture helps to create unity between the owning family and the business. Culture consists of common values, beliefs, and practices. Values are core beliefs about what is important. Beliefs define who "we" are, who "they" are, and how "we" relate to "them" (see Sorenson, 2011, 2013a, 2013b). Practices are expressions of beliefs and values. When the culture of the family is compatible with that of the business, the two institutions are likely to find it easier to cooperate in accomplishing common goals. In fact, some researchers assert that one way to determine whether a business is a family-business is to measure the similarity between family and business values (Astrachan, Klein, & Smyrnios, 2002).

Businesses and families are predisposed to place emphasis on different kinds of values. Families tend to emphasize what Rokeach (1973) calls moral values (e.g., integrity, responsible, forgiving) that maintain interpersonal relationships. Businesses tend to emphasize what Rokeach calls competence values (e.g., ambitious, capable, logical) that focus on accomplishment (see Sorenson, 2013a, 2013b). Studies find a prevalence of both kinds of values in family firms. For example, Koiranen (2002) found that 100-year old Finnish firms emphasized the moral values of "honesty," "credibility," and "obeying the law" *and* competence values of "quality" and being "industrious/hardworking." Another study (Payne, Brigham, Broberg, Moss, & Short, 2011) found significant differences in cultural values between family and non-family businesses. For example, compared to non-family firms, family firms had significantly more references to "empathy," "warmth," and "zeal."

Sorenson (2013b) indicated that family values and practices may become embedded in the business in the following ways: multiple family members work in the business (e.g., Dyer, 1986); family and business share common rituals, stories, symbols, and heroes (e.g., Parada & Viladás, 2010); the founder promotes family values in the business (see Schein 1983, 1985); the owning family collaborates to create vision, goals, policies, and practices, which may be included in a family charter or constitution; and the family organizes events that recognize and celebrate the values of the founder and the founding family (e.g., see Shepard, 2011).

Entities that have common cultures may also have common identities. Eddleston (2011) suggests that families and businesses can have strong but separate cultures and identities. When they share common cultures, family businesses can develop a common family-firm identity. That is, when families and businesses have similar values, they can identify with and be committed to one another (Mahto et al., 2010).

Summary.

In family businesses, the family and the business are more likely to work cooperatively to obtain desired outcomes when 1) the owning family is clear about family mission, goals and values; 2) when the owning family works with business managers, the board and employees to define business strategy, mission, goals, and values that are compatible with those of the owning family; and 3) when owning family beliefs, values and practices are compatible with those of the business. In other words, the family and the business are more likely to identify with one another and be aligned about important goals and outcomes when they share a common culture.

Human resources

Human resources management research examined outcomes associated with the practices, processes, and rules related to recruitment, development, management and retention of employees (see Yu, Chapter 1).[7] The outcome variables summarized by Yu indicate that human resources policies and practices are important for family businesses, especially when the owning family employs family members in the business. Human relations policies help define expectations for employment and guidelines for mentoring, career development, appropriate wages and benefits, and performance evaluation. From a family governance perspective, human resources practices include the owning family being good stewards, engaging in fair process, being flexible and supportive, developing human capital in the next generation, and avoiding stagnation that can occur when family members have extended tenure. Below, I provide an overview of human resources research that addresses the relationship between human resources policies and practices, and long-term and family outcomes.

One potential human resource advantage of family ownership is the family capital (human, social, and financial capital) that the owning family brings to a business (Danes, Stafford, Haynes, & Amarapurkar, 2009; Sorenson & Bierman, 2009). According to Sirmon and Hitt (2003), important family resources may include human capital, social capital, patient capital, and survivability capital, as well as family governance. They note that families often have unique tacit abilities that strengthen a business. These tacit abilities are implicit and difficult to duplicate, but they can be transferred across generations.

Other scholars suggest that because family owners control their businesses, they are in a position to better manage human resources problems that plague non-family businesses. For example, two articles summarize the work-family conflict literature and outline how owning families are in a position to manage work-family conflicts (Rothausen, 2009; Rothausen & Sorenson, 2011). One owner, for instance, indicated that her family business supports a work-family balance – the firm limits work demands placed on employees and excuses both family and non-family employees when they must attend to family needs (McEnaney, 2011).

However, family businesses also have human resource challenges. In an early article, Lansberg (1983) summarized the human resources problems that occur when business and family institutions overlap, including tensions regarding employee selection, compensation, appraisal, and training and development.

Family relationships can negatively impact human resources practices in family firms. For example, in a study of 276 newspapers owned by families, researchers (Gómez-Mejía et al., 2001) found a significant positive improvement in firm performance when low-performing non-family executives were relieved from their positions. However, the performance of CEOs from owning families was rarely assessed, and the CEOs stayed on the job longer than was justified by performance. What approaches do owners of family firms use to manage family-based human resources conflicts? Often owners develop formal governance policies that outline the qualifications required to be hired and retained in the business. In addition, they may specify an age for retirement.

Within the business, many family-business owners use clan controls to help manage human resources (Moores & Mula, 2000). Clan controls promote desired behavior by emphasizing common values and beliefs, developing deep levels of agreement about acceptable behavior, promoting high commitment to socially prescribed behaviors, and developing mutual understanding that individual interests are best served by group interests. Over time, employees become socialized in expected behavior much as they would if they had an extended stay with a family. Moores and Mula indicate, however, that larger family firms tend to adopt bureaucratic controls.

Another study of SMEs found a tendency to use social and clan types of control (emphasis on common values, beliefs, and norms) and that when organizations become larger and more complex, they adopt standardized human resource practices (de Kok, Uhlaner, & Thurik, 2006). Similarly, an additional study of SMEs found that almost all small firms tend to rely on informal training. But as they grow, they adopt more formal, structured, and development-oriented training (Kotey & Folker, 2007).

Astrachan and Kolenko (1994) examined the relationship between firm survival and success, and formal human resources practices in larger family firms. Of the five practices they assessed, Astrachan and Kolenko found that employee reviews, compensation plans, employee policy manuals, and written job descriptions were used significantly more frequently than were written succession plans or formal entry requirements for family members. They also found that use of these practices was positively related to gross firm revenues. And, they found that human resources practices were positively related to level of owner education and to the use of formal governance practices. And formal governance practices were positively related to firm longevity.

Summary.
Combining family ownership with business creates some human resources advantages. Families that have considerable family capital (e.g., human, social, and financial) tend to have more successful and enduring family businesses. And owners of family businesses may be more able to avoid problems such as work-family conflict compared with non-family businesses. Moreover, within small family businesses, human resources tend to be managed informally using family-based social and clan-type influence to socialize employees. Within larger family firms, more formal and standardized policies and practices and used. And there is evidence that firm longevity is positively related to formal human resources practices.

Discussion

This chapter is based upon a study by Yu et al. (2012) that summarized outcome variables used in family business research. They found that a business/family dimension and a short-term/long-term dimension underlie a broad range of potential outcomes in family-business. A cluster of governance outcomes was centrally located in the Landscape Map, suggesting that it has a central role in guiding and coordinating the family firm to obtain desired outcomes. This chapter has provided an overview of research within each of the outcome categories that were included in the governance cluster.

At the end of the research overview for each element of Governance, I provided a brief summary that might prompt more research inquiry or practitioner applications. Below, I provide additional comments for researchers based on reflection about the overall family business landscape. Then, I summarize potential applications for practitioners.

Researchers

Governance is centrally located within the two dimensions of the Landscape Map and includes seven clusters of outcome variables. The outcome category most centrally located in the overall family business landscape is decision-making. Those who make governance decisions determine the extent to which the family business will seek long-term and family outcomes. The background and interests of decision-makers will likely influence the extent to which they seek those outcomes and other outcomes available within the family business landscape. Researchers might explore several areas about decision-making, including who makes decisions, the decision process, and the extent to which the owning family pursues business and family, and long- and short-term outcomes.

Unique to family businesses, concentrated family owner control increases the range of values and about which families can agree. Given that owning family values are often cited as a defining characteristic of family-businesses (e.g., Astrachan et al., 2002), we know very little about them and the effect they have on both business and family outcomes for the short- and the long-term. Thus, researchers might explore more specifically how values are formed in the family and the business, and how they are sustained across generations.

While the Landscape Map (see Figure 2.1) includes governance structure as an important element of Governance, we know very little about *family* governance structures. Family governance structures that have been identified include owner councils, assemblies, annual shareholder meetings, retreats, and reunions. We would better understand governance structure if we understood the role *family* governance structures in overall family-business governance. In addition, as the numbers of family-business owners increase across generations, the owning family seems challenged to sustain unity, trust and commitment. Researchers might examine the governance structures and processes that promote or limit trust in these owning families.

The mission and goals statement provides direction for the family business (e.g., Alavi & Karami, 2009; Bart, Bontis, & Taggar, 2001; Mustakallio, et al., 2002; Nam & Herbert, 1999). Researchers might examine the relationships among mission statements and decision-making processes, decision-makers, and influential advisors. For example, researchers might examine whether the content of mission and goals statements differs when the owning family has more decision influence.

The research cited above suggests that lone owners of large, public firms seek short-term business growth and profitability (e.g., Miller et al., 2011). Researchers might explore the extent to which sole owners in small, private firms focus on profitability and growth. And they might explore the broader question of what percentage of sole owners could be classified as family businesses. Questions about sole owners might include the following: When the only decision-maker is a sole owner or when influential advisors are non-family members, is the focus primarily on short-term business performance and growth? When decision-makers or influential advisors are multiple family members, is more attention given to long-term and family outcomes?

One indicator of decision influence is board membership. Most family businesses have family members on their boards (Bartholomeusz & Tanewski, 2006; Fiegener et al., 2000; Voordeckers et al., 2007). Future research might examine the extent to which having multiple family members involved in decision-making is positively associated with 1) an increased focus on family outcomes, 2) effectiveness in producing favorable family outcomes, and 3) a long-term focus, including an emphasis on succession and a long-term strategy.

In family firms, there is evidence that CEOs have long tenure, even when firms have poor business performance (e.g., Gómez-Mejía et al., 2001; Westhead et al., 2001). Future research might examine factors associated with long-term tenure, including sole ownership, ownership control, and levels of family member influence on CEOs. Does the long-term tenure of family CEOs produce better family and long-term outcomes? Or does it simply reflect the entrenched position of the CEO, who may be the sole or majority owner?

Second-generation sibling owners have high levels of conflict and considerable difficulty in making governance decisions (Ensley & Pearson, 2005). Apparently, beyond the second generation, owners are better prepared to make decisions. Researchers could compare the family governance practices of owners in first, second, and third generations and beyond to better understand what produces successful governance and why. It could be that in the second generation the owning family has not yet learned to separate family governance from business governance.

As the number of family-business owners increases across generations, those who govern the business seem challenged to retain owner trust and commitment. Researchers might examine the governance processes that promote or limit trust in these owning families.

Finally, succession has long been a primary area of interest in family business. Researchers might assess the extent to which long-term and family discussions early in the formation of businesses is associated with succession of leadership and ownership later on. In addition, researchers might examine the extent to which family members are included in family business discussions and the extent to which they discuss succession.

Practitioners

One of the contributions of the Landscape Map is the visual representation of important outcomes. Governing owners can benefit from giving attention to potential outcomes in all four quadrants of the Landscape Map. For example, an owning family might begin by developing mission and goals for the business that take into account desired business *and* family outcomes for both the short- and the long-term that might be expressed as a family mission statement.

In addition, the owning family might consider how best to include family members in governance decisions. If the family is most concerned about professionalizing the business for growth, it might include non-family industry and business experts on its board to guide decision-making. Such experts can help the owning family to move beyond clan controls and practices to more professional practices that might be expected in a broad market.

If owners desire to prepare family members to become future owners and leaders, it might include family representatives on its board. Family board members can indicate the extent to which family members are satisfied with the business and its leaders, identify family members who are committed to the business and who have human capital to make contributions, discuss potential roles for family members, and design early experiences to promote understanding and interest in the business. In addition, family members can establish human resources policies that define expectations for family members interested in joining the business. Moreover, both non-family and family board members can help during transitions. Non-family board members can provide perspective and an external assessment of leader candidates.

To prepare for succession, lone owners can seek out the best transition practices. They can seek advice in from other owning families and from external experts in structuring ownership and governance so the business succeeds and the family retains good relationships. If multiple children will become owners, current owners can prepare them to work together in making governance decisions. If only one child is given ownership or controlling ownership, the owner can seek advice to establish an estate plan and decision policies that promote family harmony. In addition, by thinking ahead, owners can begin next generation education early by discussing the family business and providing appropriate work opportunities for children.

In general, if owners are thinking about making theirs a multi-generational family business, they can put in place the governance structure that will prepare owners and potential owners for the future. For example, they might organize family meetings to educate potential owners about the business. And they might invite future owners to board meetings, hire them as employees, or find other ways to involve them in the business.

Conclusion

Based on the research that led to Yu et al.'s (2012) publication on the landscape of family business outcomes, this chapter examined the Governance cluster, the outcome categories within the cluster, and the dimensions underlying family business outcomes. The most central outcome category in the Landscape Map is decision-making, which is within the Governance cluster. Closely associated with decision-making are the individuals, structures, and agreements that guide decisions.

In a family business, family members have ownership and therefore the ultimate decision control. Controlling owners select the individuals who participate in making decisions. They develop decision-making structures, including boards of directors or advisors, owner counsels or assemblies, and networks of advisors. Owners develop family mission and goals and the human resources policies that help to guide decision-making.

In this chapter, I suggest the defining characteristic of a family business is that in addition to seeking short-term business outcomes, owners seek long-term and family outcomes. Business owners who focus on long-term and family outcomes are more likely to establish a multi-generational family business.

Notes

1. This is the summary of outcome variables by Yu (Chapter 1) and the number of studies that used the outcomes variable (noted in parentheses): strategic investment decisions; start-up decision; allocation of financial resources; the future leader's perception of the business; intention to join the family business (5); dependence on a single decision-maker; internalization process; management transfer; fair process; familiness; generational differences among family businesses; succession planning activities (2); merger and acquisition; decision quality and decision commitment; management and ownership; the intermingling of family and business finance (3); the purchase of child care service; women's pathways to participation and leadership; foreign direct investment behavior; probability of new venture start-up.
2. This is the summary of outcome variables by Yu (Chapter 1) and the number of studies that used the outcomes variable (noted in parentheses): Ownership (7); corporate governance structure (2); allocation of financial resources; intention/behavior of the family; control sales; management (2); perceived control; fair process; piercing the corporate veil; issues about family relationship during the succession process; characteristics and key success factors; continuity; equity financing; interest rate premium; business collateral and personal collateral.
3. This is the summary of outcome variables by Yu (Chapter 1) and the number of studies that used the outcomes variable (noted in parentheses): Family control (2); control sales; types of family relationships in top management team; intention/behavior of the family; organizational flexibility; market; bureaucratic and clan control in organizational life-cycle stages; existence of board of directors; percentage of family members in the top management team.
4. This is the summary of outcome variables by Yu (Chapter 1) and the number of studies that used the outcomes variable (noted in parentheses): Corporate governance structure (4); informal cooperation; management and ownership; executive tenure (3); agency costs; transaction costs; types of family relationships in top management team; board composition (2); family business structure; issues about family relationship during the succession process; continuity; existence of board of directors; percentage of family members in the top management team.
5. This is the summary of outcome variables by Yu (Chapter 1) and the number of studies that used the outcomes variable (noted in parentheses): network composition; interfirm cooperation capability in the context of networking family firms; business group formation; group membership; family business' response to merger or takeover process; survival strategies in a hostile environment; establishment and growth of an entrepreneurial family business; congruity between business and family.
6. This is the summary of outcome variables by Yu (Chapter 1) and the number of studies that used the outcomes variable (noted in parentheses): business practices/goals (5); company objectives; culture; merger and acquisition; continuity
7. This is the summary of outcome variables by Yu (Chapter 1) and the number of studies that used the outcomes variable (noted in parentheses): employee training programs; professional human resource management practices; strategic human resource; fair process; flexibility; the purchase of child care service; mentoring in family businesses; human capital; opportunism; group cohesion; amount of perceived benefits for the next generation (educational and relational); stewardship; stagnation.

References

Alavi, M.T, & Karami, A. (2009). Managers of small and medium enterprises: Mission statement and enhanced organizational performance. *Journal of Management Development*, *28*(6), 555–62.

Anderson, A.A., Jack, S.L., & Dodd S.D. (2005). The role of family members in entrepreneurial networks: Beyond the boundaries of the family firm. *Family Business Review*, *18*(2), 135–54.

Anderson, R.C., & Reeb, D.M. (2003). Founding-family ownership and firm performance: Evidence from the S&P 500. *The Journal of Finance*, *58*, 1301–28.

Anderson, R.C., & Reeb, D.M. (2004). Board composition: Balancing family influence in S&P 500 firms. *Administrative Science Quarterly*, *49*, 209–37.

Andres, C. (2008). Large shareholders and firm performance – An empirical examination of founding-family ownership. *Journal of Corporate Finance*, *14*, 431–45.

Aronoff, C.E., & Ward, J.L. (1996). *Family business governance: Maximizing family and business potential*. Marietta, GA: Business Owner Resources.

Arosa, B., Iturralde, T., & Amaia, M. (2010). Ownership structure and firm performance in non-listed firms: Evidence from Spain. *Journal of Family Business Strategy, 1*(1) 88–96.

Astrachan, J.H., & Kolenko, T.A. (1994). A neglected factor in explaining family business success: Human resource practices. *Family Business Review, 7*(3), 251–62.

Astrachan, J.H., & Shanker, M.C. (2003). Family businesses' contribution to the U.S. economy: A closer look. *Family Business Review, 16*(3), 211–19.

Astrachan, J.H, Klein, S.B., & Smyrnios, K.H. (2002). The F-PEC scale of family influence: A proposal for solving the family business definition problem. *Family Business Review, 15*(1), 45–58.

Bain & Co., Inc. (1996). *Management tools and techniques: An executive's guide.* Boston, MA: Bain & Co.

Bammens, Y., Voordeckers, W., & van Gils, A. (2008). Boards of directors in family firms: A generational perspective. *Small Business Economics, 31*(2), 163–80.

Bammens, Y., Voordeckers, W., & van Gils, A. (2011). Boards of directors in family businesses: A literature review and research agenda. *International Journal of Management Reviews, 13*, 134–52.

Bart, C.K., Bontis, N., & Taggar, S. (2001). A model of the impact of mission statements on firm performance. *Management Decision, 39*(1), 19–35.

Bartholomeusz, S., & Tanewski, G.A. (2006). The relationship between family firms and corporate governance. *Journal of Small Business Management, 44*, 245–67.

Basco, R., & Rodriguez, M.J.P. (2009). Studying family enterprise holistically: Evidence for integrated family and business systems. *Family Business Review, 22*, 82–95.

Beckhard, R., & Dyer, W.G., Jr. (1983). Managing continuity in the family-owned business. *Organizational Dynamics, 12*(1), 4–11.

Boyd, J., Upton, N., & Wircenski, M. (1999). Mentoring in family firms: A reflective analysis of senior executives' perceptions. *Family Business Review, 12*, 299–309.

Boyle, E.H., Jr., Pollack, J.M., & Rutherford, M.W. (2012). Exploring the relationship between family involvement and firms' finance performance: A meta-analysis of main and moderator effects. *Journal of Business Venturing, 27*, 1–18.

Carney, M. (2005). Corporate governance and competitive advantage in family-controlled firms. *Entrepreneurship Theory and Practice, 29*(3), 249–65.

Carney, M., & Gedajlovic, E. (2002). The coupling of ownership and control and the allocation of financial resources: Evidence from Hong Kong. *Journal of Management Studies, 39*, 123–46.

Corbetta, G., & Montemerlo, D. (1999). Ownership, governance, and management issues in small and medium-size family businesses: A comparison of Italy and the United States. *Family Business Review, 12*(4), 361–74.

Corbetta, G., & Salvato, C. (2004). Self-serving or self-actualizing? Models of man and agency costs in different types of family firms: A commentary on "Comparing the agency costs of family and non-family firms: Conceptual issues and exploratory evidence." *Entrepreneurship Theory and Practice, 28*(4), 355–62.

Craig, J.B.L., & Moores, K. (2006). A 10-year longitudinal investigation of strategy, systems, and environment on innovation in family firms. *Family Business Review, 19*, 1–10.

Daily, C.M., & Dollinger, M.J. (1992). An empirical examination of ownership structure in family and professionally managed firms. *Family Business Review, 5*(2), 117–36.

Danes, S.M., Haberman, H.R., & McTavish, D. (2005). Gendered discourse about family business. *Family Relations, 54*(1), 116–30.

Danes, S.M., Rueter, M.A., Kwon, H.K., & Doherty, W. (2002). Family FIRO model: An application to family business. *Family Business Review, 15*, 31–44.

Danes, S.M., Stafford, K., Haynes, G., & Amarapurkar, S. (2009). Family capital of family firms: Bridging human, social, and financial capital. *Family Business Review, 22*(3), 199–215.

Danes, S.M., Zuiker, V., Kean, R., & Arbuthnot, J. (1999). Predictors of family business tensions and goal achievement. *Family Business Review, 12*, 241–52.

Davis, J.H., Allen, M.R., & Hayes, H.D. (2010). Is blood thicker than water? A study of stewardship perceptions in family business. *Entrepreneurship Theory and Practice, 34*(6), 1093–115.

de Kok, J.M.P., Uhlaner, L.M., & Thurik, A.R. (2006). Professional HRM practices in family owned-managed enterprises. *Journal of Small Business Management, 44*, 441–60.

Dyer, W.G., Jr. (1986). *Cultural change in family firms: Anticipating and managing business and family transitions.* San Francisco, CA: Jossey-Bass, Inc..

Dyer, W.G., Jr., & Mortensen, S.P. (2005). Entrepreneurship and family business in a hostile environment: The case of Lithuania. *Family Business Review, 18*(3), 247–58.

Eddleston, K. (2011). The family as an internal and external resource of the firm: The importance of building family-firm identity. In R.L. Sorenson (Ed.), *Family business and social capital* (pp. 186–97). Cheltenham, UK, and Northampton, MA, USA: Edward Elgar Publishing.

Eddleston, K., & Kellermanns, F.W. (2007). Destructive and productive family relationships: A stewardship theory perspective. *Journal of Business Venturing, 22*(4), 545–65.

Ensley, M.D., & Pearson, A.W. (2005). An exploratory comparison of the behavioral dynamics of top management teams in family and nonfamily new ventures: Cohesion, conflict, potency, and consensus. *Entrepreneurship, Theory and Practice, 29*, 267–84.

Feltham, T.S., Feltham, G., & Barnett, J.J. (2005). The dependence of family businesses on single decision-maker. *Journal of Small Business Management, 43*, 1–15.

Fiegener, M.K. (2010). Locus of ownership and family involvement in small private firms. *Journal of Management Studies, 47*(2), 296–391.

Fiegener, M.K., Brown, B.M., Dreux, D.R., IV, & Dennis, W.J., Jr. (2000). CEO stakes and board compositions in small private firms. *Entrepreneurship, Theory and Practice, 24*, 5–24.

Gómez-Mejía, L.R., Larraza-Kintana, M., & Marianna, M. (2003). The determinants of executive compensation in family-controlled public corporations. *Academy of Management Journal, 46*(2), 226–37.

Gómez-Mejía, L.R., Núñez-Nickel, M., & Gutierrez, I. (2001). The role of family ties in agency contracts. *Academy of Management Journal, 44*, 81–95.

Gómez-Mejía, L.R., Takács Haynes, K., Núñez-Nickel, M., Jacobson, K.J.L., & Moyano-Fuentes, J. (2007). Socio-emotional wealth and business risks in family-controlled firms: Evidence from Spanish olive oil mills. *Administrative Science Quarterly, 52*, 106–137.

Habbershon, T.G., & Williams, M.L. (1999). A resource-based framework for assessing the strategic advantages of family firms. *Family Business Review, 12*(1), 1–25.

Hatum, A., & Pettigrew, A. (2004). Adaptation under environmental turmoil: Organizational flexibility in family-owned firms. *Family Business Review, 17*, 237–58.

Jaffe, D.T., & Lane, S.H. (2004). Sustaining a family dynasty: Key issues facing complex multigenerational business-and investment-owning families. *Family Business Review, 17*(1), 81–98.

Jensen, M.C., & Meckling, W.H. (1976). Theory of the firm: Managerial behavior, agency costs and ownership structure. *Journal of Financial Economics, 3*, 305–60.

Karra, N., Tracey, P., & Phillips, N. (2006). Altruism and agency in the family firm: Exploring the role of family, kinship, & ethnicity. *Entrepreneurship, Theory and Practice, 30*, 861–77.

Kertesz, R., & Atalaya, C.I. (1999). Family businesses in Argentina: Current issues. *Community, Work and Family, 2*(1), 93–103.

Klein, S.B., Astrachan, J.H., & Smyrnios, K.X. (2005). The F-PEC scale of family influence: Construction, validation, and further implication for theory. *Entrepreneurship Theory and Practice, 29*(3), 321–39.

Klein, P., Shapiro, D., & Young, J. (2005). Corporate governance, family ownership and firm value: The Canadian evidence. *Corporate Governance: An International Review, 13*(6), 769–84.

Koiranen, M. (2002). Over 100 years of age but still entrepreneurially active in business: Exploring the values and family characteristics of old Finnish family firms. *Family Business Review, 15*(3), 175–87.

Kotey, B. & Folker, C. (2007). Employee training in SMEs: Effect of size and firm type-family and non-family. *Journal of Small Business Management, 47*, 214–38.

Lambrecht, J., & Lievens, J. (2008). Pruning the family tree: An unexplored path to family business continuity and family harmony. *Family Business Review, 21*(4), 295–313.

Lansberg, I.S. (1983). *Organizational Dynamics, Summer,* 39–46.

La Porta, R., Lopez-de-Silanes, F., & Shleifer, A. (1999). Corporate ownership around the world. *Journal of Finance, 54*, 471–517.

Ling, Y., & Kellermanns, F.W. (2010). The effects of family firm specific sources of TMT diversity: The moderating role of information exchange frequency. *Journal of Management Studies, 47*, 322–44.

Livingston, L. (2007). Control sales in family firms. *Family Business Review, 20*, 49–67.

Mahto, R.V., Davis, P.S., Pearce, J.A., & Robinson, R.B. (2010). Satisfaction with firm performance in family businesses. *Entrepreneurship Theory and Practice, 34*, 985–1001.

Marshall, J.P., Sorenson, R., Brigham, K., Wieling, E., Reifman, A., & Wampler, R.S. (2006). The paradox for the family firm CEO: Owner age relationship to succession-related processes and plans. *Journal of Business Venturing, 21*, 348–68.

Martin-Reyna, J.M.S., & Duran-Encalada, J.A. (2012). The relationship among family business, corporate governance and firm performance: Evidence for the Mexican stock exchange. *Journal of Family Business Strategy, 3*, 106–17.

McConaughy, D.L. (2000). Family CEOs vs. non-family CEOs in the family controlled firm: An examination of the level and sensitivity of pay to performance. *Family Business Review, 13*(2), 121–31.

McConaughy, D.L., Matthews, C.H., & Fialko, A.S. (2001). Founding family controlled firms: Performance, risk, and value. *Journal of Small Business Management, 39*, 31–49.

McEnaney, T. (2011). Our family enterprise. In R.L. Sorenson (Ed.), *Family business and social capital* (pp. 170–77). Cheltenham, UK, and Northampton, MA, USA: Edward Elgar Publishing.

Miller, D., & Le Breton-Miller, I. (2005). Management insights from great and struggling family business. *Long Range Planning, 38*, 517–30.

Miller, D., & Le Breton-Miller, I. (2006). Family governance and firm performance: Agency, stewardship, and capabilities. *Family Business Review, 19*(1), 73–87.

Miller, D., Le Breton-Miller, I., & Lester, R.H. (2010). Family ownership and acquisition behavior in publically-traded companies. *Strategic Management Journal, 31*, 201–23.

Miller, D., Le Breton-Miller, I., & Lester, R.H. (2011). Family and lone founder ownership and strategic behavior: Social context, identity, and institutional logics. *Journal of Management Studies, 48*(1), 1–25.

Miller, D., Le Breton-Miller, I., & Scholnick, B. (2008). Stewardship vs. stagnation: An empirical comparison of small family and non-family businesses. *Journal of Management Studies, 45*(1), 51–78.

Moores, K., & Mula, J. (2000). The salience of market, bureaucratic, and clan controls in the management of family firm transitions: Some tentative Australian evidence. *Family Business Review, 23*, 91–106.

Morck, R., & Yeung, B. (2003). Agency problems in large family business groups. *Entrepreneurship Theory and Practice, 27*(4), 367–82.

Mustakallio, M., Autio, E., & Zahra, S.A. (2002). Relational and contractual governance in family firms: Effects on strategic decision making. *Family Business Review, 15*, 205–22.

Nam, Y.H., & Herbert, J.I. (1999). Characteristics and key success factors in family business: The case of Korean immigrant businesses in metro-Atlanta. *Family Business Review, 12*, 341–52.

Neubauer, F., & Lank, A.G. (1998). *The family business. Its governance and sustainability.* London, UK: Macmillan.

Parada, M.J., & Viladás, H. (2010). Narratives: A powerful device for values transmission in family businesses. *Journal of Organizational Change Management, 23*(2), 166–72.

Payne, G.T., Brigham, K.H., Broberg, J.C., Moss, T.W., & Short, J.C. (2011). Organizational virtue orientation and family firms. *Business Ethics Quarterly, 21*(2), 257–85.

Perry, J., & Ring, J.K. (2013, January). *Who are the most trusted family business advisors?* Paper presented at the Annual Conference of the United States Association for Small Business and Entrepreneurship, San Francisco, CA.

Poza, E.J., & Messer, T. (2004). Spousal leadership and continuity in family firms. *Family Business Review, 14*, 25–36.

Rahim, M.A. (1983). A measure of styles of handling interpersonal conflict. *Academy of Management Journal, 26*, 368–76.

Reynolds, P.D., Bygrave, W.D., Autio, E., Cox, L.W., & Hay, M. (2002). Global entrepreneurship monitor; 2002 executive report. Kansas City, MO: Ewing Marion Kauffman Foundation.

Rokeach, M. (1973). *The nature of human values*. New York: Free Press.

Rothausen, T. (2009). Management work – family research and work – family fit: Implications for building family capital theory in family business. *Family Business Review*, *22*(3), 220–34.

Rothausen, T. & Sorenson, R.L. (2011). Leveraging family member capacity in for the business and the family. In R.L. Sorenson (Ed.), *Family business and social capital* (pp. 155–69). Cheltenham, UK, and Northampton, MA, USA: Edward Elgar Publishing.

Salvato, C. & Internationella handelshögskolan. (2002). *Antecedents of entrepreneurship in three types of family firms*. Jönköping, Swe.: Jönköping International Business School.

Schein, E.H. (1983). The role of the founder in creating organizational culture. *Organizational Dynamics*, *12*(1), 13–28.

Schein, E.H. (1985). *Organizational culture and leadership*. San Francisco, CA: John Wiley & Sons.

Schulze, W.S., Lubatkin, M.H., & Dino, R.N. (2002). Altruism, agency, and the competitiveness of family firms. *Managerial and Decision Economics*, *23*, 247–59.

Schulze, W.S., Lubatkin, M.H., & Dino, R.N. (2003a). Toward a theory of agency and altruism in family firms. *Journal of Business Venturing*, *18*, 473–90.

Schulze, W.S., Lubatkin, M.H., & Dino, R.N. (2003b). Exploring the agency consequences of ownership dispersion among the directors of private family firms. *Academy of Management Journal*, *46*, 179–94.

Shepard, S. (2011). Reclaiming our identity as a business-owning family. In R.L. Sorenson (Ed.), *Family business and social capital* (pp. 198–208). Cheltenham, UK, and Northampton, MA, USA: Edward Elgar Publishing.

Shepherd, D.A., & Zacharakis, A. (2000). Structuring family business succession: An analysis of the future leader's decision making. *Entrepreneurship Theory and Practice*, *24*, 25–39.

Sirmon, D.G., & Hitt, M.A. (2003). Managing resources: Linking unique resources, management and wealth creation in family firms. *Entrepreneurship Theory and Practice*, *27*, 339–58.

Smyrnios, K.X., and Walker, R.H. (2003). *Australian family and private business survey*. Melbourne: The Boyd Partners and RMIT University.

Sonfield, M.C., & Lussier, R.N. (2004). First-, second-, and third-generation family firms: A comparison. *Family Business Review*, *17*, 189–202.

Sorenson, R.L. (1999). Conflict strategies used by successful family businesses. *Family Business Review*, *12*, 325–39.

Sorenson, R.L. (2000). The contribution of leadership styles and practices to family and business success. *Family Business Review*, *13*(3), 183–200.

Sorenson, R.L. (2011). Social capital and family business. In R.L. Sorenson (Ed.), *Family business and social capital*, (pp. 1–30). Cheltenham, UK, and Northampton, MA, USA: Edward Elgar Publishing.

Sorenson, R.L. (2013a). How moral and social values become embedded in family firms. *Journal of Management, Spirituality & Religion*, (ahead-of-print), 1–22.

Sorenson, R.L. (2013b). Values in family business. In P. Sharma, M. Nordqvist & L. Melin (Eds.), *The SAGE handbook of family business* (forthcoming). London, UK: SAGE Publications, Ltd.

Sorenson, R.L., & Bierman, L. (2009). Family capital, family business, and free enterprise. *Family Business Review*, *22*(3), 193–95.

Sorenson, R.L., Folker, C.A., & Brigham, K.H. (2008). The collaborative network orientation: Achieving business success through collaborative relationships. *Entrepreneurship Theory and Practice*, *32*(4), 615–34.

Stavrou, E.T. (1999). Succession in family businesses: Exploring the effects of demographic factors on offspring intentions to join and take over the business. *Journal of Small Business Management*, *37*, 43–61.

Stavrou, E.T., & Swiercz, P.M. (1998). Securing the future of the family enterprise: A model of offspring intentions to join the business. *Entrepreneurship Theory and Practice*, *23*, 19–39.

Steen, A., & Welch, L.S. (2006). Dancing with giants: Acquisition and survival of the family firm. *Family Business Review*, *19*, 289–300.

Steier, L. (2001). Family firms, plural forms of governance, and the evolving role of trust. *Family Business Review*, *14*, 353–67.

Tsai, W.H., Hung, J.H., Kuo, Y.C., & Kuo, L. (2006). CEO tenure in Taiwanese family and nonfamily firms: An agency theory perspective. *Family Business Review*, *19*, 11–28.

Uhlaner, L. (2013). Family businesses and corporate governance. In M. Wright, D.S. Siegel, K. Keasey, & I. Filatotchev (Eds.). *Oxford Handbook of Corporate Governance* (forthcoming). Oxford, UK: Oxford University Press.

Voordeckers, W., Van Gils, A., & Van den Heuvel, J. (2007). Board composition in small and medium-sized family firms. *Journal of Small Business Management*, *45*, 137–56.

Ward, J., & Dolan, C. (1998). Defining and describing family business ownership configurations. *Family Business Review*, *11*, 305–309.

Westhead, P., Cowling, M., & Howorth, C. (2001). The development of family companies: Management and ownership imperatives. *Family Business Review*, *14*, 369–85.

Westhead, P., & Howorth, C. (2006). Ownership and management issues associated with family firm performance and company objectives. *Family Business Review*, *19*, 301–14.

Wu, Z., Chua, J.H., & Chrisman, J.J. (2007). Effects of family ownership and management on small business equity financing. *Journal of Business Venturing*, *22*, 875–95.

Yu, A., Lumpkin, G.T., Sorenson, R.L., & Brigham, K.H. (2012). The landscape of family business outcomes: A summary and numerical taxonomy of dependent variables. *Family Business Review*, *25*(1), 33–57.

Zahra, S.A., Hayton, J.C., Neubaum, D.O., Dibrell, C., & Craig, J. (2008). Culture of family commitment and strategic flexibility: The moderating effect of stewardship. *Entrepreneurship Theory and Practice*, *32*(6), 1035–54.

3. Performance in the family business: Financial and socio-emotional outcomes

Mary Schmid Daugherty

Introduction

A new business venture started around the kitchen table is often the beginning of a family business. The business grows, and over time a decision is made for a son, daughter, or other relative to pitch in at the business. The founder, who often does not even consider himself or herself an entrepreneur, realizes that this business venture is now something more than just a business. It is his or her business, his or her legacy, and his or her chance to make a stamp on the world. The business at this point can be considered a success for the mere fact that it still exists – approximately 85 percent of all new businesses fail within their first five years of operation (Poza, 2010). Yet the founder may not be content with the knowledge that the business "still exists," the quest now is to successfully manage the business, to steer the ship, to provide for the family in various ways, hopefully for generations. But what is success, and how is it measured?

All businesses strive for financial success, but in family businesses, there is often more to success than financial gain. Most families embrace socio-emotional considerations that are of value to the family and need to be considered in a measure of success, among them family harmony (Astrachan & Jaskiewicz, 2008; Sharma, Chrisman, Pablo, & Chua, 2001), family social status, (Dyer & Whetten, 2006; Zellweger 2007), family reputation (Milton, 2008), and family legacy (Gómez-Mejía, Haynes, Núñez-Nickel, Jacobson, & Moyano-Fuentes, 2007). These goals are specifically tied to the emotional value of owning a business together as a family. And these socio-emotional goals become even more important as the number of generations involved in the firm increases (Chrisman, Chua, Pearson, & Barnett, 2010). Socio-emotional goals, often referred to as private benefits of control, can be valued as highly as monetary returns on capital (Ehrhardt & Nowak, 2003). It is the socio-emotional goals that differentiate family from non-family firms (Chrisman, Chua, & Sharma, 2005; Sharma, 2004; Westhead & Howorth, 2006).

This chapter is written with the business family in mind. It is a summary of the research on best practices. It addresses the unique challenges and opportunities a family business faces in the quest for successful performance – performance that includes both financial measures and the socio-emotional aspects of owning a business together.* These two goals require a commitment to stewardship. The owners, as stewards of the business,

---

* Performance is one of the main clusters found in "A Map of the Landscape of Family Business" (also referred to as the Landscape Map) which can be found on the page just inside the cover of this book and in the Yu, Lumpkin, Sorenson, and Brigham (2012) article published in *Family Business Review*. Following the Landscape Map, the "Outcome Categories by Chapter Table" (also referred to as the Outcome Categories

must carefully craft a set of governance policies and practices that promote positive financial and socio-emotional outcomes for the entire enterprise. This chapter should be shared with the entire family group to help them continue to develop in their roles as responsible owners. Responsible owners should see themselves as stewards of the family business, they should educate themselves about the business, and they must commit to adding value to the business (Ward, 1997). Evaluating best practices and modifying them to the family's own personal business situation is a positive step towards responsible stewardship of the family business.

This chapter will proceed as follows. It starts with a discussion of the family business as a distinct business structure. The chapter then continues with a discussion of performance as seen from both the more traditional financial view, as well as from an overall success perspective incorporating socio-emotional outcomes. The next section addresses some of the many risks that can impact the overall success of the business. The final section concludes with a practical discussion of best practices that have proven to go hand-in-hand with successful performance for the family and the business.

I have had the opportunity to observe first-hand the benefits of incorporating best practice into the operations of family firms. As a third-generation owner of an operating business, I have helped my family incorporate family and business governance over the past two decades. My background in investments and my position as a finance professor have also given me unique insight into how to enhance the value of a family business beyond a stellar balance sheet. In addition, in my consulting practice, I have worked with a number of family ownership groups as they work through the challenges and opportunities faced as they professionalize their family and their business. As these family firms implemented the suggestions addressed in this chapter they enhanced the financial and socio-emotional performance of their family and their business.

Family business as a distinct business structure

Family business research is replete with references to the unique nature of family-controlled business. Many research studies have identified differences between family and non-family businesses (Gallo, Tapies, & Cappuyns, 2004; Habbershon & Williams, 1999; Shanker & Astrachan, 1996). It is clear that once an enterprise self-identifies as a family business, it reflects a complicated nexus of business ambition, family values, family relationships, and long-term wealth-building goals. All businesses need to remain competitive to be successful. For the family business, this fact is particularly poignant as the business needs to support a growing family base. The business often needs to grow to remain competitive and generate cash flow, for not only the business but for the family itself. Performance in terms of financial success is necessary to meet growth and cash flow needs. It is equally important to consider the owner's socio-emotional goals as a necessary component to keep the family business intact.

The need for funding continued growth may require family business owners to look for ways to raise capital. Capital may come from within the business, the family, debt markets, or through other creative sources of capital, depending on how much control

Table) is provided. This table shows all chapters that contain content about the outcome categories that appear in this chapter.

they are willing to relinquish. Family businesses are very reluctant to give up family control, even in situations where the outside funding provides a better probability of business survival (Gómez-Mejía et al., 2007). In addition, many family firms are willing to limit growth in the business to avoid debt, and some family firms avoid debt entirely (Galve-Gorriz & Salas-Fumas, 1996; Mishra & McConaughy, 1999). Possibly because most financing for family firms comes from family members reinvesting in the business, evidence shows that family firms try to limit their capital exposure by making low investment in capital expenditures (Gallo et al., 2004). It is estimated that privately held businesses in which families hold significant ownership or management positions represent 80 percent of all firms in the US. Sectors such as retail services and wholesaling, which require less investment in capital expenditures, represent a significantly higher percentage (James, 1999; Shanker & Astrachan, 1996).

The reality is that family businesses face significant disadvantages regarding their ability to raise capital, manage risk, and grow (Carney & Gedajlovic, 2002). The challenge of raising funds can cause family firms to be shortsighted in their needs for cash, accepting investment decisions that have quicker payback periods to manage cash flow. But if the payback period is used as the sole criterion on a capital investment decision, the family firm may reject projects that offer significant returns beyond the payback period (Brigham & Houston, 2009). And that assumes the business can actually raise the cash needed to fund growth. However, family businesses may be able to offset the disadvantage of raising capital with patient capital. Patient capital is equity provided by family owners willing to balance the current return on their business investment with the merits of a long-term strategy (de Visscher, 2007). The patient capital that the family has invested over one or more generations provides more than just financial capital; it also builds on the socio-emotional attributes relating to family heritage and fiduciary duty to the business, which business owners often pass on to the next generation (de Visscher, 2007).

Performance: Financial success

Financial success is important for business sustainability. Because of the private nature of family businesses, the research on financial success has been limited to evaluating family-controlled but publicly traded companies. Various studies have indicated that family-controlled businesses in the public markets outperform non-family-controlled business. A seminal study by Anderson and Reeb (2003) evaluated family ownership in the S&P 500, and found that one-third of the companies were family controlled businesses and that these firms accounted for 18 percent of the outstanding equity. Their study drew some significant conclusions. Using profitability-based measures of performance (ROA), the study found that family-controlled firms were significantly better performers than non-family-controlled firms. And in terms of market-based measures of performance, the firms that exhibited significant family ownership performed at least as well as non-family firms.

Various studies have evaluated why family firms perform better than non-family firms. One view suggests that family ownership creates value when the firm is managed by the owner. When the founder serves as the Chief Executive Officer (CEO) or as the chairman of the board when there is a non-family CEO, family management appears to add value (Villalonga & Amit, 2006). Other research suggests that firms that remain in control of the founding family are generally run more efficiently, carry less debt, and report higher market equity/book equity ratios than non-family firms (McConaughy, Matthews, & Fialko, 2001). Lower use of debt is a more conservative financing approach but is consistent with the view that family businesses consider non-economic factors when making decisions. Families have reputations and identity at stake and, therefore, are not willing to put their family business in any danger of default. Yet, even with this bias against using debt, i.e., less risk, family firms report higher financial performance.

There is also the possibility that the ability of family firms to outperform their non-family counterparts depends on the distribution of family ownership (Maury, 2006; Maury & Pajuste, 2005). Family ownership concentrated in a few controlling shareholders' hands can potentially hurt not only financial success but socio-emotional success if minority shareholders feel disenfranchised. If the dominant shareholder(s) in the family business exert control and dictate key decision-making to the detriment of the minority shareholders, it can lead to litigation among family members. Minority investors run the risk that the majority owners use their control rights to expropriate private benefits of control at the expense of the minority shareholder (LaPorta, Lopez-De-Silanes, Shleifer, & Vishny 1999; Shleifer & Vishny, 1997). Not only is litigation costly from a financial standpoint, but the damage to the socio-emotional aspect of the family is likely irreparable. Many real life cases illustrate the emotional havoc along with the financial damages wreaked by family conflicts (Gordon & Nicholson, 2008). But these cases are not limited to the rich and famous. Unfortunately, there are examples of this litigation in many family businesses regardless of fame or size.

In an attempt to evaluate family firm financial success, data was differentiated more specifically between ownership types (Miller, Le Breton-Miller, Lester, & Cannella, 2007). When the data was evaluated by owner type, it was determined that performance is better in a business that is owned by a sole founder/entrepreneur versus a family ownership group. So what was missing in previous studies that caused variations in results? In previous studies, firms that were 100 percent owned and operated by the founder were also classified as family firms. Yet these two types of firms differ in the social context of their ownership. Family firms have significant family influences while the lone founder may have more diverse relationships with non-family constituents (bank relationships, outside investors, partners, etc.). These non-family relationships may be more highly financially motivated (Miller, Le Breton-Miller, & Lester, 2011). But many lone founders operate in the role of family founder, i.e., the founder currently has, or intends to have, other family members as owners. This type of founder will exhibit a blend of entrepreneurial (extensive business relationships outside the family) and family roles, viewing himself or herself as a business builder and family nurturer. This middle role provides a balance between the risk-taking nature of an entrepreneur and the conservative nature of a family owner trying to blend the needs and wants of the family and the business. When financial performance is measured against these three types of owners (sole owner, family owner, and blended family/owner), the results suggest that lone founders earned superior shareholder returns, the family owner earned average shareholder returns, and the blended family founder earned returns between the other two returns (Miller et al., 2011).

The results of these studies may tempt us to conclude that family businesses' financial performance is in some aspects "better," or at least "as good as" non-family controlled firms. However, I would hesitate to do so. These studies focused on larger, well-established firms that have strong corporate governance and audit controls. The results may not translate to smaller, less structured, privately held family businesses. What we can draw from the studies is that the results do suggest that the expense of adding governance and audit controls did not hurt long-term financial performance. In fact, these studies may suggest that those family firms that remain private can enjoy significant overall success in performance, satisfying not just financial but socio-emotional goals, by establishing some formal governance procedures.

Overall success

Many research studies have evaluated financial performance as a measure of business success – it is the most researched topic identified in the area of family business (Yu, Lumpkin, Sorenson, & Brigham, 2012) – but far fewer studies look specifically at the issue of family business' socio-emotional outcomes (Gómez-Mejía et al., 2007). The whole idea of what constitutes family business "success" is difficult to nail down and can mean something very different from one family firm to another. It is very likely that families who wholly own and run businesses have their identities so intertwined with the overall success of the business that they embrace a strategy towards long-term growth to protect the family asset for generations (Miller & Le Breton-Miller, 2005). The family ownership gives the family the power to influence the firm goals. Indeed, family business research suggests that family involvement creates distinct goals, behavior, and performance outcomes for the business that often include non-economic considerations (Chrisman et al., 2005; Dyer & Whetten, 2006; Gómez-Mejía, Larraza-Kintana, & Makri, 2003).

Stewardship theory supports the notion that family businesses define success more broadly by considering family-centered socio-emotional goals (Corbetta & Salvato, 2004). Stewardship focuses on trust, culture, and personal connections between management and the business. It is widely believed that family business owners care very much about the long-term prospects of the business because the business impacts the family's wealth, reputation, and future well-being (Miller, Le-Breton-Miller, & Scholnick, 2008). This connection between the family and the business is likely to create a strong sense of stewardship. Family members' identification with the business, sense of kinship obligation, and source of personal and social fulfillment are all likely to contribute to an elevated sense of stewardship toward the well-being and continuity of the enterprise (Arregle, Hitt, Sirmon & Very, 2007).

It is widely accepted that family firms embrace different priorities than non-family firms (Gersick, Davis, Hampton, & Lansberg, 1997). These priorities impact the choices of types and levels of investment the family business makes in developing and acquiring resources over time. Resources include tangible "traditional" assets such as property, equipment, and cash, as well as intangible assets such as reputation, social networks, intellectual property, and employee loyalty. These resources are combined to produce the competitive package the firm employs to build success. Various studies have used a resource-based view to evaluate how family involvement may produce differences in terms of how resources are developed and deployed (Arregle et al., 2007; Chrisman et al., 2005; Sirmon & Hitt, 2003). Miller and LeBreton-Miller (2005) have characterized the various capabilities exhibited by family firms into four priorities (the 4-C model): continuity, command, connection, and community. Obviously these four characteristics are not exclusive to family firms, but family firms, due to the family involvement in pursuing these goals, often weigh these four goals differently from their non-family counterparts. Even when family and non-family businesses "own" the same resources, the results in terms of performance can vary. Some authors propose that it is the way family businesses combine these four priorities that make some family businesses great (Chrisman, Chua, & Kellermanns, 2009; Miller & LeBreton-Miller, 2005).

Another widely accepted assertion describing performance differences between family businesses and non-family businesses is explained by agency theory (Ward, 1997). What is essential in any definition of family business is the fact that, due to their ownership, family members enjoy certain control rights over the firm's assets and use these rights to exert influence regarding business decisions (Carney, 2005). According to this theory, the fundamental difference in performance between the two types of firms is the potentially divergent interests of the shareholders as owners versus "professional" managers as employees, not owners. In family businesses, strong family relationships between the owners and the managers often lower agency costs for the family firm, and allow for a longer-term perspective (Chrisman, Chua, & Litz, 2004). In other words, the family business can reflect an ownership-control alignment that meets the needs of both the business and the owners (Carney, 2005) while eliminating an agency problem disconnect between the non-owner manager and the owner. Non-family businesses, on the other hand, are forced to incur additional expenses to make sure the agent, such as the manager, adheres to the interests of the owner. Evidence of this advantage is shown by numerous studies that indicate owner-managed businesses are more efficient and valuable than similar non-family businesses in terms of size and industry exposure (McConaughy, 1994).

Is it as simple as saying family businesses, due to their agency advantage, have better performance than non-family businesses? The answer, of course, is no. It is not clear that the agency advantage translates into better performance for firms that wish to grow and compete on a larger scale. For example, Gallo et al. (2004) reported that family businesses with a family member as Chief Financial Officer (CFO) achieve higher margins and return on equity (ROE). Yet their data also indicated that these firms had not grown as much as they could have if they had captured more market share. Family businesses with non-family CFOs were older, had greater market share, and were bigger businesses in terms of sales. Interestingly, when the non-family CFO had influence in strategic decisions, those firms also reported ROE levels higher than family CFO firms. This is consistent with results that show that the family business with a non-family CFO reported higher return on equity (Schulze, Lubatkin, Dino, & Buchholtz, 2001). Therefore, the driver of successful business performance for family businesses isn't necessarily the lack of agency conflict. Instead, this research suggests that one of the metrics for successful business performance lies in allowing the CFO, family member or not, to participate in strategic decisions.

Risk and performance in family firms

A family business is at its basic level a business, which means that the business must compete and meet the challenges of the marketplace. Furthermore, the owner, as an investor in the business, requires some type of return on his or her investment. Return is a function of the amount of risk the owner is willing to take; in order to earn returns, the investor must accept a certain degree of risk. Thus, entrepreneurs, or what we refer to as the founders of family business, need to be risk-takers in their goals to maximize return. However, the research at the individual level has found little empirical evidence to support the idea that entrepreneurs are risk-takers (Naldi, Nordqvist, Sjoberg, & Wiklund, 2007). What the research does indicate is that family business entrepreneurs have a commitment to quality, tradition, and service, although that should not be antithetical to taking the necessary risks to be competitive (Gallo et al., 2004). Researchers have attempted to highlight the difference in risk-taking among entrepreneurs based on entrepreneurial orientation (Lumpkin & Dess, 1996; Lyon, Lumpkin, & Dess, 2000; Wiklund & Shepard, 2003). This research has helped explain some of the conflicting results regarding risk-taking. For example, innovative and proactive business strategies are positively associated with risk-taking, while the more widely dispersed the family ownership, the less risk the firm is willing to take (Naldi et al., 2007). Surprisingly, in family firms that are more risk-oriented, research suggests that the risk has negative implications for their performance (Naldi et al., 2007).

How do family businesses approach factors that typically involve risk? Family businesses tend to use less debt, hire fewer full-time employees, and invest less in long-term research and development; for example, family businesses may remain focused on the short-term payback. (Gallo et al., 2004; Gómez-Mejía et al., 2003). The potential reason for this behavior is that the level of risk a manager is willing to take is directly related to his or her equity ownership (Eisenhardt, 1989; Shleifer & Vishny, 1997; Zajac & Westphal, 1994). This suggests that the risk of losing accumulated family wealth, and therefore losing the financial/social well-being of the family legacy for future generations, accentuates the tendency of managers of family firms to take less risk than managers of other entrepreneurial firms (James, 1999; McConaughy et al., 2001; Schulze, Lubatkin, & Dino, 2002). Regardless of whether firms take more or less financial risk, research suggests that family firms won't take actions that they believe will have a negative socio-emotional value (Gómez-Mejía et al., 2007). Thus, risk aversion can prove to be static over time in a family firm. Many family businesses do business in the way that reflects the risk profile of the founder carried through the generations. The founder's influence is direct if he or she is still alive, but it can be just as strong in death through the tradition carried on by the family successors. Therefore, a tendency to avoid risk can and does carry on through the generations (Gallo et al., 2004).

Family related determinants of performance

Along with the roles that investment risk or entrepreneurial risk might play in family-firm performance, there are many challenges to overall success that may be an unintentional consequence of a family firm's desire to maintain a sense of family harmony. The family business often does not use or have interest in developing formal control systems (Daily & Dollinger, 1992; Randøy & Goel, 2003), has few if any outside board members (Cowling, 2003; Schulze et al., 2001), and has little in the way of external forces demanding account-ability and transparency (Carney, 2005). One study found that family firms are focused on generational ownership and allow key business decisions to be influenced by family (Chua, Chrisman, & Sharma, 1999). Key business decisions are often made in relatively informal, less analytical ways using the social controls developed within the family. These social controls, i.e., clan controls, help sustain socio-emotional outcomes but may not allow for any discourse on strategic decision-making (Moores & Mula, 2000).

Many of the threats to performance faced by family business are based on the inter-relationships between the family members themselves. A study that analyzed data from the 1997 National Family Business Survey found several significant factors that impact performance. By far the most important factor in terms of business performance was determined to be the process for dealing with disruptions, i.e., conflict resolution (Olson et al., 2003). This tension can originate at either the family or the business level, but the interaction between the two necessitates a well-thought-out response. Destructive conflict within the family and/or within the business, both from a financial and socio-emotional perspective, will affect the sustainability of the family business (Danes & Amarapurkar, 2005). For example, the less functional the family, the more likely the business will have cash flow problems (Danes & Amarapurkar, 2001).

By their very nature, families face various conflicts. Within the context of a business family, the sources of conflict can be magnified. There are questions of who should work for the company, how much should family members be paid, what titles/roles do family members hold, and, perhaps most importantly, who is accountable to whom? Family relationships make it difficult to address these questions which present challenges unique to family firms and confront the notion that there is no agency conflict in family businesses (Schulze et al., 2001; Schulze, Lubatkin, & Dino, 2003). The way a family addresses these questions has everything to do with the success of the family business. For example, if a family currently has a family CEO, eventually a family is faced with the challenge of deciding on a new CEO. Who should be chosen and why? The research on the succession process stresses the benefits of adherence to meritocracy, including external evaluation, coaching, and work experience (Chrisman, Chua, & Sharma, 1998; Sharma et al., 2001). The research indicates that smooth management succession from a family member to a non-family professional manager is likely to lead to superior business performance (Chittoor & Das, 2007). The studies overwhelmingly suggest that the family should make the CEO succession decision in the best interest of the business, although evidence shows this may require choosing among family members or, alternatively, going outside the family to fill this position.

Succession, or any family employment, raises the challenging issue of how to evaluate the work performance of family members. Family relationships can make it more difficult to adequately evaluate family employees' performance. It is generally thought that family-owned firms have little if any agency costs due to family members being altruistic toward each other as relatives (Eisenhardt, 1989, Schulze et al., 2003). But while altruism can mitigate some agency costs, it can lead to economic costs by the entrenchment of ineffec-tive managers (Morck & Yeung, 2004). How do you pass over your child for a promotion? Or ask your father to step down? It is clearly difficult to identify family members who are ineffective in their job and then follow up with appropriate action. Because of these relationship problems, family businesses are not immune to principal-agent dysfunction that can hurt performance. In fact, family relationships can potentially increase agency costs as a result of executive entrenchment (Gómez-Mejía, Núñez-Nickel, Gutierrez, 2001). However, these same research studies suggest that family firms gain economic performance benefits by using some agency cost control mechanisms, such as annual evaluations for all employees, family or not (Gómez-Mejía et al., 2001; Schulze, Labatkin, Dino, & Buchholtz, 2001, Schulze et al., 2003).

To be clear, it is only an agency cost if the owner managers pursue their own interests contrary to the goals of the other owners (Chrisman et al., 2004). For example, if the family has a non-economic goal of hiring all family members, keeping the incompetent family member on the payroll is not an agency problem. It becomes an agency problem if the family firm has a meritocracy family employment policy, but the CEO decides to keep his child on the payroll in direct defiance of the family policy. Based on this definition, if family employment is a goal of the family business, it is not an agency problem if the employee is "less than optimal." However, most would agree that it is clearly poor stewardship. Altruism may bias the perception of parent owners regarding the performance of family employees, particularly when such judgments have spillover effects on family relationships outside of the business (Chrisman et al., 2004; Schulze et al., 2003). Parents' altruism can lead them to be generous with their children even if the children lack the competence to add value to the business over time.

This is not to suggest that family employees are necessarily a negative for the company, but it does suggest good stewardship of the business requires formal governance practices with written policies and guidelines for both the business and the family. An in-depth analysis of two national surveys conducted by Mass Mutual in 1993 and 1994 found that family employees "earned" their salary by generating additional business revenue; the marginal effect of a family employee was found to be 100 times greater than a non-family employee. However, that same study reported that employee reviews, compensation plans, appraisal, and personal development plans were often used for non-family employees but not for family member employees (Astrachan & Kolenko, 1994). This information suggests that even though two detailed national surveys found family employees are significantly more productive, many family firms don't put their family employees through an extensive review process. This allows the misperception that family employees are a weak link in the employee ranks to continue. This data may explain why the owner manager's self-reported perception of business success went up with every non-family member hired, but went down with every family member employed; they simply assume that family members are a drag on performance (Olson et al., 2003). The owner managers who participated in this study clearly have a negative view of the work performance of family employees, but perhaps not of themselves.

There is a positive relationship between family business revenues and the use of formal work policies (Leon-Guerrero, McCann, & Haley, 1998). Family businesses should encourage good stewardship by promoting formal governance practices, including written policies and guidelines for all employees regardless of ownership status. Five critical human resource practices are positively related to performance in family businesses: 1) training and development, 2) performance appraisals, 3) recruitment packages, 4) morale maintenance, and 5) competitive compensation structures (Carlson, Upton,

& Seaman, 2006). As stewards of the business' and the family's socio-emotional goals, family members should promote written job descriptions, fair compensation plans, and formal employee reviews for all employees. There should be a written family employment policy that identifies requirements for family members wishing to work for the family business (Ward, 1997).

Best practices for success

Clearly there is no one "best" way to manage a family business. However, after reviewing the literature on family business performance, we can draw from some common themes to manage and enhance the overall success of a family business in both financial and socio-emotional terms. The key themes family business should consider are: 1) focusing on stewardship as a positive approach to being responsible owners, and 2) establishing formal controls and governance for the family and the business.

The research suggests that many family businesses use an informal process for decision-making. This works well for founders but is problematic for the next generation of family members, especially those who may not work in the business, yet need to be "heard." The family members need to articulate their goals for the business, and the managers, whether family members or not, need to have one "master." Family businesses should implement formal control and governance systems including active, independent business boards, specific financial controls, and formal governance systems for the family. Schulze et al. (2001) build a compelling case that the additional agency costs are worth it. Additionally, we can refer to the results from Anderson and Reeb's (2003) study that indicate that the stringent formal controls and governance required in the public market do not hurt financial performance. Family businesses performed at least as well as their non-family controlled, public counterparts. Non-economic influences that exist in most family firms don't appear to hurt the financial performance either.

Stewardship theory is perhaps the most appropriate way to address a more formal governance structure for the family and the business (Blumentritt, Keyt, & Astrachan, 2007). Stewardship theory focuses on trust, culture, and personal connections between management and the business. The goal should be to have the CEO (family or non-family CEO) supported by a strong board consisting of family and non-family members, and a functioning family council. Stewardship is necessary to allow the family to acknowledge and address some of the unique risk factors that the family business is likely to face. One of the most challenging issues is the need to move to a meritocracy for the sake of the business. If family businesses can employ capable, qualified family members in management positions, then the firms should certainly do so. However, the family business should look for the best-qualified employees to fill top management positions. In a family acting as true stewards of their business, management systems can be adopted for non-family managers to fill important employment roles. A family business moving towards a system of meritocracy in hiring practices alleviates some of the risk unique to a family-owned business.

Family conflict can create excessive concern about family issues that divert attention from the needs of the business and often hurt productivity. Research is clear that managing conflict is important to the success of a family business and that firms resolving issues in a collaborative way provide more positive family and business outcomes (Sorenson, 1999). Families that develop a formalized process for responding to business and/or family issues create an environment of stewardship for the family and the business. This formalized process often takes the form of family policies determined through a collaborative, give and take effort of all the participating family members (often in the family council). A governance structure that allows for this formalized process can decrease family conflict, and allows the business and the family to enhance performance overall.

Family businesses should also seriously tackle the challenge of defining the amount of return and related risk the owners collectively are willing to accept. Generally speaking, the more dispersed the family ownership, the more risk averse the owners tend to become. As stewards of the business, the owners want to protect the family legacy. Yet by minimizing the risk owners are willing to take, they may actually be putting the business at greater risk by not allowing the business to meet the competitive challenges in the marketplace. In addition, in many family businesses, the founder was unwilling to accept debt and passed on the legacy of risk aversion through the generations. This legacy of not using debt can actually create more risk for the family business by putting pressure on the company's ability to fund growth.

In summary, a more formal business structure allows for a systematic review of risk. This can lead to better outcomes for the business, which in term helps the family achieve its financial and socio-emotional goals. Family businesses would benefit from a formal process for dealing with the tension that inevitably arises in the family and in the business. At the business level, there should be a board of directors (advisors) that includes family and independent members. At the family level, there should be a family council, or at a minimum a family group, that works through the inevitable family conflicts. All family members should embrace the notion of stewardship. When family members act as stewards they participate as responsible owners. They encourage education about the business and promote collective participation with the business. Thus, the familiness of the business can then be effectively nurtured and developed to ensure the business and the family can thrive through the generations.

References

Anderson, R.C., & Reeb, D.M. (2003). Founding-family ownership and firm performance: Evidence from the S&P 500. *The Journal of Finance, 58*(3), 1301–28.

Arregle, J.L., Hitt, M.A., Sirmon, D.G., & Very, P. (2007). The development of organizational social capital: Attributes of family firms. *Journal of Management Studies, 44*(1), 73–95.

Astrachan, J.H., & Jaskiewicz, P. (2008). Emotional returns and emotional costs in privately held family businesses: Advancing traditional business valuation. *Family Business Review, 21*(2), 139–49.

Astrachan, J.H., & Kolenko, T.A. (1994). A neglected factor explaining family business success: Human resource practices. *Family Business Review, 7*(3), 251–62.

Blumentritt, T.P., Keyt, A.D., & Astrachan, J.H. (2007). Creating an environment for successful non-family CEOs: An exploratory study. *Family Business Review, 20*(4), 321–35.

Brigham, E.F., & Houston, J.F. (2009). *Fundamentals of financial management* (12th ed.). Mason, OH: South-Western Cengage Learning.

Carlson, D., Upton, N., & Seaman, S. (2006). The impact of human resource packages and compensation design on performance: An analysis of family-owned SMEs. *Journal of Small Business Management, 44*(4), 531–43.

Carney, M., & Gedajlovic, E. (2002). The coupling of ownership and control and the allocation of financial resources: Evidence from Hong Kong. *Journal of Management Studies, 39*(1), 123–46.

Carney, M. (2005). Corporate governance and competitive advantage in family-controlled firms. *Entrepreneurship Theory and Practice, 29*(3), 249–65.

Chittoor, R., & Das, R. (2007). Professionalism of management and succession performance – A vital linkage. *Family Business Review, 20*(1), 65–79.

Chrisman, J.J., Chua, J.H., & Kellermanns, F. (2009). Priorities, resource stocks, and performance in family and non-family firms. *Entrepreneurship Theory and Practice, 35*(5), 739–60.

Chrisman, J.J., Chua, J.H., & Litz, R. (2004). Comparing the agency costs of family and non-family firms: Conceptual issues and exploratory evidence. *Entrepreneurship Theory and Practice, 28*(4), 335–54.

Chrisman, J.J., Chua, J.H., Pearson, A.W., & Barnett, T. (2010). Family involvement, family influence, and family-centered non-economic goals in small firms. *Entrepreneurship Theory and Practice, 36*(5), 1–27

Chrisman, J.J., Chua, J.H., & Sharma, P. (1998). Important attributes of successors in family businesses: An exploratory study. *Family Business Review, 11*(1), 19–34.

Chrisman, J.J., Chua, J.H., & Sharma, P. (2005). Trends and directions in the development of a strategic management theory of the family firm. *Entrepreneurship Theory and Practice, 29*(5), 555–75.

Chua, J.H., Chrisman, J.J., & Sharma, P. (1999). Defining the family business by behavior. *Entrepreneurship Theory & Practice, 23*, 19–39.

Corbetta, G., & Salvato, C. (2004). Self-serving or self-actualizing? Models of man and agency costs in different types of family firms: A commentary on "Comparing the agency costs of family and non-family firms: Conceptual issues and exploratory evidence." *Entrepreneurship Theory and Practice, 28*(4), 355–62.

Cowling, M. (2003). Productivity and corporate governance in smaller firms. *Small Business Economics, 20*, 335–44.

Daily, C.M., & Dollinger, M.J. (1992). An empirical examination of ownership structure in family and professionally managed firms. *Family Business Review, 5*(2), 117–36.

Danes, S., & Amarapurkar, S. (2001). Business tensions and success in farm family business. *Family Economics and Research Management Biennial, 4*, 178–90.

Danes, S., & Amarapurkar, S. (2005). Farm business-owning couples: Interrelationships among business tensions, relationship conflict quality, and spousal satisfaction. *Journal of Family and Economic Issues, 26*(3), 419–41.

de Visscher, F.M. (2007, November/December). What to consider when selling the family business. *Capital Eyes, de Visscher Newsletter*.

Dyer, W., & Whetten, D. (2006). Family firms and social responsibility: Preliminary evidence from the S&P 500. *Entrepreneurship Theory and Practice, 30*(6), 785–802.

Ehrhardt, O., & Nowak, E. (2003, June). *Private benefits and minority shareholder expropriation (or What exactly are private benefits of control?)*. Paper presented at the EFA 2003 Annual Conference (Paper No. 809). Retrieved from http://papers.ssrn.com/sol3/papers.cfm?abstract_id=423506

Eisenhardt, K.M. (1989). Agency theory: An assessment and review. *Academy of Management Review, 14*, 57–74.

Gallo, M.A., Tapies, J., & Cappuyns, K. (2004). Comparison of family and non-family business: Financial logic and personal preferences. *Family Business Review, 17*(4), 303–18.

Galve-Gorriz, C., & Salas-Fumas, V. (1996). Ownership structure and firm performance: Some empirical evidence from Spain. *Managerial and Decision Economics, 17*, 587–94.

Gersick, K.E., Davis, J.A., Hampton, M.M., & Lansberg, I. (1997). *Generation to generation: Life cycles of the family business*. Boston, MA: Harvard Business School.

Gómez-Mejía, L.R., Larraza-Kintana, M., & Makri, M. (2003). The determinants of executive compensation in family-controlled public corporations. *Academy of Management Journal, 46*(2), 226–37.

Gómez-Mejía, L.R., Núñez-Nickel, M., & Gutierrez, I. (2001). The role of family ties in agency contracts. *Academy of Management Journal*, *44*, 81–95.

Gómez-Mejía, L.R., Takács Haynes, K., Núñez-Nickel, M., Jacobson, K.J.L., & Moyano-Fuentes, J. (2007). Socioemotional wealth and business risks in family-controlled firms: Evidence from Spanish olive oil mills. *Administrative Science Quarterly*, *52*, 106–37.

Gordon, G., & Nicholson, N. (2008). *Family wars: The real stories behind the most famous family business feuds*. London, UK: Kogan Page.

Habbershon, T.G., & Williams, M.L. (1999). A resource-based framework for assessing the strategic advantages of family firms. *Family Business Review*, *13*(1), 1–25.

James, H.S. (1999). Owners as manager, extended horizons and the family firm. *International Journal of the Economics of Business*, *6*(1), 41–55.

La Porta, R., Lopez-de-Silanes, F., Shleifer, A., & Vishny, R.W. (1999). The quality of government. *Journal of Law Economics and Organization*, *15*(1), 222–79.

Leon-Guerrero, A.Y., McCann, J.E., and Haley, J.D., Jr. (1998). A study of practice utilization in family businesses. *Family Business Review*, *11*(2), 107–20.

Lumpkin, G.T., & Dess, G.G. (1996). Clarifying the entrepreneurial orientation construct and linking it to performance. *Academy of Management Review*, *21*, 135–72.

Lyon, D.W., Lumpkin, G.T., & Dess, G.G. (2000). Enhancing entrepreneurial orientation research: Operationalizing and measuring a key strategic decision-making process. *Journal of Management*, *26*(5), 1055–85.

Maury, B. (2006). Family ownership and firm performance: Empirical evidence from Western European corporations. *Journal of Corporate Finance*, *12*(2), 321–41.

Maury, B., & Pajuste, A. (2005). Multiple large shareholders and firm value. *Journal of Banking and Finance*, *29*, 1813–34.

McConaughy, D.L. (1994). *Founding-family-controlled corporations: An agency-theoretic analysis of corporate ownership and its impact upon performance, operating efficiency and capital structure*. (Doctoral dissertation). Retrieved from ProQuest Dissertations and Theses. (304112247).

McConaughy, D.L., Matthews, C., & Fialko, A. (2001). Founding family controlled firms: Performance, risk, and value. *Journal of Small Business Management*, *39*(1), 31–49.

Medoza, D., & Ward, J. (2011). *Family business ownership: How to be an effective shareholder*. New York: Family Business Press

Miller, D., & LeBreton-Miller, I. (2005). *Managing for the long run: Lessons in competitive advantage from great family businesses*. Boston, MA: Harvard Business School.

Miller, D., Le Breton-Miller, I., & Lester, R.H. (2011). Family and lone founder ownership and strategic behavior: Social context, identity and institutional logics. *Journal of Management Studies*, *48*(1), 1–25.

Miller, D., LeBreton-Miller, I., Lester, R.H., & Cannella, A.A. (2007). Are family firms really superior performers? *Journal of Corporate Finance*, *13*, 829–58.

Miller, D., LeBreton-Miller, I., & Scholnick, B. (2008). Stewardship vs. stagnation: An empirical comparison of small family and non-family businesses. *Journal of Management Studies*, *45*(1), 51–78.

Milton, L.P. (2008). Unleashing the relationship power of family firms: Identity confirmation as catalyst for performance. *Entrepreneurship Theory and Practice*, *32*, 1063–81.

Mishra, C.S., & McConaughy, D.L. (1999). Founding family control and capital structure: The risk of loss of control and the aversion to debt. *Entrepreneurship Theory and Practice*, *23*(4), 53–65.

Moores, K., & Mula, J.M. (2000). The salience of market, bureaucratic, and clan controls in the management of family firm transitions: Some tentative Australian evidence. *Family Business Review*, *13*(2), 91–106.

Morck, R., & Yeung, B. (2004). Family control and the rent-seeking society. *Entrepreneurship Theory and Practice*, *28*(4), 391–409.

Naldi, L., Nordqvist, M., Sjoberg, W., & Wiklund, J. (2007). Entrepreneurial orientation, risk taking, and performance in family firms. *Family Business Review*, *20*(1), 33–47.

Olson, P.D., Zuiker, V.S., Danes, S.M., Stafford, K., Heck, R.K.Z., & Duncan, K.A. (2003). The impact of the family and the business on family business sustainability. *Journal of Business Venturing*, *18*, 639–66.

Poza, E. (2010). *Family business* (3rd ed.). Mason, OH: South-Western Cengage Learning.

Randøy, T., & Goel, S. (2003). Ownership structure, founder leadership, and performance in Norwegian SMEs: Implications for financing entrepreneurial opportunities. *Journal of Business Venturing, 18*, 619–37.

Schulze, W.S., Lubatkin, M.H., & Dino, R.N. (2002). Altruism, agency and the competitiveness of family firms. *Managerial and Decision Economics, 23*, 247–59.

Schulze, W.S., Lubatkin, M.H., & Dino, R.N. (2003). Toward a theory of agency and altruism in family firms. *Journal of Business Venturing, 18*, 473–90.

Schulze, W.S., Lubatkin, M.H., Dino, R.N., & Buchholtz, A.K. (2001). Agency relationships in family firms: Theory and evidence. *Organization Science, 12*(2), 85–105.

Shanker, M.C., & Astrachan, J.H. (1996). Myths and realities: Family businesses' contribution to the US economy. *Family Business Review, 9*, 107–123.

Sharma, P. (2004). An overview of the field of family business studies: Current status and directions for the future. *Family Business Review, 17*(1), 1–36.

Sharma, P., Chrisman, J.J., Pablo, A., & Chua, J.H. (2001). Determinants of initial satisfaction with the succession process in family firms: A conceptual model. *Entrepreneurship Theory and Practice, 25*(3), 1–19.

Shleifer, A., & Vishny, R.W. (1997). A survey of corporate governance. *The Journal of Finance, 52*(2), 737–83.

Sirmon, D.G., & Hitt, M.A. (2003). Managing resources: Linking unique resources, management and wealth creation in family firms. *Entrepreneurship Theory and Practice, 27*(4), 339–58.

Sorenson, R.L. (1999). Conflict management strategies used in successful family businesses. *Family Business Review, 12*(2), 133–46.

Villalonga, B., & Amit, R. (2006). How do family ownership, control and management affect firm value? *Journal of Financial Economics, 80*, 385–417.

Ward, J.L. (1997). Growing the family business: Special challenges and best practices. *Family Business Review, 10*(4), 323–37.

Westhead, P., & Howorth, C. (2006). Ownership and management issues associated with family firm performance and company objectives. *Family Business Review, 19*(4), 301–16.

Wiklund, J., & Shepherd, D. (2003). Knowledge-based resources, entrepreneurial orientation, and the performance of small- and medium-sized businesses. *Strategic Management Journal, 24*(13), 1307–14.

Yu, A., Lumpkin, G.T., Sorenson, R.L., & Brigham, K.H. (2012). The landscape of family business outcomes: A summary and numerical taxonomy of dependent variables. *Family Business Review. 25*(1), 33–57.

Zajac, E., & Westphal, J. (1994). The costs and benefits of managerial incentives and monitoring in large U.S. corporations: When is more not better? *Strategic Management Journal, 15*, 121–43.

Zellweger, T. (2007). Time horizon, costs of equity capital, and generic investment strategies of firms. *Family Business Review, 20*(1), 1–15.

4. Social and economic impact of family business

Keith H. Brigham

Introduction

Do family firms matter? While there is a growing interest in family business studies, there is an ongoing debate as to the effectiveness of the family firm as an organizational configuration. The overarching purpose of this chapter is to increase our understanding of the social and economic contribution of family firms. More specifically, I will address how existing research can inform us about the effectiveness of family firms and where there are gaps in our knowledge and understanding. Therefore, this chapter has a descriptive element that relates to what we know, and a prescriptive element that relates to what we need to know to achieve more positive family business outcomes.

In order to provide some boundaries around the scope of the discussion, I will use the framework presented by Yu, Lumpkin, Sorenson, and Brigham (2012) as the foundation of this chapter.* Yu et al. (2012) conducted a review of the family business literature covering the period from 1998–2009. Their analysis focused on the dependent variables (outcomes) that researchers had examined. These outcomes were then plotted along two dimensions and grouped into different, broader outcome categories; this resulted in a figure containing a systems dimension (business vs. family) and a temporal dimension (short-term vs. long-term), and seven general clusters identified and labeled as Performance, Strategy, Social and Economic Impact, Governance, Succession, Family Business Roles, and Family Dynamics (see Landscape Map).

This chapter focuses on the broader cluster of Social and Economic Impact which contains four outcome variables labeled *entrepreneurship*, *social capital and knowledge transfer*, *regulatory and business environment*, and *economic contribution*. I will distill some of the key findings from the reviewed studies in Yu et al., (2012) that relate to each of these four outcome categories and identify where gaps in our knowledge still remain. Again, the intent is that this chapter, albeit necessarily limited in scope, can provide a better understanding of both the current state of knowledge with respect to these important outcomes and how they may relate to more positive organizational outcomes.

---

* "A Map of the Landscape of Family Business" (also referred to as the Landscape Map) can be found on the page just inside the cover of this book and in the Yu, Lumpkin, Sorenson, and Brigham (2012) article published in *Family Business Review*. Following the Landscape Map, the "Outcome Categories by Chapter Table" (also referred to as the Outcomes Categories Table) is provided. This table shows all chapters that contain content about the outcome categories that appear in this chapter.

Social and Economic Impact and component outcomes

Based on the first of four studies (Study 1, 1998–1997) detailed in the Yu et al. (2012) analysis, the Social and Economic Impact cluster was the least researched. Researchers reviewed 212 articles and only 8 percent of the 393 identified outcome variables (some articles had multiple outcome variables) fell within the Social and Economic Impact cluster. Based on the distribution of the variables within the cluster, the outcomes were grouped into four categories: entrepreneurship 12/393 (3.05 percent), social capital and knowledge transfer 8/393 (2.04 percent), economic contribution 5/393 (1.27 percent), and regulatory and business environment 7/393 (1.78 percent). Given that Social and Economic Impact is the least researched of the seven identified clusters, there are several interesting questions about it that need to be answered. Furthermore, the position of the cluster – centered within the short-term business quadrant within the Landscape Map – positions the research toward the traditional business system domain versus the family system domain. Thus, many of the research questions related to the outcomes in this cluster are often viewed and treated as general management questions instead of unique family business questions. In the remainder of this section, I will provide a more in-depth look at the four outcome categories that comprise the Social and Economic Impact cluster.

Entrepreneurship

The entrepreneurship category was based on a number of specific dependent variables found within the 212 family-business articles reviewed. These include entrepreneurial orientation, strategic persistence, corporate entrepreneurship, innovation, entrepreneurial risk-taking, familiness, family forces on entrepreneurship, and the future leader's perception of the business. In a general sense, many of the articles that addressed these variables were exploring the question of whether family firms are entrepreneurial.

The examination of entrepreneurship in family firms is driven by the premise that all firms need to be somewhat entrepreneurial to survive in today's business environment. The competitive landscape that all firms face is increasingly dynamic and uncertain (Hamel, 2000). Faced with rapidly increasing pressures of globalization and technological change, it is imperative that family firms develop an entrepreneurial mindset to identify and exploit opportunities in their environments (Sirmon & Hitt, 2003). In this hypercompetitive environment (D'Aveni, 1994), industry boundaries are blurred, and increased competition and change may come from all directions.

The question of whether family firms are more or less entrepreneurial than non-family firms is unresolved in the research literature. Zahra, Hayton, and Salvato (2004), illustrate the arguments for family firms being entrepreneurial in the following excerpt:

> Family firms are an important source of economic development and growth. These firms create value through product, process, and service innovations that fuel growth and lead to prosperity. The long-term nature of family firms' ownership allows them to dedicate the resources required for innovation and risk taking, thereby fostering entrepreneurship. Furthermore, the kinship-ties that are unique to family firms are believed to have a positive effect upon entrepreneurial opportunity recognition (Barney, Clark, & Alvarez, 2003). Owner managers also understand that their family firms' survival depends on their ability to enter new markets and revitalize

existing operations in order to create new businesses (Ward, 1987). Entrepreneurial activities increase the distinctiveness of the family firms' products and therefore enhance their profitability and growth (Zahra, 2003). Thus, it is important that family firms are able to innovate and aggressively pursue entrepreneurial activities. (p. 363)

This passage suggests that family firms recognize the need to act entrepreneurially and that they may possess certain characteristics that foster entrepreneurship. However, in the following excerpt, Zahra et al. (2004) also acknowledge that certain characteristics of family firms may serve to inhibit entrepreneurial activity.

Yet, over time some family firms become conservative, unwilling or unable to take the risks associated with entrepreneurship (Autio & Mustakallio, 2003; Dertouzos, Lester, & Solow, 1989). Founders of family firms, who desire to build a lasting legacy, may become more conservative in their decisions because of the high risk of failure of entrepreneurial ventures (Morris, 1998), as well as the risk of destruction of family wealth (Sharma, Chrisman, & Chua, 1997). Family firms may also choose conservative strategies as a result of their organizational cultures (Dertouzos et al., 1989), defined as the enduring values that shape the firms' characters and how they adapt to the external environment. These cultures embody the beliefs, aspirations, histories, and self-concepts that are likely to influence firms' disposition to support and undertake entrepreneurial activities. (p. 364)

This excerpt illustrates the counter argument and popular perception that family firms tend to be more conservative and less entrepreneurial than non-family firms. Thus, in the face of rising environmental pressures on all firms to adopt a more entrepreneurial mindset, more researchers are beginning to examine the factors either promoting or discouraging entrepreneurial activity in family firms. Currently, there is no clear resolution regarding whether family firms, on average, are more or less entrepreneurial than non-family firms. Researchers acknowledge that individual firms will vary with respect to their level of entrepreneurial activity. Some family firms will be more entrepreneurial than non-family firms while others will be less entrepreneurial than non-family firms. However, some characteristics of family firms may be somewhat distinctive, and these could influence, either positively or negatively, levels of entrepreneurial activity.

Within the articles identified by Yu et al. (2012) that relate to the entrepreneurship category, several examine factors within family firms that might influence the level of entrepreneurship (Craig & Moores, 2006; Hall, Melin, & Nordqvist, 2001; Kellermanns & Eddleston, 2006; Litz & Kleysen 2001; Zahra, 2005; Zahra et al., 2004). These articles also offer some directions for future research that would improve our understanding of this important line of inquiry. A number of these articles adopt the general premise that in today's competitive landscape, family firms need to be able to act more entrepreneurially. Kellermanns and Eddleston (2006) employ the concept of corporate entrepreneurship, which includes firm activities designed to reframe the company's business approach or to emphasize innovation. Corporate entrepreneurship may consist of product or process innovations, research and development, and the entering of new markets. Kellermanns and Eddleston (2006) found that the ability to recognize technological opportunities, willingness to undergo organizational change, and the use of strategic planning processes to pursue opportunities all increase corporate entrepreneurship in family firms. Family firms are often criticized for being resistant to change and unable to act entrepreneurially. Kellermanns and Eddleston (2006) conclude that family firms must foster a culture that promotes and accommodates change and entrepreneurship. Future research should examine how willingness to change is developed and how it may affect other family firm outcomes.

Zahra et al. (2004) propose that dimensions of culture will have a stronger influence on entrepreneurship in family firms versus non-family firms. Family firms often have distinctive cultures that are difficult to imitate and thus may bestow strategic advantages. Specifically, Zahra et al. (2004) found that the cultural dimensions relating to an external orientation, decentralization, and a longer-term perspective, all of which can be argued to be more prevalent in family firms, were positively related to entrepreneurship. They conclude that the distinctive cultures of family firms may be advantageous and play a particularly strong role in promoting entrepreneurship in family firms. Future research should further examine the links between dimensions of culture and entrepreneurship.

Hall et al. (2001) posit that entrepreneurial family firms are characterized by explicit and open cultures. Family firms possessing these types of cultures will be better prepared for the uncertainty and speed of change that is characteristic of the new competitive landscape. Hall et al. (2001) state that "family firms do not have to be characterized as inflexible, resistant to change, and burdened by traditions. Quite the contrary: family firms can arrive at characteristics that *encourage* entrepreneurship rather that *stifle* it through transformation of their cultural patterns" (p. 206). Hall et al. (2001) also states the following:

> Moreover, entrepreneurship as radical, strategic change is characterized by a situation where the historical harmony between strategy, structure, culture, and leadership tends to be broken and reestablished in a new way. This characterization implies changes in both the organizational culture and the dominant strategic ways of thinking (Melin & Alvesson, 1989; Melin & Hellgren, 1994; Hellgren & Melin, 1993).
>
> Radical change is a difficult process in any company – family dominated or not. In the family business, change is, however, likely to be more heavily resisted than in other organizations because "the feelings and emotions related to change are likely to be deeper and more intense than those in nonfamily businesses" (Dyer, 1994, p. 125). (p. 197)

Through this article, Hall et al. (2001) reinforce the apparent importance of culture on entrepreneurship in family firms and the key role that willingness to change plays in the entrepreneurial process for family firms.

Litz and Kleysen (2001) parse the broader question of entrepreneurship in family firms by examining how intergenerational family involvement affects the outcome of innovation. Innovation is a central component in most conceptualizations of entrepreneurship. Litz and Kleysen (2001) provide a definition of family firm innovation to distinguish it from more general innovation, stating that "Family firm innovation is the intentional generation or introduction of novel processes and or products resulting from the autonomous and interactive efforts of members of a family firm" (p. 341). They go on to emphasize that "the crucial variable in family firm innovation is, therefore, the interaction *between* family members resulting in collaborative and innovative outcomes" (p. 341).

Litz and Kleysen (2001) highlight the role that intergenerational processes may play in family firms' ability to act innovatively. They suggest that the onus is on the younger generations to reach their innovative potential. As discussed in some of the previous articles we have examined, the overarching nature of the family firm culture may play a key role in family firm innovation. This point is emphasized by Litz and Kleysen (2001) in the following statement of future research directions:

> Another more macro research issue concerns the role of family culture. Given observed differences between families (Minuchin, 1974), a more comprehensive theory of family firm innovation must grapple with the relationship between a family's system dynamics and the firm's innovative behavior. In particular, what kinds of family cultures support innovation and what cultures frustrate it? Furthermore, how do particular aspects of family culture, such as structure, emotional climate, and intergenerational projection processes, impact innovation? (p. 348)

Family culture and innovation in family firms are strongly linked, and the nature of the relationship is complex. The culture of the family firm may either promote or arrest innovative behavior.

Zahra (2005) explored the factors likely to influence entrepreneurial risk-taking in family firms. Using multiple measures of entrepreneurial activity and risk-taking, Zahra (2005) found that higher levels of family ownership and more generational involvement served to promote entrepreneurship. On the other hand, longer CEO tenures inhibited entrepreneurial risk-taking. Different characteristics of family firms may influence entrepreneurship in opposite directions.

Finally, Craig and Moores (2006) examined the entrepreneurial behavior of family firms through the outcome of innovation. Their study provides a rare longitudinal (over time) look at the level of innovation in established family firms. They report that within their sample of family firms, those facing greater environmental uncertainty had higher levels of innovation. Furthermore, firms with structural characteristics such as less formalization and more decentralization had higher levels of innovation. Craig and Moores (2006) argue that, despite perceptions that established family firms tend to be conservative, they do place substantial importance on innovation practices and strategies. Established family firms adapt to environmental pressures through altering their innovation approaches and certain drivers of innovation (especially in samples considered more innovative such as high-technology firms); thus, innovation may have stronger effects in family firms. The authors conclude, based on their findings, that "the linkages between established family firms and innovation may be substantially stronger than currently assumed by many" (p. 8).

Key points.
It may be helpful to summarize what we know based on the articles related to the entrepreneurial behavior of family firms and to point out what we can do to apply what we already know.

- In the new competitive landscape, the ability of family firms to act more entrepreneurially is viewed as crucial for both survival and growth.
- There is still an ongoing debate as to whether family firms are more or less entrepreneurial than non-family firms.
- Certain distinctive characteristics of family firms may serve to both promote and inhibit innovative and entrepreneurial behaviors.

Practitioner points.

While there are pressures to avoid risks that might undermine the survival of a family firm, there are also risks of becoming obsolete. Family firms might do the following to remain entrepreneurial.

- They might regularly assess their firm's ability to compete by benchmarking their innovative activities against close competitors.
- The family might provide education for family members in the latest technologies and innovations.
- Firm leaders might develop or refine the ability to recognize and screen entrepreneurial opportunities.

Social capital and knowledge transfer

In the family business literature, much of the research is spurred by the overarching question of whether family firms out-perform non-family firms. To address this question, a growing body of research focuses on the potential set of resources that may be unique to family firms and potentially bestow a competitive advantage over non-family firms. One of the most prevalent of these resources is social capital, which is determined by the levels of trust, reciprocity, and interaction that form ties among members of a group (Nahapiet & Ghosal, 1998). Greater social capital can lead to an enhanced sharing of information and tacit knowledge (Marsh & Stock, 2006), and foster the successful exploitation of that knowledge in the competitive environment (Cohen & Levinthal, 1990; Zahra & George, 2002).

Researchers have recognized that the integration of family and business systems, a unique aspect of family firms, may lead to enhanced social capital. In fact, they have even termed the type of social capital generated by the family dynamic as family capital (Hoffman, Hoelscher, & Sorenson, 2006) or family social capital (Arregle, Hitt, Sirmon, & Very, 2007). Family capital is embedded in family relationships and may be a source of unique competitive advantage for family firms. The social capital created by the nature of family relationships may not be easily imitated by non-family firms. Family capital can foster the type of knowledge integration and transfer that form dynamic capabilities and, ultimately, competitive advantage (Chirico & Salvato, 2008; Salvato & Melin, 2008).

The social capital and knowledge transfer category was based on a number of specific dependent variables from the 212 reviewed articles including: mentoring in family firms, predecessor roles during and after instatement of the successor, family business self-efficacy scale in succession, internationalization process, interfirm cooperation capability in the context of networking family businesses, socialization processes and patterns, transfer and management of social capital, and continued involvement and knowledge transfer. Several of the articles that address these variables are discussed below.

Niemela (2004) developed a model of interfirm cooperation capability, which consists of social networking capabilities, management capabilities, and learning capabilities. The empirical results from this study suggest that interfirm cooperation is a simultaneous learning process for family firms and their owners. Steier (2001) examines social capital (conceptualized as the resources embedded in relationships), which is often a strength of family firms. While social capital is an asset, it is an intangible resource that is difficult to manage and transfer. This study details the different approaches that family firms employ to manage and transfer social capital in family firms. Steier (2001) suggests that future research should explore how social capital is transferred and affected by the succession process.

Boyd, Upton, and Wircenski (1999) surveyed 76 senior executives of family firms to ascertain their perceptions of mentoring. On the whole, the respondents had favorable opinions regarding the value of mentoring processes. However, different types of mentoring, depending on levels of formality and family membership, may be more appropriate based on the unique characteristics of the participants in the process. Boyd et al. (1999) suggest that future research should include the role of gender and the establishment of links to family firm performance. Tsang (2001) found that family firms may often utilize a "learning-by-doing" approach when diversifying or expanding internationally.

Key points.
Based on the prior discussion, several noteworthy points include:

- Family firms, with the presence of the family system, have unique relational patterns.
- These patterns can be a potential strength for family firms, but may also need to be managed differently than what is typically prescribed for non-family firms.
- The manner in which knowledge and relational assets are transferred between family members may affect a number of important individual and firm outcomes.
- Despite the potential strong influence on family firm outcomes, this area appears to be severely under-researched.

Practitioner points.
Sustaining family social patterns and tacit knowledge across generations requires social contact and time. Here are some things owners of family businesses can do.

- Hold regular family social gatherings that help sustain relationships.
- Celebrate and repeatedly tell stories that celebrate family values and identity.
- Provide opportunities to next generation leaders to participate in business meetings and business leadership, with many opportunities to discuss the family business, and how it maintains relationships with key internal and external stakeholders.

Economic contribution

The economic contribution outcome grouping consisted of specific dependent variables including: prevalence of family firms, economic impact on economies, the domain of family business, and family business groups. Next, I will present some of the key findings from the articles incorporating these outcomes.

A handful of articles in the study attempted to systematically ascertain the number and proportion of businesses that are family firms. Often, the motivation of these types of studies is to confirm more piecemeal estimates of family firm prevalence and to call attention to the predominance of family firms as an organizational form. One such article, Anonymous (2003), used surveys of 60 family business experts (through the auspices of IFERA) to gather estimates of the prevalence of family firms throughout the world. While the methodology appears to use mixed data sources and is thus confusing, the authors reported the following estimates for the percentages of family firms: US (95 percent), Germany (60 percent), Netherlands (74 percent), UK (70 percent), Spain (75 percent), Italy (93 percent), and Brazil (90 percent). Heck and Trent (1999) employed a unique methodology based on sampling households to estimate the prevalence of US family firms. They found that one out of ten households owned a family business.

Astrachan and Shanker (2003) provide an analysis of the prevalence and impact of family firms in the US. They present a bull's-eye framework that looks at family business prevalence and impact. Based on three different definitional criteria, the analysis is represented in the figure of a bull's-eye with the outer ring representing the least restrictive and the inner ring representing the most restrictive definitions. Using their broadest definition of a family business (requiring family control and participation), they estimated that there were 24.2 million family businesses, accounting for 89 percent of business tax returns. These family firms employed 82 million individuals (62 percent of the workforce) and contributed $5.9 trillion (64 percent) to the GDP. Using a middle definition (also requiring that a founder/descendant run the firm with the intention to keep the business in the family), Astrachan and Shanker (2003) estimated that there were 10.8 million family businesses, accounting for 39 percent of business tax returns. These family firms employed 77 million individuals (58 percent of the workforce) and contributed $5.5 trillion (59 percent) to the GDP. Applying the narrowest definition (further requiring multiple generation participation and multiple family members in management), they estimated that there were 3 million family businesses, accounting for 11 percent of business tax returns. These family firms employed 36 million individuals (27 percent of the workforce) and contributed $2.6 trillion (29 percent) to the GDP. The authors do suggest some caveats and limitations in interpreting these numbers.

Specific studies have measured the prevalence and economic impact of family firms outside of the US. For example, Flören (1998), using a broad definition, reported that 83 percent of all incorporated firms in the Netherlands were family firms. Family firms in the Netherlands are responsible for the creation of between 59 percent and 68 percent of all private sector jobs and account for between 39 percent and 46 percent of total employment. Family firm contributions are responsible for 54 percent of the Dutch GDP. These results are fairly close to those reported for the broad definition of family firms in the US, and suggest that the prevalence and impact of family firms is a global phenomenon.

While we see that the prevalence and economic impact of family businesses is significant, their social impact is also likely significant. Interestingly, the social impact of family businesses has not been systematically addressed in the research literature. Anecdotal evidence suggests that family businesses are highly committed to their employees and devoted to community development. However, research has not yet examined the extent of the social impact and whether family firms differ significantly from non-family firms.

Key points.

Several main points can be culled from the previously discussed articles:

- Family firms are pervasive, and even by the most stringent definitions, they have a significant impact on economies throughout the world.

- Several researchers suggest that despite the fundamental importance of family firms to the world's economies, their numbers and influence are often underestimated and discounted.
- Definitional issues limit the ability to conduct comparative studies, aggregate results, or calculate definitive rates and statistics that easily convey the importance of family firms to other parties (e.g., policy-makers).

Practitioner points.
Even though family businesses are pervasive and provide much social and economic good, family businesses often overlook or understate their own contributions. Here are some things they might do to counteract these oversights:

- Keep family members abreast of economic contributions. Talk about overall profits, numbers of employees, and the effects of products and services.
- Involve family members in community outreach and philanthropy.
- Acknowledge that yours is a family business. Owners of family businesses may limit themselves when they do not recognize that theirs is a family business and that there are many other family businesses like their own in their community. These businesses have common problems and issues. By talking about common issues, family business owners and members can learn from one another about handling unique issues related to family ownership.

Regulatory and business environment

The regulatory and business environment outcome grouping comprises specific dependent variables including: perceptions of nascent entrepreneurs towards the environment, issues facing family firms, survival strategies in hostile environments, and family business dominance in industries. Several relevant studies that investigate these outcomes are presented in the remainder of this section.

In a particularly unique study, Chrisman, Chua, and Steier (2002) examined how cultural influences swayed entrepreneurs' perceptions of the business environment. Using a state-by-state approach, they found that the prevalence of family businesses in a state influenced entrepreneurs' perceptions of the business environment more than other cultural factors. This relationship was negative for a number of perceived business environment outcomes (e.g., government regulation, access to capital, workforce skills). Chrisman et al. (2002) conclude that:

> From the perspective of practice, entrepreneurs and managers should understand that the incidence of family versus non-family businesses in an industry or community may have a large influence on perceptions and these perceptions may affect buyer, supplier, and competitive dynamics. (p. 124)

Dyer and Mortensen (2005) studied the survival strategies of family and non-family firms when faced with a hostile environment. Though based on a small sample, the results suggested that family firms, based on their ability to draw on family resources including social capital and broader networks, were more likely to survive. Murphy and Murphy (2001) noted the recent trend of US courts in piercing the corporate veil for limited liability companies. This trend may be particularly problematic for family firms. Murphy (2005) surveyed private family firms regarding managers' perceptions of the most important issues facing their firms. Based on a list of 20 potential issues, corporate taxation was ranked as the most important issue by the greatest number of respondents. Murphy (2005) concludes that despite espoused concerns for some family-related issues, family firms "are struggling with more fundamental issues such as profitability and growth" (p. 132).

Key points.
There does not appear to be an overarching theme emerging from the few articles addressing the regulatory and business environment outcomes. However, some critical observations are the following:

- Family businesses, despite their unique family characteristics, are still businesses. They may have similar concerns as other businesses and, at the end of the day, strive for profitability and survival like all firms.
- However, particular legal and tax issues may impact family firms to a greater degree, particularly estate taxes that are a major liability for family firms.

Practitioner points.
Work with other family businesses to influence government regulations that influence business success. For example, one issue that consumes much time and money is handling estate issues when passing the business to the next generation. Family business owners can join organizations such as Family Enterprise USA that will help them lobby to influence government laws and regulations.

Linking the outcomes within the Social and Economic Impact cluster

While I explored some of the main findings and areas for future development with respect to the four outcome groupings that comprise the Social and Economic Impact cluster, a question emerged – How do the outcome categories (entrepreneurship, social capital and knowledge transfer, regulatory and business environment, and economic contribution) really relate to one another in a practical sense? In the Yu et al. (2012) study, the outcomes (see Landscape Map) were plotted based on how they scored and clustered on the systems dimension (business vs. family) and temporal dimension (short-term vs. long-term). This approach was theoretically grounded and provided valuable insights for the purposes of the authors' research. However, from a more applied perspective, I considered how these outcomes might be connected in a practical sense.

At first blush, the four categories appeared disparate to me. The outcomes crossed levels of analysis (e.g., firm to macro-environment), and I wondered, as is sometimes evident in cluster analysis, if the regulatory and business environment category might have been the "potpourri" grouping, where extraneous items that didn't fit well anywhere else were forced together. The good news is that as I delved into the outcomes a clearer pattern of connections was revealed.

Numerous articles reviewed in this chapter stressed the importance of culture on entrepreneurship in family firms, and stressed the key role that a willingness to change beliefs and cultures plays in promoting entrepreneurial behaviors within family firms (e.g., Hall et al., 2001; Kellermanns & Eddleston, 2006). Hall et al. (2001) conclude that, "to support entrepreneurial processes, managers need to foster a process of high-order learning in which old cultural patterns are continuously questioned and changed" (p. 193). This high-order learning is described as the ability of the organization to question taken-for-granted beliefs and to contemplate its ability to learn (Argyris & Schön, 1981). Thus, entrepreneurship and learning (through social capital and knowledge transfer) appear to be linked; to achieve a culture that fosters entrepreneurial behavior the firm must be able to adopt a learning approach that reflects a willingness to change and that can challenge existing cultures. This type of a learning approach would likely be enhanced in a family firm with high family capital and open exchanges of information.

There is general consensus that in the new competitive landscape the ability to think and act more entrepreneurially is of crucial importance to the survival and growth of family firms. Therefore, the prevalence and economic contribution of family firms is tied to entrepreneurial behaviors and learning. If, as numerous articles referenced in this chapter propose, the very survival of many family firms depends on their ability to adopt a more entrepreneurial posture, then the failure to do so would have adverse effects on the family firm as a viable organizational form. Conversely, if family firms are able to adapt to changes in the environment, then they can survive and prosper. Either way, entrepreneurial behavior and the future prevalence and economic contribution of family firms appear to be conjoined.

The final connection is between the prevalence and economic contribution of family firms, and the regulatory and business environment. In the strategic management literature, the firm's general external environment is often comprised of six segments under which different types of trends or changes can be classified. These are labeled the demographic, socio-cultural, political/legal, economic, global, and technological segments. Trends and changes in these segments can greatly influence the performance and survival of industries and firms. While changes in most of these segments are too broad and powerful for an industry to alter (e.g., demographic shifts in the ethnic make-up of the US), the political/legal segment can be shaped by firms and industries. To be proactive in shaping laws and regulations that may affect their industry, firms often form trade groups that "lobby" for favorable outcomes. The regulatory aspect of the family firm environment could be altered through a much more clear and forceful statement on the prevalence and economic contribution of family firms.

I would hazard a guess that most people are surprised when shown some of the figures like those presented earlier in this chapter on the high prevalence and impact of family firms – regardless of how strict the definition. However, while definitional debates have kept researchers from coming to a consensus and providing some simple and straightforward figures, they have not prohibited researchers from ubiquitously citing the failure rates of family firms by generation (30 percent survive to the second generation and 12 percent to the third generation); however, there is no such clarity on the positive numbers relating to incidence, employment, or contribution towards GDP. A simple but effective step would be for researchers to form consensus on these numbers and disseminate them to the public and policy-makers. Effectively conveying the existing prevalence and economic impact of these statistics could greatly influence policy-makers, especially in today's economic environment, by shaping regulations that are more favorable to family firms (e.g., estate tax policies). The relationship between prevalence and the regulatory environment may also be somewhat reciprocal in that favorable regulatory environment changes for family firms could also have a positive impact on future family firm prevalence and economic contribution.

In sum, what at first seemed to be four disparate outcome categories are upon further analysis intertwined and connected. High-order learning, achieved through high levels of family social capital and knowledge transfer, can reshape culture and promote entrepreneurial behavior in family firms. The general ability to become more entrepreneurial in the new competitive landscape may likely determine the overall prevalence and economic contribution of family firms. More clearly defining the scope and aggregate economic influence of family firms can assist in proactively shaping the regulatory and business environment for family firms, and reciprocally influence the prevalence and economic contribution of family firms in the future.

A central idea that emerged from several articles is that it may be imperative that family firms be able to adopt and implement more entrepreneurial postures. Family firms have distinctive cultures and characteristics, which may serve to both promote and inhibit entrepreneurship. Culture is a broad and somewhat messy construct. Prescribing that a family firm owner who wants to make his or her firm more entrepreneurial must manage the culture of the firm is very general. Therefore, I would like to briefly highlight a management concept that might be more specific and helpful to the family firm practitioner.

In 1986, Prahalad and Bettis introduced the concept of dominant logic. They defined dominant logic as,

> a mind set or a world view or conceptualization of the business and the administrative tools to accomplish goals and make decisions in that business. It is stored as a shared cognitive map (or set of schemas) among the dominant coalition. It is expressed as a learned, problem-solving behavior. (p. 491)

Dominant logic evolves over time, and it is learned and reinforced through organizational processes and outcomes (Prahalad & Bettis, 1986).

Chua, Chrisman, and Sharma (1999) define a family business as a,

> business governed and/or managed with the intention to shape and pursue the vision of the business held by a dominant coalition controlled by family members of the same family or a small number of families in a manner that is potentially sustainable across generations of the family or families. (p. 4)

This definition suggests that the dominant logic in the family business is likely tied to the vision of the dominant coalition to preserve and pass the business on to future generations. This may be much different than a start-up venture with the dominant logic of establishing a viable market opportunity or of a large public firm focused on maximizing shareholder wealth.

Since many family firms began as small entrepreneurial ventures, they may have at one time possessed a more entrepreneurial dominant logic. However, as firms grow and mature, the dominant problems change (Kazanjian, 1988) and so may their dominant logic(s). Once a dominant logic is entrenched, it can be very difficult to replace. The old

dominant logic must be "unlearned," and significant changes made to existing organizational systems and processes before it can be replaced (Bettis & Prahalad, 1995). Changes
in a dominant logic and the unlearning process may tend to be punctuated and acceler-
ated by crises (Bettis & Prahalad, 1995). Some firms, despite facing external changes
and pressures that clearly demand a new logic, may find it impossible to unlearn the old
dominant logic and will fail (Bettis & Prahalad, 1995). Family firms may face particular
obstacles in trying to replace an existing dominant logic because "the feelings and emotions related to change are likely to be deeper and more intense than those in nonfamily
businesses" (Dyer, 1994, p. 125).

Hall et al. (2001) provide the following prescriptive statement:

> Because culture has a great impact on the thoughts and actions of individuals, it is very impor-
> tant, especially for strategic actors, to be aware of and be able to question taken-for-granted
> values, norms, and traditions. Entrepreneurship as radical change can come about only if
> individuals question and challenge what is taken for granted. Thus, "uncovering the taken-for-
> granted action could help organizations with business strategizing and change" (see Smircich,
> 1983, p. 349). For such uncovering to take place, actors must not only be able to make sense of
> and put culture into words, but also feel encouraged to question the dominating ways of think-
> ing and patterns of action in the organization. (p. 204)

As this statement suggests, culture and dominant logic are intertwined. If to survive and
thrive in the new competitive landscape family businesses must develop an entrepreneurial mindset (Sirmon & Hitt, 2003), then the ability to adopt an entrepreneurial dominant
logic may be of paramount importance. The challenge for the dominant coalition of the
family firm is to employ high-order learning in questioning and thinking about how they
think.

Conclusion

The purpose of this chapter was to offer my perspective regarding what we know and
what we ought to know with respect to the four outcome categories within the Social
and Economic Impact cluster of the Landscape Map. By using the Yu et al. (2012)
framework, I have articulated some of the more interesting research findings associated
with the outcomes and distilled key points from the research literature and to make this
chapter more useful to family firm owners. I also provided specific practitioner points of
action related to each of the outcome categories and provide a summative section that
links the outcome categories to the Landscape clusters in a way I hope will further the
application of the research.

In summary, as previously discussed, family firms need to be entrepreneurial, which
can be facilitated through the concept of higher-order learning and the challenging of
established dominant logics that may hinder entrepreneurship. Family firms are prevalent and have positive economic and social impacts on their communities. The impact of
family businesses as an economic and social force needs to be systematically researched
and documented, and the findings shared so that government policies, which in turn
shape the business environment, can reflect policies that will encourage and support
family business to achieve more positive outcomes.

References

Anonymous. (2003). Family businesses dominate: International family enterprise research academy (IFERA). *Family Business Review, 16*, 235–40.

Argyris, C., & Schön, D.A. (1981). *Organizational learning*. Reading, MA: Addison-Wesley.

Arregle, J.L., Hitt, M.A., Sirmon, D.G., & Very, P. (2007). The development of organizational social capital: Attributes of family firms. *Journal of Management Studies, 44*, 73–95.

Astrachan, J.H., & Shanker, M.C. (2003). Family businesses' contribution to the U.S. economy: A closer look. *Family Business Review, 16*, 211–19.

Bettis, R.A., & Prahalad, C.K. (1995). The dominant logic: Retrospective and extension. *Strategic Management Journal, 16*, 5–14.

Boyd, J., Upton, N., & Wircenski, M. (1999). Mentoring in family firms: A reflective analysis of senior executives' perceptions. *Family Business Review, 12*, 209–309.

Chirico, F., & Salvato, C. (2008). Knowledge integration and dynamic organizational adaptation in family firms. *Family Business Review, 21*, 169–81.

Chrisman, J.J., Chua, J.H., & Steier, L.P. (2002). The influence of national culture and family involvement on entrepreneurial perceptions and performance at the state level. *Entrepreneurship Theory & Practice, 26*, 113–30.

Chua, J.H., Chrisman, J.J., & Sharma, P. (1999). Defining the family business by behavior. *Entrepreneurship Theory & Practice, 23*, 19–39.

Cohen, W.M., & Levinthal, D.A. (1990). Absorptive capacity, A new perspective on learning and innovation. *Administrative Science Quarterly, 35*, 128–52.

Craig, J.B.L., & Moores, K. (2006). A 10-year longitudinal investigation of strategy, systems, and environment on innovation in family firms. *Family Business Review, 19*, 1–10.

D'Aveni, R.A. (1994). *Hypercompetition*. The Free Press: New York.

Dyer, W.G., Jr. (1994). Potential contributions of organizational behavior to the study of family-owned businesses. *Family Business Review, 7*, 109–31.

Dyer, W.G., Jr., & Mortensen, S.P. (2005). Entrepreneurship and family business in a hostile environment: The case of Lithuania. *Family Business Review, 18*, 247–58.

Flören, R.H. (1998). The significance of family business in the Netherlands. *Family Business Review, 11*, 121–34.

Hall, A., Melin, L., & Nordqvist, M. (2001). Entrepreneurship as radical change in the family business: Exploring the role of cultural patterns. *Family Business Review, 14*, 193–208.

Hamel, G. (2000). *Leading the revolution*. Boston: Harvard Business School Press.

Heck, R.K.Z., & Trent, E.S. (1999). The prevalence of family business from a household sample. *Family Business Review, 12*, 209–19.

Hoffman, J., Hoelscher, M., & Sorenson, R. (2006). Achieving sustained competitive advantage: A family capital theory. *Family Business Review, 24*, 137–46.

Kazanjian, R.K. (1988). Relation of dominant problems to stages of growth in technology based new ventures. *Academy of Management Journal, 31*, 257–79.

Kellermanns, F.W., & Eddleston, K.A. (2006). Corporate entrepreneurship in family firms: A family perspective. *Entrepreneurship Theory & Practice, 30*, 809–30.

Litz, R.A., & Kleysen, R.F. (2001). Your old men shall dream dreams, your young men shall see visions: Toward a theory of family firm innovation with help from the Brubeck family. *Family Business Review, 14*, 335–51.

Marsh, S.J., & Stock, G.N. (2006). Creating dynamic capability: The role of intertemporal integration, knowledge retention, and interpretation. *Journal of Product Innovation Management, 23*, 422–36.

Murphy, D.L. (2005). Understanding the complexities of private family firms: An empirical investigation. *Family Business Review, 18*, 123–33.

Murphy, D.L., & Murphy, J.E. (2001). Protecting the limited liability feature of your family business: Evidence from the US court system. *Family Business Review, 14*, 325–34.

Nahapiet, J., & Ghosal, S. (1998). Social capital, intellectual capital, and the organizational advantage. *Academy of Management Review, 23*, 242–66.

Niemela, T. (2004). Interfirm cooperation capability in the context of networking family firms: The role of power. *Family Business Review, 17*, 319–30.

Prahalad, C.K., & Bettis, R.A. (1986). The dominant logic: A new linkage between diversity and performance. *Strategic Management Journal, 7*, 485–501.

Salvato, C., & Melin, L. (2008). Creating value across generations in family-controlled businesses: The role of family social capital. *Family Business Review, 21*, 259–76.

Sirmon, D.G., & Hitt, M.A. (2003). Managing resources: Linking unique resources, management and wealth creation in family firms. *Entrepreneurship Theory and Practice, 27*, 339–58.

Smircich, L. (1983). Concepts of culture and organizational analysis. *Administrative Science Quarterly, 28*, 339–58.

Steier, L. (2001). Next-generation entrepreneurs and succession: An exploratory study of modes and means of managing social capital. *Family Business Review, 14*, 259–76.

Tsang, E.W.K. (2001). Internationalizing the family firm: A case study of a Chinese family business. *Journal of Small Business Management, 39*, 88–94.

Yu, A., Lumpkin, G.T., Sorenson, R.L., & Brigham, K.H. (2012). The landscape of family business outcomes: A summary and numerical taxonomy of dependent variables. *Family Business Review, 25*, 33–57.

Zahra, S.A. (2005). Entrepreneurial risk taking in family firms. *Family Business Review, 18*, 23–40.

Zahra, S.A., & George, G. (2002). Absorptive capacity: A review, reconceptualization, and extension. *Academy of Management Review, 27*, 185–203.

Zahra, S.A., Hayton, J.C., & Salvato, C. (2004). Entrepreneurship in family vs. non-family firms: A resource-based analysis of the effect of organizational culture. *Entrepreneurship Theory & Practice, 28*, 363–81.

5. Strategy in family business: Recent findings and future challenges

G.T. Lumpkin and Gregory G. Dess

Introduction

Family firms represent a major engine of economic growth and wealth creation (Astrachan & Shanker, 2003). Young, small firms represent a substantial portion of the new job creation and innovation in the US economy (Birch, Haggerty, & Parsons, 1994), and many of today's new ventures are family-based. A growing body of research indicates that family-controlled businesses outperform non-family businesses (e.g., Anderson & Reeb, 2003). Compared to firms in general, however, less is known about the strategic orientations and organizational processes that drive family firms (Sharma, Chrisman, & Chua, 1997). Although a few studies have investigated family firm strategic postures (e.g., Daily & Thompson, 1994), the strategic methods employed by family firms, many of which are highly entrepreneurial, are not well understood.

A growing body of research suggests that family businesses are fundamentally different from non-family businesses (e.g., Miller & Le Breton-Miller, 2005). Beneath this important conclusion, however, questions persist about how family firms behave and what makes them different. The Landscape framework, set forth in the paper by Andy Yu and colleagues (Yu, Lumpkin, Sorenson, & Brigham, 2012), highlights the importance of strategy in a family business context; it also illustrates how strategy relates to other features and forces which affect family business outcomes.*

Strategy is located in the upper-left quadrant of the Landscape Map (Yu et al., 2012), which indicates that it is a long-term (upper) issue for family businesses and chiefly a business (left side) concern. Many of the long-term considerations that family businesses face are family related, such as issues of succession and the long-term involvement of family members in the business. When it comes to the survival and success of the business itself, strategy-making and strategic planning guide managerial behavior and ensure the family firm's future prospects (Sharma et al., 1997).

In the sections below, we will address the major topical areas identified in the Yu, Lumpkin, Sorenson and Brigham (2012) study that pertain to the Strategy cluster's outcome categories of survival and growth, strategy content, internationalization, financial structure, and investment policies. In the strategy content section, we elaborate on

---

* "A Map of the Landscape of Family Business" (also referred to as the Landscape Map) can be found on the page just inside the cover of this book and in the Yu, Lumpkin, Sorenson, and Brigham (2012) article published in *Family Business Review*. Following the Landscape Map, the "Outcome Categories by Chapter Table" (also referred to as the Outcomes Categories Table) is provided. This table shows all chapters that contain content about the outcome categories that appear in this chapter.

three familiar approaches to achieving strategic advantage – low-cost leadership, differentiation, and focus – and explore both "familiness" (Habbershon & Williams, 1999) and family-based brands (Craig, Dibrell, & Davis, 2008) as key family resources that can enhance strategic advantages. Then we consider the importance of entrepreneurship as a type of strategic activity that can strengthen the strategic management and performance of family firms. To do so, we draw on entrepreneurial orientation (EO), a popular approach to conceptualizing entrepreneurship that is derived from the strategic management literature (Lumpkin & Dess, 1996). Using an EO framework, we also propose a number of questions designed to challenge owners and managers to improve the strategic performance of their family firms.

Survival and growth

The importance of strategy to the management of family firms can best be understood by considering the question, "Why do some family businesses succeed and others do not?" In a family business context, there could be many ways to address the issue of what constitutes success. But at the most basic level, issues of survival, growth, and financial sustainability are paramount. Small- and medium-size family enterprises (SMEs) may face serious resource constraints that threaten cash flow or inhibit business development and growth. Large family firms may have sufficient resources but face challenges such as how to remain viable in competitive markets and how to achieve the operational efficiencies needed to sustain ongoing profitability. Hence, the question of how to survive and grow is a constant concern for strategic decision-makers in family firms.

With regard to survival, the family system surrounding a family business is thought to provide strategic advantages that may be unavailable to non-family firms. Family businesses that have the support of spouses or other family members are able to withstand dips in sales or financial shortfalls that might pitch other firms into failure (Poza & Messer, 2001). Families can also be an important source of resources – financial and otherwise – that can extend a family firm's ability to survive during startup or difficult periods. For more mature family businesses, the availability of patient capital (Sirmon & Hitt, 2003) – that is, investments that are made without expectations of quick returns – can bolster a family firm's chance of long-term survival.

Recent research has highlighted one of the key advantages that many family businesses have over non-family firms: the strategic benefits of a long-term orientation. In their book *Managing for the Long Run*, based on an in-depth study of 40 high-performing family-controlled businesses (FCBs), Miller and Le Breton-Miller (2005) noted that family firms tend to be financially stronger and more effective than their non-family counterparts. Among the conclusions they reached about why this is the case, the author's wrote that, "the only way to sustain good performance is to act in the long-run interests of the company and all of its stakeholders" (2005, p. 232). Indeed, FCBs have been found to outperform non-family businesses on a range of performance outcomes including traditional profitability measures (Anderson & Reeb, 2003; Villalonga & Amit, 2006), efficiency (McConaughy, Matthews, & Fialko, 2001), and sales growth (Chrisman, Chua, & Steier, 2002; Lee, 2006; Zahra, 2003). Hence, there is clear evidence that family businesses with a long-term orientation are capable of achieving superior performance.

Beyond mere survival, the role of strategic management involves understanding why some firms outperform others. Thus, managers of family firms need to determine how to compete in order to create competitive advantages that are lasting and inimitable. These concerns have led family business researchers to investigate two important elements of strategic management in family firms. The first concern involves asking which business-level strategies are needed to maintain a competitive advantage. For example, family firms need to determine if it is best to pursue a low-cost producer strategy or to develop products and services that are unique and enable the business to charge premium prices. Related questions involve whether to focus on a niche market or to compete more broadly. The second concern involves understanding the kind of valuable, rare, or difficult-to-copy resource endowments a family business can deploy to remain competitive. For example, family businesses may need to ask whether using the family name in advertising will give the company an advantage over other competitors.

It is these two topics that we turn to next.

Business-level strategies

Many of the strategic management issues family businesses face involve business-level strategies, that is, the strategic decisions and actions firms use to gain competitive advantages in specific product markets. The most common approach to characterizing competitive business strategies is Porter's (1980) generic strategies framework, which includes low-cost leadership, differentiation, and focus strategies. In the sections below, we will investigate each of these three avenues to achieving competitive advantage. Note that several studies of the strategic practices and policies of family firms have led many family business researchers to conclude that there are very few differences in the methods and requirements of family versus non-family firms when it comes to how they approach business-level strategy (e.g., Daily & Thompson, 1994).

Low-cost leadership.

Porter's (1996; 1980) low-cost leadership strategy concentrates on cost control in order to be the lowest-cost producer relative to other competitors. It achieves cost savings by pursuing efficient scale economies and minimizing expenditures on product innovation and advertising. Cost leaders are also often price leaders offering no-frills products to customers who prefer cost savings over service or brand image. To succeed, firms with an overall goal of cost leadership must restrict their emphasis to controlling costs and place their attention on attaining production economies.

Cost leadership is the competitive strategy typically pursued by Hambrick's (1985) cost leaders or efficient misers, and Treacy and Wiersema's (1995) companies that compete on the basis of "operational excellence." These approaches require that successful organizations develop consistency among, a) their strategy; b) the business models they adopt; c) their choice of technology; and, d) their organizational capabilities, including their human resource capabilities (Ghoshal, 2003). A conservative strategy based on maintaining close control of operations and limiting new expenses is an avenue to competitive advantages for many family businesses (Carney, 2005).

Differentiation.

A differentiation strategy (Porter, 1996; 1980) emphasizes unique products or services based on innovativeness in product development, original applications of new technologies, and/or the offering of distinctive bundles of attractive features such as convenience, image, and service. The strategy depends on effective marketing, quality, creativity, a strong image, and a good reputation. Differentiators use their unique position to build customer loyalty, which serves as a competitive barrier and enables them to charge above-average prices.

Differentiation is central to strategies pursued by Miller and Friesen's (1984) innovative firms, and Treacy and Wiersema's (1995) companies that highlight "product leadership." Such firms are usually at the forefront of change and create uncertainties with which rivals must contend. A recent study of Australian family businesses found that both early stage and older family businesses compete by using frequent innovations and market-leading introductions of new products and services consistent with a differentiation strategy (Craig & Moores, 2006).

Focus.

The use of a focus strategy (Porter, 1996; 1980) suggests concentration on a narrow domain such as a limited customer group, a specialized product line, or a particular geographical area. The essence of a focus strategy is the exploitation of a particular market niche. A focuser may attempt to achieve a cost advantage or a product/service advantage through differentiation, but will do so within a targeted market segment.

Firms pursuing a focus strategy use an approach similar to Miller and Friesen's (1978) niche strategy. McDougall and Robinson (1990) found that firms focus in different ways, including small markets, limited growth markets, small order size, and narrowly defined product lines. Each of these approaches is characteristically narrow in scope, thus providing focus strategy firms with an ability to succeed by single-minded focus on a novel product or service that can capture above-average returns (Miller, 1986). Family business researchers have identified market segment focus or niche strategies as an important avenue for family firms to create competitive advantages (Harris, Martinez, & Ward, 1994).

To summarize, family businesses may choose from several different approaches in pursuit of a strategic direction and plan of action aimed at ensuring their long-term survival and success. Cost leaders obtain advantages by minimizing expenses and seeking operating efficiencies; differentiators highlight unique product attributes and customer service to achieve advantages; and focusers compete by zeroing in on narrow market segments where they can attain distinct advantages. Combinations of these strategies can also be deployed to realize superior advantages.

Familiness and family-based branding

In prior family business and family firm performance research, several authors have identified characteristics or attributes that are uniquely "family oriented" (e.g., Lumpkin, Martin, & Vaughn, 2008). Drawing on the resource-based view of the firm (RBV), Habbershon and Williams (1999) developed the concept of "familiness" to distinguish family firms from non-family firms. They define familiness as "the unique bundle of resources a particular firm has because of the systems interaction between the family, its individual members, and the business" (1999, p. 11). Habbershon and Williams see familiness as the strategic capabilities that a family firm derives from its human capital, physical capital, and organizational and process capital resources. They argue that familiness affects a number of things, including goal setting and acceptance, relationships and alliances, international partner selection criteria, and ownership of knowledge-based resources. In a follow-up article, the authors expand on the RBV-based model and introduce a new term, "the *f*-factor," to encompass those resources and capabilities that give a family a "distinctive familiness" (Habbershon, Williams, & MacMillan, 2003).

Drawing on a familiness perspective, research has been conducted to investigate the importance of family members as unique resources that contribute positively to family business success. During an era of liberalization in India's emerging economy, family personnel were able to adapt their family business groups to the new environment more effectively by making strategic use of family-based resources (Manikutty, 2000). Another study found that familiness qualities in 21 managers at eight family-owned firms enabled them to develop a more market-oriented culture that was positively associated with strategic focus, customer orientation, family relationships, and operational efficiency (Tokarczyk, Hansen, Green, & Down, 2007). Hence, family-centric resources such as familiness provide a promising avenue for building strategic competitive advantages.

Family-based branding is closely related to the idea of familiness in that it builds on a family's name or its characteristics to develop a unique identity. The use of a family name as a company name creates strong associations in the minds of consumers and other stakeholders. Prior research indicates that family branding can be used to strengthen perceptions of a family firm's customer orientation (Craig et al., 2008) or to convey a strong sense of the family's values (Post, 1993). In general, these associations are positive because "family brand identity may act as a proxy of the virtuous qualities that customers associate with family membership" (Craig et al., 2008, p. 364). Hence, when a company such as S.C. Johnson, the fifth-generation consumer products company, brands itself as "A Family Company" it is endeavoring to gain a strategic advantage based on family characteristics – quality, reliability, and stability. Other families, by contrast, often build on the celebrity power of a family name or its members. Recently, for example, Parmentier (2011) studied Victoria and David Beckham, and how their growing visibility and distinctiveness contributed to strengthening their family brand. In contrast to a celebrity endorsement, celebrity capital suggests actual involvement with a business and provides an even more potent source of strategic advantages (Hunter, Burgers, & Davidsson, 2009).

In summary, family businesses are often able to use the fact that they are a family or elements of their family identity as strategic assets. Such family-based assets can be leveraged for various types of advantages, including reputational benefits and a stronger customer orientation.

Internationalization

Opportunities in global markets are spurring more and more family businesses to become involved with international trade. In prior decades, internationalization was thought to be the domain of large multinational corporations (Davis & Harveston, 2000). Today, statistics indicate that 98 percent of all US exporters are SMEs (U.S. Small Business Administration, Office of Advocacy, 2012). Considering that a large majority of those businesses are family-controlled (Astrachan & Shanker, 2003), it is clear that internationalization has become an important component of family businesses' success. Exporting is only one of several types of international trade; family businesses are also engaged in foreign direct investment (Tsang, 2002); joint ventures (Okoroafo, 1999); strategic alliances (Fernandez & Nieto, 2005); and outsourcing (Kayser & Wallau, 2002). Hence, internationalization is playing an increasingly important role in the strategic plans of family firms.

There are many motivations for a family business to engage in internationalization:

- To increase the size of potential markets – International trade affords attractive opportunities to provide goods and services to untapped markets, including rapidly growing markets such as China and India.
- To attain economies of scale in operations – Spreading the costs of manufacturing or operations over more units of production helps reduce costs; other economies can be achieved by pooling purchases or sharing research and development expenses.
- To extend the life-cycle of a product – When domestic markets become saturated or when a product has reached maturity in one's home country, sales and growth potential may still exist in an international market.
- To optimize the physical location for every activity in the value chain – Locating manufacturing or warehousing facilities near markets, accessing a more economical work force, and reducing risks associated with exchange rates and political instability can contribute to more efficient and effective value chain activities.

Many avenues are available to family businesses to achieve some or all of these goals. In addition to outsourcing and offshoring (shifting a value-creating activity to a foreign location), companies can participate via exporting, licensing, franchising, strategic alliances, joint ventures, and wholly owned subsidiaries. Each of these approaches can help family businesses create strategic advantages from internationalization.

To be successful, international activities typically require companies to deploy resources and develop strategic capabilities beyond those needed to be successful in domestic markets (Peng, 2001). Further, engaging in international business is often associated with having less control over operations, a condition that many family businesses are unwilling to accept. As a result, several studies have found that internationalization occurs relatively less frequently among family businesses as compared to non-family businesses (e.g., Okoroafo, 1999; Zahra, 2003). A recent study of exporting by Spanish family firms, for example, found a negative relationship between family ownership and internationalization (Fernandez & Nieto, 2005). A study of Australian family businesses indicated that the managerial capabilities needed for competing effectively in international markets was lacking in family businesses compared to their non-family counterparts (Graves & Thomas, 2006).

Overall, the primary reason family firms internationalize is strictly business – to enjoy greater quality and cost benefits (Okoroafo, 1999). But among family firms involved in international business, a few family business characteristics influence how they internationalize. In a study of overseas venturing, Tsang (2002) found that the approach of Chinese family firms typically involves more highly centralized control over management and strategic decision-making than in non-family firms. Further, family businesses that made investments in information technology and Internet usage were more likely to internationalize (Davis & Harveston, 2000).

The role of generational differences is unclear, however. Okoroafo (1999) found that if early generations of a family business did not engage in internationalization, it was unlikely that later generations would either; Fernandez and Nieto (2005) found essentially the opposite: the presence of second and subsequent generations in the family business was associated with greater international involvement. Despite uncertainty about the role of subsequent generations, research suggests that older, larger, and more sophisticated family firms are more likely to be engaged in international business (Zahra, 2003). The increased pace of globalization makes it likely that many more family businesses will engage in internationalization in the future, regardless of their size or the generation in charge.

In summary, internationalization is a viable strategy that offers important advantages for many types of family businesses and can be undertaken using several different approaches – exporting, licensing, franchising, strategic alliances, joint ventures, and wholly owned subsidiaries. To internationalize successfully, family firms may have to develop new capabilities and deploy resources beyond those needed for domestic markets.

Financial structure

For businesses of all types, access to resources is a critical success factor. Financial resources are especially important; the ability to fund operations or invest in new initiatives is an essential component of firm survival and growth. For SMEs, obtaining funding is one of the most serious challenges. Because SMEs tend to have smaller operations, limited cash flow, less collateral, and fewer market opportunities, they often find it more difficult to attract financing relative to large organizations with "deep pockets." Family businesses are no different than other businesses in their need for financial resources. However, research indicates that the financial structures of family businesses may enhance their ability to obtain funding as well as reduce the amount of funding needed to effectively manage operations and growth.

The types of funding that family and non-family businesses utilize are generally similar. In a study comparing family business versus non-family business use of five different credit products – lines of credit, financial leases, commercial mortgages, motor vehicle loans, and equipment loans – no differences were found between family and non-family businesses with the exception of motor vehicle loans: family businesses were more likely to use motor vehicle loans (Coleman & Carsky, 1999). The same study found no differences in the amount of leverage used by family and non-family businesses despite a general belief that family-controlled businesses are averse to debt financing.

Indeed, the use of debt by family businesses is complex and depends on several factors including, firm size, the use of strategic planning, the business objectives, and the nature and extent of family control (Romano, Tanewski, & Smyrnios, 2000). For example, publicly held family businesses have greater access to financing than private family firms (Maherault, 2000). Further, large firms are more likely to use bank financing than are small firms (Coleman & Carsky, 1999), and family firms controlled by the founding family tend to have less debt (McConaughy et al., 2001). This suggests that the more closely controlled a family business is, both in terms of private ownership and the number of family members involved in management, the less likely the family business will be to use debt financing. Schulze and colleagues found that the patterns of ownership by family firms – from closely controlled to widely dispersed – affected the level of debt used by family firms (Schulze, Lubatkin, & Dino, 2003).

The financial practices and ownership structures of family businesses may also affect how much financing a family business needs. Smaller, private family businesses often use family loans or intermingle household funds with business funds in order to meet short-term financing needs, thus minimizing the need for external funding (Haynes, Walker, Rowe, & Hong, 1999; Yilmazer & Schrank, 2006). Larger, more established family businesses with non-family members in senior decision-making roles have been shown to use more sophisticated financial planning techniques (capital budgeting and working capital management) and practices aimed at helping companies make more efficient use of resources (Filbeck & Lee, 2000).

Despite this apparent contrast between smaller, private and larger, professionally managed family businesses, McConaughy et al. (2001) found that family firms controlled by the founding family operated more efficiently than management-controlled family firms. Separately, Carney and Gedajlovic (2002) found that when ownership and control of a family business are coupled, short-term profitability is greater and financial liquidity is higher, but capital expenditures are lower. Hence, greater family control tends to be associated with more profitability and efficiency in the short run, but may inhibit long-term growth plans or investment in the future. This view is supported by research that indicates that the more owners prefer to maintain family control of the family business, the less likely the family firm will be to use equity financing aimed at growing the business (Romano et al., 2000). Overall, this suggests that the financial structures of family business have an important influence on the strategic planning and decision-making of family firms.

To summarize, the financial needs of family businesses are quite similar to those of non-family firms. Nevertheless, there are key differences in how family firms obtain funding. In general, the patterns of family ownership are likely to affect the use of debt financing: smaller, private family firms use less debt compared to non-family firms and tend to rely on family loans; larger family firms' financial structures are more similar to their non-family counterparts. Family firms that maintain close financial control often enjoy higher short-term profitability.

Investment policies

In the context of family businesses, the topic of investment policies has several different meanings. One of those topics is the extent to which family businesses welcome or invite other entities to invest in them. That is, to what extent are family businesses owned or financed by equity investors? A second set of questions revolves around the issue of what family firms invest in. This research covers a number of topics ranging from family businesses investing in other family firms (e.g., Steier, 2003) to investments by family businesses in professionalization of management and succession planning (e.g., Chittoor & Das, 2007).

The capital structure of any business can be viewed broadly as the ratio of debt to equity on its balance sheet. The previous section, Financial Structure, addressed family business perspectives on debt; in this section, we focus on the role and strategic implications of equity investments in the ownership regime of a family business. In general, equity financing, especially of SMEs, is a less popular and less commonly used financing option (Wu, Chua, & Chrisman, 2007). One reason for this is known as pecking order theory (Myers, 1984), which holds that private companies needing funding for operations will make financial decisions in a hierarchical fashion: the first choice is internal financing, followed by debt, and finally, external equity. In a study of the use of venture capital by SMEs in the UK, Poutziouris (2001) found support for a pecking order decision rule and concluded that "Family companies are not enthusiastic about widening the equity base – with venture capital – at the cost of relinquishing family business control" (p. 288). However, owning a share of control seems to be critical to equity investors, as demonstrated by Maherault's (2000) study of French family firms, in which he found that family businesses were not especially attractive to equity investors unless they were publicly traded.

One investment that family businesses may slightly favor is investment in other family businesses. Steier (2003) used agency theory to address different approaches to family-firm investing. Agency theory refers to differences in attitudes and preferences toward risk that occur when managers of a business (agents) are separated from its owners. He argued that investors who use a familial "altruistic" rationale for investing will have significantly different risk preferences, governance expectations, and investment objectives than those who invest with a more business-minded "market" rationale. Some support for this is evident in research of "family angels," angel investors who prefer to invest in family firms. A study comparing family angels to other informal investors found them willing to take greater risks, to be more actively involved in business decisions, and less concerned with an exit strategy (Erikson, Sorheim, & Reitan, 2003).

One more type of investing is worth noting: the extent to which family firms make strategic investments in assets, capabilities, and plans that can affect the future well-being of the business. Factors such as the professionalization of management, succession planning, training and development of future managers, and investments in R&D, equipment and/or real estate can contribute to business longevity (see Chittoor & Das, 2007). Nevertheless, family business researchers suggest "a peculiar financial logic" that favors low debt and close family control may be a substitute for future planning and a long-term investment policy in many family firms (Gallo, Tapies, & Cappuyns, 2004). Such a conservative approach may help such firms enjoy short-term financial success, but failure to make more far-sighted investments in the business may limit their long-run prospects.

To summarize, equity financing is less popular among family firms in part because firms prefer to maintain control and in part because investors may find closely held family firms less attractive to invest in. However, research indicates that family firms may favor investing in other family businesses. Further, family firms often make strategic investments – in assets and capabilities that impact their long-term business success.

Entrepreneurial orientation

Consistent with the view of other family business researchers, we believe there is a natural link between entrepreneurship and family business, and that family firms may benefit from entrepreneurial practices (Dyer & Handler, 1994; Hoy & Verser, 1994). How can family firms be more entrepreneurial? To address this, we draw on the notion of entrepreneurial orientation (EO), an entrepreneurial-type strategy (Wiklund & Shepherd, 2005) that many firms engage in to launch new ventures and revitalize their organizations. EO refers to the policies, practices, and strategy-making processes that firms use to enact their organizational purpose, sustain their vision, and create competitive advantages. EO provides family firms with an avenue to strategic renewal and growth that can improve performance and ensure their long-term future.

Prior research suggests that the EO construct provides an effective tool for capturing evidence of entrepreneurial decision-making and action across a wide variety of organizational and geographic contexts (e.g., Kreiser, Marino, & Weaver, 2002; Tan & Tan, 2005). Family business researchers have found EO to be a useful framework for investigating entrepreneurship in family businesses (e.g., Naldi, Nordqvist, Sjoberg, & Wiklund, 2007; Nordqvist, Habbershon, & Melin, 2008; Zahra, 2005). Entrepreneurial orientation consists of five dimensions, including innovativeness, risk-taking, proactiveness, competitive aggressiveness, and autonomy. While the empirical research on entrepreneurship in family business is limited, there has been some convergence regarding the use of different dimensions of entrepreneurial orientation in a family business context (Nordqvist et al., 2008). In the sections below, we briefly discuss each of these dimensions in terms of how they are used in the entrepreneurship literature and their role in prior family business research.

Innovativeness

Innovativeness refers to a firm's efforts to introduce newness through experimentation and creativity aimed at developing new products, services, and processes (Lumpkin & Dess, 1996). It represents a willingness to depart from familiar capabilities or practices, and venture beyond the current state of the art. Innovativeness is viewed as essential to maintaining a company's viability because it is a key source of the new ideas that lead to product introductions, service improvements, and managerial practices that advance and sustain a thriving company.

Many family firms highlight innovativeness in their strategy making. For example, Daily and Dollinger (1992) found that a Prospector strategy, characterized by researching and introducing innovative new products and services (Miles & Snow, 1978), was a common strategic type among family firms. This finding was supported in a study by McCann, Leon-Guerrero, and Haley (2001), which found that family firms were more likely to identify themselves as Prospectors than any other type. Additionally, Ward (1988) suggested that the relative stability of family firms placed them in a strong position to engage in experimentation.

Risk-taking

Risk-taking refers to bold decisions and actions made in the face of uncertainty, including borrowing heavily and/or committing significant resources to ventures in uncertain environments (Lumpkin & Dess, 1996). Risk-taking is considered a defining feature of entrepreneurial behavior even though prior research suggests that many entrepreneurs either do not perceive their actions as risky (Simon, Houghton, & Aquino, 2000) or take action only after significantly reducing uncertainty through research and planning (Bhide, 2000).

Risk-taking is a defining feature of many family firms because, like early entrepreneurs, it refers to those who work for themselves rather than working for someone else for wages (e.g., Cantillon, 1931). The nature and extent of risk-taking in family firms seems to range widely, depending on how risk is defined. On the one hand, risk-taking, such as the risks necessary to grow a family business, may require a relatively high degree of boldness in strategy-making (Daily & Dollinger, 1992). On the other hand, risk-taking that involves incurring debt to venture into new areas may be less common in family firms, especially if there is a risk of losing control of the business (Mishra & McConaughy, 1999). Additionally, firm members who have greater vested interests in the business, as is often the case with family firms, may be more cautious when making financial decisions (Oswald & Jahera, 1991). Indeed, in a study of 696 Swedish SMEs (265 family and 431 non-family), Naldi et al. (2007) found that family firms take significantly fewer risks than non-family firms.

Proactiveness

Proactiveness refers to an opportunity-seeking and forward-looking qualities that are characteristic of a marketplace leader who has the foresight to act in anticipation of changes in demand or emerging market trends (Lumpkin & Dess, 2001). Proactiveness involves tracking and monitoring changes in the business environment, consumer tastes, and technologies. It reflects the kind of vision and future orientation that enables firms to take fast action with minimal planning when opportunities appear.

Because successfully pursuing opportunities ahead of the competition often involves a long-time horizon, proactiveness is a common feature of many family firms (Ward, Leong, & Boyer, 1994). Upton, Teal, and Felan (2001) found that 44 percent of the family firms that had been Ernst & Young Entrepreneur of the Year winners employed a first-to-market strategy. However, even though proactiveness has been associated with strong performance in previous EO studies (Miller, 1983), this is not always the case with family firms. Daily and Thompson's (1994) study of strategic postures found that committing resources to entering new markets was not a strong predictor of firm growth in family firms.

Competitive aggressiveness

Competitive aggressiveness refers to the intensity of a firm's efforts to outperform industry rivals and improve its position in a competitive marketplace (Lumpkin & Dess, 2001). It is characterized by a strong offensive posture or a combative response. Competitive aggressiveness may also involve energetically leveraging the results of other entrepreneurial activities such as innovativeness or proactiveness to build or sustain competitive advantages.

Family firms are often perceived to be competitively aggressive. Two studies using the Miles and Snow (1978) typology found that the Defenders mode, characterized by a strong defensive posture designed to protect against competitive threats, was the second most common type among family firms (Daily & Dollinger, 1992; McCann et al., 2001). Even though Ward (1988) suggested that family firms may need to be more aggressive to avoid being under-performers, there is mixed evidence that competitive aggressiveness by family firms will lead to stronger outcomes. As a result, family businesses may be less rivalrous than their non-family counterparts, especially if too much aggression can be damaging to a firm's reputation (Harris et al., 1994). Nonetheless, effective strategic management sometimes demands that firms use competitive aggressiveness to combat industry trends that threaten their survival or market position (Miller & Camp, 1985).

Autonomy

Autonomy refers to the independence that is needed to explore opportunities, bring forth business concepts, and carry them through to completion (Lumpkin, Cogliser, & Schneider, 2009). Prior research supports the view that autonomy encourages innovation, promotes the launching of entrepreneurial ventures, and increases the competitiveness and effectiveness of firms (Brock, 2003; Kanter, 1983). Research also indicates that autonomous individuals, operating outside their usual work routines and practices, represent an important source of creativity and entrepreneurial development (Gebert, Boerner, & Lanwehr, 2003).

In their study of the cultural conditions that family businesses need to bring about entrepreneurial change as a business is maturing, Hall, Melin, and Nordqvist (2001) found that the most effective family firms "create an atmosphere in which employees feel encouraged to express their ideas and criticism" (p. 205). Further, well-aligned and more concentrated ownership allows family business principals to make investments in key personnel and vest them with decision-making authority (Daily & Dollinger, 1992; Zahra, 2005).

Many family business researchers have argued that family firms would benefit from employing more entrepreneurial approaches (e.g., Eddleston, Kellermans, & Sarathy, 2008; Habbershon & Pistrui, 2002), but few studies have investigated the role of each of the five dimensions of EO in either promoting or suppressing entrepreneurship. In the table below, we set forth several broad questions that family business owners and managers should ask when seeking to develop an entrepreneurial orientation. We believe addressing these issues can enhance a family firm's ability to achieve superior strategic performance.

To summarize, research indicates that family firms can use entrepreneurial-type strategies to launch new initiatives, strategically renew their operations, and improve their overall performance. An entrepreneurial orientation – consisting of innovativeness, risk-taking, proactiveness, competitive aggressiveness, and autonomy – provides an avenue that many family firms have found useful for achieving long-term survival and growth by fostering entrepreneurial decision-making and action.

Table 5.1 Strategic discussion questions

Strategic discussion questions:
How to enhance a family firm's entrepreneurial orientation

Innovativeness
- Does your family firm encourage technological, product-market, and administrative innovation?
- How does your family firm stimulate creativity and experimentation?
- Does your family firm properly invest in new technology, R&D, and continuous improvement?
- Are your family firm's innovative initiatives hard for competitors to successfully imitate?
- Does your family firm "safeguard" investments in R&D during difficult economic periods, or are they generally the first area where significant cuts are made?

Risk-taking
- Does your family firm foster and encourage a proper level of business, financial, and personal risk-taking?
- Does you family firm enhance its competitive risk position by researching and assessing risk factors in order to minimize uncertainty?
- Does your family firm invest in techniques and processes that have not been properly vetted ahead of time?
- Overall, does your family firm carefully manage risks and avoid taking actions without sufficient forethought, research, and planning?

Proactiveness
- Does your family firm continuously monitor trends and identify future needs of customers and/or anticipate future demand conditions?
- Does your family firm strive to be a "first mover" to capture the benefits of being an industry pioneer?
- Is your family firm aware of the downside of being a first mover, such as customer resistance to novel ideas and bearing the costs associated with unforeseen technological problems?
- Does your family firm effectively use the following methods to act proactively: introducing new products and technologies ahead of the competition and continuously seeking out new product or service offerings?

Competitive Aggressiveness
- Does your family firm effectively use an aggressive posture to combat industry trends that may threaten your survival or competitive position?
- Does your family firm enhance its competitive position by, for example, entering markets with drastically lower prices, countering the business practices or techniques of successful competitors, or making timely announcements of new products or technologies?
- Does your family firm know when it is in danger of acting overly aggressively, and avoid such actions that can lead to erosion of firm reputation and retaliation by competitors?

Autonomy
- Does your family firm foster the necessary culture, rewards, and processes to support product champions and others who take initiative independently?
- Does your family firm implement necessary structural changes to stimulate "out-of-the-box" thinking?
- Does your family firm consider developing independent work units to enhance creative thinking?
- Does your family firm have a proper balance between patience and tolerance for autonomous groups or individuals, and the forbearance to reduce and eliminate initiatives that are not succeeding?
- Does your family firm ensure adequate coordination to minimize inefficiencies and duplication of efforts?

Discussion

When it comes to strategic management, there are many similarities between family and non-family businesses. Both use similar strategic content; both need financing to operate effectively; both are engaged in internationalization. But there are also important differences in how they deploy family-based resources, how they make funding and investment decisions, and how they turn entrepreneurial attributes into organizational strengths. In this chapter, we have explored these topics and provided a set of challenging questions for owners and managers to address to improve their family firms' strategic performance and overall well-being. The topics we have highlighted have important implications, both for practitioners and future family business researchers.

Future research directions

The topic of strategic management in a family business context presents numerous promising and worthwhile questions that warrant future research. In general, family business research could benefit from a more in-depth look at each of the categories that fall within the Strategy cluster. In particular, researchers might ask how family firms strategize differently as the role and influence of the family system changes. For example, in a study of founders' value systems, García-Álvarez and López-Sintas (2001) revealed that founders who were more focused on firm growth also emphasized individual (self) values. However, founders who were more concerned about the family as a group and about family relationships tended to be less focused on growth and preferred conservative approaches to debt and risk. Such research suggests that issues such as family values, a family-first versus business-first orientation (Ward, 1988), and the structure of family business ownership could reveal important insights about how owning families strategically use their resources.

Future family business researchers might also examine more thoroughly the temporal role of strategy given its position in the long-term quadrant of the Landscape Map. In prior research on the role of a long-term orientation (LTO), Lumpkin and Brigham state that, "[T]here is compelling evidence that an LTO bestows strategic advantages that contribute positively to the financial well-being of family firms" (2011, p. 1149). For example, family firms that invest in projects with a long-time horizon before returns are realized have an advantage when compared to firms that seek shorter-term investment pay-offs (Zellweger, 2007). Future research into these and other investment policies can enhance understanding of how family firms can use strategic management to gain competitive advantages.

Regarding EO, family scholars could explore what factors may enhance (or inhibit) the strength of the relationship between EO and firm performance. For example, family business culture is often influenced by conservative investment policies and a tendency to closely control finances. Might such practices lead to core rigidities (Hamel & Prahalad, 1996) and subsequently erode innovation or discourage risk taking? How might the emotional intelligence (Goleman, 1998) of the family and non-family members who lead family businesses improve an organization's willingness to take risks and engage in more proactive behaviors? And how do reward systems (e.g., behavioral-based or outcome-based) facilitate (or retard) such behaviors? Such research might also help scholars understand how family business owners perceive risk and their willingness to bear perceived uncertainty (McMullen & Shepherd, 2006). Further, researchers could also incorporate different perspectives on risk-taking given the increasing role of knowledge in the global economy.

Research indicates that family firms are often relatively stronger performers than are non-family firms (McConaughy et al., 2001). However, as Habbershon et al. (2003) note, past research has largely identified the factors that are unique to family businesses but then has recommended traditional strategy models. Future researchers should investigate whether there are elements of a family enterprise that provide a substitute to traditional strategic or entrepreneurial approaches and, by so doing, contribute to stronger performance. Longitudinal and fine-grained research into the effectiveness of leveraging attributes of the family itself – its name or reputation or celebrity appeal – could enhance understanding of whether familiness qualities bestow strategic advantages.

Implications for practitioners

The role of strategy suggested by the Landscape Map (Yu et al., 2012) has a number of important implications for family business owners, managers, and consultants. To begin, the fact that the Strategy cluster emerged as one of the seven important arenas of family business is worth noting. Effective strategizing and strategic management are important elements of success for any purposeful enterprise. Without forecasting, planning, thoughtful policies and practices, awareness of resources and capabilities and how to leverage them, and a sense of direction and purpose, an organization cannot expect to perform effectively or achieve lasting success. Applying the tools and principles of strategic management to family businesses can boost performance and provide them with a comparative advantage. This includes utilizing proven business-level strategies such as low-cost leadership, differentiation, and focus.

Beyond those approaches to strategic management that any business can employ, research indicates that a family business can achieve comparative advantages by leveraging its unique attributes. The family system itself, by offering financial support, loyal and trustworthy human capital, and an emotional safety net, can provide the initial stability and resources that will enable a family business to survive and prosper in its early years or during periods of financial hardship. The family identity may also contribute to differential advantages. It is worthwhile for family businesses to market test whether the family name itself or claims that a company is family-owned enhance or detract from customer appeal. Compared to non-family businesses, a family firm's relatively more efficient operations, preference for conservative financing, and tendency to maintain ownership control can enhance the perception among both customers and strategic partners that the family business is stable and reliable.

With regard to the EO of family firms, we believe it is important for family firms to maintain a strong entrepreneurial orientation over time. Business founders often have an EO that shapes their priorities and decisions. Yet a founder's entrepreneurial drive may not pass on to successive generations. In practical terms, family firms that want to survive across generations and remain successful may need to strengthen their entrepreneurial orientation. Creating a climate in which it is important to maintain a strong EO and urging family business owners in successive generations to increase their EO, should help increase their chances of surviving beyond the first or second generation.

To do so, the values, norms, and shared beliefs that are embedded in family business culture need to consistently reflect the benefits of entrepreneurial activity for strategic advantage and effective performance. In an entrepreneurial culture, acting innovatively and seeking venture opportunities are part of the organization's "way of life." In contrast to an entrepreneurial mindset, the risk aversion and strategic conservatism that is often found among later generations of family business owners could lead family firms to make decisions that impede growth or miss lucrative opportunities. In organizations that are unaccustomed to internationalization or corporate venturing or that are just starting to act more entrepreneurially, it may take years for the culture to become entrepreneurial if the entrepreneurial spirit of the founder is lost. Strong and consistent leadership is needed to create a climate favoring entrepreneurial behavior that helps family firms make strategically savvy decisions aimed at preserving wealth or outlasting competitors.

In conclusion, the appearance of Strategy as one of the key clusters in landscape of family business highlights the importance of the cluster in a family firm's ability to achieve financial viability and long-term success. For family businesses that are aiming to coordinate their strategic activities with the other demands of running a business, the topics discussed in this chapter will have both practical and theoretical implications.

References

Anderson, R.C., & Reeb, D.M. (2003). Founding-family ownership and firm performance: Evidence from the S&P 500. *The Journal of Finance, 58,* 1301–328.

Astrachan, J.H., & Shanker, M.C. (2003). Family businesses' contribution to the U.S. economy: A closer look. *Family Business Review, 16*(3), 211–20.

Bhide, A.V. (2000). *The origin and evolution of new businesses.* New York: Oxford University Press.

Birch, D., Haggerty, A., & Parsons, W. (1994). *Who's creating jobs?: 1994.* Cambridge, MA: Cogentics, Inc.

Brock, D.M. (2003). Autonomy of individuals and organizations: Towards a strategy research agenda. *International Journal of Business and Economics, 2,* 57–73.

Cantillon, R. (1931). *Essay on the nature of trade in general* (H. Higgs, Trans.). London, UK: Macmillan (Original work published 1755).

Carney, M. (2005). Corporate governance and competitive advantage in family-controlled firms. *Entrepreneurship Theory and Practice, 29*(3), 249–65.

Carney, M., & Gedajlovic, E. (2002). The coupling of ownership and control and the allocation of financial resources: Evidence from Hong Kong. *Journal of Management Studies, 39*(1), 123–46.

Chittoor, R., & Das, R. (2007). Professionalization of management and succession performance – a vital linkage. *Family Business Review, 20*(1), 65–79.

Chrisman, J.J., Chua, J.H., & Steier, L.P. (2002). The influence of national culture and family involvement on entrepreneurial perceptions and performance at the state level. *Entrepreneurship Theory and Practice, 26,* 113–30.

Coleman, S., & Carsky, M. (1999). Source of capital for small family-owned businesses: Evidence for the national survey of small business finances. *Family Business Review, 12*(1), 73–85.

Craig, J.B., Dibrell, C., & Davis, P.S. (2008). Leveraging family-based brand identity to enhance firm competitiveness and performance in family businesses. *Journal of Small Business Management*, *46*, 351–71.

Craig, J.B., & Moores, K. (2006). A 10-year longitudinal investigation of strategy, systems, and environment on innovation in family firms. *Family Business Review*, *19*(1), 1–10.

Daily, C., & Dollinger, M. (1992). An empirical examination of ownership structure in family and professionally managed firms. *Family Business Review*, *5*(2), 17–136.

Daily, C., & Thompson, S.S. (1994). Ownership structure, strategic posture, and firm growth: An empirical examination. *Family Business Review*, *7*(3), 237–49.

Davis, P.S., & Harveston, P.D. (2000). Internationalization and organizational growth: The impact of Internet usage and technology involvement among entrepreneur-led family businesses. *Family Business Review*, *13*(2), 107–20.

Dyer, W.G., & Handler, W. (1994). Entrepreneurship and family business: Exploring the connections. *Entrepreneurship Theory and Practice*, *19*(1), 71–83.

Eddleston, K., Kellermans, F.W., & Sarathy, R. (2008). Resource configuration in family firms: Linking resources, strategic planning and technological opportunities to performance. *Journal of Management Studies*, *45*(1), 26–50.

Erikson, T., Sorheim, R., & Reitan, B. (2003). Family angels vs. other informal investors. *Family Business Review*, *16*(3), 163–71.

Fernandez, Z., & Nieto, M.J. (2005). International strategy of small and medium-sized family businesses: Some influential factors. *Family Business Review*, *18*(1), 77–89.

Filbeck, G., & Lee, S. (2000). Financial management techniques in family businesses. *Family Business Review*, *13*(3), 201–16.

Gallo, M.A., Tapies, J., & Cappuyns, K. (2004). Comparison of family and nonfamily business: Financial logic and personal preferences. *Family Business Review*, *17*(4), 303–18.

García-Álvarez, E., & López-Sintas, J. (2001). A taxonomy of founders based on values: The root of family business heterogeneity. *Family Business Review*, *14*(3), 209–30.

Gebert, D., Boerner, S., & Lanwehr, R. (2003). The risks of autonomy: Empirical evidence for the necessity of a balance management in promoting organizational innovativeness. *Creativity and Innovation Management*, *12*, 41–9.

Ghoshal, S. (2003). Miles and Snow: Enduring insights for managers. *Academy of Management Executive*, *17*, 109–14.

Goleman, D. (1998). What makes a leader? *Harvard Business Review*, *76*: 92–105.

Graves, C., & Thomas, J. (2006). Internationalization of Australian family businesses: A managerial capabilities perspective. *Family Business Review*, *19*(3), 207–24.

Habbershon, T.G., & Pistrui, J. (2002). Enterprising families domain: Family-influenced ownership groups in pursuit of transgenerational wealth. *Family Business Review*, *15*, 223–38.

Habbershon, T.G., & Williams, M.L. (1999). A resource-based framework for assessing the strategic advantages of family firms. *Family Business Review*, *12*, 1–25.

Habbershon, T.G., Williams, M.L., & MacMillan, I.C. (2003). A unified systems perspective of family firm performance. *Journal of Business Venturing*, *18*, 451–66.

Hall, A., Melin, L., & Nordqvist, M. (2001). Entrepreneurship as radical change in the family business: Exploring the role of cultural patterns. *Family Business Review 14*, 193–208.

Hambrick, D. (1985). Strategies for mature industrial product businesses. In J.H. Grant (Ed.), *Strategic management frontiers* (pp. 320–56). Greenwich, CT: JAI Press.

Hamel, G., & Prahalad, C.K. (1996). Competing in the new economy: Managing out of bounds. *Strategic Management Journal*, *17*: 232–42.

Harris, D., Martinez, J.I., & Ward, J.L. (1994). Is strategy different for the family-owned business? *Family Business Review*, *7*(2), 159–74.

Haynes, G.W., Walker, R., Rowe, B.R., & Hong, G.S. (1999). The intermingling of business and family finances in family-owned businesses. *Family Business Review*, *12*(3), 225–39.

Hoy, F., & Verser, T. (1994). Emerging business, emerging field: Entrepreneurship and the family firm. *Entrepreneurship Theory and Practice*, *19*(1), 9–23.

Hunter, E.J., Burgers, J.H., & Davidsson, P. (2009). Celebrity capital as a strategic asset: Implications for new venture strategies. In G.T. Lumpkin & J.A. Katz (Eds.), *Advances in entrepreneurship, firm emergence, and growth, Vol. 11: Entrepreneurial strategic content* (pp. 137–60). Oxford, UK: Elsevier/JAI.

Kanter, R.M. (1983). *The change masters: Innovation and entrepreneurship in the American corporation.* New York: Simon & Schuster.

Kayser, G., & Wallau, F. (2002). Industrial family businesses in Germany – Situation and future. *Family Business Review, 15*(2), 111–15.

Kreiser, P.M., Marino, L.D., & Weaver, K.M. (2002). Assessing the psychometric properties of the entrepreneurial orientation scale: A multi-country analysis. *Entrepreneurship Theory and Practice, 26,* 71–94.

Lee, J. (2006). Family firm performance: Further evidence. *Family Business Review, 19,* 103–14.

Lumpkin G.T., & Brigham, K.H. (2011). Long-term orientation and intertemporal choice in family firms. *Entrepreneurship Theory & Practice, 35*(6): 1147–67.

Lumpkin, G.T., Cogliser, C.C., & Schneider, D.R. (2009). Understanding and measuring autonomy: An entrepreneurial orientation perspective. *Entrepreneurship Theory and Practice, 33*(1), 47–69.

Lumpkin, G.T., & Dess G.G., (1996). Clarifying the entrepreneurial orientation construct and linking it to performance. *Academy of Management Review, 21,* 135–72.

Lumpkin, G.T., & Dess G.G., (2001). Linking two dimensions of entrepreneurial orientation to firm performance: The moderating role of environment and industry life cycle. *Journal of Business Venturing, 16,* 429–51.

Lumpkin, G.T., Martin, W., & Vaughn, M. (2008). Family orientation: Individual-level influences on family firm outcomes. *Family Business Review, 21*(2), 127–38.

McCann, J.E., Leon-Guerrero, A.Y., & Haley, J.D. (2001). Strategic goals and practices of innovative family businesses. *Journal of Small Business Management, 39*(1), 50–9.

McConaughy, D.L., Matthews, C.H., & Fialko, A.S. (2001). Founding family controlled firms: Performance, risk, and value. *Journal of Small Business Management, 39*(1), 31–49.

McDougall, P., & Robinson, R.B., Jr. (1990). New venture strategies: An empirical identification of eight "archetypes" of competitive strategies for entry. *Strategic Management Journal, 11,* 447–67.

McMullen, J.S., & Shepherd, D.A. (2006). Entrepreneurial action and the role of uncertainty in the theory of the entrepreneur. *Academy of Management Review, 31*(1): 132–52.

Maherault, L. (2000). The influence of going public on investment policy: An empirical study of French family-owned businesses. *Family Business Review, 13*(1), 71–9.

Manikutty, S. (2000). Family-based groups in India: A resource-based view of the emerging trends. *Family Business Review, 13*(4), 279–92.

Miles, R.E., & Snow, C.C. (1978). *Organizational strategy, structure, and process.* New York: McGraw-Hill.

Miller, A., & Camp, B. (1985). Exploring determinants of success in corporate ventures. *Journal of Business Venturing, 1,* 87–105.

Miller, D. (1983). The correlates of entrepreneurship in three types of firms. *Management Science, 29,* 770–91.

Miller, D. (1986). Configurations of strategy and structure: Towards a synthesis. *Strategic Management Journal, 6,* 233–49.

Miller, D., & Friesen, P. (1978). Archetypes of strategy formulation. *Management Science, 24,* 921–33.

Miller, D., & Friesen, P. (1984). *Organizations: A quantum view.* Englewood Cliffs, NJ: Prentice-Hall.

Miller, D., & Le Breton-Miller, I. (2005). *Managing for the long run.* Boston, MA: Harvard Business School Press.

Mishra, C., & McConaughy, D. (1999). Founding family control and capital structure: The risk of loss of control and the aversion to debt. *Entrepreneurship Theory and Practice, 23*(4), 53–64.

Myers, S.C. (1984). The capital structure puzzle. *Journal of Finance, 39,* 575–92.

Naldi, L., Nordqvist, M., Sjoberg, K., & Wiklund, J. (2007). Entrepreneurial orientation, risk taking, and performance in family firms. *Family Business Review, 20,* 33–58.

Nordqvist, M., Habbershon, T.G., & Melin, L. (2008). Transgenerational entrepreneurship: Exploring entrepreneurial orientation in family firms. In H. Landström, D. Smallbone, H. Crijns,

& E. Laveren (Eds.), *Entrepreneurship, sustainable growth and performance: Frontiers in European entrepreneurship research* (pp. 93–116). Cheltenham, UK, and Northampton, MA, USA: Edward Elgar.

Okoroafo, S.C. (1999). Internationalization of family businesses: Evidence form Northwest Ohio, U.S.A. *Family Business Review, 12*(2), 147–58.

Oswald, S.L., & Jahera, J.S. (1991). The influence of ownership on performance: An empirical study. *Strategic Management Journal, 12*(4), 321–26.

Parmentier, M.A. (2011). When David met Victoria: Forging a strong family brand. *Family Business Review, 24*(3), 217–32.

Peng, M. (2001). The resource-based view and international business. *Journal of Management, 27*(6), 803–29.

Porter, M.E. (1980). *Competitive strategy.* New York: Free Press.

Porter, M.E. (1996). What is strategy? *Harvard Business Review, 74*(6), 61–81.

Post, J.E. (1993). The greening of the Boston Park Plaza Hotel. *Family Business Review, 6*(2), 131–48.

Poutziouris, P.Z. (2001). The views of family companies on venture capital: Empirical evidence from the UK small to medium-size enterprising economy. *Family Business Review, 14*(3), 277–91.

Poza, E.J., & Messer, T. (2001). Spousal leadership and continuity in the family firm. *Family Business Review, 14*(1), 25–35.

Romano, C.A., Tanewski, G.A., & Smyrnios, K.X. (2000). Capital structure decision making: A model for family business. *Journal of Business Venturing, 16*, 285–310.

Schulze, W.S., Lubatkin, M.H., & Dino, R.N. (2003). Exploring the agency consequences of ownership dispersion among the directors of private family firms. *Academy of Management Journal, 46*(2), 179–94.

Sharma, P., Chrisman, J.J., & Chua, J.H. (1997). Strategic management of the family business: Past research and future challenges. *Family Business Review, 10*(1), 1–35.

Simon, M., Houghton, S.M., & Aquino, K. (2000). Cognitive biases, risk perception, and venture formation: How individuals decide to start companies. *Journal of Business Venturing, 14*, 113–34.

Sirmon, D.G., & Hitt, M.A. (2003). Managing resources: Linking unique resources, management and wealth creation in family firms. *Entrepreneurship Theory and Practice, 27*, 339–58.

Steier, L. (2003). Variants of agency contracts in family-financed ventures as a continuum of familial altruistic and market rationalities. *Journal of Business Venturing, 18*, 597–618.

Tan, J., & Tan, D. (2005). Environment-strategy coevolution and coalignment: A staged-model of Chinese SOEs under transition. *Strategic Management Journal, 26*, 141–57.

Tokarczyk, J., Hansen, E., Green, M., & Down, J. (2007). A resource-based view and market orientation theory examination of the role of "familiness" in family business success. *Family Business Review, 20*(1), 17–31.

Treacy, M., & Wiersema, F. (1995). *The discipline of market leaders.* Reading, MA: Addision Wesley.

Tsang, E.W.K. (2002). Learning from overseas venturing experience: The case of Chinese family businesses. *Journal of Business Venturing, 17*, 21–40.

Upton, N., Teal, E.J., & Felan, J.T. (2001). Strategic and business planning practices of fast growth family firms. *Journal of Small Business Management, 39*(1), 60–72.

US Small Business Administration, Office of Advocacy. (2012). Advocacy issues updated, expanded frequently asked questions [Press release]. Retrieved from http://www.sba.gov/advocacy/809/287981.

Villalonga, B., & Amit, R. (2006). How do family ownership, control, and management affect firm value? *Journal of Financial Economics, 80*, 385–417.

Ward, J.L. (1988). The special role of strategic planning for family businesses. *Family Business Review, 1*(2), 105–17.

Ward, P.T., Leong, G.K., & Boyer, K.K. (1994). Manufacturing proactiveness and performance. *Decision Sciences, 25*, 337–58.

Wiklund, J., & Shepherd, D. (2005). Entrepreneurial orientation and small business performance: A configurational approach. *Journal of Business Venturing, 20*, 71–91.

Wu, Z., Chua, J.H., & Chrisman, J.J. (2007). Effects of family ownership and management on small business equity financing. *Journal of Business Venturing, 22*, 875–95.

Yilmazer, T., & Schrank, H. (2006). Financial intermingling in small family businesses. *Journal of Business Venturing, 21*, 726–51.

Yu, A., Lumpkin, G.T., Sorenson, R.L., & Brigham, K.H. (2012). The landscape of family business outcomes: A summary and numerical taxonomy of dependent variables. *Family Business Review, 25*, 1, 33–57.

Zahra, S. (2003). International expansion of I.S. manufacturing family businesses: The effect of ownership and involvement. *Journal of Business Venturing, 18*, 495–512.

Zahra, S. (2005). Entrepreneurial risk taking in family firms. *Family Business Review, 18*, 23–40.

Zellweger, T. (2007). Time horizon, costs of equity capital, and generic investment strategies of firms. *Family Business Review, 20*(1), 1–15.

6. Family business roles

Pramodita Sharma and Frank Hoy

Introduction

Yu, Lumpkin, Sorenson, and Brigham (2012) – the editors of this book – painstakingly reviewed 257 empirical studies on family business published between 1998 and 2009 in nine journals. The studies revealed 327 different dependent variables. Next, they sought input from family business advisors, owners, and scholars, mapping the identified variables into seven clusters that form the Landscape Map.* Each cluster is the subject of a chapter in this book. Three clusters labeled Performance, Strategy, and Social and Economic Impact are largely focused on the business system of family enterprises. Performance anchors the business end of the map. The three clusters of Succession, Family Dynamics, and Family Business Roles relate to the family-system of family enterprises. The family end of the Landscape Map is anchored by the Family Business Roles cluster. The Governance cluster falls in the middle of the map as this cluster includes variables that balance the needs of the family and the business systems.

The focus of this chapter is on the Family Business Roles cluster, which Yu et al. (2012) define as the "roles and attitudes of family business members and non-members." Thus, studies that aim to understand the roles played by different family and non-family members in business, as well as the attitude toward the family business held by these members, are part of this cluster. The related topic of "family involvement in business" is also part of this cluster. Of the identified variables, when Yu et al. (2012) asked 22 family business scholars to list variables that distinguish family business research from other disciplines, only that variable – family involvement in business – received unanimous support, indicating the integral role of this variable in the field. Two other variables – "family values" and "family business characteristics" – came close as they were listed as being domain distinguishing dependent variables by 20 out of the 22 surveyed scholars.

In addition to the importance of the category "family involvement in business," the integral role the categories, "attitudes of the controlling family" and the "roles played by family members," play in the family business is generally accepted. Curiously, however, the cluster in which these three categories of variables belong is *the smallest of all seven clusters* with only 37 out of the 257 reviewed articles focused on these topics. The category "attitudes towards family business" is the least researched in the literature (Yu et al.,

---

* "A Map of the Landscape of Family Business"(also referred to as the Landscape Map) can be found on the page just inside the cover of this book and in the Yu, Lumpkin, Sorenson, and Brigham (2012) article published in *Family Business Review*. Following the Landscape Map, the "Outcome Categories by Chapter Table" (also referred to as the Outcome Categories Table) is provided. This table shows all chapters that contain content about the outcome categories that appear in this chapter.

2012). This means that our empirically based knowledge of roles and attitudes of families in business is sparse. The dearth of research on these important topics may partly be explained by the "wide and shallow" character of family business studies at this early stage in the field's development, as scholars are focused on understanding how family involvement and influence on business impact a wide array of dependent or outcome variables with only a handful of articles exploring each topic in depth (Zahra & Sharma, 2004; Yu et al., 2012). Nevertheless, given the importance of the roles and attitudes on family enterprises and the importance of these enterprises on the global economy, more research on these topics is needed.

In tracing the evolution of family business research and education, Sharma, Hoy, Astrachan, and Koiranen (2007) observed that in its formative years this field was largely driven by practice. The large majority of organizational research was focused on non-family enterprises as scholars operated under the tacit assumptions that "members of an organization are not and should not be related by blood and, therefore, familial relationships do not significantly influence behavior in the workplace" (Dyer Jr., 2003, p. 403). Meanwhile a parallel body of knowledge on family enterprises emerged outside the mainstream scientific research arena. This literature took shape in the form of autobiographies or biographies such as *Father, Son & Co.*, and *The Arms of Krupp*, or writings of consultants to family firms such as *Beyond Survival*. As a result, we have anecdotal observations and normative prescriptions of how family enterprises function or could function to be more effective and successful. Business owners, therefore, may adopt practices that appear to be intuitively obvious and supported by published work that may have applied in only a limited number of cases. This leads to owners, their consultants, and even educators advocating policies and behaviors that they only think they know, not ones for which there may be empirical evidence resulting from rigorous research studies.

The purpose of this chapter is to provide a comprehensive overview of the body of knowledge related to attitudes toward family and business, family involvement in business, and the roles adopted by family and non-family members in relation to family enterprises. In developing this review, we depend heavily on the knowledge developed through peer-reviewed empirical research on family firms – the research that formed the Yu et al.'s (2012) Family Business Roles cluster. In addition, three other sources are used to supplement these insights: 1) writings based on experiences and observations of practitioners, 2) research on the concepts of attitudes and roles conducted outside the context of family firms, and 3) theories proposed by family business scholars published in peer-reviewed outlets, although these propositions have yet to be empirically validated. Because family business scholars and practitioners need to exercise caution in using findings from non-family firms, experiential observations, and untested theories proposed in the literature, we indicate where further empirical work is needed. In taking this approach, we differentiate between what we know and what it is we only think we know.

The cluster Family Business Roles has three major categories of topics: Family involvement in business (F_{IB}), attitudes toward family and toward business (A), and roles of family and non-family members in business (R). To begin to understand all three of these categories, we must start with a definition of family; this is the topic of our next section. The subsequent three sections discuss what we know about the three major topical categories, F_{IB}, A, R, in this cluster. The following section postulates some relationships between these three categories of variables. The concluding section highlights what we can say with confidence about the roles and attitudes in family business, what we think we know or can venture a calculated guess about, and issues on which there is virtually no knowledge at this stage of the field's development.

What is a family?

In the inaugural issue of the *Family Business Review* (FBR), the editors declared they would not impose a particular definition to the term "family business" (Lansberg, Perrow, & Rogolsky, 1988). Their position was not to imply that definitions are unimportant; rather, it was to acknowledge the complexity of the context. In order to understand what a family business is, we must begin questioning what people consider a family to be, then, shift to what level a family's involvement in business should be for an enterprise to be called a family business. How much ownership of the company should they have? Must multiple family members play active roles in the management and/or the governance of the business? Do at least two generations have to be involved? The editors understood, however, that definitions are critical. Both scholars and practitioners must know what type of organization is being described in order to determine whether results may be applicable to their situations. Lansberg et al. (1988) encouraged researchers to clearly define the entity of focus in their research with hopes that evidence-based knowledge will help define the domain, distinctiveness, and boundaries of this new field of study.

Twenty-five years since the launch of FBR, we can look back and see that some progress has been made in regard to the definition of family business (Sharma, Chrisman, & Gersick, 2012). Two approaches have emerged in the literature: *components-of-involvement* and *essence* approaches (Chua, Chrisman, & Sharma, 1999). The components approach focuses on the extent and nature of family involvement in business within the three dimensions of ownership, management, and governance that is used to distinguish family firms from their non-family counterparts. The essence approach focuses on understanding the behavioral distinctiveness of family firms from their non-family counterparts. This approach considers components of family involvement in business as a necessary, but an insufficient condition to define a family business. Instead, the essence approach contends that the combination of family involvement in the business and distinctive behaviors, such as the intention to pursue the controlling family's vision for the business or desire to sustain the business across generations, distinguish family firms from other organizational forms (e.g., Chua et al., 1999). The literature seems to have settled into using the essence approach for conceptual definitions and the components approach for operational definitions of family firms.

Although the issue of defining family business has received attention in the literature, it is somewhat surprising that there has been virtually no discussion about the definition of a family (Sharma & Salvato, 2012). Even in scales such as the Family Climate or F-PEC (Power, Experience, Culture) that aim to measure prevailing family processes or family influence on business, respectively, the decision to define family is left to the respondents (Björnberg & Nicholson, 2007; Klein, Astrachan, & Smyrnios, 2005). While some research studies ask the participants about the gender and generation mix of the family involved in business, most tend to silently assume family to be a homogenous entity. Moreover, many other components of family considered important by family science scholars have been largely neglected in family business research (Danes, in press; James, Jennings, & Breitkruz, 2012).

While the archeological and anthropological studies of agrarian societies show us that the existence of family units working together cooperatively predates historical documentation, the concept of family can refer to disparate phenomenon in society. In a broad sense, family is generally thought of as a kinship relationship that typically encompasses a network of genealogical relationships, social ties, and biological and affinity-based relationships derived from marriage (Stewart, 2003). However, the concept of family changes over time. At this stage of human evolution, families and their involvement in business may vary on the following dimensions, leaving each enterprising family to make its own decisions along these lines (e.g., Bengtson, Acock, Allen, Dilworth-Anderson, & Klein, 2005; Bernandes, 1985; Hoy & Sharma, 2010; Sharma & Salvato, in press):

- Consanguinity – Can non-blood relatives own, manage, or govern a family firm? What is the status of in-laws?
- Gender – Is involvement in business open to family members of one or both genders?
- Birth order – Are there any distinctions or expectations from older or younger family members in terms of their involvement in the family firm?
- Generations – How many generations can own, manage, or govern the firm at any point in time?
- Legal status – What rights and responsibilities do children of a previous marriage have? Must an individual be legally married or adopted in a family before s/he can own, manage, or govern the family firm?
- Cohabitation – What is the status of individuals who are cohabitating with a blood relative of the controlling family? Can they own, manage, or govern a family firm?

With the myriad of possible variations along the above dimensions, finer distinctions in family are likely to influence research findings. Following a cue from the lessons learned in defining a family business, the components and essence approaches might be helpful in defining a family as well. While the above dimensions can form the *components of a family*, the following definition suggested by Hoy and Sharma (2010) implies the *essence of a family*: "Family is a group of people affiliated through bonds of shared history and a commitment to share a future together while supporting the development and well-being of individual members" (p. 49).

Each controlling family has underlying beliefs about the mix of components that define a family and the norms for the involvement of family members in business. While these prevailing assumptions are rarely discussed within business families,[1] they are often tested during life-cycle transitional stages in the family and its enterprise, leading to either the reinforcement of or change in the prevailing beliefs (Hoy & Sharma, 2010). In designing research, care must be taken to add indicators to understand what the prevailing beliefs and behaviors of a "family" are along these component dimensions so the heterogeneity of family can be captured and understood. In addition to shedding light on the heterogeneity in families in the sample studied and the related implication on the variables of interest, such an approach will enable advisors and practitioners to understand the applicability of findings in their work. Knowledge of how business owners and their relatives see themselves as families is important to advisors to the companies and families. Varying beliefs affect structures such as family business councils, constitutions, codes of ethics, and even boards of directors. Next, we discuss the literature related to the distinguishing feature of family business studies: family involvement in business.

Family involvement in business (F_{IB})

Scholars agree that the "family involvement in business" (F_{IB}) outcome category distinguishes family business studies from all other disciplines (e.g., Craig & Salvato, 2012; Yu et al., 2012). This belief has persisted over the years as F_{IB} has been used in the literature to distinguish family from non-family enterprises, both conceptually and empirically. For example, when Shanker and Astrachan (1996) set out to determine the extent of influence of family enterprises on the US economy, they divided these enterprises into broad, middle, and narrow categories based on the extent of the family's involvement in business. Their broadest category required families to have some degree of effective control over the business with the intention to retain the business in the family. The middle category consisted of firms in which the founder or descendent has legal control of the voting stock with some family involvement in the business. In the narrow category, multiple generations of the family had to be involved in daily operations, and more than one family member must have significant management responsibility. As can be expected, the impact of family enterprises in the US is varied based on the definitions used. It is noteworthy, however, that even when using the most stringent definition Shanker and Astrachan (1996) found a significant economic and social impact of family enterprises in the US – a finding replicated in most other nations of the world.

As we discussed in the last section, the operational and conceptual definitions of family business are based on family involvement in business. While the former definition identifies family involvement in ownership, management, and governance of the enterprise, the latter adds a behavioral dimension to this involvement, asking questions related to the impact of such involvement. F_{IB} has not only played a critical role in unequivocally establishing the significance of family enterprises in the global economy, it has also helped to distinguish family from non-family firms and understand the heterogeneity within these enterprises. It is therefore a bit puzzling why Yu et al.'s (2012) review revealed a limited amount of focus on F_{IB} as a dependent variable. Perhaps researchers have been more interested in understanding how F_{IB} explains the variance of other dependent variables rather than in why we observed varied levels of F_{IB}.

Indeed, we find that family's involvement in ownership and management has been used to understand financial performance, which is the most studied dependent variable, Governance, which is the largest cluster in the Landscape Map, and other strategic decisions such as employee retention. For example, in a study of 620 randomly selected privately held Italian firms, Sciascia and Mazzola (2008) found that an average family's involvement in ownership (measured as percentage of equity held by family members) was 77.24 percent, while family involvement in management (percentage of firm's managers who were family members) was 63.22 percent. This study revealed that while there was no impact of family ownership on firm performance, there was a negative non-linear relationship between family's involvement in management and firm performance. That is, higher levels of family involvement in management were associated with decreased firm performance. The authors interpret these results to indicate that:

> The presence of family managers does not seem to compensate for disadvantages deriving from a nonmonetary goal orientation or the costs deriving from the need to solve conflicts between family managers and the limits on enlarging the company's social and intellectual capital through the employment of nonfamily managers. Moreover, the quadratic nature of the relationship calls for greater attention to be paid to these effects by family business owners, especially in those cases where family involvement in management is high. (Sciascia and Mazzola, 2008, p. 331)

While Sciascia and Mazzola's (2008) research is focused on privately held firms, several studies have been conducted to understand how F_{IB} influences firm performance in publicly held firms (e.g., Miller, Le-Breton Miller, Lester, & Cannella, 2007; Villalonga & Amit, 2006). These studies confirm that the relationship between F_{IB} and firm performance is contingent on the definition of family business used. Anderson and Reeb (2003), in what has become one of the most frequently cited studies, reported the founder's role as positive on profitability measures, market performance, and cost of debt financing, although the positive performance declined for publicly traded firms when families held more than a third of the equity. Family ownership had a positive influence on firm performance, but the impact of family management on performance varies depending on the CEOs identity. Founder-led firms outperformed while descendent-led firms underperformed non-family CEO-led firms. Two comprehensive reviews of F_{IB} on firms' financial performance are provided by Amit and Villalonga (in press) and Stewart and Hitt (2012).

The impact of F_{IB} on governance of the firm is revealed in a study of 2,365 private incorporated US firms with fewer than 500 employees (Fiegener, Brown, Dreux, & Dennis Jr., 2000). By law, such firms are required to have boards of directors. CEOs with greater ownership and family stakes were found to have smaller boards with less outsider representation and a larger percentage of family directors. However, one unexpected finding indicated that:

> when the family stakes entail more complex family-business overlap, with greater potential for conflict between family needs and business needs, CEOs tend to expand board membership to accommodate greater family involvement in governance, perhaps as a means to manage these complex family business issues. (Fiegener et al., 2000, p. 19)

In addition to influencing firm performance and governance decisions, F_{IB} has been found to impact strategic decisions such as downsizing. In his study of the largest 500 publicly listed companies in the US, Block (2010) found that the extent of family ownership decreases the likelihood of deep job cuts. Family managers are less likely to consider downsizing as a reaction to low profitability. These findings indicate "that family owners care more about their reputation for social responsibility than do other owners, motivating them to avoid deep job cuts" (Block, 2010, p. 109).

In reviewing this research, we note that F_{IB} is perhaps the most critical variable in family business studies. Not only has it helped to establish the domain of the field and distinguish it from other disciplines, but also empirical research suggests varied levels of F_{IB} have significant performance and behavioral implications for business families and their enterprises. While some progress has been made by studying family involvement in ownership and management of business, the system of family is largely treated as a homogeneous entity. This assumption gets challenged when we discuss the significantly different attitudes of families towards business and the impact such differences have on the roles family members might play both in business and in family.

Our discussion to this point indicates that future research is needed along three paths: 1) When developing research studies to understand the consequences of F_{IB}, it will be useful to collect more information about the controlling family so as to begin developing finer-grained usable knowledge; 2) Given how influential the beliefs of the controlling family are on behavior, studies are needed that measure beliefs about the family, the business, and the relationship between family and business; and, 3) Causal factors that lead to varied levels of F_{IB} at different points in the life of business families and their enterprises will need to be identified and understood. Findings from studies along these research paths will have direct application for controlling families, instructing the families as to the importance of belief systems and how they affect transitions in both families and enterprises over life-cycles. It is our hope that the components of family listed in this chapter will provide a start along the first and second paths. While there is limited empirical work on the third path, as noted by Yu et al. (2012), it is our hope that the following discussion on the attitudes toward family business and the roles adopted by family members is likely to help make some progress in this regard.

Attitudes toward family business (A)

Organizational behavior researchers have described attitude as "a fairly stable evaluative tendency to respond consistently to some specific object, situation, person, or category of people" (Johns & Saks, 2005, p. 109). While attitudes influence the behavior of individuals within organizations, they, in turn, are influenced by beliefs and values. Johns and Saks (2005) explained that beliefs govern the pathways that we think will lead to the desired outcomes. Values, on the other hand, are broad tendencies to prefer certain states of affairs to others and determine what an individual considers to be good or bad. Beliefs and values, and, thus, attitudes and behaviors, are acquired early in life and influenced by family (e.g., Hoy & Sharma, 2010).

```
Beliefs / Values ──────▶ Attitudes ──────▶ Behaviors (such as adopted roles)
```

As revealed in the following discussion, empirical research on attitudes towards family business is sparse regardless of whether we view it from an outsider's perspective, or from an insider's perspective as a member of the family or of the business sub-system (cf. Yu et al., 2012).

Outsiders' attitudes towards family enterprises

Despite the prevalence and persistence of family enterprises since prehistoric years, the attention of researchers, advisors, media, and even government on these firms is a relatively recent phenomenon. Earlier perceptions of family enterprises focused on nepotism, which assumed the hiring and promotion decisions in these firms were largely based on kinship rather than on ability. Thus, it is no surprise that one of the earliest empirical investigations of attitudes towards family enterprises focused on nepotism (Ewing, 1965). The article, published in *Harvard Business Review*, reported the results of a survey of 2,700 leaders of public and private companies regarding their attitudes toward nepotism. While the word had negative connotations in general, respondents in this study delineate both advantages and disadvantages of nepotism, thereby providing a more balanced view. The following advantages were highlighted:

- stronger sense of public responsibility;
- better fit;
- more interest in company;
- morale stimulated when relative is competent;
- more loyal and dependable; and
- continuity of policies.

The identified disadvantages were the following:

- jealousy and resentment among non-family employees;
- discourages outsiders from joining company;
- cannot be fired/demoted as readily as non-family;
- lack of objectivity by relatives;
- family interests above corporate interests; and
- loss of respect for top management.

While little empirical research on nepotism has followed this pioneering study, Adam Bellow's 2003 book, *In Praise of Nepotism*, marks a notable exception. Drawing insights from evolutionary theory, he notes the biological roots of nepotism as the favored treatment of kin has served as glue that binds human society. The deep history of nepotism over time and societies is reviewed to conclude that kinship bonds and transmission of legacies has prevailed throughout and will likely continue to shape societies of the future. Bellow (2003) makes a strong case for dealing with nepotism openly as it has both its positive and negative dimensions. Empirical research on family enterprises confirms this view as F_{IB} by itself has neither a negative nor a positive valence. Instead, it is the degree and nature of this involvement and how it is managed that impacts other outcome variables of interest.

We tend to think about nepotism in terms of the attitudes outsiders and non-family managers and employees may have regarding family members, as well as the equity and fairness issues that follow. However, one conclusion of Ewing's study, and hinted in the Bellow's book, is that there are serious self-perception issues on the part of the family member who joins the firm. The relative can suffer from self-image and self-esteem problems. One respondent summarized the problem in the statement, "He'll never know . . . if he's worth half his salary or twice the amount" (Ewing, 1965, p. 40). Thus, in addition to understanding the outsider's perspective on F_{IB}, it is important to understand the related family attitudes as well.

Insiders' attitudes towards family enterprises

While empirical research on attitudes of insiders (family and non-family members) is rather limited, from the beginnings of the field, scholar practitioners observed different philosophical orientations guiding family enterprises. For example, in one of the classic books on family businesses, *Keeping the Family Business Healthy*, Ward (1987) noted that all families have to make a basic choice regarding the relative role of family and business in order to resolve the competing demands and needs of the two social institutions of family and business. Ward (1987) observed that depending on whether family or business needs are given precedence in decision-making, firms can be described as having *family-first, business-first*, or *family-enterprise-first* orientations. Surmising the relationship between these attitudes and F_{IB}, Ward suggested that those businesses with family-first orientation would employ all family members seeking to join the enterprise regardless of their qualifications or contributions to the business. The ownership of the enterprise would remain with family members. Firms with business-first orientation would employ family members only if the benefits to the business of such employment are higher than the involved costs. Ownership may be shared with non-family outsiders in these cases. Family-enterprise orientation leads to an equal importance given to both family and business. Such orientation in firms might attempt to develop opportunities within or related to the business that best utilize the inherent strengths and interests of family members who desire to contribute to the business. Similar guiding beliefs are used when determining the distribution of dividends or absorbing losses that might occur in the business, or the extent of investment of time, money, and emotional capital that family members might be willing to devote into a new venture created by a family member (cf. Hoy & Sharma, 2010).

Birley (2001; 2002) led a large multi-national empirical study of 6,631 firms in 16 countries on the attitudes of owner-managers and next generation members toward the family and business and used the labels family-in, family-out, and family business jugglers to describe the three orientations within family businesses, thus confirming Ward's (1987) prior descriptions. Birley noted the importance of attitudes in understanding family enterprises and the F_{IB} stating that:

> the set of attitudes towards the family and the business consistently combine to divide owner-managers. These attitudes are primarily concerned with the early involvement of the children with the business, the importance of family managerial succession, the continuing involvement of more than one generation, and the transfer of shares only to family members. (Birley, 2001, pp. 74–75)

In a study of 732 Spanish small- and medium-sized family firms (50–500 employees), Basco and Rodríguez (2009) found about 46 percent of firms followed a family-enterprise-first orientation, emphasizing both family and business concerns; 26 percent used business-first orientation, while another 28 percent placed limited importance on both family and business issues in their management and governance. In comparison to the business-first firms, firms with the family-enterprise-first orientation performed better on family dimensions. Furthermore, these firms performed equally well compared to business-first firms on the business dimensions. This study is the first evidence suggesting the importance of the tangible performance implications of different orientations in family firms.

In the works of Ward (1987), Birley (2001; 2002), and Basco and Rodríguez (2009), we have evidence of confirmatory findings from empirical research and reflective advisors. Despite some differences in the authors' chosen terminology, the three identified mindsets seem to have passed the test of time (from 1987 to 2009), and have been confirmed across generations and geographical regions.

In short, we can say with confidence that there are at least three broad orientations of enterprising families' attitudes towards business: that business exists to serve the family's needs (family-first); that family exists to serve the business's needs (business-first); and that both family and business needs are equally important and must be balanced (family-enterprise-first). However, there is a lot more we need to know. For example, while the organizational behavioral researchers suggest attitudes to be "fairly stable" tendencies that guide behaviors, it is unclear when and how attitudes change (Johns & Saks, 2005). Over the last few decades, we have experienced significant sociological and demographic changes that have modified prevailing attitudes. Perhaps the most visible are the changing roles of gender and birth order as more women are attaining higher levels of education and participating in the work force. Are some family enterprises more adept at adopting and perhaps reaping advantages of such changes than others? If so, what factors influence such variations? Does a proactive or reactive stance lead to performance implications on the family or business dimensions? Research is needed to understand these questions.

Another stream of research might be aimed to understand the factors that influence the formation of family-first, business-first, or family-enterprise-first orientations. While there is some theoretical work that suggests that the role of family structure and community culture might influence such orientations and related strategic decisions (e.g., Sharma & Manikutty, 2005), more theory development and empirical research is needed to understand the process and factors that impact the formation of specific orientations towards family and business.

Can a family's orientation regarding the relative role of family and business change over time? If so, why? And how is such change accomplished? Longitudinal studies conducted under the rubric of the Successful Transgenerational Entrepreneurship Practices (STEP) project are beginning to shed light on some of these issues. For example, a study tracing the history of an Italian group from 1833 to 1996 revealed the critical role of far-sighted "family champions" in changing the family's attitudes toward the founder's business (Salvato, Chirico, & Sharma, 2010). A combination of high regard for this family member, and the leader's business savvy and ability to show a bright future for the family and business while working closely with astute non-family executives helped modify the attitudes of family members and change the course of business. Thus, the largest steel company in Italy transformed and became a leader in the renewable energy business, thereby creating trans-generational value. Given its "fairly stable" nature, attitudinal changes are likely to occur over an extended period of time. Thus, longitudinal studies in family enterprises are likely to improve our related understanding because we can observe factors that lead to changed attitudes in a relatively closed system. STEP represents an effort to bring about collaborations of families in business with research scholars to identify entrepreneurial behaviors that practitioners can use in fostering both survival and prosperity of enterprises across generations.

Roles of family and non-family members in business (R)

Since the early 1980s, scholars and practitioners have been interested in understanding the variations in and complexities of roles played by family and non-family members in the hybrid identity system of family business that combines two fundamental human institutions of family and business. As if following the principle that "a picture is worth a thousand words," researchers and practitioners used pictorial depictions to understand various roles of family and non-family members in these firms. Sharma and Nordqvist (2008) have provided a comprehensive review of the different models used over time. Here we focus on the one model that has gained widespread acceptance: Davis's three-circle model (1982), which overlays the circles of family members, owners, and managers/employees (Figure 6.1). Gersick, Davis, Hampton, and Lansberg (1997) explain that:

> the reason the three-circle model has met with such widespread acceptance is that it is both theoretically elegant and immediately applicable. It is a very useful tool for understanding the source of interpersonal conflicts, *role dilemmas*, priorities, and boundaries in family firms. Specifying different roles and subsystems helps to break down the complex interactions within a family business and makes it easier to see what is actually happening, and why. (p. 7, *italics added*)

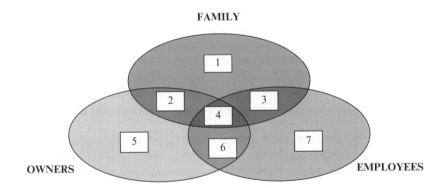

POSSIBLE ROLES OF FAMILY MEMBERS (Individuals in areas 1–4):
1. Family members NOT involved in business at this time
2. Family members owners who are NOT involved in business at this time
3. Family member employees with no ownership
4. Family member owners involved in business at this time

POSSIBLE ROLES OF NON-FAMILY MEMBERS (Individuals in areas 5–7):
5. Non-family owners not involved in operations of the business
6. Non-family owners also involved in operations of the business
7. Non-family employess in business with no ownership stake

Figure 6.1   Possible roles for family and non-family members in family enterprises (cf. Davis, 1982)

Over the years, researchers and practitioners have modified this model further by adding axes to capture the co-evolution of the three systems over time (Gersick et al., 1997) and to measure the family influence along the three dimensions of ownership (Power), management (Experience), and family (Culture) through the F-PEC scale (e.g., Klein et al., 2005). Models, however good, are invariably simplifications of the complex realities. This model is no exception. As we will note below, while it is useful in under-standing the possible roles of family and non-family members at a point in time, it tends to veil the heterogeneity of occupants within each of the seven areas. Researchers are now beginning to capture these realities by highlighting the nuances and finer variations within each area. A good example of this is Santiago's (2011) research on in-laws in family enterprises, which we discuss later in this section.

Despite its limitations, we find the three-circle model useful in structuring our discus-sion on the roles of family and non-family members in business. And perhaps equally significant, such organizing of discussion helps to highlight stakeholder roles that need more research attention. We will start our discussion with the circle that has received the most attention in family business literature – the family circle. Within this circle, the fol-lowing four stakeholder roles have been the focus of research attention:

- incumbent leader(s): we discuss leaders who may be founders or descendants, lone entrepreneurs or copreneurs, and their role in creating the culture of their enter-prise and how their role changes during and after the leadership transition process;
- next generation members: we discuss how their role changes during and after lead-ership transition and why these members join the family enterprises;
- gender roles in family enterprises: we discuss how they have changed in the last few decades; and
- in-laws: we discuss their position in the family circle and how this position may be precarious in some enterprising families and their firms but quite central in others.

After completing this discussion related to the family circle, we move to the employee circle wherein we touch upon the limited research on non-family employees. Our knowl-edge of the ownership circle is limited to an understanding of the major versus minor owners; passive versus active owners; and responsible versus irresponsible owners. But beyond these labels, there is not much work to shed light on the intricacies of each type of owner role, suggesting the need for more research on this front. These circles represent more than academic exercises. They also help both advisors and practitioners recognize and evaluate how various stakeholders relate to and interact with one another.

Incumbent leaders in family firms

Leaders have been a target of research attention in several management disciplines including organizational behavior, strategy, and entrepreneurship. These literatures focused on characteristics of leaders, reasons they become leaders, their styles, and effectiveness. But with its interest in the potential continuity (or closure) of an enterprise beyond the founder or incumbent leader's tenure, family business research has focused on various factors that influence leadership transition. Examples include culture created by first-generation family firms; the incumbent's role during and after succession, and the related topic of departure styles of family business leaders; and factors that influence next generation's decision-making and role in business. Researchers interested in gender issues have studied the roles adopted by copreneurs – that is, couples who launch a business together, the role they play, and how their roles change if the marriage or romantic relationship is dissolved. Research findings on these topics are discussed below.

Culture in first-generation firms

Based on a study of more than 40 family firms, Dyer Jr. (1988) identified four types of culture in first-generation family firms: paternalistic, laissez-faire, participative, and professional. Not only are these cultures based on different assumptions about human nature, relationships, and the environment, but they also provide a framework for analyzing relationships between family members and non-members, and they play an important role in determining whether a firm continues beyond the founder's tenure.

The *paternalistic culture* is the most commonly found culture in first-generation family firms studied in this research. Power and decision-making is centered in the incumbent leader. Other family and non-family members involved in the business largely carry out the decisions of this leader. While the leader is at the top of the hierarchy, family members are given a preferential treatment as compared to non-family members. The latter are not trusted and are closely supervised by family members. Carrying on the founder's legacy is the primary aim of this type of an organization. First-generation firms following the *laissez-faire culture* are similar to the paternalistic firms as these too are hierarchical and afford preferential treatment to family members. However, non-family members in these firms are given more decision-making authority wherein they can choose the means to accomplish the goals set by the family. *Participative culture* was found in only four of the 40 firms studied. Relationships between family and non-family members are more egalitarian as power of family is de-emphasized. An environment is created to magnify the talents of employees. In family firms with the *professional culture*, there is generally a separation of ownership and management. While family controls the ownership, non-family managers have the operational responsibilities. Competition among managers is intense as individual performance is encouraged and promoted.

Although the issue of roles adopted by founders or incumbent leaders in firms with different cultures has not been elaborated upon in the literature, one can reasonably expect differences. Culture established by the founder is sticky as revealed both by Davis and Harveston (1999) and Sonfield and Lussier (2004) in their respective studies of 1,002 and 161 firms in the US.

It is interesting to note that the identified cultures parallel the three attitudes of insiders towards the family firms discussed in the last section. The paternalistic and laissez-faire cultures mirror family-first orientation; the professional culture is similar to the business-first orientation; and the participative culture parallels the family-enterprise-first orientation.

Contradictions can be found in empirical studies. The family-enterprise-first culture was the least frequently found culture in Dyer Jr.'s (1988) study. In contrast, with 338 family-enterprise firms, this category formed the largest cluster of firms in Basco and

Rodríguez's (2009)'s study. In this sample 205 firms placed limited importance on both business and family activities and 189 were business-first firms. These authors reported that the family-enterprise-first firms achieved better family results and similar business results in comparison with the other clusters. Research is needed to deepen our understanding of factors that hinder and support the development of family-enterprise-first orientation and participative cultures in first-generation firms. Second, both Dyer Jr.'s and Ward's studies were conducted over 20 years ago. But there has been no follow-up work to understand the relationship between attitudes toward family and business, and the culture established by the founders. Moreover, questions such as the relationship between founder's attitudes or established culture, and individual variables such as the founder's personality, or family-related variables such as family structure or cohesion, or contextual variables such as industry or location in which the enterprise operates need research attention. Furthermore, the question of the role of established culture on promoting or hindering the longevity of an enterprise needs investigation.

Incumbent's role during and after succession

The relative roles played by an incumbent leader and a successor have perhaps best been described by Handler (1990) based on her study of 32 successors of family firms. She shows that during the transition process the role played by the predecessor changes from being the sole operator to king to supervisor and finally to becoming consultant for the successor. In turn, the successor moves through the roles of an assistant to manager to leader. While this study nicely describes the roles during the transition process, it stops short of explaining the roles of the predecessor once the new leader has taken charge and becomes the firm's leader.

A survey of 1,155 family business owners suggests that leaders with higher education and income who work longer hours per week and have tax-deferred income expect to retire partially rather than take full retirement (Kim & De Vaney, 2003). What roles do they play during this stage of partial retirement? Cadieux's (2007) exploratory study of five family firms from Canada suggests that predecessors' roles may either be more related to the organization or to the successors. Examples of the former types of roles are chairperson of the board, protector, intermediary, tech support, and consultant. Roles more related to the successor include advisor, supervisor, teacher, introducer, mobilizer, and confidant.

On the related topic of the departure styles of family business leaders, there is only one study that relies on several different sources of data. Findings are extremely interesting. Sonnenfeld and Spence (1989) identified four departure styles of leaders: *monarchs, generals, governors*, and *ambassadors*. Monarchs are most troubled by the lost power and do not leave office voluntarily. Generals also leave office only when forced out, but in the end they do so willingly. However, they plan their return to power to "rescue" the firm from the real or imagined inadequacy of their successor. Ambassadors make a graceful exit and maintain contact with the firm in an advisory capacity, often in a governance role. Governors lead a firm for a bounded term and make a clean break maintaining virtually no contact with the firm. While all four departure styles are found in family firms, the first two are more prevalent and troubling for the next-generation leaders. The best departure style for a family business leader is that of the ambassador, who leads the organization to moderate levels of growth, recognizes the time to step down, and maintains contact with the organization as advisor. Sharma, Chrisman, and Chua (1997) note that:

> While the ambassador style can appear to be conceptually superior, this has not been empirically proven. And whether it is or not, the existing literature provides few clues as to how a departing leader can be persuaded to follow the appropriate departure style, or how successors can minimize the deleterious effects of a leader who cannot be so persuaded. (p. 15)

Overall, while this research provides hints of possible types of roles incumbents, successors, and predecessors might take during and after the succession process, more research is needed to determine the generalizability of these findings and factors that influence the adopted roles.

Next-generation family members

Research on roles of next-generation family members is rather limited to the findings from Handler's (1990) study described above that shows next-generation members moving from the role of an assistant, to that of a manager, and eventually to the leader of a firm. Part-time involvement of next-generation members in the firm has been observed to aid their socialization in business. However, not all next-generation members consider joining their family enterprise to be their first career choice. Studies largely focused on university students suggest that weak economy and poor market conditions for employment, personal needs and goals, and perception of sunk costs in the business have a positive effect on the next generation's decision to join their family business (e.g., Shepherd & Zacharakis, 2000; Stavrou & Swiercz, 1998). A desire to build their self-confidence, efficacy, and to discover their interests propels next-generation members to experience work life outside their family enterprises as they graduate out of college (Handler, 1990; Ward, 1987). Children of business families have been found to have a less clear sense of their career identity, goals, and interests than others who do not come from business backgrounds (Eckrich & Loughead, 1996). Scholars and practitioners are unified in their prescription that "it may be beneficial for these young individuals, their family, and the business, if they do not join the family business until they explore their abilities and discover their interests" (Stavrou & Swiercz, 1998, p. 34).

Research on commitment of next-generation family members sheds some light on the different reasons next-generation family members decide to join their family firms (Sharma & Irving, 2005). These are:

- affective commitment based on a strong alignment of identity and career interests with opportunities in the business;
- normative commitment based on obligations and family's expectations for next generation's role related to the family and their business;
- continuance commitment based on individual's fear of losing inherited financial wealth through the family business; and
- imperative commitment based on perceived inability to find alternate employment.

Evidence from 199 Canadian and Swiss firms suggests that individuals who join based on their own desire or obligation to family exhibit lower turnover intentions as compared to those who join based on other reasons (Dawson, Sharma, Irving, Marcus, & Chirico, 2012). Although we can extrapolate that next-generation family members who join based on affective commitment will likely follow the three successor roles described by Handler (1990) – assistant, manager, and leader – more research is needed to understand reliably if the roles followed by these members vary based on their underlying reasons for joining the business.

Gender roles in family business

Significant changes in attitudes related to gender have been observed since the influential writings of Léon Danco in the seventies. His books, *Beyond Survival: A Guide for the Business Owner and his Family* (1975), *Inside the Family Business* (1980), *Someday It'll All Be . . . Who's?* (1990), and others, brought the family firm out from the shadows as a legitimate form of enterprise that plays a significant role in society. His writings reflect his experiences and the times in which he wrote. For example, when we look at the full *Beyond Survival* (1975) title the pronoun "his" leaps out at us. Danco identifies stereotypical roles of family business stakeholders with labels including:

- Old Dad: hard working, secretive, autocratic;
- Momma: first employee, bookkeeper, protective of son;
- Sons: inheritor, over-sold, under-developed;
- Daughters: inherit stock, recruiter of successor (perhaps husband) if no son, acknowledgement of competent women being considered;
- Family Managers: long service, lacking managerial experience elsewhere, resentful of successors;
- Greedy Kids: push dad out, grandchildren as hostages, compounded by spouse;
- Wives of Sons: status based on husband's position, generally primogeniture;
- Advisors: "Rasputins", lawyers, accountants, bankers, insurance agents, consultants, "hangers-on", immense influence;
- Directors: non-existent in family firms (fictional), may include managers, becoming a management committee, not board.

Danco's books have sold well and have been reissued over the years, with appropriate updates to reflect changing times and viewpoints. But stereotypes die hard. They often originate because they reflect someone's observation of actual behavior. Even today, we could find examples of each of Danco's descriptions.

In a more recent book written in collaboration with the Family Firm Institute by two principals in a marketing consulting company, the changing role of women in the family firm is given prominence (Raphel & Raye, 2009). The authors offered three categories for women: leader, owner, or disinterested and entitled. They suggested that although women continue to have problems, there are also new choices available. The problems they listed are reflective of women in the workplace: pay differentials, the need to prove themselves, attempts to be superwomen, and the pulls of the separate demands of the family and the business. Among the available choices is a greater social acceptance of women as leaders, opportunities to succeed in non-traditional occupations, increased achievement in college and graduate education, and, becoming more recognized, the need for women family members to take leadership roles in the firm.

We mentioned the evolving roles of women as reported in the practitioner literature. The composite review of three books on this topic by McCollom-Hampton in *Family Business Review* (2009) may be of interest. Gender issues have received considerable attention in the scholarly literature as well. In one study of 485 Canadian family firms, incumbent leaders were asked to rate the importance of 30 attributes they consider important in making their decision when appointing their successor (Chrisman, Chua, & Sharma, 1998). It was interesting to find that gender and birth order were listed as the two least important factors in their decision. Integrity and commitment to business were the two most desirable attributes. Similar findings were revealed when this study was replicated in India (Sharma & Rao, 2000), signaling a change in attitudes in terms of primogeniture (oldest son is the selected heir) in east and west.

Researchers have observed that female entrepreneurs have had close connections with other self-employed persons, especially a parent (Hisrich & Brush, 1984; Waddell, 1983). Hisrich and Brush suggested that "the ability to conceive of the possibility of becoming an entrepreneur may be grounded in family background and household environment" (p. 8). Egan (1997) found that when a family highly regards goal-setting and achieving success through self-initiated efforts, it reinforces women centered entrepreneurial activities. A study of women entrepreneurs in Singapore reported that their family environments encouraged creative thinking and independence (Lee, 2005).

Based on a thorough review of 48 research works published since 1985 on women in family firms, Jimenez (2009) summarized the obstacles and opportunities for women's involvement in family enterprises as follows:

Obstacles

- invisibility
  - roles and loyalties
  - relationships with parents, siblings, non-family members
  - struggles for power and authority
  - directly involved, but not recognized
- emotional leadership (chief emotional officer)
  - caretaker, peacemaker, conflict solver
  - communications
  - preserve values
  - family unity
- succession and primogeniture
  - rarely seriously considered candidates for leadership
  - expectations of family role

Opportunities

- professional career in family firm
  - flexible schedules
  - job security

- personal growth
- supportive environment
- father as natural mentor
- reactive, proactive, evolving roles
- running the family firm
  - outside experience gives credibility and self-confidence
  - well-defined internal position
  - loyalty to firm and family

Jimenez's work corresponds with findings reported by others who see multiple and conflicting roles for women in family enterprises (e.g., Curimbaba, 2002; Dumas, 1998; Poza & Messer, 2001). They suffer inter-role conflict, and triggers of the conflicts can be bi-directional (Netemeyer, Boles & McMurrian, 1996). According to Rogers (2005), however, role conflict is less intense for women without children.

While it is one thing to describe data collected on women and conditions they face, it is another to compare women in their family business roles with men to determine if differences exist. Aldrich (1989) found that social structures and societal expectations differ for men and women entrepreneurs. Alternatively, independence and self-achievement are primary motives for both men and women (Orhan, 2005). According to Matthews and Moser (1996), the parental role model was more significant for men than women, related to their entry into business ownership. Conversely, other studies report female entrepreneurs had a close connection with other self-employed persons, especially a parent (Hisrich & Brush, 1984; Waddell, 1983). After examining the roles of men and women in family firms, Jimenez (2009) concluded that:

> Families with rigid or more segregated gender roles may make it more difficult for women and for men with feminine or balanced values or leadership styles to be included fully in family business. If the family business itself has a culture of masculine norms embedded in its job customs and norms (e.g., long hours implying commitment, aggressive or competitive internal culture), it may also build unintended barriers to full involvement for family members with balanced or feminine values, which equates to barriers to the full use of the human and social capital of those members for the business. (p. 224)

The issue of respective roles of men and women in family enterprises provides an interesting twist in the context of copreneurial ventures, that is, married couples or couples in marriage-like relationships who have joint ownership, commitment, and responsibility for a business enterprise (Barnett & Barnett, 1988). Findings from the 1997 National Family Business Study reveal that copreneurs typically live in a rural area and have home-based lifestyle businesses that report lower levels of financial success than other comparative enterprises (Fitzgerald & Muske, 2002). Copreneurs enter and exit from this role with changes in their lives and relationships indicating the dynamic nature of such enterprises (Muske & Fitzgerald, 2006).

What happens to copreneurial enterprises after the dissolution of the romantic relationship between the couple? Research on nine divorced couples who had run enterprises that employed between 2–700 employees and had been in a marital (or similar) relationship ranging from 2–32 years, suggests that couples who trusted each other's business acumen felt they had synergistic abilities, felt an emotional connection, were satisfied with their respective roles and power in the enterprise, and continued to work effectively together post-divorce (Cole & Johnson, 2007). This study was conducted in the US. Given the increasing instances of divorce and separation in many countries today, it would be interesting to understand whether such continuity of enterprise owned and operated jointly by a divorced couple works effectively over the long term in different cultural and family contexts.

In-laws in business families

Another category of special roles in a family is the in-laws. Some firms have been found to resist the involvement of in-laws, implementing policies that prohibit in-laws from joining the firm (Hubler, 1996). Similar to the blood relatives, the values and attitudes of in-laws are shaped by the families in which they are raised. They will naturally have different values resulting from being raised in different families. Roles of in-laws range from true partnership in the enterprise, as in the case of copreneurs discussed above, to no involvement at all in the business. Focusing on the spouses, Bieneman (1997) identified the following possible roles in a business:

1) involvement (no universal rules);
2) participation in the family council (sometimes they resist, but should be important members);
3) membership on board of directors (generally not unless also active in management. Board should include outside directors);
4) ownership and voting control (wealth distribution, tax planning, estate plan);
5) picking a successor (seldom decide but often influence); and
6) combined roles (acting as a spouse, parent, and business advisor can create the potential for conflict – spouses should have an understanding of goals and motives of other family members).

Some practitioners find the "Wives of Sons" and other in-laws to be of value to the firm. Hubler (1996) observes that in-laws bring the following positive qualities into the firm:

- a dose of objectivity;
- the ability to keep family members on their best behavior;
- help for spouses to understand emotionally charged messages;
- prevention of distortion of information; and
- help for resolving spousal concerns and issues.

Hubler proposed a ground rule for owners to follow: *allow in-laws to attend and participate in selected family business planning meetings*. He contended that there is nothing worse than second-hand information, especially coming from someone emotionally involved. To this, Bieneman (1997) added some further guidelines for dealing with in-laws:

1) fair treatment;
2) extra (careful) communication;
3) avoid a double standard;

4) clear rules of the game;
5) less emotional baggage;
6) talent; and
7) balance.

While the above descriptions are largely based on experiential insights of advisors and tend to discuss in-laws as a homogenous category of family members, research by Santiago (2011) based on in-depth interviews with 300 individuals, 114 of whom were in-laws in 82 Philippine business families, highlights the heterogeneity within "in-law" category of family members. Santiago (2011) observed the precarious role of in-laws in family enterprises, arguing for a need to modify the three-circle model to reflect this role. She demonstrated this by adding a dotted circle outside the family circle, indicating that while some in-laws may never be fully assimilated into the family, others may be welcomed into management and ownership roles. Moreover, in-laws may move in and out of the family, ownership, and management circles based on their performance in business and in marriage, and other key family relationships.

Being new additions to the family, all in-laws must earn their position both in the family and in the business. At first, while they may be welcomed into the family, they hold a tentative position related to the family's business. The strength of their relationship is not enough to earn them the same rights and privileges related to the business as are afforded to members of the family-of-origin (Hoy & Sharma, 2010). Further, Santiago (2011) found differences between parents-in-law, siblings-in-law, and children-in-law. While parents-in-law were limited to being given secondary management positions, sons- and daughters-in-law were more easily welcomed into the ownership positions, although some contextual variations apply for this category of in-laws too. Perhaps the category of in-laws with the subtlest distinction is that of sibling-in-laws. In this category, the gender, business requirements, and the side that the in-law is from significantly influence whether his or her involvement in business is accepted and/or expected. Financial, human resources, and technical needs combined with related abilities of the in-laws determined whether or not this category of in-laws was tapped to provide these resources. Another interesting finding of this study is that greater trust was placed on the siblings of the spouse than the spouse of the siblings (Santiago, 2011, p. 349).

This path-breaking study questions the sweeping usage of the term *family* by highlighting the distinctions between different categories of in-laws. It also sheds light on various stages of acceptance of different categories of in-laws in a family and the varying beliefs of families regarding such acceptance, as indicated by the following quote from this article:

> Although in-laws may be warmly accepted into homes, often they cannot immediately say they are part of the family. The feeling of oneness, of being trusted, comes with time. . . .. It is earned, not a right. However, like all types of relationships, trust can be lost.
>
> Some families would rather not put that trust to a test. If a family business can run well on its own, then in-law participation is actually discouraged. As one interviewee quips, "It is better to hire a stranger than my son-in-law. At least if he doesn't perform, I can fire him. If I hire and then fire my son-in-law, I may lose my daughter's love. Why risk it?" (Santiago, 2011, p. 356)

This quote exemplifies how beliefs held within a family cross over to establish a policy for a company.

Family roles

The foregoing discussions of incumbent leaders, next generation, gender, and in-laws reported findings primarily associated with direct involvement in the family firm. This reflects the weight of the research, which has focused more on the business than the family side of the equation. Rothausen and Sorenson (2011) contended that the focus on business and family should be more balanced, that scholars should examine how the functioning of the family influences value formation that may subsequently impact the firm. And they argue that both spouses should be involved in family issues, avoiding a parenting default by one spouse due to being consumed by the demands of the business. This view was reinforced by the direct experience of McEnaney (2011). Danes, Stafford, Haynes, and Amarapurkar (2009) proposed that a spouse not actively working in the business, who may or may not have an ownership position, should take on the role of "household manager." This designation highlights how the family provides a developmental context in preparing members for their future relationships with the firm.

The point being made here is that there is a dearth of scholarship on family members not employed in the business regarding how they function, both individually and as a unit distinct from the business, yet simultaneously influencing the business. Such influences can occur on a daily basis, but also over time, to shape attitudes and behaviors. Although some models have been introduced to address these issues (c.f., Stafford, Duncan, Danes, & Winter, 1999), there are few empirical studies in the current body of knowledge to provide guidance.

Non-family employees

Non-family employees and managers are critical to the growth of family enterprises. Dyer Jr. (1988) contended that outside, non-family members can play significant roles in effecting productivity and satisfaction in both family and business. These members have been observed to help in bringing objectivity to discussions, providing technical competencies lacking within the business family, and helping to professionalize the enterprise. Some non-family managers rise to the level of becoming the most trusted advisor of the controlling family (Strike, 2012).

But the role of non-family members is more complex than their counterparts in non-family firms. Based on interviews with 27 family and non-family members in US family firms to understand factors that lead to the success of non-family CEOs, Blumentritt, Keyt, and Astrachan (2007) note that while non-family members are assigned to lead the business, they often find themselves in the roles of management trainers, counselors, confidants, and supervisors of individuals who sit on boards and evaluate their performances. Non-family members may be tasked with managing, developing, and even firing the children of the family that owns the firm (Blumentritt et al., 2007). Thus, they need both business and interpersonal competencies. This finding resonates with the observation of Hall and Nordqvist (2008). Based on in-depth interviews with 96 family and non-family members in five Swedish firms, Hall and Nordqvist (2008) found that:

> Professional management in family businesses means an in-depth enough understanding of the owner family's dominant goals and meanings of being in business (i.e., cultural competence) to

be able to make effective use of relevant education and experience (i.e., formal competence) in a particular family business. (p. 63)

These scholars suggest that professional non-family managers are likely to benefit from "reciprocal role taking" – that is, developing an ability to view the situation from the perspective of the key representatives of the owning family (Hall & Nordqvist, 2008). To this, Blumentritt et al. (2007) add that while compassion is important for non-family members, having a strong board helps.

Just as with in-laws, non-family employees are not a homogenous category. Their roles may vary from that of a junior employee, to a functional manager, to a CFO or a CEO, to becoming the most trusted advisor of the family (Salvato, Minichilli, & Piccarreta, 2012; Strike, 2012). And these roles are dynamic, as the same individual may move through different roles over time as indicated by the following comment made by a non-family CEO who had spent many years as a manager in the same family business and felt he had built a "tremendous amount of credibility with the family":

> When you change roles and become CEO, you're running the business and the situation is different. You can lose that credibility very rapidly because now you have to make choices, you have to make decisions, you have to run the business and make sure it's going in a direction which some of the family members may not be on board with. (Blumentritt et al., 2007, p. 332)

Thus, the role of non-family members in business is integral, dynamic, and complex. Consultants have frequently been called in to help family businesses recruit and retain non-family managers. Family business owners recognize that key personnel may lose enthusiasm and look elsewhere if they perceive that there is a glass ceiling restricting their advancement in favor of relatives of the owner. Some research has examined the role of non-family managers, giving attention to retention of such managers, who may perceive limited advancement opportunities. Crego (1996) listed a set of motivators for those in non-family management roles:

- strong set of core values permeating the firm's culture;
- clearly stated and implemented mission;
- professional work environment;
- objective recognition and reward systems;
- commitment to the customer; and
- innovative and entrepreneurial behavior.

In the company, however, hiring and retaining personnel are presumed to be based on competence and skills. The norms of fairness are based on merit. Living and working in both circles makes holding those distinctions difficult. Applying the value systems can lead to confusion with regard to authority, leadership, compensation, promotion, and discipline. Barnett and Kellermanns (2006) argue that "Securing the commitment and cooperation of nonfamily employees is likely to be more difficult if they do not perceive that decision outcomes, decision processes, and decision-makers are fair and just" (p. 838).

In short, we know that non-family employees are critical to the growth and success of a family enterprise and that their role in such firms is more complex than similar roles in non-family enterprises. In addition to having superior technical skills, they must be aware of the family's attitudes towards business and the respective role of family and non-family members in business. Overall, while some progress has been made to understand the role of non-family employees, much more work remains. It will be useful to keep in mind the heterogeneity of non-family employees and their roles when designing future research studies.

As we alluded to in the beginning of this section on roles, the best-developed aspect of the three-circle model is the family circle, where researchers and practitioners have studied and observed the roles of incumbent leaders, next-generation family members, women in family firms, and, more recently, in-laws. Missing pockets of understanding remain, however, not only with regard to these family stakeholders but others as well. For example, the role of grandparents or great-grandparents has received virtually no attention. In today's landscape of generational stack up in workplaces (Green, 2011), the role of these senior family members, both within the family and the enterprise, deserves careful attention. Another integral category of family members who have not been subjected to research attention are the next-generation family members who are not the anointed heirs but may play critical roles in the family and the enterprise. The involvement of siblings in the business may vary from nil to joint leadership of the enterprise. Work is needed to understand these roles and dynamics.

Regarding the other two circles, empirical research has provided only preliminary understanding of the complex roles of these stakeholders in family enterprises. For the employees' circle, research has examined recruitment, retrenchment, and advancement issues. Finer variations between junior employees versus middle managers versus non-family CEOs, or between employees with and without ownership have not been studied yet.

As we mentioned earlier, there is not much scientific research-based knowledge on the ownership circle. Ownership is often assumed to be a single family or family member. In practice, however, as the intertwining of the circles suggests, non-family employees may have ownership stakes. It is not unusual for multiple unrelated individuals to form enterprises together, sometimes with multiple families interacting. Some of those founding owners or others who obtain equity positions later may not work in the firm, but they certainly have a stake in how relatives of the owner-manager team influence the allocation of company resources. Clearly, there are many interesting opportunities for future investigation.

Conclusion

So why do we want to know what research tells us about family businesses? More to the point, why do we want to know how the roles and attitudes of family business stakeholders relate to the business? An obvious answer is that the success of family firms over time suggests that kinship offers benefits outweighing costs. It is important to add that benefits are not always defined as financial. They may be emotional, they may be reflected in mental health, or they may be played out in the firm through group cohesion (Stewart, 2003). Other benefits that have been documented in terms of successfully operating the business include sources of capital, pooled resources, lower employee turnover, cohesion, and social support (Peredo, 2003). In his review of prior studies, Stewart also observed that in recommending behavioral and performance actions to business owners, there needs to be some consideration of to whom the benefits accrue – to both the family and the firm? Equally, do they accrue only to family members or to both family and non-family? These questions imply that both managing and advising family firms should rely on sound research findings that assess the complexity of the situation.

Keeping in mind that the cluster of Family Business Roles is the smallest of all seven clusters of empirical research, identified by Yu et al. (2012), what can we confidently say that we know about family business roles? And what do we think we know? In this section, we summarize insights based on our review of the scholarly and practitioner literatures on these questions. Although we suggest in the heading below that some truths have been established regarding family businesses, it is important to acknowledge the limitations associated with research to date. Most studies are cross-sectional rather than longitudinal, which could result in conclusions that have a short-term bias. This represents a dilemma for advisors who are positioned to apply research findings in training programs or practitioners who are devising incentive systems. One purpose of the STEP in-depth multi-generational case study approach is to provide advisors and practitioners with a longer-term view. At present, however, our most substantiated conclusions follow.

What we know for sure about family business roles

- Variations in the composition of family along the dimensions of consanguinity, gender, birth order, number of generations co-habiting in a single household, and legal status of the focal couple currently exist in our society.
- Family involvement in business (F_{IB}) is the single most important factor that distinguishes family business studies from other related disciplines.
- Three dimensions of F_{IB} are important to keep in mind when trying to understand the unique dynamics and sources of conflict in a family. These three dimensions are family's role in ownership, management, and governance of the enterprise.
- Attitudes of outsiders toward family enterprises are changing. While nepotism had negative connotations even as recently as the seventies, with the increasing knowledge about success of long-lived family enterprises, the positive aspects of nepotism are becoming more visible.
- Family enterprises can be divided broadly into three categories based on their attitudes towards family and toward business. These are family-first, business-first, and family-enterprise-first. Evidence suggests that while it is extremely difficult to tread the family-enterprise-first path that gives equal importance to balance the needs of family and of the business, those who can do so successfully enjoy performance advantages over other enterprises on both family and business dimensions.
- Each internal stakeholder (i.e., family or non-family member involved with the business) can play in one of the seven areas of the three-circle model (Figure 6.1). Within each of these areas, however, there are finer distinctions, some of which have been studied. Good examples are the varied roles played by women in family enterprises or different categories of in-laws and their roles in family firms.
- Incumbent leaders, especially founders, create a unique culture for their enterprise. This culture has a long shadow and persists over generations. While family cham-

pions of change can modify existing cultures and beliefs, it takes a high degree of skill to accomplish such a feat, especially in family enterprises.

- Next-generation family members have varied motivations in joining their family enterprise. What are the long-term performance implications of these different motivating factors?
- Not all in-laws are alike. Several categories of in-laws have been identified in the literature: children-in-law, siblings-in-law, and parents-in-law. Furthermore, there are finer distinctions within each of these categories of in-laws.
- Non-family employees play a critical role in family enterprises. However, this role is complex.

These points represent what scholarship has to offer practice. Advisors to families and business owners acquire knowledge through education within their disciplines and through experience. Not all disciplines have developed bodies of knowledge about families in business. And personal experience with specific clients cannot necessarily be generalized to broader populations. While it may appear intuitively obvious that family involvement is a distinguishing characteristic in family businesses or that in-laws are not all alike, it is important for advisors to rely on research confirmations beyond anecdotal evidence. Additionally, these findings add support to advice offered by experts regarding how influential family beliefs and behaviors are in the success of the family enterprise.

What we think we know, but need more research to empirically validate our thoughts

- The composition of family is changing. A family can be defined either based on its components such as the gender of the focal couple, number of generations living in the same household, legal status, etc., or based on its essence. What components are more or less important in understanding the heterogeneity of business families? In this chapter, we proposed a definition of family based on shared history and commitment to share the future – is this how families describe their essence? Do the components and essence of family change over time? If so, what are their implications on family's involvement in business?
- What causes varied degrees and modes of families' involvement in ownership, management, and governance of their enterprise(s)? Can family businesses be clustered into a few categories based on these factors? If so, what do these clusters look like? Do these clusters vary over time and across regions of the world? If so, are there implications for performance of the firm on financial and socio-emotional dimensions? Performance of the family?
- If the family-enterprise attitude leads to high performance on family and business dimensions, what factors hinder or support family business leaders to adopt and pursue this attitude over generations?
- What are the finer distinctions of roles within each of the seven areas of the three-circle model (Figure 6.1)? For example, can there be attitudinal or role differences within owners in area 5 or between family employees currently residing in area 3? Similar questions need to be asked and addressed for all seven areas in the circle to provide a realistic understanding of the family business roles.

- What is the relationship between the nature of the culture developed by a founder or an incumbent leader, and (a) his/her departure style, (b) the motivation of next generation to join the business, and (c) the roles played by family and non-family members in the enterprise?
- Is there a relationship between the personality of an in-law and his/her acceptance into different roles in a family enterprise? If so, how do families monitor the behavior and performance of in-laws in comparison to similar performance of a family member?
- What factors enable a non-family employee to success in family firms? Are these factors different at different levels of seniority?
- What is the relationship among family involvement in business, family's attitudes toward business, and roles played by family and non-family members in business? Is this relationship stable or variable over time?

The questions raised above represent cautionary notes to both advisors and practitioners. Much of the early literature on family firms was written by owners and consultants. Descriptions and opinions reflected the eye of the beholder rather than scientific methodology. Much of what we think we know about healthy family enterprises has yet to be confirmed through rigorous research. In this summary, we urge skepticism in practice and activism by scholars.

Note

1. The terms family business and business families are often used interchangeably. It is more precise to define the latter as a subgroup of family members who own or work in the business.

References

Aldrich, H. (1989). Networking among women entrepreneurs. In O. Hagan, C. Rivchun & D. Sexton (Eds.), *Women-owned businesses* (pp. 103–13). New York: Praeger.

Amit, R., & Villalonga, B. (2013). Financial performance of family firms. In P. Sharma, M. Nordqvist & L. Melin (Eds.), *The SAGE handbook of family business* (forthcoming). London, UK: SAGE Publications, Ltd.

Anderson, R.C., & Reeb, D.M. (2003). Founding-family ownership and firm performance: Evidence from S&P 500. *Journal of Finance, 58*(3), 1301–27.

Barnett, F., & Barnett, S. (1988). *Working together: Entrepreneurial couples.* Berkeley, CA: Ten Speed Press.

Barnett, T., & Kellermanns, F.W. (2006). Are we family and are we treated as family? Nonfamily employees' perceptions of justice in the family firm. *Entrepreneurship Theory and Practice, 30*(6), 837–54.

Basco, R., & Rodríguez, M.J.P. (2009). Studying family enterprise holistically: Evidence for integrated family and business systems. *Family Business Review, 22*(1), 82–95.

Bellow, A. (2003). *In praise of nepotism: A natural history.* New York: Doubleday.

Bengtson, V.L., Acock, A.C., Allen, K.R., Dilworth-Anderson, P., & Klein, D.M. (2005). *Sourcebook of family theory and research.* Thousand Oaks, CA: SAGE Publications, Inc.

Bernandes, J. (1985). Do we really know what "the family" is? In P. Close & R. Collins (Eds.), *Family and economy in modern society* (pp. 192–227). London, UK: Macmillan Publishers.

Bieneman, J.N. (1997). *The Horwath international guide to total planning in the family and owner managed business.* New York: Horwath International.

Birley, S. (2001). Owner-manager attitudes to family and business issues: A 16 country study. *Entrepreneurship Theory and Practice, 25*(1), 63–76.

Birley, S. (2002). Attitudes of owner-managers' children towards family and business issues. *Entrepreneurship Theory and Practice, 26*(1), 5–19.

Block, J. (2010). Family management, family ownership, and downsizing: Evidence from S&P 500 firms. *Family Business Review, 23*(2), 109–30.

Blumentritt, T.P., Keyt, A.D., & Astrachan, J.H. (2007). Creating an environment for successful nonfamily CEOs: An exploratory study of good principals. *Family Business Review, 20*(4), 321–35.

Björnberg, Å., & Nicholson, N. (2007). The family climate scales – Development of a new measure for use in family business research. *Family Business Review, 20*(3), 229–46.

Cadieux, L. (2007). Succession in small and medium-sized family businesses: toward a typology of predecessor roles during and after instatement of the successor. *Family Business Review, 20*(2), 95–109.

Chrisman, J.J., Chua, J.H., & Sharma, P. (1998). Important attributes of successors in family businesses: An exploratory study. *Family Business Review, 11*(1), 19–34.

Chua, J.H., Chrisman, J.J., & Sharma, P. (1999). Defining the family business by behavior. *Entrepreneurship: Theory & Practice, 23*(4), 19–39.

Cole, P.M., & Johnson, K. (2007). An exploration of successful copreneurial relations post divorce. *Family Business Review, 20*(3), 185–98.

Craig, J., & Salvato, C. (2012). The distinctiveness, design, and direction of family business research: Insights from management luminaries. *Family Business Review, 25*(1), 109–16.

Crego, E.T., Jr. (1996). Motivating your nonfamily managers. In M. Fischetti (Ed.), *The family business management handbook* (pp. 49–50). Philadelphia: Family Business Publishing.

Curimbaba, F. (2002). The dynamics of women's roles as family business managers. *Family Business Review, 15*(3), 239–52.

Danco, L.A. (1975). *Beyond survival: A guide for the business owner and his family.* Cleveland, OH: Reston Publishing.

Danco, L.A. (1980). *Inside the family business.* Cleveland, Ohio: Center for Family Business Press.

Danco, L.A. & Jonovic, D.J. (1990). *Someday it'll all be. . .who's?* Cleveland, Ohio: Center for Family Business Press.

Danes, S.M. (2013). The future of family business research through the family scientist's lens. In P. Sharma, M. Nordqvist & L. Melin (Eds.), *The SAGE handbook of family business* (forthcoming). London, UK: SAGE Publications, Ltd.

Danes, S.M., Stafford, K., Haynes, G., & Amarapurkar, S.S. (2009). Family capital of family firms: Bridging human, social and financial capital. *Family Business Review, 22*(3), 199–215.

Davis, J.A. (1982). *The influence of life stage on father-son work relation in family companies.* Ann Arbor, MI: University Microfilms.

Davis, P.S., & Harveston, P.D. (1999). In the founder's shadow: Conflict in the family firm. *Family Business Review, 12*(4), 311–23.

Dawson, A., Sharma, P., Irving, G., Marcus, J., & Chirico, F. (2012). Predictors of next generation family members' commitment to family. Working paper.

Dumas, C. (1998). Women's pathways to participation and leadership in the family owned firm. *Family Business Review, 11*(3), 219–28.

Dyer, W.G., Jr. (1988). Culture and continuity in family firms. *Family Business Review, 1*(1), 37–50.

Dyer, W.G., Jr. (2003). The family: The missing variable in organizational research. *Entrepreneurship Theory and Practice, 27*(4), 401–16.

Eckrich, C.J., & Loughead, T.A. (1996). Effects of family business membership and psychological separation on the career development of late adolescents. *Family Business Review, 9*(4), 369–86.

Egan, M. (1997). Getting down to business and off welfare: Rural women entrepreneurs. *Journal of Women and Social Work, 12*(2), 215–28.

Ewing, D.W. (1965). Is nepotism so bad? *Harvard Business Review, 43*(1), 223–36.

Fiegener, M.K., Brown, B.M., Dreux, D.R., IV, & Dennis, W.J., Jr. (2000). CEO stakes and board composition in small private firms. *Entrepreneurship Theory & Practice, 24*(1), 5–24.

Fitzgerald, M.A., & Muske, G. (2002). Copreneurs: An exploration and comparison to other family businesses. *Family Business Review, 15*(1), 1–16.

Gersick, K.E., Davis, J.A., Hampton, M.M., & Lansberg, I. (1997). *Generation to generation: Life cycles of the family business.* Boston, MA: Harvard Business School Press.

Green, M. (2011). *Inside the multigenerational family business: Nine symptoms of generational stack-up and how to cure them.* New York: Palgrave Macmillan Publishers.

Hall, A., & Nordqvist, M. (2008). Professional management in family businesses: Toward an extended understanding. *Family Business Review, 21*(1), 51–69.

Handler, W. (1990). Succession in family firms: A mutual role adjustment between entrepreneur and next generation family members. *Entrepreneurship Theory & Practice, 15*(1), 37–51.

Hisrich, R.D., & Brush, C.G. (1984). The woman entrepreneur: Management skills and business problems. *Journal of Small Business Management, 22*(1), 30–37.

Hoy, F., & Sharma, P. (2010). *Entrepreneurial family firms.* Upper Saddle River, NJ: Pearson Prentice Hall.

Hubler, T. (1996). Making room for in-laws. In M. Fischetti (Ed.), *The family business management handbook* (pp. 29–30). Philadelphia, PA: Family Business Publishing.

James, A.E., Jennings, J.E., & Breitkruz, R. (2012). Worlds apart? Re-bridging the distance between family science and family business research. *Family Business Review, 25*(1), 87–108.

Jimenez, R.M. (2009). Research on women in family firms: Current status and future directions. *Family Business Research, 22*(1), 53–64.

Johns, G., & Saks, A.M. (2005). *Organizational behavior: Understanding and managing life at work.* Toronto: Pearson Prentice Hall.

Kim, J., & De Vaney, S.A. (2003). The expectation of partial retirement among family business owners. *Family Business Review, 16*(3), 199–210.

Klein, S.B., Astrachan, J.H., & Smyrnios, K.X. (2005). The F-PEC scale of family influence: Construction, validation, and further implication for theory. *Entrepreneurship Theory and Practice, 29*(4), 321–39.

Lansberg, I., Perrow, E.L., & Rogolsky, S. (1988). Family business as an emerging field. *Family Business Review, 1*(1), 1–8.

Lee, J. (2005). Women entrepreneurs in Singapore. In S.L. Fielden & M.J. Davidson (Eds.), *International handbook of women and small business entrepreneurship* (pp. 178–92). Cheltenham, UK, and Northampton, MA, USA: Edward Elgar.

McCollom-Hampton, M. (2009). Composite review of three books on women in family firms. *Family Business Review, 22*(4), 366–69.

McEnaney, T. (2011). Our family enterprise. In R.L. Sorenson (Ed.), *Family business and social capital* (pp. 170–77). Cheltenham, UK, and Northampton, MA, USA: Edward Elgar Publishing.

Manchester, W. (1968). *The arms of Krupp, 1587–1968.* London, UK: Little Brown

Matthews, C.H., & Moser. S.B. (1996). A longitudinal investigation of the impact of family background and gender on interest in small firm ownership. *Journal of Small Business Management, 34*(2), 29–43.

Miller, D., Le-Breton Miller, I., Lester, R.H., & Cannella, A.A. (2007). Are family firms really superior performers? *Journal of Corporate Finance, 13*(5), 829–58.

Muske, G., & Fitzgerald, M.A. (2006). A panel study of copreneurs in business: Who enters, continues, and exits? *Family Business Review, 19*(3), 193–205.

Netemeyer, R., Boles, J., & McMurrian, R. (1996). Development and validation of work-family conflict and family-work conflict scales. *Journal of Applied Psychology, 81*(4), 400–10.

Orhan, M. (2005). Why women enter into small business ownership. In S.L. Fielden & M.J. Davidson (Eds.), *International handbook of women and small business entrepreneurship* (pp. 3–16). Cheltenham, UK, and Northampton, MA, USA: Edward Elgar Publishing.

Peredo, A.M. (2003). Nothing thicker than blood? *Entrepreneurship Theory and Practice, 27*(4), 397–400.

Poza, E., & Messer, T. (2001). Spousal leadership and continuity in the family firm. *Family Business Review, 14*(1), 25–36.

Raphel, N., & Raye, J. (2009). *The complete idiot's guide to a successful family business*. New York: Penguin Group.

Rogers, N. (2005). The impact of family support on the success of women business owners. In S.L. Fielden, & M.J. Davidson (Eds.), *International handbook of women and small business entrepreneurship* (pp. 91–102). Cheltenham, UK, and Northampton, MA, USA: Edward Elgar Publishing.

Rothausen, T.J., & Sorenson, R.L. (2011). Leveraging family member capacity for the business and the family. In R.L. Sorenson (Ed.), *Family business and social capital* (pp. 155–69). Cheltenham, UK, and Northampton, MA, USA: Edward Elgar Publishing.

Salvato, C., Chirico, F., & Sharma, P. (2010). A farewell to the business: Championing exit and continuity in entrepreneurial family firms. *Entrepreneurial and Regional Development*, *22*(3/4), 321–48.

Salvato, C., Minichilli, A., & Piccarreta, R. (2012). Faster route to the CEO suite: Nepotism or managerial proficiency? *Family Business Review*, *25*(2), 206–24.

Santiago, A.L. (2011). The family in family business: Case of the in-laws in Philippine businesses. *Family Business Review*, *24*(4), 343–61.

Sciascia, S., & Mazzola, P. (2008). Family involvement in ownership and management: Exploring nonlinear effects on performance. *Family Business Review*, *21*(4), 331–45.

Shanker, M.C., & Astrachan, J.H. (1996). Myths and realities: Family businesses' contribution to the U.S. economy – A framework for assessing family business statistics. *Family Business Review*, *9*(2), 107–23.

Sharma, P., Chrisman, J.J., & Chua, J.H. (1997). Strategic management of the family business: Past research and future challenges. *Family Business Review*, *10*(1), 1–35.

Sharma, P., Chrisman, J.J., & Gersick, K.E. (2012). 25 years of *Family Business Review*: Reflections on the past and perspectives for the future. *Family Business Review*, *25*(1), 5–15.

Sharma, P., Hoy, F., Astrachan, J.H., & Koiranen, M. (2007). The practice-driven evolution of family business education. *Journal of Business Research*, *60*, 1012–21.

Sharma, P., & Irving, G. (2005). Four bases of family business successor commitment: Antecedents and consequences. *Entrepreneurship Theory and Practice*, *29*(1), 13–33.

Sharma, P., & Manikutty, S. (2005). Strategic divestments in family firms: Role of family structure and community culture. *Entrepreneurship Theory and Practice*, *29*(3), 293–312.

Sharma, P., & Nordqvist, M. (2008). A classification scheme for family firms: From family values to effective governance to firm performance. In J. Tàpies & J.L. Ward (Eds.), *Family values and value creation: The fostering of enduring values within family-owned* businesses (pp. 71–101). New York: Palgrave Macmillan Publishers.

Sharma, P., & Rao, S.A. (2000). Successor attributes in Indian and Canadian family firms: A comparative study. *Family Business Review*, *13*(4), 313–30.

Sharma, P., & Salvato, C. (2012). Family firm longevity: A balancing act between continuity and change. In P. Fernández Pérez & A. Colli (Eds.), *A Global Revolution: The endurance of large family businesses in the world*. Cambridge University Press.

Shepherd, D.A., & Zacharakis, A. (2000). Structuring family business succession: An analysis of the future leader's decision making. *Entrepreneurship Theory and Practice*, *24*(1), 25–39.

Sonfield, M.C., & Lussier, R.N. (2004). First-, second-, and third-generation family firms: A comparison. *Family Business Review*, *17*(3), 189–202.

Sonnenfeld, J.A., & Spence, P.L. (1989). The parting patriarch of a family firm. *Family Business Review*, *2*(4), 355–75.

Stafford, K., Duncan, K.A., Danes, S.M., & Winter, M. (1999). A research model of sustainable family businesses. *Family Business Review*, *12*(3), 197–208.

Stavrou, E.T., & Swiercz, P.M. (1998). Securing the future of the family enterprise: A model of offspring intentions to join the business. *Entrepreneurship Theory and Practice*, *23*(2), 19.

Stewart, A. (2003). Help one another, use one another: Toward an anthropology of family business. *Entrepreneurship Theory and Practice*, *27*(4), 383–96.

Stewart, A., & Hitt, M.A. (2012). Why can't family business be more like a nonfamily business? Modes of professionalization in family firms. *Family Business Review*, *25*(1), 58–86.

Strike, V. (2012). Advising the family firm: Reviewing the past to build the future. *Family Business Review*, *25*(2), 156–77.

Villalonga, B., & Amit, R. (2006). How do family ownership, control and management affect firm value? *Journal of Financial Economics*, *80*, 385–417.

Waddell, F.T. (1983). Factors affecting choice, satisfaction, and success in the female self-employed. *Journal of Vocational Behavior*, *23*, 294–304.

Ward, J.L. (1987). *Keeping the family business healthy: How to plan for continuing growth, profitability, and family leadership*. San Francisco, CA: Jossey-Bass.

Watson, T.J., & Petre, P. (2000). *Father, son & co.: My life at IBM and beyond*. New York: Bantam Publishers.

Yu, A., Lumpkin, G.T., Sorenson, R.L., & Brigham, K.H. (2012). The landscape of family business outcomes: A summary and numerical taxonomy of dependent variables. *Family Business Review*, *25*(1), 33–57.

Zahra, S., & Sharma, P. (2004). Family business research: A strategic reflection. *Family Business Review*, *17*(4), 331–46.

7. Family dynamics in the family business

Kirby Rosplock

Introduction

One of the special aspects of the family firm is the unique involvement, influence, and interplay of the family within the business context. The manners in which the family dynamics enhance the family business as an organizational form differentiate it from other mainstream corporations. Family dynamics can be both an enhancement and sometimes a liability to the business. Because the family business is the most prevalent form of business (La Porta, Lopez-de-Silanes, & Shleifer, 1999; Shanker & Astrachan, 1996), the field of study is still relatively young, and better understanding of the role of family dynamics in the business is crucial.

I approach this chapter from the perspective of a family business owner, scholar, and advisor. I was fortunate to be born into a multi-generational family lumber business and am currently a fourth-generation owner. My interest and passion extended beyond the confines of my family's enterprise, and I have been a student of family business studies for over a decade, earning an MBA and a doctorate in organizational systems. I am fortunate to work with and advise a number of family enterprises as the Director of Research and Development in a multi-family office, GenSpring Family Offices. GenSpring is the leading registered investment advisor in the US serving over 700 enterprising and affluent families nationally and internationally. Thus, my perspective is shaped not only by my experiences of growing-up and being part of a large, complex family business, but also as a researcher and advisor to family businesses.

In this chapter, I explore existing studies and research as they relate to family dynamics in the family business, and focus on the optimal family dynamics that enhance the family business. I begin the chapter with a brief look back at the evolution of family business study and discuss some notable characteristics of family business. I then move into a discussion of the body of knowledge surrounding family characteristics, values, and concerns within the family business and those that enhance family dynamics. The discussion then moves to the concepts of family capital, family brand, patient capital, familiness, and why family involved with the business may be a unique advantage in the family business. Finally, I address concerns such as sibling rivalry, nepotism, gender bias, the phenomenon of the "shirtsleeves-to-shirtsleeves" cycle, and how these issues impact the business and become disruptive to family dynamics.

The chapter then moves into a review of the various attributes of conflict and how it impacts the family business. Understanding the root of most conflict in the family business, along with some of the best practices associated with managing conflict, may provide opportunities to build practices and protocols to deal with conflict before it arises. The chapter also addresses the concept of commitment in family business, and explores the notion of satisfaction and how it is manifested in the family business. Commitment and satisfaction are important areas for family business owners to foster in order to build continuity, shared values, and a sense of unity in the family.

Finally, I provide suggestions to practitioners on how to apply some of the research findings and address the opportunities to academics for further research that will help family business owners enhance family dynamics. The chapter closes with a review of some of the key takeaways regarding family dynamics in the family business.

Defining family dynamics and family business

Although some entrepreneurs start a business with no intention of growing it into a family business (Ward & Aronoff, 1990), others have family in mind as an important driver for starting a business. In some instances, this intention is explicit, such as a husband and wife or two siblings wanting to work together; other times, it may be implicit, such as an early founder who encourages family members to participate and take ownership responsibility to carry the business forward to future generations. Regardless of the intent, family dynamics truly differentiate family businesses from non-family businesses in terms of behavior and decision-making.

What do we mean by family dynamics in the family business? What are some of the innate goals of a family enterprise, and how do they differ from mainstream, corporate America? It is the goal of this chapter to explore more deeply what family business researchers have learned; from that knowledge, families and practitioners may benefit in their endeavor to foster generative family dynamics in the business, and researchers may better understand family businesses.

As mentioned in the introduction to this chapter, family dynamics are one of the key factors that differentiate family businesses from non-family businesses. But what *are* family dynamics? I define family dynamics as the complex interplay of family relationships and the strong emotional ties that bind family member to family member and also to the business. Several dependent variables are associated with family dynamics, including commitment, family values and concerns, conflict, satisfaction, and family business characteristics. These variables are more deeply discussed in the framework, the Landscape of Family Business Outcomes, developed by Yu, Lumpkin, Sorenson, and Brigham (2012).* In fact, of the seven clusters identified in their family business framework, Family Dynamics was the second most-studied area.

Family businesses are as old as, if not older than, recorded time. It is likely that a family business was the first form of business, predating recorded history (Colli, 2003). Because family businesses are the most prevalent organizational form, understanding them as a unique area of study is imperative.

Considerable progress has been made by family business researchers to examine,

---

* "A Map of the Landscape of Family Business"(also referred to as the Landscape Map) can be found on the page just inside the cover of this book and in the Yu, Lumpkin, Sorenson, and Brigham (2012) article published in *Family Business Review*. Following the Landscape Map, the Outcome Categories by Chapter Table (also referred to as the Outcomes Categories Table) is provided. This table shows all chapters that contain content about the outcome categories that appear in this chapter.

assess, and identify those characteristics that make family businesses special, unique, and, sometimes, idiosyncratic. Despite these efforts, variations of the definition of family business abound (Astrachan & Shanker, 2003), and the field continues to grapple with a single definition of family business (Astrachan, Klein, & Smyrnios, 2002; Upton, Vinton, Seaman, & Moore, 1993) and how to study the family enterprise in an integrated and holistic fashion (Basco & Rodriquez, 2009). Scholars have noted that without a widely accepted and adopted definition of family business, the field will struggle to advance (Chrisman, Chua, & Sharma, 2003). But why is it so important for researchers to define family business? By defining the "unit of analysis" (a.k.a. family business), researchers are ensuring that the field is uniformly researching the same subject matter. Put more simply, if we aren't comparing apples to apples, then what have we really learned, particularly if what one person calls an apple is to another an orange? In fact, researchers have discovered that, depending on which definition of family business is applied to a given sample, "the sample size can differ in size between 15 and 81 percent" (Westhead & Cowling, 1997, p. 23). As a result, many academicians in the field over the past decade have dedicated significant effort to assessing, defining, and further exploring the unique characteristics of the family firm (Basco & Rodriquez, 2009; Björnberg & Nicholson, 2007; Chittoor & Das, 2007; Chua, Chrisman, & Chang, 2004; Chua, Chrisman, & Sharma, 1999; Denison, Lief, & Ward, 2004; Litz, 1995; Klein, Astrachan, & Smyrnios, 2005; Murphy, 2005; Rutherford, Muse, & Oswald, 2006; Uhlaner, 2005; Westhead & Cowling, 1998; Westhead & Horworth, 2006).

How have those studying the field gone about defining the family firm? There are a number of different features that these investigators have identified that distinguish a business as a family business. They have looked at ownership of the firm by family and the involvement of family members in management roles as criteria that help define a family business (Handler, 1989). Some researchers believe that a family business comes into being if or when there is intent to pass the enterprise on to a successive generation of family (Barach & Ganitsky, 1995; Birley, 1986; Heck & Scannell Trent, 1999; Ward, 1987, 1988), or when a successor is identified (Churchill & Hatten, 1987). Other researchers have looked at family influence as it pertains to power, experience, and culture to help define whether the enterprise is a family business. Klein et al. (2005) defined power in terms of how the family finances the business, structures the ownership, and continues to lead and control the business through management and governance practices. They define experience as the involvement of the family in the business. And they define culture as "the values and commitment exhibited in the business" (Klein et al., 2005). Thus, Klein et al. (2005) specifically include the family influence on the business in their definition.

Chua et al. (1999) proposed a theoretical definition of family business after reviewing some 250 family business papers that mention a definition of the family business. They determined that most family business definitions incorporate three qualifying combinations of ownership and management. Chua et al. (1999) determined that the business is either:

(A) family-owned and family-managed;
(B) family-owned but not family-managed; and
(C) family-managed but not family-owned. (p. 20)

Interestingly, all of the definitions studied by Chua et al. (1999) include qualification (A) as a family business, but not necessarily combinations of qualifications (B) or (C). Specifically, Chua et al. (1999) admit that "once one deviates from the nuclear family-owned and managed business, there is considerable disagreement and ambiguity about which other combination still makes up a family business" (p. 24). However, it is important to note that Chua et al. (1999) recognize the importance of understanding vision and intention when defining the family business. Does the family view itself as a family enterprise? Do they intend to promote and foster being a family enterprise to their constituents, shareholders, clients, and business relationships? How does the family business function as compared to an independently owned and operated business? Chua et al. (1999) posit that understanding a family's vision and intention to operate as a family enterprise may be one of the best ways to define the family business.

In my experience families that overtly define themselves as a family business hold family values dear in their business and have a strong rapport with their employees, customers, and vendors. There is a sense of pride, honor, and integrity in many family businesses that can translate into higher levels of trust and loyalty with their clients, employees, and business affiliations. The purpose of their business is not merely about financial profits. Upholding and conveying core family values is important. Many of these family businesses have earned the respect and admiration of those with whom they have worked; some may ultimately ascend to the "gold standard" in their industries because family values and brand are associated with how they conduct business. Businesses such as S.C. Johnson Wax, Sargento Foods, Tyson Foods, Nordstrom, and Ford Motor Company are just a few family enterprises that exhibit this sense of pride. Because their family names are associated with the business, they exceed conventional expectations or norms, and in certain instances, are willing to "right" wrongs even when they are not at fault. However, not all family businesses value their brand. In some family businesses, family dynamics include derision and humiliation, and can be extremely detrimental, damaging, and disparaging to the family enterprise. I will explore this further in my discussion of family business concerns later in the chapter.

The pride often associated with being a family business owner is exemplified by the following account related at a family business conference. In the account, a family business owner shared a story that exhibited the importance of his family's brand in relation to a quality issue that occurred with a client. The family business was contracted to provide seating for a football stadium. The family business that treated and painted the stadium seating used a batch of paint that turned out to be defective. Only a few months after installation, the pigment in the paint on the new seats faded, and the previously crimson seats bleached to a soft pink color. The owners of the stadium were greatly displeased and complained to the family business owner. Although the family business owner was not legally bound to replace the seating, he did not want his family name and reputation for quality and service to be tarnished by this incident. Realizing that the family brand was in jeopardy, the company did what was "right" and replaced the defective seating at their expense. In this account, the sense of family pride and the family's commitment to the values of integrity, honesty, and fairness, not dollars, guided the firm's actions. This small example is just one incident that supports the research related to reputation and family brand identity. A family's connection to their brand and family identity is just one of the characteristics that may help define a family business.

Why is understanding the characteristics of what constitutes a family business important to business-owning families? The domain of family business study provides the theoretical and empirical constructs to better understand the phenomenon of family enterprise. Once we have an agreed upon a definition of what constitutes a family business, the field has a solid foundation upon which to build further research. In practical terms, business owners will have more substantiating evidence of good and bad practices, opportunities, and threats to aid in the management, development, and approach to their family business strategy.

Family business characteristics, values, and concerns

As mentioned earlier in this chapter, of seven clusters identified by Yu et al. (2012), Family Dynamics was the second most-studied area. This indicates a transition from a proliferation of research on succession and performance to a greater interest in the unique characteristics of family business (Yu, 2009). By better understanding how family businesses are defined, their unique qualities and characteristics, and their values and concerns, researchers hope to discover new insights that may enhance the performance of families who own businesses.

Notable characteristics and values of the family business

In the following, I explore some of the important and notable characteristics of the family business. One of the most-referenced characteristics of the family business as it relates to family dynamics is the intention that the business be sustained for future generations (Aronoff, 2004; Beckhard & Dyer Jr., 1983; Gersick, Davis, McCollom Hampton, & Lansberg, 1997; Habbershon & Pistrui, 2002; Hughes Jr., 2007; Jaffe & Lane, 2004; Lansberg, 1999; Sorenson, 2000; Ward, 1987). This long-term, multi-generational perspective relates to a unique and important characteristic of the family business – that of family capital. Hoffman, Hoelscher, and Sorenson (2006) relate many of the strategic advantages and unique attributes of the family business to the concept of family capital. More specifically, they describe family capital as "limited to information channels among family members. The relational component is a distinguishing characteristic in family capital and includes obligations and expectations, reputation, identity and moral infrastructure" (Hoffman, Hoelscher, & Sorenson, 2006, p. 137). Thus, the dominant family group has significant influence on how the business is operated, owned, managed, and directed, which is unique and materially different than a non-family-owned firm. That influence can be a disadvantage or liability when family relationships are not valued or properly fostered, and as a result, can create dysfunction or conflict in the family business. When family capital is *not* managed, the dynamics of the family can turn sour and hinder performance and company culture, which can lead to loss of employees and/or clients.

Stafford, Duncan, Danes, and Winter (1999) define the concept of family capital somewhat differently. In their view, family capital is the stock and flow of the combined resources shared by the family business, including its human, financial, and social capital (Stafford et al., 1999). Danes, Lee, Stafford, and Heck (2008) have advanced the concept of sustainability in their Sustainable Family Business Theory (SFBT-I & SFBT-II), which posits that a firm's sustainability is a function of the integration of the firm's success, the family's functioning, and the method of utilizing resources across each of these interlocking systems. Other studies empirically tested SFBT-I and SFBT-II, first with cross-sectional data and then with longitudinal data (Danes, Stafford, Haynes, & Amarapurkar, 2009; Olson, Zuiker, Danes, Stafford, Heck, & Duncan, 2003). Although these studies provided initial insight into family capital, researchers have yet to settle on a precise definition of family capital, and further empirical studies are required (Danes et al., 2009).

Other practitioners in the field have looked at family capital as comprising intellectual capital in addition to human and financial capital (Collier, 2002; Hughes, 2004). Hughes defines human capital within the family as who you are and what you can contribute to the family, and intellectual capital as what you know. It is important to understand that family capital and its associated subset of capitals is an important characteristic that differentiates how the family business is managed. The family's values, their emphasis on developing human and intellectual capital, and the deployment of it in the enterprise can provide family capital. What we know of multi-generational families who employ a long-term perspective and embrace their family capital is that they are more likely to have greater ability to weather "storms" (i.e., family conflict, environmental challenges, and competition) because their focus looks beyond the short-term toward the impact of the enterprise on and for future generations. This characteristic – patient capital – is unique, and to some, idiosyncratic, to family business.

Families who understand and appreciate their patient capital are better equipped to endure and persevere during the difficult times that inevitably arise in the business world. This ability to adapt in a sometimes adversarial environment helps achieve the longer-term outcome (de Visscher, Aronoff, & Ward, 1995; Gersick et al., 1997; Poza, Hanlon, & Kishida, 2004; Ward, 1997). Furthermore, these family businesses generally operate on a longer-term horizon because their shareholders – primarily family members – have a cross-generational perspective which contrasts with, for example, a publicly traded company that must answer daily to its shareholders. Patient capital creates continuity and a bridge between generations of family owners as the firm evolves, and it can temper expectations, particularly in times of duress.

The family brand and identity, as mentioned earlier, are often cited as yet other unique characteristics of a family business (Tagiuri & Davis, 1996; Zellweger, Eddleston, & Kellermanns, 2010). For some family businesses, the family brand is the family's identity. For others, families may identify themselves as family businesses, but have no family brand associated with their businesses. To those who identify their business as a family business and have a strong sense of family brand, this deep connection to the family business image is what Ward (1987) described as creating a shared identity. Through a greater understanding and expression of the family's values one generation can link itself to the next by sharing the family's business history, core values, and milestone stories of the family founders. The core values of the family enterprise are embedded in these stories. Hughes (2007) discusses how a family may evolve into a "family of affinity," tied together not just by bloodlines, but by the shared values, personal history, and desire to remain a working unit. From perseverance and risk-taking to hard work and caring for the family and the family business employees, much of the family's core values are tied to those of the founder and the business. The founder's values can have a profound effect on the culture and community established in the family business (Dyer Jr., 1986; García-Álvarez & López-Sintas, 2001; Schein, 1983).

The family brand, shared identity, and culmination of values associated with the firm are contributing factors that can lead to positive family dynamics. A family's mission statement or vision statement often illustrate their shared values, identity, and brand. Researchers have linked these three characteristics to social responsibility in the family business. Dyer Jr. and Whetten (2006) explore the concept of social responsibility in the family enterprise in a preliminary study that looks at the degree of social responsibility in family and non-family firms. By comparing the social performance of family and non-family firms from the S&P 500 over a ten-year period, they learned that family firms are typically more socially responsible on a number of fronts related to image, reputation, and intention to preserve the family's shared assets. Similarly, Niehm, Swinney, and Miller (2008) studied community social responsibility in relationship to the family business; they learned that commitment to the community explained much of the perceived family business performance and that community support explained financial performance. This may indicate that socially responsible businesses are good not only for the communities in which they reside, but also for the long-term viability and sustainability of the business in small rural communities. Future studies on social responsibility may look at its relationship to frameworks such as SFBT, among others. There are also ideal opportunities to look at the role of social, ethical, and cultural differences of family businesses and the impact on social responsibility within communities.

Another important characteristic associated with the family business is that of familiness. First introduced in 2002 by Habbershon and Williams as the "idiosyncratic firm level bundle of resources and capabilities resulting from the systems' interactions" (as cited in Habbershon, Williams, & MacMillan, 2003, p. 451), familiness is further defined by Habbershon et al. (2003) as the unique synergy created by the interactions among family and the business. It is important to note that this synergy can be either a positive or negative force in and on the family business (Björnberg & Nicholson, 2007; Habbershon et al., 2003). Following Chua et al. (1999), Habbershon et al. (2003) maintain that one of the unique characteristics of familiness is how the family intention is set in order to collectively pursue a vision that spans multiple generations. Another definition of familiness refers to the "resources and capabilities related to family involvement and interactions" (Chrisman, Chua, & Litz, 2003, p. 468). Each of these definitions of familiness explains it as a positive attribute that is a generative, cohesive influence of the family on the business.

Historically, academics such as Alfred Chandler (1977) and Max Weber (1947) called for managerial capitalism in the family business, whereby managers with little or no equity were responsible for running the business with owners acting as financiers and/ or investors (Chandler, 1990). Since then researchers have found that the interface of the business and the family is actually a strategic advantage that allows family businesses to outperform their non-family corporate counterparts (Anderson, Mansi, & Reeb, 2003; Miller & Le Breton-Miller, 2006; Villalonga & Amit, 2006). The family business is able to create a unique family culture (Denison, Lief & Ward, 2004) that has its own individual strengths and values (Aronoff, 2004; Denison et al., 2004). Researchers have found that the family business culture is distinctly different from non-family firms and is performance-enhancing (Aronoff, 2004; Denison et al., 2004). Understanding the implications of family business culture on performance is another area ripe for further study. In general, the concepts of familiness, family capital, patient capital, family brand, and family identity are relatively newer concepts within the family business literature. Opportunities abound to empirically test constructs and hypotheses around these newer areas of study, particularly as they relate to practice. For example, how do families with businesses foster and exhibit family capital or familiness in their family business? What are the distinguishing characteristics of patient capital of a multi-generational family enterprise? Does family brand and family identity foster a positive working culture and, if so, how? These are just a few questions that, if answered, would demonstrate and illuminate the actual practice of these concepts.

Family business concerns

Along with positive values, concerns, and negative family dynamics associated with family business also abound. Frequently cited concerns focus on relational family dysfunction (Kellermanns & Eddleston, 2006), and the study of relationships in the family firm is extensive (Danes, Leichtentritt, Metz, & Huddleston-Casas, 2000; Danes, Stafford & Loy, 2007; Klein, 2008; Marshack, 1994; Milton, 2008; Sciascia & Mazzola, 2008; Wang, 2005; Werbel & Danes, 2010). Particularly, relationships in leadership and ownership succession are a primary area of family business research (Cater & Justis, 2010; Chua, Chrisman, & Sharma, 2003; Lee, 2006). In certain cases, when nepotism occurs, succession is viewed as a family business concern.

Nepotism, or the favoritism of a family member in a family enterprise, is one of the most frequently discussed phenomena of family business practitioners and researchers. In these instances, the successive generation feels entitled to ownership, control, inheritance, leadership role, or other special privileges associated with the family business without actually earning them. Frequently associated with nepotism is the challenge of professionalizing a family leader and preparing them for succession. Some successors are open and willing to be mentored, guided, and educated; those associated with nepotism, however, may be uninterested in doing the work to earn the job and rely instead on their family laurels and their perceived birthright. This can create tension in the workplace, particularly with key non-family employees and managers who may become frustrated, disincentivized, or disenchanted in the face of nepotism.

The process of leadership succession in general is an area of concern for many family businesses (Winter, Danes, Koh, Fredricks, & Paul, 2003). It is also a significant focal point in family business research because a family firm that does not successfully manage its leadership succession can create a significant negative financial impact on the business (Chua et al., 2003). Gersick et al. (1997) discuss the shirtsleeves-to-shirtsleeves cycle, whereby one generation of family creates the wealth vis-à-vis the family business and the second generation spends down the wealth or mismanages the business, leaving the third generation to start a new enterprise or go back to work, rolling up their proverbial shirtsleeves to rebuild the wealth. Hughes (2004) notes that this phenomenon is universal; it extends across cultures. In certain instances, the shirtsleeves-to-shirtsleeves cycle may be impacted by the need to "prune" the family tree (Lambrecht & Lievens, 2008). Lambrecht and Lievens learned from their study that simplifying the ownership, governance, and/or management structures in a family enterprise by eliminating nonproductive, non-contributing, or disenfranchised family member owners can enhance the family harmony and continuity. Unfortunately, research into the impact of pruning the family tree or consolidating family business ownership has not been widely studied and is opportune for further inquiry. Lambrecht and Lievens (2008) refute the previously held assumption that buying out family shareholders is too expensive; however, it continues to be a phenomenon that rarely occurs. In fact, the opportunity cost of not removing certain discontented family owners as early as possible may increase the longer they remain in the business.

In other situations, the shirtsleeves-to-shirtsleeves phenomenon is more widespread when a family fails to embrace a stewardship ethos. Instead, the momentum in the family enterprise stagnates and can become parochial and riddled with conflict that is subject to conservatism, cronyism, and constrained resources (Miller, Le Breton-Miller, & Scholnick, 2008). In a study of small, Canadian family- and non-family-run firms, Miller et al. (2008) discovered that family enterprises desired longevity and continuity, tended to embrace stewardship principles, and leveraged the family business whereby they fostered corporate longevity and favorable relationships with shareholders. Miller et al. (2008) uncovered far more support for the stewardship principle than the stagnation theory, which may also align with findings regarding family firms outperforming non-family firms (Anderson et al., 2003). Thus, the concerns of family business owners – particularly around continuity and longevity, and the perils of leadership and ownership succession – are valid.

Other concerns uniquely associated with multi-generational firms arise when multiple family members or siblings become rivals in the family business. Sibling rivalry is a phenomenon that typically results beyond or within the second generation. In many cases, a major concern to the incoming family leader is the controlling matriarch or patriarch who struggles with stepping down from the proverbial family business throne. With the increase in life expectancy and the delay of baby boomers in taking their retirement, there has been a slow-down in initiating succession planning. Founders staying in the business longer than expected significantly impact succession planning, and consequently it has become an important topic of research.

Frequently connected to controlling patriarchs and matriarchs is the "leadership divide." This dilemma arises because the successor is often undermined and/or disempowered when the elder generation remains in the forefront or in the shadows maintaining the controlling interests of the business. Thus, an area of concern with many first-generation family owners is whether the business will, in fact, succeed beyond the first generation (Danco, 1975; Poza, 1989; Ward, 1987). Anecdotally, practitioners and family business advisors have experienced situations where owners who do not broach the topic of succession, thus putting their family firms at risk due to poor leadership preparation, planning, and implementation (Handler & Kram, 1988; Lansberg, 1988; Leon-Guerrero, McCann III, & Haley Jr., 1988). Mazzola, Marchisio, and Astrachan (2008) examined the role that strategic planning may play in providing critical tools to bridge generations and professionally develop family members. Mazzola et al. (2008) find compelling evidence that strategic planning, when done well, can foster the development and buy-in of the next generation, create opportunities to build knowledge about the business, and cultivate relationships with next-generation members, thus developing family business continuity. A family's characteristics, values, and concerns are at the heart of the family business; in order for family businesses to thrive, unraveling these related issues and challenges and studying the "positive deviants" – those positive outliers that demonstrate success – are essential to understanding and appreciating family businesses that navigate and master these challenges to build generative family enterprises (Whitney & Trosten-Bloom, 2010).

From the review of dependent variables associated with family business characteristics, values, and concerns, we can begin to understand and appreciate why researchers are intrigued by the truly unique and differentiating characteristics of the family business that may provide strategic advantages and enhance performance (Anderson et al., 2003). For the field of family business scholars and practitioners, this opportunity to modernize the lexicon of family business terms to expand these characteristics is also a challenge. In an attempt to meet this challenge, researchers have created and named unique family business concepts such as family capital, patient capital, family brand, and familiness to begin to formally recognize and study the family dynamic that is inherent in the family firm, thus developing a whole new confluence of opportunity.

Beyond the research contributions, identifying family business values, characteristics, and concerns can directly benefit family business owners and their family enterprises. From the research, family business owners may consider the benefits of assessing how family capital is developed and/or supported in their family enterprise. They may choose to explore how the values of the family impress upon the values of the company. Family business owners may also find it helpful to understand how they identify as a family business as compared to what researchers have learned about what constitutes a family business. Even these basic steps may provide greater clarity of intention and continuity – is the family enterprise one that the owner hopes future family members will want to foster and pass on? Just as there are very positive attributes, the pitfalls and concerns identified in the family business research provide markers of what family business owners may want to avoid. From nepotism and poor succession planning, to sibling rivalry and family outlaws – family members who are married into the family, however not readily accepted and/or integrated, the research illuminates how detrimental many of the family business concerns can be on the long-term success and viability of the business. By putting off or failing to address these concerns, the family business owner is merely passing along the issues for future generations to confront; at worst, avoidance may lead to the demise of the business. It is my hope that the research will inspire family business owners to raise a mirror, and determine what positive and negative characteristics and dynamics are embodied in their own family enterprise.

Conflict in the family business

Conflict in the family business threatens cohesion and the ability of the family to build a foundation for continuity and productive family dynamics in the family enterprise. Consequently, some experts in the field have identified family business conflict as one of the fastest-growing areas of concern for the family business; thus, the need for additional research in this vein is strong (Cosier & Harvey, 1998; Sharma, 2004; Ward & Aronoff, 1994). A review of the existing scholarly literature, however, shows a lack of information in how conflict occurs, the degree to which it impacts the family and business success, and potential opportunities to mitigate conflict before it arises.

Conflict in the family enterprise has various connotations and meanings. To date, most family business conflict research focuses on substantive conflict, identified as conflict stemming from differing ideas and/or means of completing a task (Guetzkow & Gyr, 1954; Ross, 1985; Simons & Peterson, 2000; Wall & Nolan, 1986). Researchers have also studied affective conflict, a product of interpersonal or relationship strife. This type of conflict is characterized as more emotional, arousing negative feelings such as anger, rage, distrust, anxiety, jealousy, or other negative sentiments.

Davis and Harveston (1998) deeply explored issues of substantive conflict in the family business from a cross-generational perspective. Specifically, they looked at substantive conflict as it pertains to, 1) ownership continuity or change, 2) leadership succession, 3) power and asset distribution, and 4) management's vision of the family business in the community. Interestingly, Davis and Harveston (1998) concluded that family members who are not directly employed or working in the day-to-day affairs of the business may act as "peace makers" and reduce the frequency and extent of conflict among family members in the business. Davis and Harveston (1998) also found an increased incidence of conflict when increased numbers of family members work day-to-day in the business. And surprisingly, Davis and Harveston (1998) also found that increased socialization among family members correlated with an increase in family conflict. However, the researchers qualified this finding by noting that perhaps the increase in communication and interaction made the conflict more identifiable; nonetheless, an increase was noted. Finally, the study also found that the frequency and extent of substantive conflict increases with the number of generations at play. Thus, family business owners may note that as more family members become involved with the family enterprise, the likelihood for conflict increases. This should signal families to establish a conflict resolution policy and explicit governance practices to mitigate conflict before it happens.

Eddleston, Otondo, and Kellermanns (2008) found that multi-generational ownership in family firms is significantly related to the perceptions of conflict and participative decision-making. Specifically, they found that participative decision-making was linked to cognitive and relationship conflict. They deduced that when ownership is shared over three or more generations, participative decision-making is positively related to cognitive and relationship conflict; however, in one- and two-generation ownership firms, participative decision-making is negatively related to cognitive and relationship conflict (Eddleston et al., 2008). Their findings seem to support the idea that family and business health and success tend to move in parallel – a thriving family can lead to a thriving business and vice versa (Olson et al., 2003). Conflict as it relates to gender and affective conflict is also an area of interest in the field. One study looked at women's roles in the family business, and their implications for conflict and tension (Danes & Olson, 2003). Danes and Olson (2003) applied a model that looks at interpersonal relationships to understand the impact of a wife's involvement in the family business in which the husband is the primary business manager. Specifically, they sought to understand the business tensions surrounding the wife's involvement and to assess the impact of those tensions on the success of the business. The results showed that tension increased in five out of the six tension types when the wife works in the day-to-day business compared with wives who do not work daily in the business (Danes & Olson, 2003). Thus, husbands and wives working together in the business appear to generate a unique subset of conflict in the family business. Defining roles, responsibilities, and power in the both the family system and business system may help to mitigate conflict.

Another study looks into the challenges that women, and specifically daughters, face during the family business succession process (Vera & Dean, 2005). The literature reveals that women have struggled to be recognized as "viable successors" and are often passed over due to primogenitor or "age asynchrony" (Vera & Dean, 2005, p. 326). The researchers learned that there can be a preferred age for male successors (father to son) that differs from females (father to daughter) which is defined as age asynchrony. Thus, researchers ascertain that gender does have implications in terms of the smoothness of the succession process. Sibling-daughter rivalry, gender discrimination, primogenitor, and work-family balance challenges are just some of the contagions that can lead to conflict with daughters as successors.

Conflicts arising from relationships in family businesses are often moderated by the amount of altruism among family members (Kellermanns & Eddleston, 2004). Thus, if the family displays a high level of commitment, shared values, and altruistic behavior toward one another, it achieves higher levels of cohesion. This cohesion, in turn, grounds the family and may help mitigate conflict. However, too much emotional cohesion can lead the family system to become enmeshed and rigid (Beavers & Voeller, 1983; Nicholson, 2003).

Conflict may also be generated as a result of poor communication, resistance to change, and a dominant authority figure. Björnberg and Nicholson (2007) developed the Family Climate Scales to understand open communication, adaptability, intergenerational authority, intergenerational attention to needs, emotional cohesion, and cognitive cohesion. They discovered that there is a negative correlation in terms of open communication and adaptability in families with high levels of intergenerational authority – the amount of freedom or constraint perceived in the working relationships from one generation to the next. In other words, when there is a strong, controlling, dominant patriarchal or matriarchal figure, the family can struggle to communicate and change or adapt, which can lay the groundwork for family conflict. Differentiating between emotional and cognitive cohesion, Björnberg and Nicholson (2007) learned that "ruptures or conflicts in the family system may stem from an absence of shared values and ideas, rather than from a lack of positive emotional bonds" (p. 240). Their study echoes the importance of building the family capital and shared values as a way to reduce affective conflict.

Closely linked to conflict is the notion of justice in the family business. Lansberg (1999) identifies three forms of justice in the family firm. The first is *distributive* justice, where the allocation of resources and hardship is shared among stakeholders. Second is the notion of *procedural* justice, which Lansberg (1999) relates to identifying *who* is involved in the decision-making. Finally, Lansberg (1999) notes *retributive* justice, which focuses on the penalty that family members who violate family rules must pay (literally and/or figuratively). Van der Heyden, Blondel, and Carlock (2005) looked at distributive justice as a means to reduce conflict in the family business. Van der Heyden et al. (2005) assess fair process through five mini-cases that highlight the five tenets they deduce as key to fair process: 1) communication and voice; 2) clarity of information, process, and expectations; 3) consistency across people, over time, and with agreed values and norms; 4) changeability of decisions, processes, goals, and principles; and 5) commitment to fairness. In summary, Van der Heyden et al. (2005) identify that families who exercise fair process are building a platform for the family's development and ongoing survival. Giving a voice to shareholders, positively reinforcing a cycle of fair process, and making the time and commitment to follow and sometimes clarify the "family firm law" provide the basis for strong family governance (Van der Heyden et al., 2005, p. 20). As discussed in the Chapter 2 of this book, many family dynamics are enhanced with strong governance practices.

Staving off conflict and achieving a high degree of family harmony and cohesion across generations are goals of most family enterprises. The intention to create harmony within a family business is one thing, but achieving this outcome is something else entirely. Researchers have found that family harmony plays an important role in the future success of the enterprise and can make the difference in a firm's overall performance (Chrisman et al., 2003; DeNoble, Ehrlich, & Singh, 2007; Dyer Jr., 2006). One important note about the findings is that the researchers all recognize that, in terms of agency attributes, the owner must also be the manager and the business must be based upon a solid governance platform. Neubauer and Lank (1998) also discuss the importance of family harmony in assessing good governance.

A 2008 study on South African-Greek family businesses explored factors such as family harmony, trust, family commitment, family communication, and profitability and how they impacted governance. What the researchers found is that "although *Family Harmony* did not influence *Perceived Good Governance*, it did so through *Profitability* and *Family Commitment and Communication*" (Adendorff, Venter, & Boshoff, 2008, p. 40). In other words, the researchers learned that when the business is profitable, it also contributes to better communication and a sense of commitment by the family members. This insight is not shocking, for when businesses are doing well shareholders are typically satisfied and conflict may be less prevalent.

Ensley and Pearson (2003) discussed cohesion in the context of the behavioral dynamics of top management teams in family and non-family business. One unanticipated finding was that non-family top management teams actually managed their behavior dynamics much better than the familial teams. Non-family top management teams exhibit higher levels of cohesion, shared strategic consensus, and less incidence of relationship conflict (Ensley & Pearson, 2003). Instead, the family teams proved to have the highest amount of relational conflict, which the researchers deduced resulted from the social and structural context of family (Amason & Sapienza, 1997). Sorenson (1999) researched unique types of conflict that arise in the family business by looking at the correlations among conflict management strategies, business outcomes, and family outcomes. He learned that the family businesses that more often reported positive outcomes also indicated higher levels of collaboration. Thus, collaboration is an effective conflict mediation strategy in the family business (Sorenson, 1999). In addition to increased collaboration, empirical research shows that there is a connection between strong governance and the prospering of the family firm over the long term (Aronoff, 1998; Astrachan & Aronoff, 1998; Astrachan & Kolenko, 1994). Family governance may also reduce the incidence of family conflict, particularly substantive conflict, if there are explicit family rules and norms governing the family.

Thus, conflict may arise as substantive or affective in the family business and can challenge the viability of successful family dynamics. The range of conflict research indicates an interest to explore it on a multitude of levels. This is good news for family business owners, as the research provides insights about the importance of mitigating conflict through strong governance and goal alignment, for example, and how enhanced communication and information sharing can foster a culture of sharing and inclusivity. By building stronger relationships among family members and non-family members in the business and taking a collaborative approach to conflict, family enterprise can mitigate much of the relationship conflict. By identifying shared values to build continuity among different generations of family, they may be able to enhance the continuity and strength to the family business ties that bind. Understanding conflict in the realm of the family business helps identify contagions for conflict and provides pathways to mitigate it. Further emphasis to understand conflict particularly as it relates to leadership styles, management practices, governance, and family ownership is important to the field of family business study.

Commitment and satisfaction in the family business

I have shared the importance of understanding how to mitigate conflict in the family enterprise in order to build continuity and cohesion in the family enterprise, but it is equally pertinent to understand commitment and satisfaction in the family business context. Both commitment and satisfaction are key attributes that have direct implications on successful family dynamics. Commitment refers to the dedication and loyalty that a family member or employee in a family company might have to the business. Satisfaction refers to the level of fulfillment, happiness, or contentment that an individual might have for his or her employment, involvement, or possible ownership of the family business. Although the two concepts are commonly linked, they have very different connotations depending on the context and/or application of study. For example, commitment is most frequently studied from a one-dimensional perspective; however, it may also be viewed multi-dimensionally. Sharma and Irving (2005) explored commitment of family business successors identifying four types of commitment – affective, normative, calculative, and imperative. In their study, Sharma and Irving (2005) defined each of these lenses, or bases, as follows:

> *Affective commitment* is based on a strong belief in and acceptance of the organization's goals combined with a desire to contribute to these goals, and the confidence in one's ability to do so. In essence, the successor "*wants to*" pursue such a career.
>
> *Normative commitment* is based on feelings of obligation to pursue a career in the family business. By pursuing a career with the family firm, the successor attempts to foster and maintain good relationships with the senior generation. In short, successors with high levels of normative commitment feel that they "*ought to*" pursue such a career.
>
> *Calculative commitment* is based on successors' perceptions of substantial opportunity costs and threatened loss of investments or value if they do not pursue a career in the family business. Successors with high levels of calculative commitment feel they "*have to*" pursue such a career.
>
> *Imperative commitment* is based on a feeling of self-doubt and uncertainty of the ability to successfully pursue a career outside the family business. Individuals with high levels of imperative commitment perceive that they lack alternative to a career in the family business. The underlying mind-set in this case is a "*need to*" pursue a career. (p. 19)

Through a series of short cases, Sharma and Irving (2005) illustrate how these different types of commitment in successors may lead to different motivations for family members to enter the business. Understanding the underlying antecedents of successor commitment may reveal more about the successor's value set, time horizon, and fulfillment in the family business.

Pieper, Klein, and Jaskiewicz (2008) explore a related category of commitment: goal alignment of family owners with the existence of a board of directors and top management team. They found that firms that reported high levels of goal alignment between owners and the management team were less likely to have a board, which indicates that families substituted a formal decision-making structure for one that was driven by social norms. In firms that had low goal alignment and the presence of a board, they determined there were often fewer family members in the top management team. Thus, as related to commitment, lack of goal alignment may indicate a lower level of ownership commitment by family members, evidenced by the limited presence of family owners in top management.

In addition to understanding what drives commitment by a successor and the impact of goal alignment, researchers have explored how satisfaction impacts the succession process. In their 2003 study, Sharma, Chrisman, and Chua explored the predictors of satisfaction with family business succession in the family firm and discovered that there are two primary dimensions – satisfaction as it relates to the process, and the performance of the company following succession. They learned that perceptions vary widely between the incumbent and the successor in the context of the succession process. One finding of particular interest is that succession planning coupled with agreed-upon defined roles increased satisfaction by both incumbents and successors. Incumbents' satisfaction increases when they perceive that successors are willing to take on the leadership role; however, successors indicate that the incumbent's reticence to step aside strongly affects their satisfaction and desire to take over. Thus, Sharma et al. (2003) uncovered the misalignment that can occur between incumbents and successors in the succession process, and the great need for heartfelt, open communication between incumbent and successor on the entire succession process.

Several studies explore commitment as one facet in the relationship to family business (Lee & Maurer, 1999; Sorenson, 2000; Van der Heyden et al., 2005). Sorenson's (2000) study examines Dyer's (1986) study on family business cultures and derives five approaches to leadership that provide insight on the implications of satisfaction and commitment in the family business culture. Specifically, Sorenson (2000) looks at participative, autocratic, laissez-faire, expert, and referent styles of leadership and their impact on employee satisfaction and commitment. A noteworthy finding was that participative leadership, or a leadership style that promotes inclusivity of its members, promotes change and fosters commitment in small family businesses (Sorenson, 2000). This echoes a commonly accepted premise in the leadership literature that involvement of members results in commitment of those members to the organization (Bass, 1990). As well, Sorenson (2000) finds that laissez-faire leadership coupled with a strong sense of mission creates an environment of greater employee commitment and satisfaction. In other words, family owners who empower their employees to work autonomously toward strategic goals based on shared values and a strategic mission exhibit higher levels of commitment and fulfillment with their work. A further understanding of the drivers of satisfaction, leadership, succession, family ownership, and culture as they relate to commitment in the family business is a prime area for further study.

Commitment and satisfaction are two integral factors for the sustainability of a family enterprise. If a family as a whole and as a collection of individuals is not committed to and/or satisfied with the existence of the family enterprise, its longevity is at risk. Further exploration of the commitment and satisfaction of non-employed family members who are owners in the family enterprise is a valid research pursuit and may provide insights into the need to cull the proverbial family tree. Both commitment and satisfaction are broad and multi-faceted. From employee satisfaction to customer satisfaction, there are ample opportunities to expand the inquiry into these critical aspects of family business.

Applications of family dynamics for practitioners

In reflecting over the most salient takeaways for practitioners from family business research, it cannot be overstated that family dynamics are a cornerstone and a distinguishing aspect of most family enterprise. As researchers endeavor to define the characteristics of family business, certain criteria surface in importance, such as do the family members define and identify themselves as a family business? And if so, what is their strategic vision as a family business (Chua et al., 1999)? Further, how does the family influence the family enterprise in terms of ownership, involvement, management, and control (Klein et al., 2005)? When families understand what makes them a family business, they also begin to crystallize what motivates and inspires them to behave and function as a family firm. This exploration may lead a family to consider the positive and negative attributes of family dynamics in their family enterprise and which attributes will most contribute to building continuity from one generation to the next.

What does the family business conflict literature tell practitioners? First, when family businesses are in harmony and doing well financially, there is less conflict and more satisfied family members (Adendorff et al., 2008; Chrisman et al., 2003; DeNoble et al., 2007; Dyer, 2006; Sorenson, 1999). Second, family business conflict research supports the importance of families fostering positive relationships among family members to build cohesion and to encourage participatory decision-making and governance practices as mechanisms to reduce conflict (Adendorff et al., 2008; Björnberg & Nicholson, 2007; Eddleston et al., 2008; Ensley & Pearson, 2003; Kellermanns & Eddleston, 2004; Olson et al., 2003; Sorenson, 1999). Third, there is a link between family and conflict in the family business; however, the influence of family members *not* involved in the business, such as in the third or later generations, was found to reduce conflict (Davis & Harveston, 1998). In conclusion, the conflict literature reaffirms that by establishing shared values, enhanced communication, good governance, and conflict resolutions strategies, families can also positively reinforce commitment and satisfaction in the family business and thus mitigate conflict.

The family business research related to commitment and satisfaction is more limited in scope and is an area ripe for further research. Despite the limited research, there are a number of key takeaways from the studies that explore commitment as one facet in the relationship to family business (Lee & Maurer, 1999; Sorenson, 2000; Van der Heyden et al., 2005). First, family business owners may want to understand the different forms of commitment – affective, normative, calculative, and imperative – experienced by successors that drive their motivation to be engaged in the family enterprise (Sharma & Irving, 2005). Understanding what motivates a family member to come into the family business may provide insights to what will fuel their commitment.

Second, the satisfaction and commitment research provides insight into the importance of defining roles for family leadership and a process to effectively transition a successor into a leadership post. With an effective strategy for the period of succession, families may greatly enhance satisfaction and commitment for both the incumbent and successor (Sharma et al., 2003). Therefore, it is important for family business owners to define agreed-upon roles and clarify the succession steps to transition.

Third, family business owners may want to examine their family business's culture and explore how they might empower their employees to work autonomously toward strategic goals that coincide with their mission. Research indicates that family business employees have higher levels of commitment toward and fulfillment by their work in mission-focused family businesses (Sorenson, 2000). Families who focus on engendering commitment and satisfaction of family and non-family employees and owners may be better equipped to stave off conflict and foster strong family business bonds.

Although practitioners will often be challenged to resolve the conflicts and problems that arise from unproductive family dynamics, shifting the paradigm to help focus the family on what *is* working and what will enhance more generative family dynamics will help the family progress in this direction. For example, applying the theory of Appreciative Inquiry (AI) and positive psychology may be helpful. Cooperrider and Whitney (2007) founded the concept and define AI as:

> The cooperative search for the best in people, their organizations, and the world around them. It involves systematic discovery of what gives a system "life" when it is most effective and capable in economic, ecological, and human terms. AI involves the art and practice of asking questions that strengthen a system's capacity to heighten positive potential. It mobilizes inquiry through crafting an "unconditional positive question" often involving hundreds or sometimes thousands of people. (p. 245)

The Poetic Principle of AI posits that we move in the direction of what we research and study (Whitney & Trosten-Bloom, 2010). In other words, the more we learn about a topic, the more likely we are to pursue a path that engages and employs these different topical areas. For example, when one is passionate about an area, one is more likely to study it and consider how one personally relates to the topic, and as a result, one engages in the topic more fully.

Practitioners may find this a meaningful and effective tool to help families to focus on the type of positive dynamics they desire to manifest in the family business. For example, practitioners may find that simply bringing awareness to the source of angst or concern on the part of one family member and helping the individual to frame in a way that is generative and focused on the change he or she desires to see as opposed to what is not occurring can help bridge the differences. Similarly, the more family business owners are open to learning about family dynamics, for example, the greater the possibility they may want to reflect on and address family dynamics in their own family firm domain. There is tremendous opportunity and power in generative family dynamics that, when harnessed effectively by a family enterprise, can enhance the family's ability to sustain the business long term.

Opportunities for future family dynamics research

When reviewing the characteristics of family enterprise and the opportunities for further study, the research exposes prominent drivers unique to family dynamics in the business. First, most family enterprise owners wish to sustain the enterprise for future family generations and embrace stewardship (Aronoff, 2004; Beckhard & Dyer, 1983; Gersick et al., 1997; Habbershon & Pistrui, 2002; Hughes, 2007; Jaffe & Lane, 2004; Lansberg, 1999; Sorenson, 2000; Ward, 1987). Second, experts and researchers have come to appreciate the positive, generative influence of family in the family enterprise in a number of different forms: family capital (Hoffman et al., 2006; Stafford et al., 1999); patient capital(de Visscher et al., 1995; Gersick, 1997; Ward, 1997); family brand (Poza et al., 2004; Taguiri & Davis, 1996); and familiness (Chua et al., 2003; Zellweger et al., 2010), among others. Third, the broadening of the proverbial lexicon to include these new terms helps to clarify the role of family in the family business and differentiate various forms of capital. These positive characteristics help drive success in sustaining the family enterprise and overcoming the shirt-sleeves to shirt-sleeves cycle (Miller et al., 2008).

As the field of family business study continues to evolve, there are many opportunities to expand the body of knowledge. When we consider the focus of family dynamics as they relate to satisfaction, conflict, commitment, family business characteristics, and family business values and concerns, we are really looking to understand what leads to preferred and desired family dynamics and family outcomes. With this premise in mind, studying positive family dynamics may be important for family business researchers to consider.

A considerable amount of the family business research focuses on the negative characteristics associated with poor family dynamics. These negative characteristics include nepotism, sibling rivalry, strained leadership succession, poor communication and/or conflict, among others. When families are pre-emptive and anticipatory, they may be better able to address these concerns before they negatively impact the family business (Cater & Justis, 2010; Chua et al., 2003; Lee, 2006). Because conflict is one of the fastest-growing areas of family business research (Cosier & Harvey, 1998; Ward & Aronoff, 1994), the practical insights researchers can bring to the nature of substantive conflict – conflict related to a difference of ideas or how tasks are performed, compared to affective conflict – conflict based on relationships – would be very helpful to family business owners. Simply being able to understand the root nature of conflict in their family can make the difference in properly addressing the issues.

With the framework of AI in mind, which was mentioned above, researchers in the field of family business may want to consider placing greater emphasis on studying those family businesses that are the "positive outliers" (Gladwell, 2008) that have beaten the shirtsleeves-to-shirtsleeves odds and sustained their enterprises across multiple generations (Gersick et al. 1997). What are the overarching shared values of those family businesses that thrive for multiple generations? How have they handled family conflict and still maintained cohesion? How has commitment fostered continuity and unity within the family? What does satisfaction in the family business look like from one generation to the next and is it similar to that of non-family employees/stakeholders? How do families successfully create family norms and rules that encourage participation, inclusivity, and wholeness? How do families capitalize on their family capital? These are just a few questions that may aid family business owners as they endeavor towards successful family dynamics.

At the end of the day, the research of family dynamics in family business is only as useful and helpful as it translates to practitioners and their families. Practitioners need more case studies that model positive family dynamics and provide guide posts for other family businesses to emulate. Thus, researchers might develop cases of exemplar family businesses to provide broader learning and knowledge to family business owners and practitioners. Researchers could amplify and build upon these positive case studies and more deeply explore the tacit family dynamics and relationship that create growth, opportunity, and harmony within the family business.

Conclusion

The reality of a truly successful family enterprise is not measured by one singular event or outcome. Rather, it is the positive family dynamics and connections among family members that span years, decades, and even generations of family owners, shareholders, employees, and managers. How families manifest their shared values, communicate, foster commitment, drive satisfaction, mitigate conflict, self-govern, and craft conflict resolutions strategies, will undoubtedly fortify their family capital. Studying the positive outliers to better understand the underlying characteristics of these successful family businesses may enhance business owners' knowledge and provide them with the insights to overcome the shirt-sleeves to shirt-sleeves cycle.

References

Adendorff, C., Venter, E., & Boshoff, C. (2008). The impact of family harmony on governance practices in South African-Greek family businesses. *Management Dynamics*, *17*(3), 28–44.

Amason, A.C., & Sapienza, H.J. (1997). The effects of top management teams' size and interaction norms on cognitive and affective conflict. *Journal of Management*, *23*(4), 495–516.

Anderson, R., Mansi, S., & Reeb, D. (2003). Founding family ownership and the agency cost of dept. *Journal of Financial Economics*, *68*, 263–85.

Aronoff, C.E. (1998). Megatrends in family business. *Family Business Review*, *11*, 181–6.

Aronoff, C.E. (2004). Self-perpetuation family organization built on values: Necessary condition for long-term family business survival. *Family Business Review*, *17*(1), 559.

Astrachan, J.H., & Aronoff, C.E. (1998). Succession issues can signal deeper problems. *Nations's Business*, *86*(5), 723.

Astrachan, J.H., Klein, S.B., & Smyrnios, K.X. (2002). The F-PEC scale of family influence: A proposal for solving the *family business* definition problem. *Family Business Review*, *15*(1), 45–58.

Astrachan, J.H., & Kolenko, T.A. (1994). A neglected factor explaining family business success: Human resource practices. *Family Business Review*, *7*(3), 251–62.

Astrachan, J.H., & Shanker, M. (2003). Family businesses' contribution to the U.S. economy: A closer look. *Family Business Review*, *16*(3), 211–21.

Barach, J.A., & Ganitsky, J.B. (1995). Successful succession in family business. *Family Business Review*, 8(2), 131–55.

Basco, R., & Rodriquez, M.J.P. (2009). Studying the family enterprise holistically: Evidence for integrated family and business systems. *Family Business Review*, 22(1), 82–95.

Bass, B. M. (1990). *Bass and Stogdill's handbook of leadership*. New York: The Free Press.

Beavers, W.R., & Voeller, M.N. (1983). Family models: Comparing and contrasting the Olson Circumplex Model with the Beavers Systems Model. *Family Process*, 22(1), 85–97.

Beckhard, R., & Dyer, W. G., Jr. (1983). Managing continuity in the family-owned business. *Organizational Dynamics*, 12(1), 5–12.

Birley, S. (1986). Succession in the family firm: The inheritor's view. *Journal of Small Business Management*, 24(3), 36–43.

Björnberg, A., & Nicholson, N. (2007). Family climate scales: The development of a new measure of use in family business research. *Family Business Review*, 20(3), 229–46.

Cater, J.J., III, & Justis, R.T. (2010). The development and implementation of shared leadership in multi-generational family firms. *Management Research Review*, 33(6), 563–85.

Chandler, A.D. (1977). *The visible hand: The managerial revolution of American business*. Cambridge: the Belknap Press of Harvard University Press.

Chandler, A.D. (1990). *Strategy and structure: Chapters in the history of the industrial enterprise*. Boston, MA: Massachusetts Institute of Technology Press.

Chittoor, R., & Das, R. (2007). Professionalization of management and succession performance – A vital linkage. *Family Business Review*, 20(1), 65–79.

Chrisman, J.J., Chua, J.H., & Litz, R.A. (2003). A unified systems perspective of family firm performance: An extension and integration. *Journal of Business Venturing*, 18(4), 467–72.

Chrisman, J.J., Chua, J.H., & Sharma, P. (2003). Current trends and future directions in family business management studies: Toward a theory of the family firm. *Written as Part of the Coleman Foundation White Paper Series*.

Chua, J.H., Chrisman, J.J., & Chang, E.P.C. (2004). Are family firms born or made: An exploratory investigation. *Family Business Review*, 17(1), 37–54.

Chua, J.H., Chrisman, J.J., & Sharma, P. (1999). Defining the family business by behavior. *Entrepreneurship Theory & Practice*, 23(4), 19–39.

Chua, J.H., Chrisman, J.J., & Sharma, P. (2003). Succession and nonsuccession concerns of family firms and agency relationship with nonfamily managers. *Family Business Review*, 16(2), 89–108.

Churchill, N.C., & Hatten, K.J. (1987). Non-market-based transfers of wealth and power: A research framework for small businesses. *American Journal of Small Business*, 11(3), 51–64.

Colli, A. (2003). *The history of family business: 1850–2000*. Cambridge, UK: Cambridge University.

Collier, C.W. (2002). *Wealth in families*. Cambridge, MA: Harvard Press.

Cooperrider, D.L., & Whitney, D. (2007). Appreciative inquiry: A positive revolution in change. In P. Holman & T. Devane (Eds.), *The Change Handbook*, (2nd ed.), (pp. 245–63). San Francisco, CA: Berrett-Koehler.

Cosier, R.A., & Harvey, M. (1998). The hidden strengths in family business: Functional conflict. *Family Business Review*, 11(1), 75–9.

Danco, L. (1975). *Beyond survival: A business owner's guide to success*. Reston, VA: Reston Publishing Company.

Danes, S.M. Leichtentritt, R.D., Metz, M.E., & Huddleston-Casas, C. (2000). Effects of conflict styles and conflict severity on quality of life of men and women in family business. *Journal of Family and Economic Issues*, 21(3), 259–86.

Danes, S.M., & Olson, P.D. (2003). Women's role involvement in family businesses, business tensions, and business success. *Family Business Review*, 16(1), 53–68.

Danes, S.M., Stafford, K., & Loy, J.T.C. (2007). Family business performance: The effects of gender and management. *Journal of Business Venturing*, 60(10), 1058–69.

Danes, S.M., Lee, J., Stafford, K., & Heck, R.K.Z. (2008). The effects of ethnicity, families and culture on entrepreneurial experience: An extension of Sustainable Family Business Theory. *Journal of Developmental Entrepreneurship*, 13, 2229–68.

Danes, S.M., Stafford, K., Haynes, G., & Amarapurkar, S.S. (2009). Family capital of family firms: Bridging human, social and financial capital. *Family Business Review*, 22(3), 199–215.

Davis, P.S., & Harveston, P.D. (1998). The influence of family on the family business succession process: A multi-generational perspective. *Entrepreneurship Theory & Practice, 22*(3), 31–53.

Denison, D., Lief, C., & Ward, J.L. (2004). Culture in family-owned enterprises: Recognizing and leveraging unique strengths. *Family Business Review, 17*(1), 61–70.

DeNoble, A., Ehrlich, S., & Singh, G. (2007). Toward the development of a family business self-efficacy scale: A resource-based perspective. *Family Business Review, 20*(2), 127–40.

de Visscher, F.M., Aronoff, C.E., & Ward, J.L. (1995). *Financing transitions: Managing capital and liquidity in the family business.* Family Business Leadership Series, No. 7. Marietta, GA: Family Enterprise Publishers.

Dyer, W.G., Jr. (1986). *Cultural change in family firms: Anticipating and managing the business and family transitions.* San Francisco: Jossey-Bass.

Dyer, W.G., Jr. (2006). Examining the "Family Effect" on firm performance. *Family Business Review, 19*(4), 253.

Dyer, W.G., Jr., & Whetten, D.A. (2006). Family firms and social responsibility: Preliminary evidence from the S&P 500. *Entrepreneurship Theory and Practice, 30*(6), 785–802.

Eddleston, K., Otondo, R., & Kellermanns, F. (2008). Conflict, participative decision-making and generational ownership dispersion: A multi-level analysis. *Journal of Small Business Management, 46*(3), 456–84.

Ensley, M.D., & Pearson, A.W. (2003). An exploratory comparison of behavioral dynamics of top management teams in family and nonfamily new ventures: Cohesion, conflict, potency, and consensus. *Entrepreneurship Theory and Practice, 29*(3), 267–84.

García-Álvarez, E., & López-Sintas, J. (2001). A taxonomy of founders based on values: The root of family business heterogeneity. *Family Business Review, 14*(3), 209–30.

Gersick, K.E., Davis, J.A., McCollom Hampton, M., & Lansberg, I. (1997). *Generation to generation: Life cycles of the family business.* Boston, MA: Harvard Business School Press.

Gladwell, M. (2008). *Outliers.* New York: Little, Brown and Co.

Guetzkow, H., & Gyr, J. (1954). An analysis of conflict in decision-making groups. *Human Relations, 7,* 367–81.

Habbershon, T.G., & Pistrui, J. (2002). Enterprising families domain: Family-influenced ownership groups in pursuit of transgenerational wealth. *Family Business Review, 5*(3), 223–38.

Habbershon, T.G., Williams, M., & MacMillan, I.C. (2003). A unified systems perspective of family firm performance. *Journal of Business Venturing, 18,* 451–65.

Handler, W.C. (1989). Managing the family firm succession process: The next-generation family member's experience. Unpublished doctoral dissertation, School of Management Boston University, cited in W.C. Handler, 1994, Succession in family business: A review of the research. *Family Business Review, 7*(2), 133–57.

Handler, W.C., & Kram, K.E. (1988). Succession in family firms: The problem of resistance. *Family Business Review, 1*(4), 361–81.

Heck R.K.Z., & Scannell Trent, E. (1999). The prevalence of family business from a household sample. *Family Business Review, 12*(3), 257–76.

Hoffman, J., Hoelscher, M., & Sorenson, R. (2006). Achieving sustained competitive advantage: A family capital theory. *Family Business Review, 19*(2), 135–45.

Hughes, J.E., Jr. (2004). *Family wealth. Keeping it in the family.* Princeton, NJ: Bloomberg Press.

Hughes, J.E., Jr. (2007). *Family: The compact among generations.* New York: Bloomberg Press.

Jaffe, D., & Lane, S. (2004). Sustaining a family dynasty: Key issues facing complex multigenerational business- and investment-owning families. *Family Business Review, 17*(1), 5–18.

Kellermanns, F.W., & Eddleston, K. (2004). Feuding families: When conflict does a family firm good. *Entrepreneurship Theory and Practice, 28*(3), 209–28.

Kellermanns, F.W., & Eddleston, K. (2006). Destructive and productive family relationships: A stewardship theory perspective. *Journal of Business Venturing, 22,* 545–65.

Klein, S.B. (2008). Commentary and extension: Moderating the outcome of identity confirmation in family firms. *Entrepreneurship Theory and Practice, 32*(6), 321–39.

Klein, S.B., Astrachan, J.H., & Smyrnios, K.X. (2005). The F-PEC scale of family influence: Construction, validation, and further implication for theory. *Family Business Review, 29*(3), 45–58.

Lambrecht, J., & Lievens, J. (2008). Pruning the family tree: An unexplored path to family business continuity and family harmony. *Family Business Review*, *21*(4), 295–313.

Lansberg, I. (1988). The succession conspiracy. *Family Business Review*, *1*(1), 119–43.

Lansberg, I. (1999). *Succeeding generations*. Boston: Harvard Business School Press.

La Porta, R., Lopez-de-Silanes, F., & Shleifer, A. (1999). Corporate ownership around the world. *Journal of Finance*, *54*, 471–517.

Lee, J. (2006). Impact of family relationships on attitudes of the second generation in family business. *Family Business Review*, *19*(3), 175–91.

Lee, T.W., & Maurer, S.D. (1999). The effects of family structure on organizational commitment, intention to leave and voluntary turnover. *Journal of Managerial Issues*, *11*(4), 493.

Leon-Guerrero, A.Y., McCann, J.E., III, & Haley, J.D., Jr., (1988). A study of practice utilization in family businesses. *Family Business Review*, *11*(2), 107–20.

Le Breton-Miller, I., & Miller, D. (2006). Why do some family businesses out-compete? Governance, long-term orientations and sustainable capability. *Entrepreneurship Theory and Practice*, *30*(6), 731–46.

Litz, R.A. (1995). The family business: Toward definitional clarity. *Family Business Review*, *8*(2), 71–81.

Marshack, K.J. (1994). Copreneurs and dual-career couples: Are they different? *Entrepreneurship Theory and Practice*, *19*(1), 49–69.

Mazzola, P., Marchisio, G., & Astrachan, J. (2008). Strategic planning in family business: A powerful developmental tool for the next generation. *Family Business Review*, *21*(3), 239–58.

Miller, D., & Le Breton-Miller, I. (2006). Family governance and firm performance: Agency, stewardship, and capabilities. *Family Business Review*, *19*(1), 73–87.

Miller, D., Le Breton-Miller, I., & Scholnick, B. (2008). Stewardship vs. stagnation: An empirical comparison of small family and non-family businesses. *Journal of Management Studies*, *45*(1), 51–78.

Milton, L. (2008). Unleashing the relationship power of family firms: Identity confirmation as a catalyst for performance. *Entrepreneurship Theory and Practice*, *32*(6), 1063–81.

Murphy, D. (2005). Understanding the complexities of private family firms: An empirical investigation. *Family Business Review*, *18*(2), 123–33.

Neubauer, F., & Lank, A.G. (1998). *The family business – 1ˢᵗ governance for sustainability*. London, UK: MacMillan.

Nicholson, N. (2003). *Leadership, culture and change in family firms. Report of first stage survey of the leadership in family firm' research initiative (LIFBRI)*. London, UK: London Business School.

Niehm, L.S., Swinney, J., & Miller, N. (2008). Community social responsibility and its consequences for family business performance. *Journal of Small Business Management*, *46*(3), 331–50.

Olson, P.D., Zuiker, V.S., Danes, S.M., Stafford, K., Heck, R.Z., & Duncan, K.A. (2003). The impact of the family and the business on family business sustainability. *Journal of Business Venturing*, *18*(5), 639–66.

Pieper, T.M., Klein, S.B., & Jaskiewicz, P. (2008). The impact of goal alignment on board existence and top management team composition: Evidence from family-influenced businesses. *Journal of Small Business Management*, *46*, 372–94.

Poza, E.J. (1989). *Smart growth: Critical choices for business continuity and prosperity*. San Francisco, CA: Jossey-Bass.

Poza, E.J., Hanlon, S., & Kishida, R. (2004). Does the family business interaction factor represent a resource or a cost? *Family Business Review*, *17*(2), 99–118.

Ross, R.S. (1985). Issues of level in organizational research. In L.L. Cummings & B.M. Staw (Eds.), *Research in organizational behavior* (Vol. 7, pp. 1–37). Greenwich, CT: JAI Press.

Rutherford, M.W., Muse, L.A., & Oswald, S.L. (2006). A new perspective on the developmental model for family business. *Family Business Review*, *19*(4), 317–33.

Schein, E.H. (1983). The role of the founder in creating organization culture. *Organizational Dynamics, Summer*, *12*(1), 13–28.

Sciascia, S., & Mazzola, P. (2008). Family involvement in ownership and management: Exploring nonlinear effects on performance. *Family Business Review*, *21*(4), 331–45.

Shanker, M.C., & Astrachan, J.H. (1996). Myths and realities: Family businesses' contributions to the US economy – A framework for assessing family business statistics. *Family Business Review*, 9(2), 107–19.

Sharma, P. (2004). An overview of the field of family business studies: Current status and directions for the future. *Family Business Review*, 17(1), 1–36.

Sharma, P., Chrisman, J.J., & Chua, J.H. (2003). Predictors of satisfaction with the succession process in family firms. *Journal of Business Venturing*, 18(5), 667–87.

Sharma, P., & Irving, P.G. (2005). Four bases of family business successor commitment: Antecedents and consequences. *Entrepreneurship Theory and Practice*, 29(1), 13–33.

Simons, T.L., & Peterson, R.S. (2000). Task conflict and relationship conflict in top management teams: The pivotal role of intragroup trust. *Journal of Applied Psychology*, 85, 102–11.

Sorenson, R.L. (1999). Conflict strategies used by successful family businesses. *Family Business Review*, 12(4), 325–39.

Sorenson, R.L. (2000). The contribution of leadership style and practices to family and business success. *Family Business Review*, 18(3), 183–200.

Stafford, K., Duncan, K.A., Danes, S., & Winter, M. (1999). A research model of sustainable family businesses. *Family Business Review*, 12(3), 197–208.

Tagiuri, R., & Davis, J.A. (1996). Bivalent attributes of the family firm. *Family Business Review*, 9(2), 199–208.

Uhlaner, L. (2005). The use of the Guttman Scale in the development of a Family Orientation Index for small-to-medium-sized firms. *Family Business Review*, 18(1), 41–56.

Upton, N., Vinton, K., Seaman, S., & Moore, C. (1993). Research note: Family business consultants – Who we are, what we do, and how we do it. *Family Business Review*, 6(3), 301–11.

Van der Heyden, L., Blondel, C., & Carlock, R.S. (2005). Fair process: Striving for justice in family business. *Family Business Review*, 18(1), 1–21.

Vera, C.F., & Dean, M.A. (2005). An examination of the challenges daughters face in family business succession. *Family Business Review*, 18(4), 321–45.

Villalonga, B., & Amit, R. (2006). How do family ownership, control and management affect firm value? *Journal of Financial Economics*, 80, 385–417.

Wall, V., & Nolan, L. (1986). Perceptions of inequity, satisfaction, and conflict in task-oriented groups. *Human Relations*, 39, 1033–52.

Wang, Y. (2005). Balancing family relationship and financial control: The story of Peter Whitley Ltd. *International Journal of Management Practice*, 1(2), 198–214.

Ward, J.L. (1987). *Keeping the family business healthy: How to plan for continued growth and family leadership.* San Francisco, CA: Jossey-Bass.

Ward, J.L. (1988). The special role of strategic planning for family business. *Family Business Review*, 1(2), 105–17.

Ward, J.L., & Aronoff, C.E. (1990). Just what is the family business? *Nation's Business*, February 1990. In Aronoff, Astrachan, & Ward (Eds.), *Family business source book*. Marietta, GA: Family Enterprise Publishers.

Ward. J.L., & Aronoff, C.E. (1994). How successful business families get that way. *Nation's Business, September*, 42–3.

Ward, J.L. (1997). Growing the family business: Special challenges and best practices. *Family Business Review*, 10(4): 323–37.

Weber, M. (1947). *The theory of social and economic organization.* New York: Oxford University Press.

Werbel, J., & Danes, S. (2010). Work family conflict in new business ventures: The moderating effects of spousal commitment to the new business venture. *Journal of Small Business Management*, 48(3), 421–40.

Westhead, P., & Cowling, M., (1997). Performance contrasts between family and nonfamily unquoted companies in the UK. *International Journal of Entrpreneurial Behaviour & Research*, 3(1) 30–52.

Westhead, P., & Cowling, M. (1998). Family firm research: The need for a methodological rethink. *Entrepreneurship Theory & Practice*, 23(1), 31–56.

Westhead, P., & Horworth, C. (2006). Ownership and management issues associated with family firm performance and company objectives. *Family Business Review*, *19*(4), 301–16.

Whitney, D., & Trosten-Bloom, A. (2010). *The power of appreciative inquiry: A practical guide to positive change* (2nd ed.). San Francisco, CA: Berrett-Koehler Publishers.

Winter, M., Danes, S.M., Koh, S., Fredricks, K., & Paul, J.J. (2003). Tracking family businesses and their owners over time: Panel attrition, manager departure and business demise. *Journal of Business Venturing*, *19*, 535–59.

Yu, A. (2009). *Family business outcomes: Dependent variables, cultural differences, and competing outcomes in U.S. and Taiwanese family businesses* (Doctoral dissertation). Retrieved from http://hdl.handle.net/2346/19080

Yu, A., Lumpkin, G.T., Sorenson, R.L., & Brigham, K.H. (2012). The landscape of family business outcomes: A summary and numerical taxonomy of dependent variables. *Family Business Review*, *25*(1), 33–57.

Zellweger, T., Eddleston, K., & Kellermanns, F.W. (2010). Exploring the concept of familiness: Introducing family firm identity. *Journal of Family Business Strategy*, *1*(1), 54–63.

8. Succession in family firms

Massimo Baù, Karin Hellerstedt, Mattias Nordqvist and Karl Wennberg

Introduction

The process of succession in family firms is often both lengthy and complex, and is influenced by factors such as the personal goals of the owner-manager, family structure, ability and ambitions of potential successors, and legal and financial issues (Le Breton-Miller, Miller, & Steier, 2004). Scholars of family business tend to emphasize what determines successful ownership and management succession involving family members and non-family stakeholders, alongside the general characteristics of effective succession (Handler, 1994; Le Breton-Miller et al., 2004; Sharma, Chrisman, & Chua, 2003a). A majority of privately held firms in many developed countries are likely to shift ownership as the owners approach retirement. Thus, from a public policy perspective, there is a need to study the conditions surrounding successful succession of family firms and the implications of these successions in the socio-economic context.

This chapter presents a comprehensive review of the scholarly literature on ownership transition and management succession in family firms. We found that most of the literature on succession is conceptual or relies on a small number of cases and/or surveys based on convenience samples. For instance, 71 percent of the work published since the mid-1970s consists of descriptive investigations based on aggregated data or micro studies of firm succession based on small samples or a small number of illustrative cases. We see a need for more studies about the effects of succession on long-term development in privately held firms and how succession affects economic outcomes at different levels of analysis (Yu, Lumpkin, Sorenson, & Brigham, 2012).*

We conducted a literature review based upon a cluster analysis that identifies four levels of analysis that dominate the current literature on succession. These levels are important for understanding transition processes and allow us to identify three main areas that offer particular interesting avenues for future research. First, succession involves, among other things, the goals and options of several actors: The individual owners and managers, the family members, the economic environment, and the potential successors, to varying degrees, who may influence the transition process. We discuss this multilevel perspective

---

* As a result of the Yu et al. (2012) research, "A Map of the Landscape of Family Business" (also referred to as the Landscape Map) was developed. The Landscape Map, can be found on the page just inside the cover of this book and in the Yu, Lumpkin, Sorenson, and Brigham (2012) article published in *Family Business Review*. Following the Landscape Map, the "Outcome Categories by Chapter Table" (also referred to as the Outcome Categories Table) is provided. This table shows all chapters that contain content about the outcome categories that appear in this chapter.

within the context of the conceptual literature. Although it is adopted in some qualitative studies, multilevel quantitative research is generally scarce. Because succession is an inherently multilevel phenomenon, we argue that empirical research must also adopt a multilevel perspective.

Second, we note that succession research focuses primarily on management transitions. In contrast, ownership transfer has received much less attention. For many small- and medium-sized enterprises (including family businesses), these two transitions go hand in hand (Handler, 1994).[1] Yet, there are reasons to single out and more closely examine ownership transition that involves not only financial issues and asset valuation, but also emotional issues such as perceived fairness among involved actors, which may represent the most critical part of a succession.

Third, our review shows that suitable analytical techniques and representative sampling methods are lacking. There is an increased need for generalizable empirical evidence that can be used to test the limits and boundary conditions of different theoretical models, and to generate insights for owners, managers, and policy-makers.

The chapter is organized as follows. In section two, we describe the methodology. Section three reviews the extant research and discusses a selection of articles represented within the categories identified in the cluster analysis. Section four uses these insights to highlight some avenues for future research that would help to fill some of the research gaps identified by our review and analysis. We highlight areas worthy of future inquiry and discuss some of the methodological issues that need to be addressed to further the research in this area. Section five provides a brief conclusion.

Methodology

Given the abundant and eclectic literature on succession, we followed a comprehensive and systematic process in reviewing previous research. This approach should enable other researchers to follow our procedures and use our findings for their own purposes, regardless of their theoretical inclination.

Using the 30 management journals listed in Debicki, Matherne, Kellermanns and Chrisman (2009) based on reviews of the literature on entrepreneurship (MacMillan, 1993; Shane, 1997) and family business (Chrisman, Chua, Kellermanns, Matherne III, & Debicki, 2008), we conducted a three-phase examination of the articles published since the first issues of these 30 journals. Using the publishers' electronic archive, we searched for the keywords *succession*, *successor*, *predecessor*, or *transition* in the abstracts of the papers, which identified 1,068 papers. Next, we read all abstracts to exclude research focusing on CEO turnover in large publicly listed firms and retained only papers examining succession in private and/or family firms. This reduced the sample to 172 papers. Finally, we read all the papers, organizing a table of contents of the research design, sample characteristics, methods of sampling and analysis, and national context. We excluded papers with a practice-oriented focus such as simple interviews, book reviews, and teaching cases. This narrowed the sample to 125 papers published during the past 35 years; eight of which are reviews of the literature.

Therefore, our analysis focused on 117 papers. Ninety percent of the articles were published in *Family Business Review* (60.8 percent), *Journal of Small Business Management*

Table 8.1 List of journals and number of articles

	First selection	Third selection	%
Academy of Management Journal	41	1	0.8%
Academy of Management Review	22	1	0.8%
Administrative Science Quarterly	42	0	–
Business Ethics Quarterly	8	0	–
California Management Review	25	0	–
Corporate Governance: An International Review	23	0	–
Entrepreneurship and Regional Development	11	0	–
Entrepreneurship: Theory & Practice	28	11	8.8%
Family Business Review	106	76	60.8%
Harvard Business Review	144	1	0.8%
Human Relations	45	0	–
International Small Business Journal	20	8	6.4%
Journal of Applied Psychology	22	0	–
Journal of Business Ethics	44	0	–
Journal of Business Research	27	0	–
Journal of Business Venturing	37	8	6.4%
Journal of Management	13	0	–
Journal of Management Studies	31	0	–
Journal of Organizational Behavior	21	0	–
Journal of Small Business Management	26	12	9.6%
Leadership Quarterly	11	1	0.8%
Long Range Planning	30	1	0.8%
Management Science	85	0	–
Organization Science	30	1	0.8%
Organization Studies	39	0	–
Organizational Dynamics	29	0	–
Sloan Management Review	38	0	–
Small Business Economics	27	4	3.2%
Strategic Management Journal	40	0	–
Strategic Organization	3	0	–
TOTAL	1068	125	

(9.6 percent), *Entrepreneurship Theory and Practice* (8.8 percent), *Journal of Business Venturing* (6.4 percent) *and International Small Business Journal* (6.4 percent). Most were empirical research (72.3 percent) distributed fairly equally between qualitative (52 percent) and quantitative (48 percent) studies. Table 8.1 presents the journals and number of articles in the review.

To classify the 117 studies, we conducted a cluster analysis to identify specific patterns in the research on ownership transfer and succession, and grouped them according to 15 different aspects of the studies highlighted by prior research. These aspects relate to:

- **level of analysis** (four aspects, see Handler & Kram, 1988; Sharma, 2004);
- **phase of succession** (four aspects);

- **the family – or firm – members involved** (seven aspects, see Barach & Ganitsky, 1995; Le Breton-Miller et al., 2004; Sharma, 2004; Vera & Dean, 2005).

The four aspects referring to level of analysis were defined according to Handler and Kram's (1988) framework for succession research. The *individual level* focuses on the centrality of the individual in the succession process, and considers personal attributes, attitudes, perspectives, behaviors and expectations. The *group level* looks at relationships, interpersonal dynamics, influences of family members on the succession process, and reactions of non-family management to the succession process. The *firm level* is related to the dimensions of governance mechanisms and temporal influences. The fourth level, the *environmental level*, considers the impacts of the external environmental contingencies on firm structure.

The second group refers to four phases of the succession process: *pre-succession, planning succession, managing succession*, and *post-succession*.

The third group refers to the types of agents discussed in the papers: *incumbent/founder, successor, parent, offspring, manager/stakeholder, shareholder, board of directors* (Barach & Ganitsky, 1995; Le Breton-Miller et al., 2004; Sharma, 2004; Vera & Dean, 2005).

From the cluster analysis, we can identify four main groups of studies, three of which are related to Handler and Kram's (1988) level of analysis: *environmental level* studies, *individual/group level* studies, *firm-level* studies, and a new category, *multilevel studies*. The majority of the studies we analyzed fall into the individual/group cluster, which is subdivided into the four phases of succession: *pre-succession, planning succession, managing succession*, and *post-succession*. The outcome is the following seven clusters of studies that we organized in our analysis of the literature review accordingly:

1.   Environmental studies
2.   Firm-level studies
3.   Individual/interpersonal studies
3.1 Pre-succession
3.2 Planning succession
3.3 Managing succession
3.4 Post-succession
4.   Multilevel studies

Results of the literature review

This section synthesizes the findings from the literature review, the focus of current research and dominant research questions, and discusses a selection of the most important findings in each of the seven groups identified. In each cluster, we present the most significant insights for practitioners that can be derived from the selected papers. These findings are analyzed in the discussion section, which identifies a number of theoretical, empirical, and methodological gaps. We conclude by suggesting avenues for future research. Table 8.2 presents the seven clusters of studies identified and the main topics covered in each respective cluster.[2]

Table 8.2   Classification of reviewed articles

Level (no. of studies)	Main topics	Significant contributions
5.1. Environmental (14)	economic models	Ayres, 1998; Diwisch et al., 2009
	buy-in/-out	Scholes et al., 2007; Wright et al., 1992
	fiscal dimension	Bjuggren & Sund, 2001; 2002; 2005; File & Prince, 1996; McCollom, 1992
	national/ethnical aspects	Chau, 1991; Huang, 1999; Kuratko et al., 1993; Perricone, Earle, & Taplin, 2001; Santiago, 2000
5.2. Firm level (15)	preliminary considerations	Brown, 1993; Fiegener et al., 1994; Foster, 1995; Kimhi, 1997; Rogers, Carsrud, & Krueger Jr., 1996; Stavrou, 2003; Steier, 2001
	corporate governance	Barach & Ganitsky, 1995; Berenbeim, 1990; Chua et al., 2003; Corbetta & Montemerlo, 1999; Malone, 1989; Miller et al., 2003; Poza et al., 2004; Sonfield & Lussier, 2004
5.3. Individual/group level		
5.3.1. pre-succession (28)	attitudes and willingness	Birley, 1986; 2002; Cadieux et al., 2002; Dumas, Dupuis, Richer, & St-Cyr, 1995; Galiano & Vinturella, 1995; Goldberg, 1996; Mandelbaum, 1994; Shepherd & Zacharakis, 2000; Stavrou, 1998; 1999; Stavrou, Kleanthous, & Anastasiou, 2005; Stavrou & Swiercz, 1998
	predecessor/ successor	Cabrera-Suárez, 2005; Cabrera-Suárez et al., 2001; Cadieux, 2007; Chrisman et al., 1998; Hoang & Gimeno, 2010; Lee, Lim, & Lim, 2003; Marshall et al., 2006; Sharma & Irving, 2005
	national/ethnical context	Bachkaniwala, Wright, & Ram, 2001; Brenes, Madrigal, & Molina-Navarro, 2006; Bruce & Picard, 2006; Howorth & Assaraf Ali, 2001; Janjuha-Jivraj & Woods, 2002; Keating & Little, 1997; Kirby & Lee, 1996; Sharma & Rao, 2000
5.3.2. planning (22)	general	DeNoble et al., 2007; Dimsdale, 1974; Goldberg & Wooldridge, 1993; Handler, 1991; Longenecker & Schoen, 1978; Sharma et al., 2003a; Sharma et al, 2001; Westhead, 2003
	relations	Ayres, 1990; Fiegener, Brown, Prince, & File, 1996; Garcia-Álvarez, López-Sintas, & Gonzalvo, 2002; Lansberg & Astrachan, 1994; Seymour, 1993; Sharma et al., 2003b
	contingencies	Brown & Coverley, 1999; Chittoor & Das, 2007; Fahed-Sreih & Djoundourian, 2006; Harveston et al., 1997; Motwani et al., 2006; Nam & Herbert, 1999; Peay & Dyer Jr., 1989; Tatoglu et al., 2008

Table 8.2 (continued)

Level (no. of studies)	Main topics	Significant contributions
5.3.3. managing (27)	family relations	Brun de Pontet, Wrosch, & Gagne, 2007; Dunn, 1999; Harvey & Evans, 1994; Kaslow, 1998; Poza & Messer, 2001; Swagger, 1991; Vera & Dean, 2005
	internal and external transfer	Cater & Justis, 2009; Correll, 1989; De Massis et al., 2008; Handler, 1992; Howorth et al., 2004; Lambrecht, 2005; Royer et al., 2008
	'co-habitation' of predecessors and successors	Ambrose, 1983; Barnes & Hershon, 1976; Churchill & Hatten, 1997; Fox et al., 1996; Handler, 1990; Ibrahim et al., 2001; Matthews et al., 1999; Post & Robins, 1993; Sonnenfeld & Spence, 1989; Thomas, 2002
	process	Gersick et al., 1999; McGivern, 1989; Murray, 2003.
5.3.4. post-succession (5)		Dyck et al., 2002; Harvey & Evans, 1995; Haveman, 1993; Haveman & Khaire, 2004; Venter et al., 2005
5.4. Multilevel (6)		Clifford, Nilakant, & Hamilton, 1991; Davis & Harveston, 1998; Handler & Kram, 1988; Lansberg, 1988; Rubenson & Gupta, 1996; Yan & Sorenson, 2006
Reviews (8)	specific reviews	Brockhaus Sr, 2004; Handler, 1994; Le Breton-Miller et al., 2004.
	entrepreneurial perspective	Dyer Jr. & Handler, 1994; Zahra, Hayton, & Salvato, 2004
	general reviews	Aronoff, 1998; Kesner & Sebora, 1994; Wortman, 1994

Environmental level studies

Research at the environmental level has investigated the impact of factors external to the firm, such as financial and legal institutions and national cultures, which affect ownership transfers or succession. This cluster of studies contributes at the macro level by discussing policy implications in various countries. A number of studies with a financial focus consider the relationship between succession and firm performance (Ayres, 1998; Diwisch, Voithofer, & Weiss, 2009). A common theme in the interaction between various financial institutions and firms' behavior during succession emerged through studies that investigated the conditions for management buy-outs (Scholes, Wright, Westhead, Burrows, & Bruining, 2007; Wright, Thompson, & Robbie, 1992), or how taxation and legal frameworks affect ownership transitions (Bjuggren & Sund, 2002; File & Prince, 1996; McCollom, 1992). Finally, this cluster contains studies that examine how different national cultures shape attitudes to succession (Kuratko, Hornsby, & Montagno, 1993), tendencies to adopt succession plans (Huang, 1999), and the prevalence of successful successions (Chau, 1991).

The *implications for practitioners* that can be derived from this cluster of studies refer to the economic environment, such as the evaluation of policy measures to improve the performance of individual firms as well as the aggregate labor market (Diwisch et al., 2009). The financial institutions and the national institutional framework heavily influence the decision of waiting (Bjuggren & Sund, 2001) or selling the firm (Scholes et al., 2007; Wright et al., 1992). Tax neutrality is important in an institutional framework that supports welfare-enhancing successions (Bjuggren & Sund, 2002), as are the legal consequences of estate planning and how trusts are governed. Inadequate estate planning is more often associated with family business failure than poor succession planning (File & Prince, 1996), where the choice of the trust is a source of paralysis in the family business (McCollom, 1992).

Firm-level studies

The articles in this cluster focus primarily on the relationship between the firm-level dimension and ownership transfer and/or succession. A first set of studies examines the factors that influence the firm and its family leaders during the period of ownership transfer/succession, by investigating, for example, the development and transfer of social capital (Steier, 2001), or firm- and industry-specific knowledge (Fiegener, Brown, Prince, & File, 1994; Foster, 1995). A second set of articles looks at corporate governance in relation to ownership transfer (Corbetta & Montemerlo, 1999; Poza, Hanlon, & Kishida, 2004), the transition from founder to professional management (Berenbeim, 1990; Sonfield & Lussier, 2004), and relations with non-family managers in the succession phase (Chua, Chrisman, & Sharma, 2003). A third set of studies explores the reasons for firm failure during and after an ownership succession (Miller, Steier, & Le Breton-Miller, 2003). In sum, this cluster of studies provides some important insights related to the build-up and transfer of social capital and intellectual assets across generations of owners, how the involvement of family members affects governance mechanisms related to ownership transfer, and how family firms' governance evolves from entrepreneurial to professional management.

Firm-level studies present several significant *insights for practitioners*. First, they provide implications for how the succession *process* should be managed. Adopting a broad approach to the preparation of succession, Brown (1993) suggests developing plans for the loss of key players, and maintaining a clear and open line of communication with them. In defining the strategies, Fiegener and colleagues (1994) recognize significant differences between family and non-family firms. Specifically, family firms favor more personal approaches to successor development, where non-family firms prefer formalized approaches and are task-oriented. Further, Kimhi (1997) encourages parents to make the business more attractive to their children – keeping the gap between market value and succession value as small as possible – and to structure adequate insurance and pensions plans. Stavrou (2003) reinforces these considerations, underlining the necessity for firms to have an internal focus and a clear understanding of inner needs and values.

Second, we identified a solid cluster related to the governance of family firm successions, suggesting important contributions to external stakeholders involved in a succession. Two important aspects that have an impact on the governance practice are the new relations with next-generation family members and with non-family managers. Several papers highlight the importance of adopting new boards of directors or management committees, introducing more advanced reporting systems, formulating codes of conduct, restructuring capitalization and stock shares, and modifying the firm's organizational structure (Barach & Ganitsky, 1995; Corbetta & Montemerlo, 1999). Focusing on the family side, results suggest that it is necessary to foster a diffuse professional culture in family firms and show the potential family-successors that their happiness is more important than a compelled participation in the family business (Malone, 1989; Miller et al., 2003). Moreover, to earn loyalty and commitment of non-family managers, a family firm must communicate the interests of the family and seek to understand the interests of its non-family managers (Chua et al., 2003). If such a communication approach is matched with management and governance practices, the agency costs related to employment of external managers in family firms may be reduced, thus furthering the efficiency of succession to external managers (Poza et al., 2004).

Individual/interpersonal level studies

This cluster of studies includes almost 80 percent of the articles reviewed. It is distinguished by a central focus on individual entrepreneurs or family firm managers/CEOs, which are the unit of analysis in studies of ownership successions in private firms. As described in the methods section, we identified four sub-clusters in this large cluster referring to different phases in the succession process: pre-succession, planning succession, managing succession, and post-succession.

Pre-succession.
The first sub-cluster of individual/interpersonal level studies focuses on the pre-succession phase, and investigates the issues that precede planning for and managing an ownership succession, including questions related to attitudes to and willingness of family members to take on ownership.

Attitudes and willingness.   These studies include investigations of attitudes to family business and the willingness to transfer ownership. They also explore emotions, intentions (Birley, 1986; Stavrou, 1998), and opinions (Birley, 2002; Shepherd & Zacharakis, 2000) of next-generation family members toward the firm. Most of these articles are based on surveys of university students who were potential successors (Birley, 1986; Shepherd & Zacharakis, 2000; Stavrou & Swiercz, 1998). An exception is Birley (2002), who surveys the offspring of family-owners who participated in previous research projects.

This cluster presents important *implications for practitioners* about the personality and psychological perspectives of incumbents and successors. Regarding the attitude and willingness to succeed, Dumas, Dupuis, Richer, and St-Cyr (1995) stress the need for succession decisions to start at a very early stage and be firmly grounded in family roots. Further, the quality of communication and climate of trust among family members encourage the willingness to succeed in next-generation family members (Cadieux, Lorrain, & Hugron, 2002). Regarding the next generation of family firm managers, it's also important to consider the gender composition. Galiano and Vinturella (1995) find in their study that daughters often consider their founder-manager fathers as "perfect," "omnipotent," and "all-knowing." Such a view could retard the development of their own identity and executive skills, highlighting the importance of founder-managers in family firms to develop successors' personal identity regardless of gender. Specifically, Stavrou and Swiercz (1998) suggest that within-family successors should not join the family business until they explore their abilities and discover their own interests. An appropriate and satisfactory occupational choice can be reached only if one understands his or her capabilities, interests, and goals (Stavrou, 1999).

Relations between predecessor and successor. In addition to the attitudes and willingness of successors, studies of the pre-planning phase investigate the resources and actions of individual former owners and successors, those resources and actions that facilitate ownership transfers. With regard to former managers, their role during the succession process and their ability to "let go" and leave control to their successors is analyzed (Cadieux, 2007; Hoang & Gimeno, 2010). Drawing on resource-based view, Cabrera-Suárez, De Saa-Perez, and Garcia-Almeida (2001) discuss the importance of the successor's ability to acquire the key knowledge and skills of the predecessor in order to maintain and improve organizational performance. The study by Handler (1991) highlights interpersonal relationships among successors considered critical to the progression of ownership succession. Chrisman, Chua, and Sharma (1998) suggest that in long-established family firms, successor integrity and commitment are considered imperative for pre-succession planning, while successors' birth order and gender are of less importance. This confronts the popularly held belief that first-born males constitute the model successor for family firms. Another study that focuses specifically on succession in businesses run by women stresses that the quality of communication and interpersonal trust within the family is crucial for successful ownership transfer (Cadieux et al., 2002). In sum, this group of studies highlights the importance of understanding the motivations of potential successors, the alternatives to intra-family succession, and the sociological and social psychological factors that lead family firms to initiate plans for ownership succession.

These relationship studies highlight the *importance for practitioners* to consider the predecessor-successor relationship. Incumbents embody tacit knowledge that is a strategic asset a family firm can develop and transfer more effectively than can a non-family one (Cabrera-Suárez et al., 2001). Moreover, competence without integrity or commitment may not provide a basis to make decisions in the best interest of the business as well as the family (Chrisman et al., 1998). A family firm manager becomes involved in the process of training and integrating a successor, and the successor often adjusts his or her leadership style (Cadieux, 2007). This period lowers the risk of succession failure by providing successors with a more in-depth view of the real needs of the business, diminishing the likelihood that successors' decisions to join the firms will be based on convenience or an unrealistic image of an easy life in the future (Cabrera-Suárez, 2005).

Planning succession.
The second sub-cluster of individual/interpersonal level studies attends to issues related to planning for a succession. A great deal of evidence suggests that the probability of a successful succession increases if there is a well-structured succession plan in place (Sharma, Chrisman, Pablo, & Chua, 2001). For example, Goldberg and Wooldridge (1993) show that self-confidence and managerial autonomy are characteristics that are

important for effective successors, while creating the right environment for developing the successor is an important ability for a predecessor. In addition to studies examining the value of planning for succession, our review of the literature identified several studies that investigate the role of interpersonal relations and the contingencies that could affect succession planning.

General studies. Several theoretical models have been published to explain how succession should be planned and managed. Longenecker and Schoen (1978) propose a theoretical framework for succession that highlights the complexities of the succession process based on a seven-stage process from the entry of the potential successor as a full-time employee in the organization to the transfer of the leadership position. Sharma et al. (2001) develop a conceptual model for succession planning that integrates several distinct theoretical frameworks, such as agency theory and stakeholder theory. The model is tested in Sharma et al. (2003a) and shows that satisfaction with the succession process in family firms is enhanced by the willingness of the former owner to step aside, the willingness of the successor to take over, an active succession planning phase, and the agreement among family members to maintain involvement in the business and to accept their individual roles. There seems to be a consensus that active planning is related to the eventual effectiveness of ownership successions. It might be that planning enhances the self-efficacy of both predecessors and successors (DeNoble, Ehrlich, & Singh, 2007).

Considering the *implications for practitioners*, planning succession in the family business is seen as a long-term, diachronic process of socialization (Longenecker & Schoen, 1978). This opens to the necessity of recognizing that the success of a succession is a function of both the satisfaction of family members and the subsequent effectiveness of the organization in terms of economic performance (Sharma et al., 2001). Those results are significant in reinforcing the necessity of a shared vision between generations in a family firm. Incumbents and other family firm owners must be honest about the costs associated with the inability to activate formal succession decision-making (Westhead, 2003). Sharma and colleagues (2003a) recognize that too often succession planning is driven by means rather than ends. Generally, the reason for succession planning is the necessity of formalizing the presence of a trusted successor rather than the need for succession to preserve the family firm. Succession planning must be considered a critical factor because it can create an environment for the successor to develop self-confidence and managerial autonomy (Goldberg & Wooldridge, 1993).

Effects of planning upon relations. Research on the relationship aspects of planning for succession highlights the importance of family relations for the organization of a succession plan (Handler, 1991) and shows that family relationships might moderate other factors regarding succession planning (Lansberg & Astrachan, 1994). Also, relationships with non-family firm members seem to be important in planning succession. Seymour (1993) investigates the intergenerational working relationships between predecessors and potential successors in 105 US firms, and finds them to be positively related to the active training of successors, but not to formal succession planning. Sharma, Chrisman, and Chua (2003b) investigate 118 Canadian family firm owner-managers and find that succession is overwhelmingly related to the pro-activeness of a trusted successor in pushing the ownership succession process.

The relation among individuals involved in the succession planning represents an important aspect of potential *interest for practitioners*. Fiegener, Brown, Prince, and File (1996) study differences in the planning process between family and non-family firms and suggest that non-family firm leaders tend to consider "executive development seminars" and "university-level coursework" to be the most important preparatory tasks performed by successors. Conversely, family firm leaders tend to believe that "managing relations with customers and vendors" and "managing large projects" are the most important task experiences for successors. Obviously, both aspects of planning are equally important and suggest that succession plans need to include a holistic overview of both the business' needs and what is needed for any type of successors.

Effect of contingencies upon planning. Research on the planning aspect of succession contains *contingent factors* involved in planning a succession. These include a successor's or predecessor's gender, firm size or level of professionalization, and cultural context. Harveston, Davis, and Lyden (1997) examine 792 male-led and 191 female-led family firms in the US and find both similarities and differences between the genders in terms of the determinants of succession planning. Motwani, Levenburg, Schwarz, and Blankson (2006) survey 368 US SMEs and find that, regardless of firm size, releasing the identity of the successor and providing him or her with training/ mentoring are important planning steps. Chittoor and Das's (2007) comparative case study discusses potential differences in succession planning involving non-family and family managers in family firms. Peay and Dyer Jr. (1989) survey the relationship between psychological traits and succession planning in a sample of 79 US entrepreneurs, finding that their power orientation – a potential proxy for low levels of professionalization – may influence planning for succession. Some studies discuss the cultural context as a discriminating element in the planning process; Fahed-Sreih and Djoundourian's (2006) study of succession planning in 114 Lebanese family firms highlights the acceptance of females as potential successors, while Tatoglu, Kula, and Glaister's (2008) study of succession planning in 408 Turkish firms shows that it is predominantly men who are considered for succession. In sum, this group of studies demonstrates that planning is strongly correlated to eventual succession success, and that planning is contingent on the relationships within the ownership family and other more tangible factors.

We encourage *practitioners to consider* the importance of the contingent aspects of succession planning, assuming as a starting point that the absence of proper succession planning and lack of timely professionalization of the management are widely believed to be the factors responsible for non-survival. Indeed, it is important for family businesses to develop a formal plan for succession regardless of the business size (Motwani et al., 2006). On the one hand, the ability to delegate is considered a crucial skill for successors who must be able to manage and guide the environment left by the incumbent. On the other hand, the incumbent must operate a succession plan that ensures the creation of a suitable business environment for authority delegation (Tatoglu et al., 2008).

Managing succession.

The third sub-cluster of individual/interpersonal level studies focuses on the succession process as it takes place. A first set of studies in this sub-cluster considers the relationship between family members during the succession phase. A second set examines the transfer process through internal and external routes. A third set, partially connected to the first set, discusses the relationship between predecessors and successors, which emerges in a transitional stage when both are exerting some influence on the firm.

Family relations. Family members' relationships are strongly associated with the actual outcome of a succession. Dunn (1999) analyzes the nature and effects of family relations in three UK family businesses during the transfer of ownership to the next generation, and highlights the importance of mitigating the anxieties of family members. Several studies look at the potential influence of CEOs' spouses (Poza & Messer, 2001), or the relations between the owner-managers' sons and daughters and their spouses (Kaslow, 1998; Swagger, 1991; Vera & Dean, 2005) on successions.

This group of papers presents important *implications for practitioners* because it focuses upon the succession process and potential effects of unplanned development. An unclear situation may cause frustration to the successor. If the incumbent perceives more progress on succession than the successor does, this difference in perspective may contribute to the successor's dissatisfaction (Brun de Pontet, Wrosch, & Gagne, 2007). Conflict and disagreement between generations in a family business represent the most destructive forces the family business faces (Harvey & Evans, 1994). Such problems may be related to vague knowledge of parental estate planning scarcely communicated to the successor generation, non-functional or mismatched roles of family members with their interests and talents, unclear criteria for career development or dependent on parental whim, or unrealistic criteria on leadership succession based on gender or sibling position (Swagger, 1991).

Internal and external succession. Transferring a family firm involves consideration of two options: internal transfer to another member of the family or transfer to an external owner. The decision is so fundamental that the survival of the firm is often contingent on the family agreeing upon and managing to execute one of these choices (Ambrose, 1983; Wennberg, Wiklund, DeTiennne, & Cardon, 2010). While this issue has received much attention in the literature, our review indicates that empirical work is dominated by case-study evidence or simple descriptive data. Furthermore, most studies seem to focus on the management aspect of succession and not on ownership (Ambrose, 1983). The approach in De Massis, Chua, and Chrisman (2008) differs in that they propose a theoretical model to investigate the factors that *prevent* intra-family succession.

Among the studies that focus on succession within the family, Lambrecht (2005) investigates ten US firms, and suggests that in order to agree upon and execute an internal transfer, the choice needs to be anchored in the family for a long time. Another study by Cater and Justis (2009) of six US firms suggests that the development of successful management involving family successors is related to parent-child relationships, knowledge acquisition, long-term orientation, cooperation, successor roles, and risk orientation. Handler (1992) studies 32 internal successors in US family firms and finds that perceptions of succession accomplishment are related to the general ability to influence the firm's overall development. Finally, Royer, Simons, Boyd, and Rafferty (2008) analyze the motivations for internal transfer in a sample of 1,108 family firms in Australia and Tanzania. The study finds that the existence of tacit knowledge within the family, and the existence of a "favorable transaction atmosphere," which encompass all the socio-cultural and technical factors that impact the transaction costs of coordination and motivation instruments, are important. In research that focuses on external succession, Churchill and Hatten (1997) discuss the market and non-market considerations in family as opposed to external successions. Correll (1989) describes the evolution of one US family firm, discussing the opportunities and points of decision related to selling the business. Howorth, Westhead, and Wright (2004) analyze the alternatives of management buy-outs and buy-ins as routes to external succession in eight UK family firms. Similarly, Thomas (2002) follows two Australian family firms involved in external ownership transfer and finds that the time horizons for family members seeking to realize capital and those seeking to retain control of their inheritance are very different.

Directly addressing family firm managers' problem of choosing between external or internal successors, De Massis and colleagues (2008) suggest that lack of able successors, lack of motivation among potential successors, predecessors' personal attachment to the business, and conflicts between parent predecessors and their children are among the most important factors for choosing an external successor. Royer et al. (2008) recognize some different situations that may bring about opposite solutions: Specifically, if family business-specific experiential knowledge is highly relevant, family members should be the preferred choice for succession in family businesses. Further, Wennberg, Wiklund, Hellerstedt, and Nordqvist (2011) suggest that families tend to divest of firms with more "uncertain" outcomes where external owners are willing to accept that uncertainty to realize the potential of long-term financial performance, whereas internal successions often lead to less risk-taking but higher chances of ensuring the survival of the business. This highlights the need for family firm managers to decide whether their interest lies in ensuring the firm's optimal economic performance or its long-term survival.

"Co-habitation" of predecessors and successors.   The managing phase of succession generally involves a period in which incumbents and successors share control of the firm. The literature review reveals that this "co-habitation" is discussed mostly in conceptual terms and is modeled by Handler (1990) in a framework that highlights succession as a mutual adjustment of roles between entrepreneurs and next-generation family members. Matthews, Moore, and Fialko (1999) propose a similar model of succession, including a process where the parent/leader and child/successor evaluate both each other and themselves through a process of cognitive categorization. Similarly, Fox, Nilakant, and Hamilton (1996) highlight the system of relationship through which such successions are managed, proposing a framework that adds two more dimensions to the incumbent/ successor relation: those of the business and of the stakeholders. In a comprehensive Canadian case study, Ibrahim, Soufani, and Lam (2001) portray the reluctance of founders to hand over their businesses to their offspring. Murray (2003) follows five US firms and highlights the often extensive periods of transition that introduce distinct problems needing to be addressed in an intermediate time horizon in order to ensure long-term

success. In sum, this group of studies emphasizes the interactive and often prolonged nature of successions, although most of this work is conceptual.

For practitioners, these studies suggest that family business succession can be conceptualized as a mutual role adjustment between incumbents and the next-generation family members (Handler, 1990). The definition of a successful role adjustment may help develop policies for promoting effective organizational transition and can allow the diagnosis of trouble spots to reduce problematic successions. In order to support this process, succession may be facilitated through several tasks: First, facilitating appropriate personal development of the incumbent, and in particular the orientation towards social rather than personal power. Second, planning the timing of the successor's entry into the management of the business. Third, initiating the constructive dialogue between incumbent and successor, particularly where father-son relationships may have become strained. Fourth, fostering constructive participation of key stakeholders, which enables the successor to assess the management performance (Fox et al., 1996).

Post-succession.

The fourth sub-cluster of individual/interpersonal level studies focuses on the post-succession phase and especially on the impact that the succession process has on the firm. Venter, Boshoff, and Maas (2005) study 332 family firms in South Africa and show that the initial willingness of the successor to take over and the relationship between the owner-manager and his or her successor, help to explain both satisfaction with the succession process and the continued profitability of the business. Our review reveals that the risk of firm failure is rarely addressed in the literature. Dyck, Mauws, Strake, and Mischke (2002) follow a case of a failed internal succession in the US that shows how difficult it is to isolate the reasons for failure. Overall, studies examining the implications of succession on firms are seldom based on samples that allow results to be generalized. Existing work highlights the interactive and often prolonged nature of successions but is mostly conceptual rather than empirical.

This cluster of studies suggests some significant insights for practitioners: First, four dimensions that directly impact succession success are communication, timing, agreement, and sequence between the incumbent and successor (Dyck et al., 2002). Second, three important practices may directly impact the continued profitability of the business: willingness of the successor to take over the business, preparation level of the successor, and the relationship between the successor and owner-manager (Venter et al., 2005). Third, an intense organizational culture in the family business may avoid detrimental effects to succession changes, ensuring the organizations' survival chances (Haveman & Khaire, 2004). Instead of shunning firms with a strong organizational culture, our review suggests that successors should consider 1) the degree of shared beliefs between the older generation and the successor; 2) the successor's age and experience; and 3) the level of older-generation involvement in the family business after succession (Harvey & Evans, 1995).

Multilevel studies

The fifth and final cluster of studies in our review adopts a multilevel perspective. All, but one, of the articles in this cluster are conceptual. The only empirical study investigates succession in 1,616 US family firms, and finds that individual-level, family-level, and firm-level factors contribute to explaining the extensiveness of the succession planning process (Davis & Harveston, 1998). The relationships are moderated by the generation in charge, but the evidence is tentative given the single-level analytical methods employed.[3]

Theoretical multilevel studies, such as Handler and Kram (1988) and Lansberg (1988), discuss how forces at the different levels might cause resistance to succession. Handler and Kram (1988) suggest that four levels are important: 1) the individual perspective viewed through a psychosocial lens; 2) the group dimension, which distinguishes family relations from family business relations; 3) the firm perspective in terms of cultural and organizational developments; and 4) the environmental level, which draws on contingency theory and organizational ecology. In a theoretical analysis of the factors that might interfere with the succession process, Lansberg (1988) outlines a multilevel stakeholder perspective, which includes family firm managers and owners, and the environment. He notes the importance of successors establishing relationships with stakeholders by working with the predecessor, the family, and the firm managers to manage a successful succession.

The conceptual papers in the multilevel cluster focus mainly on the relations between context and the agents involved in the succession process, suggesting a potential interplay between a family firm's generational stage and the current owner-manager's characteristics in terms of the likelihood of engaging in succession planning. This work calls for empirical tests of the models proposed, suggesting the importance of including variables from multiple levels of analysis and of correctly specifying multilevel influences in analyses of firm succession.

These multilevel papers also offer important *suggestions to practitioners*. Davis and Harveston (1998) recognize that efforts to engage in effective succession planning will be affected by factors that can only be observed at different levels of analysis, suggesting that family firm managers as well as potential successors need to "look outside the box" of their own perspectives. Handler and Kram (1988) recognize that such a multilevel perspective is important for practitioners since resistance to succession from various stakeholders at different levels represents a key reason for failure to plan for succession in family firms. Lansberg (1988) proposes a number of operational strategies for managing succession that refer to founder, owner, family, and managers, highlighting the need for a multilevel perspective for practitioners who work with succession processes.

Discussion and suggestions for future research

This chapter identified several studies on succession in the context of family firms. These cases fall into three main areas: the topic of succession (management or ownership transition), the context in which succession takes place, and the methods and research designs employed. The latter two are related to the multilevel nature of succession. We believe that more attention will improve our understanding of the phenomenon of firm succession and suggest new research directions to further the cross-fertilization of theories, concepts, and methods from the family business literature, and other related fields such as entrepreneurship, strategy, and organizational behavior. Below, we outline some areas identified in our literature review as ones previously given limited attention. Finally, we collect ten aspects that we would like to consign to practitioners interested in better understanding the succession dynamics within family firms.

Succession as management and/or ownership transitions

Our review shows that most studies focus on management succession, with only 19 percent of the published works addressing ownership transition. There is no clear distinction between management and ownership succession, although there is a need for such a differentiation – both empirically and theoretically. We identified only three papers that make a distinction (Churchill & Hatten, 1997; Gersick, Lansberg, Desjardins, & Dunn, 1999; Handler, 1994). Generally, the problem of succession seems to be discussed at management level, while the problem of ownership succession is most often viewed as a legal problem (Bjuggren & Sund, 2002; Howorth et al., 2004; McCollom, 1992). The co-existence of ownership and management succession is a topic that requires more attention in order to provide a better understanding of the complexity of the succession process from a multilevel perspective. While studies at family level can generate insights into how family relations affect ownership succession (Dunn, 1999; Kaslow, 1998), research is scarce at the intersection between ownership and management succession that examines, for example, how the potential for strategic, market, and entrepreneurial orientations can be maintained across successions. Our review and analysis of the literature suggest there is a gap in relation to the impact of family characteristics on the type of ownership transition and its consequences for strategic choices, financial performance, and survival.

The succession context

The succession context can be thought of as economic, demographic, or institutional factors that shape the process and outcome of ownership and management transfers in family firms. Our literature review indicates that the vast majority of the published works on firm succession pay very limited attention to context and that most empirical work consists of single-region or single-industry studies. Other work investigates succession predominantly in Anglo-Saxon countries.[4] Our review identifies six cross-country comparison studies (Berenbeim, 1990; Chau, 1991; Corbetta & Montemerlo, 1999; Scholes et al., 2007; Sharma & Rao, 2000; Stavrou, 1998), which suggests that the country context is important for the evolution of ownership succession, especially in relation to systems of corporate governance (Tylecote & Visintin, 2008), firm demographics (Motwani et al., 2006), and cultural-institutional factors (Chau, 1991; Kuratko et al., 1993). Most of the existing studies are heavily decontextualized in terms of industry and region of study, and there is a lack of consideration about how variation in the economic, demographic, or institutional context may shape the succession process and its implications for different family and organizational outcomes. Thus, succession research could benefit from the increased attention to context. We believe the lack of attention to context is probably attributable to the lack of data, time, and resources devoted to research designs that follow individuals and firms over time and that compare effects across space, such as industries, regions, countries, or other institutional settings. Economic factors may influence firm succession, exemplified by the lack of external funding to finance transfers due to the recent global financial crisis. Demographic aspects may also influence successions in that firms in regions with aging populations may experience more successful transition/succession processes if outsiders are considered. Institutional aspects may also have an impact on succession processes in that high taxes on ownership transfers may encourage external handovers of family firms (Henrekson, 2005).[5]

Effects of ownership transitions and successions on firm level outcomes

Our review reveals that very few studies investigate the impact of family versus non-family succession on the strategic or organizational development of the firm. How the firm is affected if a family member takes over ownership compared to when an outsider steps in is important with regard to both the organizational behavior and strategic management of family firms (Astrachan, 2010; Dyer Jr. & Handler, 1994; Sharma, 2004). Recent evidence suggests that firms taken over by outsiders perform financially better than firms that remain within the family (Bennedsen, Nielsen, Pérez-González, & Wolfenzon, 2007; Cucculelli & Micucci, 2008). Indeed, new owners can bring additional resources and infuse entrepreneurial energy into an established firm (Nordqvist & Melin, 2010). However, there are several methodological challenges for research to isolate the impact of family versus outsider succession on outcomes at firm level. For example, Block, Jaskiewicz, and Miller (2011) argue that, due to the strong correlation between family ownership and family management in most family firms, Gaussian statistics, relying on significance testing, might be inherently inappropriate research methods. Hence, there is a clear need for more knowledge on the performance effects of succession processes. Several interesting questions remain.

For example, it is frequently argued that family firms take a long-term view of firm development (James, 1999; Lumpkin, Brigham, & Moss, 2010). In their review of the family business literature, Yu and colleagues (2012) present a numerical taxonomy of 34 different dependent variables categories frequently studied in the literature. Basing on cluster analyses and expert ratings (a modified Delphi method), they suggest that the different dependent variables can be categorized depending on long-term vs. short-term outcomes, and their analysis highlights that dependent variables related to succession in family business are the most long-term issues. Among these variables, Yu and colleagues specifically suggest that "Succession processes," and "Succession/transition events" are the most long-term outcomes in family business literature. This insight has implications for the research designs used to investigate the outcomes of firm succession. Outcomes measured too close to the succession point mean that no long-term view is accounted for, and furthermore, outcomes from succession may differ in the intermediate- and long-term (Wennberg et al., 2011).

Our review also suggests there is a lack of research on the specific determinants of various types of ownership transitions and successions. In particular, it would be of interest to know what specific skills, resources, and relations (or lack thereof) make family successors less able than outsiders (Bennedsen et al., 2007). The existing research does not go beyond an insider/outsider view of succession in order to investigate what human, social, or other resources are important for successors – outsiders or insiders.

The effects of ownership transitions on macro level economic development

A growing body of work at the intersection of economics, geography, and entrepreneurship research investigates how micro-level economic action leads to macro-level economic change (Carree & Thurik, 2003; Van Praag & Versloot, 2007). The potential for many family firms to close down rather than undergo a successful ownership transfer is alarming from a public policy point of view. Few studies address these issues, underlining the urgent need for more research to investigate how and under what conditions firms might transfer to new ownership rather than close down.

It is also possible that the aggregate turnover in firm ownership rates might be larger than is generally known. DeTienne (2010) shows that a conservative estimate of the transfer of wealth by trade among US privately held companies in the first six months of 2006, amounted to $100 billion. Despite the obvious societal and economic ramifications of such large-scale changes among family owner-managers, little is known about the impact of such firm ownership transitions on economic development (Mason & Harrison, 2006). A lack of research in this area means that the wider economic consequences of succession in family firms are unclear. While our review shows that several studies address *specific mechanisms* of ownership transitions and succession in privately held firms, little work has been done on the wider societal outcomes of these processes.

Methods and research designs

The literature on succession in private firms is often seen as fragmented because it covers a wide variety of topics (Le Breton-Miller, Miller, & Steier, 2004). Our review also shows that the field is fragmented in terms of the empirical settings and analytical and methodological approaches. Most importantly, 30 percent of published studies are theoretical or conceptual contributions that have never been empirically tested, and among empirical articles there is an apparent dearth of longitudinal studies. Hence, there is a need for more sophisticated approaches to explain the organizational, family, and individual aspects of succession, moving to a meso level of analysis in order to generalize assumptions and intuitions from the theoretical and qualitative literature.

Suggestion for practitioners

Facing succession, practitioners must consider the real essence of this process. Succession is a multilevel process with individual, interpersonal and organizational consequences. Succession represents the synthesis between intergenerational family relations and organizational culture. Succession is the match point of an incumbent's, a successor's and a firm's life cycles. Focusing on the implications of the studies that we have examined and previously discussed, we identified a list of ten significant issues that practitioners working with succession need to be aware of.

First, *culture*, represents the family roots. The owner-family embodies tacit knowledge that can be transferred to family successors (Cabrera-Suárez et al., 2001). A high degree of shared beliefs between generations favor the survival of the firms (Harvey & Evans, 1995).

Second, *education*, serves the development of the human capital of the family members and potential non-family successors. Successors must explore their abilities and discover their own interests before joining or taking over a family business (Stavrou & Swiercz, 1998). The right choice can be made only by understanding personal capabilities, interests, and goals (Stavrou, 1999). Moreover, a constructive participation of key stakeholders should support the successor's preparation (Fox et al., 1996).

Third, *communication*, and the quality of communication controls the climate of trust among family members which are essential factors determining the succession outcomes (Cadieux et al., 2002). Succession must be seen as a long-term process of socialization between family members and stakeholders (Longenecker & Schoen, 1978). Therefore success of a succession implies the necessity of reinforcing a shared vision between generations in a family firm and the appropriate involvement of the key stakeholders.

The fourth, *discussion*, is a critical aspect related to the interaction between individuals. In particular, personality and psychological perspectives of incumbents and successors must be considered in a way that favors a process of training and integration of the successor, as well as a stepping aside of the incumbent. This offers the possibility of the successor to adjust the leadership style according to the organizational characteristics (Cadieux, 2007). An unclear situation may cause frustration to both the successor and the key stakeholders.

The fifth issue is *willingness*. The importance of considering the attitude and willingness of an individual to take over or let go (Dumas et al., 1995) must be balanced with the family expectations and the capability of the next generation of family members (Galiano & Vinturella, 1995).

The sixth issue, *commitment*, is strictly connected to communication and willingness: commitment is formed and reinforced through culture and communication. The sensation of being part of the company and desire to contribute to its success are fundamental characteristics of successful successors. Indeed, competence without commitment may not provide a basis to make decisions in the best interest of the business as well as the family (Chrisman et al., 1998).

The seventh, *planning*. The importance of this aspect is well known. In particular, the absence of proper succession planning and lack of timely preparation of the management are widely believed to be the factors responsible for problems in succession processes. Indeed, it is fundamental for family businesses to develop a formal plan for succession regardless of the business size (Motwani et al., 2006). Therefore, planning must be considered a critical factor, favoring a successor's development of self-confidence and managerial autonomy (Goldberg & Wooldridge, 1993).

The eighth issue is *timing*. Any succession process risks failure if the schedule is not prepared and respected. Respecting the right timing in passing the baton is a critical issue in supporting successor's willingness and commitment to succeed (Brun de Pontet et al., 2007).

The ninth issue, *agreement*, uses both aspects of communication and discussion to lead to an agreement that involves the incumbent, successor, family members and key stakeholders. Indeed, conflicts between generations represent the most destructive force the family business faces (Harvey & Evans, 1994). The agreement must be sought not only within the family, but also recognize resistance from various stakeholders, as they could represent a key reason for failure (Handler & Kram, 1988). Here, the ability to delegate must be considered crucial for successors to be effective.

The tenth and final aspect *involvement*, presents the necessity of balancing the incumbent's and successor's roles. Indeed, succession can be conceptualized as a mutual role adjustment between incumbents and the next-generation family members (Handler, 1990), jointly reinforcing the power of the successor and reducing the involvement of older-generations in the family business after succession (Harvey & Evans, 1995).

Conclusion

This chapter provides a review of the published research on succession in family businesses and an agenda for future research. Our review and discussion of the literature shows that most prior research consists of either descriptive investigations based on aggregated data, or micro studies of firm succession based on small samples or a number of illustrative cases. Most articles make their recommendations to practitioners on small samples without the potential to draw general conclusions. We suggest there is a strong need for a research approach that bases implications on theoretically motivated research designs with the potential to draw more general conclusions.

Our synthesis of the literature identifies several areas for future research that is of interest for both managers and public policy. Based on our review and synthesis of the literature, we suggest the following areas as being particularly promising: First, the specific topic of ownership transition is worthy of more attention since most attention in previous studies has been on management succession. By focusing more on the role and impact of ownership for both succession *processes* and succession *outcomes*, researchers can make important contributions. Second, arguments related to the multilevel nature of the succession process need to be reflected in the research design employed, particularly within the stream of quantitative work. Third, the local and regional contexts need to be incorporated within the study of ownership transitions and successions since our literature review indicates these processes may be contextually contingent. In sum, although the topic of succession in family firms has attracted significant research attention, there are still vast opportunities to advance the research on ownership transitions and successions – theoretically, conceptually, and methodologically – and generate insights relevant for theory, practitioners, and policy-makers.

Notes

1. The correlation between ownership and management in empirical studies of family firms often amounts to between 0.5 and 0.7 (Block, Jaskiewicz, & Miller, 2011).
2. At the end of Table 8.2, we list prior literature reviews not considered in the cluster analysis.
3. Multilevel is the term used in social science to describe a phenomenon that unfolds or is under the influence of different levels of analysis (i.e., individual, family, firm, region). This is different from the multilevel model, which refers to a statistical model whose parameters vary on more than one level (Kozlowski & Klein, 2000).
4. Almost 50 percent of empirical studies in our review concern the US while 10 percent focuses on Canada or the UK.

5. Although the role of taxes is investigated in Bjuggren and Sund (2002) and File and Prince (1996), these are within-country studies and hence exclude variations in institutional settings.

References

Ambrose, D. (1983). Transfer of the family-owned business. *Journal of Small Business Management*, *21*(1), 49–56.*

Aronoff, C. (1998). Megatrends in family business. *Family Business Review*, *11*(3), 181–6.*

Astrachan, J.H. (2010). Strategy in family business: Toward a multidimensional research agenda. *Journal of Family Business Strategy*, *1*(1), 6–14.

Ayres, G. (1990). Rough family justice: Equity in family business succession planning. *Family Business Review*, *3*(1), 3–22.*

Ayres, G. (1998). Rough corporate justice. *Family Business Review*, *11*(2), 91–106.*

Bachkaniwala, D., Wright, M., & Ram, M. (2001). Succession in South Asian family businesses in the UK. *International Small Business Journal*, *19*(4), 15.*

Barach, J., & Ganitsky, J. (1995). Successful succession in family business. *Family Business Review*, *8*(2), 131.*

Barnes, L., & Hershon, S. (1976). Transferring power in the family business. *Harvard Business Review*, *54*(4), 105–14.*

Bennedsen, M., Nielsen, K.M., Pérez-González, F., & Wolfenzon, D. (2007). Inside the family firm: The role of families in succession decisions and performance. *The Quarterly Journal of Economics*, *122*(2), 647–91.

Berenbeim, R. (1990). How business families manage the transition from owner to professional management. *Family Business Review*, *3*(1), 69–110.*

Birley, S. (1986). Succession in the family firm: The inheritor's view. *Journal of Small Business Management*, *24*(3), 36–43.*

Birley, S. (2002). Attitudes of owner-managers' children towards family and business issues. *Entrepreneurship Theory and Practice*, *26*(3), 5–20.*

Bjuggren, P.O., & Sund, L.G. (2001). Strategic decision making in intergenerational successions of small- and medium-size family-owned businesses. *Family Business Review*, *14*(1), 11–24.*

Bjuggren, P.O., & Sund, L.G. (2002). A transition cost rationale for transition of the firm within the family. *Small Business Economics*, *19*(2), 123–33.*

Bjuggren, P.O., & Sund, L.G. (2005). Organization of transfers of small and medium-sized enterprises within the family: Tax law considerations. *Family Business Review*, *18*, 305–19.*

Block, J.H., Jaskiewicz, P., & Miller, D. (2011). Ownership versus management effects on performance in family and founder companies: A Bayesian reconcilation, *Journal of Family Business Strategy*, *2* (4), 232–45.

Brenes, E., Madrigal, K., & Molina-Navarro, G. (2006). Family business structure and succession: Critical topics in Latin American experience. *Journal of Business Research*, *59*(3), 372–74.*

Brockhaus, R., Sr. (2004). Family business succession: Suggestions for future research. *Family Business Review*, *17*(2), 165–77.*

Brown, F. (1993). Loss and continuity in the family firm. *Family Business Review*, *6*(2), 111–30.*

Brown, R., & Coverley, R. (1999). Succession planning in family businesses: A study from East Anglia, UK. *Journal of Small Business Management*, *37*(1), 93–8.*

Bruce, D., & Picard, D. (2006). Making succession a success: Perspectives from Canadian small- and medium-sized enterprises. *Journal of Small Business Management*, *44*(2), 306–9.*

Brun de Pontet, S., Wrosch, C., & Gagne, M. (2007). An exploration of the generational differences in levels of control held among family businesses approaching succession. *Family Business Review*, *20*(4), 337–54.*

Cabrera-Suárez, K. (2005). Leadership transfer and the successor's development in the family firm. *The Leadership Quarterly*, *16*(1), 71–96.*

Cabrera-Suárez, K., De Saa-Perez, P., & Garcia-Almeida, D. (2001). The succession process from a resource-and knowledge-based view of the family firm. *Family Business Review*, *14*(1), 37–46.*

Cadieux, L. (2007). Succession in small- and medium-sized family businesses: Toward a typology of predecessor roles during and after instatement of the successor. *Family Business Review*, *20*(2), 95–109.*

Cadieux, L., Lorrain, J., & Hugron, P. (2002). Succession in women-owned family businesses: A case study. *Family Business Review*, *15*(1), 17–30.*

Carree, M., & Thurik, A. (2003). The impact of entrepreneurship on economic growth. In Z. Acs & D. Audretsch (Eds.), *Handbook of entrepreneurship research* (pp. 437–72). Dordrecht, Neth.: Kluwer Academic Publishers.

Cater, J., & Justis, R. (2009). The development of successors from followers to leaders in small family firms: An exploratory study. *Family Business Review*, *22*(2), 109–24.*

Chau, T. (1991). Approaches to succession in East Asian business organizations. *Family Business Review*, *4*(2), 161–79.*

Chittoor, R., & Das, R. (2007). Professionalization of management and succession performance– A vital linkage. *Family Business Review*, *20*(1), 65–79.*

Chrisman, J., Chua, J., Kellermanns, F., Matherne III, C., & Debicki, B. (2008). Management journals as venues for publication of family business research. *Entrepreneurship Theory and Practice*, *32*(5), 927–34.

Chrisman, J., Chua, J., & Sharma, P. (1998). Important attributes of successors in family businesses: An exploratory study. *Family Business Review*, *11*(1), 19–34.*

Chua, J., Chrisman, J., & Sharma, P. (2003). Succession and nonsuccession concerns of family firms and agency relationship with nonfamily managers. *Family Business Review*, *16*(2), 89–107.*

Churchill, N., & Hatten, K. (1997). Non-market-based transfers of wealth and power: A research framework for family business. *Family Business Review*, *10*(1), 53–67.*

Clifford, M., Nilakant, V., & Hamilton, R. (1991). Management succession and the stages of small business development. *International Small Business Journal*, *9*(4), 43–55.*

Corbetta, G., & Montemerlo, D. (1999). Ownership, governance, and management issues in small and medium-size family businesses: A comparison of Italy and the United States. *Family Business Review*, *12*(4), 361–74.*

Correll, R. (1989). Facing up to moving forward: A third-generation successor's reflections. *Family Business Review*, *2*(1), 17–29.*

Cucculelli, M., & Micucci, G. (2008). Family succession and firm performance: Evidence from Italian family firms. *Journal of Corporate Finance*, *14*(1), 17–31.

Davis, P., & Harveston, P. (1998). The influence of family on the family business succession process: A multi-generational perspective. *Entrepreneurship Theory and Practice*, *22*(3), 31–3.*

De Massis, A., Chua, J., & Chrisman, J. (2008). Factors preventing intra-family succession. *Family Business Review*, *21*(2), 183–99.*

Debicki, B., Matherne, C., Kellermanns, F.W., & Chrisman, J. (2009). Family business research in the new millennium. *Family Business Review*, *22*(2), 151–66.

DeNoble, A., Ehrlich, S., & Singh, G. (2007). Toward the development of a family business self-efficacy scale: A resource-based perspective. *Family Business Review*, *20*(2), 127–40.*

DeTienne, D.R. (2010). Entrepreneurial exit as a critical component of the entrepreneurial process: Theoretical development. *Journal of Business Venturing*, *25*(2), 203–15.

Dimsdale, P. (1974). Management succession. Facing the future. *Journal of Small Business Management*, *12*(4), 42–6.*

Diwisch, D., Voithofer, P., & Weiss, C. (2009). Succession and firm growth: Results from a non-parametric matching approach. *Small Business Economics*, *32*(1), 45–56.*

Dumas, C., Dupuis, J., Richer, F., & St-Cyr, L. (1995). Factors that influence the next generation's decision to take over the family farm. *Family Business Review*, *8*(2), 99–120.*

Dunn, B. (1999). The family factor: The impact of family relationship dynamics on business-owning families during transitions. *Family Business Review*, *12*(1), 41–57.*

Dyck, B., Mauws, M., Starke, F., & Mischke, G. (2002). Passing the baton: The importance of sequence, timing, technique and communication in executive succession. *Journal of Business Venturing*, *17*(2), 143–62.*

Dyer, W., Jr., & Handler, W. (1994). Entrepreneurship and family business: Exploring the connections. *Entrepreneurship Theory and Practice*, *19*(1), 71–83.*

Fahed-Sreih, J., & Djoundourian, S. (2006). Determinants of longevity and success in Lebanese family businesses: An exploratory study. *Family Business Review, 19*(3), 225–234.*

Fiegener, M., Brown, B.M., Prince, R.A., & File, K.M. (1994). A comparison of successor development in family and nonfamily businesses. *Family Business Review, 7*(4), 313–29.*

Fiegener, M., Brown, B.M., Prince, R.A., & File, K.M. (1996). Passing on strategic vision: Favored modes of successor preparation by CEOs of family and non-family firms. *Journal of Small Business Management, 34*(3), 15–26.*

File, K.M., & Prince, R.A. (1996). Attributions for family business failure: The heir's perspective. *Family Business Review, 9*(2), 171–84.*

Foster, A. (1995). Developing leadership in the successor generation. *Family Business Review, 8*(3), 201–9.*

Fox, M., Nilakant, V., & Hamilton, R. (1996). Managing succession in family-owned businesses. *International Small Business Journal, 15*(1), 15–25.*

Galiano, A., & Vinturella, J. (1995). Implications of gender bias in the family business. *Family Business Review, 8*(3), 177–88.*

Garcia-Álvarez, E., López-Sintas, J., & Gonzalvo, P. (2002). Socialization patterns of successors in first- to second-generation family businesses. *Family Business Review, 15*(3), 189–203.*

Gersick, K., Lansberg, I., Desjardins, M., & Dunn, B. (1999). Stages and transitions: Managing change in the family business. *Family Business Review, 12*(4), 287–97.*

Goldberg, S. (1996). Research note: Effective successors in family-owned businesses: Significant elements. *Family Business Review, 9*(2), 185–97.*

Goldberg, S., & Wooldridge, B. (1993). Self-confidence and managerial autonomy: Successor characteristics critical to succession in family firms. *Family Business Review, 6*(1), 55–73.*

Handler, W. (1990). Succession in family firms: A mutual role adjustment between entrepreneur and next-generation family members. *Entrepreneurship Theory and Practice, 15*(1), 37–51.*

Handler, W. (1991). Key interpersonal relationships of next-generation family members in family firms. *Journal of Small Business Management, 29*(3), 21–32.*

Handler, W. (1992). The succession experience of the next generation. *Family Business Review, 5*(3), 283–307.*

Handler, W. (1994). Succession in family business: A review of the research. *Family Business Review, 7*(2), 133–57.*

Handler, W., & Kram, K. (1988). Succession in family firms: The problem of resistance. *Family Business Review, 1*(4), 361–81.*

Harveston, P., Davis, P., & Lyden, J. (1997). Succession planning in family business: The impact of owner gender. *Family Business Review, 10*(4), 373–96.*

Harvey, M., & Evans, R. (1994). The impact of timing and mode of entry on successor development and successful succession. *Family Business Review, 7*(3), 221–36.*

Harvey, M., & Evans, R. (1995). Life after succession in the family business: Is it really the end of problems? *Family Business Review, 8*(1), 3–16.*

Haveman, H. (1993). Ghosts of managers past: Managerial succession and organizational mortality. *Academy of Management Journal, 36*(4), 864–881.*

Haveman, H., & Khaire, M.V. (2004). Survival beyond succession? The contingent impact of founder succession on organizational failure. *Journal of Business Venturing, 19*(3), 437–63.*

Henrekson, M. (2005). Entrepreneurship: A weak link in the welfare state? *Industrial and Corporate Change, 14*(3), 437–67.

Hoang, H., & Gimeno, J. (2010). Becoming a founder: How founder role identity affects entrepreneurial transitions and persistence in founding. *Journal of Business Venturing, 25*(1), 41–53.*

Howorth, C., & Assaraf Ali, Z. (2001). Family business succession in Portugal: An examination of case studies in the furniture industry. *Family Business Review, 14*(3), 231–44.*

Howorth, C., Westhead, P., & Wright, M. (2004). Buyouts, information asymmetry and the family management dyad. *Journal of Business Venturing, 19*(4), 509–34.*

Huang, T. (1999). Who shall follow? Factors affecting the adoption of succession plans in Taiwan. *Long Range Planning, 32*(6), 609–16.*

Ibrahim, A., Soufani, K., & Lam, J. (2001). A study of succession in a family firm. *Family Business Review, 14*(3), 245–58.*

James, H.S. (1999). Owner as manager, extended horizons and the family firm. *International Journal of the Economics of Business*, *6*(1), 41–55.

Janjuha-Jivraj, S., & Woods, A. (2002). Successional issues within Asian family firms: Learning from the Kenyan experience. *International Small Business Journal*, *20*(1), 77–94.*

Kaslow, F. (1998). Handling transitions from mother to son in the family business: The knotty issues. *Family Business Review*, *11*(3), 229–38.*

Keating, N., & Little, H. (1997). Choosing the successor in New Zealand family farms. *Family Business Review*, *10*(2), 157–71.*

Kesner, I.F., & Sebora, T.C. (1994). Executive succession: Past, present & future. *Journal of Management*, *20*(2), 327–72.*

Kimhi, A. (1997). Intergenerational succession in small family businesses: Borrowing constraints and optimal timing of succession. *Small Business Economics*, *9*(4), 309–18.*

Kirby, D., & Lee, T. (1996). Research note: Succession management in family firms in northeast England. *Family Business Review*, *9*(1), 75–85.*

Kozlowski, S., & Klein, K. (2000). A multilevel approach to theory and research in organizations: Contextual, temporal, and emergent issues. In S. Kozlowski and K. Klein (Eds.), *Multilevel theory, research, and methods in organizations: Foundations, extensions, and new directions* (pp. 391). San Francisco, CA: Jossey-Bass.

Kuratko, D., Hornsby, J.S., & Montagno, R. (1993). Family business succession in Korean and US firms. *Journal of Small Business Management*, *31*(2), 132–136.*

Lambrecht, J. (2005). Multigenerational transition in family businesses: A new explanatory model. *Family Business Review*, *18*(4), 267–282.*

Lansberg, I. (1988). The succession conspiracy. *Family Business Review*, *1*(2), 119–143.*

Lansberg, I., & Astrachan, J. (1994). Influence of family relationships on succession planning and training: The importance of mediating factors. *Family Business Review*, *7*(1), 39–59.*

Le Breton-Miller, I., Miller, D., & Steier, L. (2004). Toward an integrative model of effective FOB succession. *Entrepreneurship Theory and Practice*, *28*(4), 305–28.*

Lee, K., Lim, G., & Lim, W. (2003). Family business succession: Appropriation risk and choice of successor. *The Academy of Management Review*, *28*(4), 657–66.*

Longenecker, J., & Schoen, J. (1978). Management succession in the family business. *Journal of Small Business Management*, *16*(3), 1–6.*

Lumpkin, G., Brigham, K.H., & Moss, T.W. (2010). Long-term orientation: Implications for the entrepreneurial orientation and performance of family businesses. *Entrepreneurship & Regional Development*, *22*(3), 241–64.

MacMillan, I.C. (1993). The emerging forum for entrepreneurship scholars. *Journal of Business Venturing*, *8*(5), 377–81.

Malone, S. (1989). Selected correlates of business continuity planning in the family business. *Family Business Review*, *2*(4), 341–53.*

Mandelbaum, L. (1994). Small business succession: The educational potential. *Family Business Review*, *7*(4), 369–75.*

Marshall, J., Sorenson, R., Brigham, K., Wieling, E., Reifman, A., & Wampler, R. (2006). The paradox for the family firm CEO: Owner-age relationship to succession-related processes and plans. *Journal of Business Venturing*, *21*(3), 348–68.*

Mason, C., & Harrison, R. (2006). After the exit: Acquisitions, entrepreneurial recycling and regional economic development. *Regional Studies*, *40*(1), 55–73.

Matthews, C.H., Moore, T., & Fialko, A. (1999). Succession in the family firm: A cognitive categorization perspective. *Family Business Review*, *12*(2), 159–69.*

McCollom, M. (1992). The ownership trust and succession paralysis in the family business. *Family Business Review*, *5*(2), 145–60.*

McGivern, C. (1989). The dynamics of management succession: A model of chief executive succession in the small family firm. *Family Business Review*, *2*(4), 401–11.*

Miller, D., Steier, L., & Le Breton-Miller, I. (2003). Lost in time: Intergenerational succession, change, and failure in family business. *Journal of Business Venturing*, *18*(4), 513–31.*

Motwani, J., Levenburg, N., Schwarz, T., & Blankson, C. (2006). Succession planning in SMEs: An empirical analysis. *International Small Business Journal*, *24*(5), 471–95.*

Murray, B. (2003). The succession transition process: A longitudinal perspective. *Family Business Review, 16*(1), 17–33.*

Nam, Y., & Herbert, J. (1999). Characteristics and key success factors in family business: The case of Korean immigrant businesses in metro-Atlanta. *Family Business Review, 12*(4), 341–52.*

Nordqvist, M., & Melin, L. (2010). Entrepreneurial families and family firms. *Entrepreneurship & Regional Development, 22*(3), 211–39.

Peay, T., & Dyer, W., Jr. (1989). Power orientations of entrepreneurs and succession planning. *Journal of Small Business Management, 27*(1), 47–52.*

Perricone, P., Earle, J., & Taplin, I. (2001). Patterns of succession and continuity in family-owned businesses: Study of an ethnic community. *Family Business Review, 14*(2), 105–21.*

Post, J., & Robins, R. (1993). The captive king and his captive court: The psychopolitical dynamics of the disabled leader and his inner circle. *Family Business Review, 6*(2), 203–21.*

Poza, E.J., Hanlon, S., & Kishida, R. (2004). Does the family business interaction factor represent a resource or a cost? *Family Business Review, 17*(2), 99–118.*

Poza, E.J., & Messer, T. (2001). Spousal leadership and continuity in the family firm. *Family Business Review, 14*(1), 25–36.*

Rogers, E., Carsrud, A., & Krueger, N., Jr. (1996). Chiefdoms and family firm regimes: Variations on the same anthropological themes. *Family Business Review, 9*(1), 15–27.*

Royer, S., Simons, R., Boyd, B., & Rafferty, A. (2008). Promoting family: A contingency model of family business succession. *Family Business Review, 21*(1), 15–30.*

Rubenson, G., & Gupta, A. (1996). The initial succession: A contingency model of founder tenure. *Entrepreneurship Theory and Practice, 21*(2), 21–35.*

Santiago, A. (2000). Succession experiences in Philippine family businesses. *Family Business Review, 13*(1), 15–35.*

Scholes, M., Wright, M., Westhead, P., Burrows, A., & Bruining, H. (2007). Information sharing, price negotiation and management buy-outs of private family-owned firms. *Small Business Economics, 29*(3), 329–49.*

Seymour, K. (1993). International relationships in the family firm: The effect on leadership succession. *Family Business Review, 6*(3), 263–81.*

Shane, S. (1997). Who is publishing the entrepreneurship research? *Journal of Management, 23*(1), 83–95.

Sharma, P. (2004). An overview of the field of family business studies: Current status and directions for the future. *Family Business Review, 17*(1), 1–36.

Sharma, P., Chrisman, J., & Chua, J. (2003a). Predictors of satisfaction with the succession process in family firms. *Journal of Business Venturing, 18*(5), 667–87.*

Sharma, P., Chrisman, J., & Chua, J. (2003b). Succession planning as planned behavior: Some empirical results. *Family Business Review, 16*(1), 1–15.*

Sharma, P., Chrisman, J., Pablo, A., & Chua, J. (2001). Determinants of initial satisfaction with the succession process in family firms: A conceptual model. *Entrepreneurship Theory and Practice, 25*(3), 17–35.*

Sharma, P., & Irving, P. (2005). Four bases of family business successor commitment: Antecedents and consequences. *Entrepreneurship Theory and Practice, 29*(1), 13–33.*

Sharma, P., & Rao, S. (2000). Successor attributes in Indian and Canadian family firms: A comparative study. *Family Business Review, 13*(4), 313–30.*

Shepherd, D., & Zacharakis, A. (2000). Structuring family business succession: An analysis of the future leader's decision making. *Entrepreneurship Theory and Practice, 24*(4), 25–39.*

Sonfield, M., & Lussier, R.N. (2004). First-, second-, and third-generation family firms: A comparison. *Family Business Review, 17*(3), 189–202.*

Sonnenfeld, J., & Spence, P. (1989). The parting patriarch of a family firm. *Family Business Review, 2*(4), 355–75.*

Stavrou, E. (1998). A four factor model: A guide to planning next generation involvement in the family firm. *Family Business Review, 11*(2), 135–42.*

Stavrou, E. (1999). Succession in family businesses: Exploring the effects of demographic factors on offspring intentions to join and take over the business. *Journal of Small Business Management, 37*(3), 43–4.*

Stavrou, E. (2003). Leadership succession in owner-managed firms through the lens of extraversion. *International Small Business Journal, 21*(3), 331–47.*

Stavrou, E., Kleanthous, T., & Anastasiou, T. (2005). Leadership personality and firm culture during hereditary transitions in family firms: Model development and empirical investigation. *Journal of Small Business Management, 43*(2), 187–206.*

Stavrou, E., & Swiercz, P. (1998). Securing the future of the family enterprise: A model of offspring intentions to join the business. *Entrepreneurship Theory and Practice, 23*(2), 19–21.*

Steier, L. (2001). Next-generation entrepreneurs and succession: An exploratory study of modes and means of managing social capital. *Family Business Review, 14*(3), 259–76.*

Swagger, G. (1991). Assessing the successor generation in family businesses. *Family Business Review, 4*(4), 397–411.*

Tatoglu, E., Kula, V., & Glaister, K. (2008). Succession planning in family-owned businesses: Evidence from Turkey. *International Small Business Journal, 26*(2), 155–80.*

Thomas, J. (2002). Freeing the shackles of family business ownership. *Family Business Review, 15*(4), 321–36.*

Tylecote, A., & Visintin, F. (2008). *Corporate governance, finance and the technological advantage of nations.* Abingdon, UK: Routledge.

Van Praag, C.M., & Versloot, P.H. (2007). What is the value of entrepreneurship? A review of recent research. *Small Business Economics, 29*(4), 351–82.

Venter, E., Boshoff, C., & Maas, G. (2005). The influence of successor-related factors on the succession process in small and medium-sized family businesses. *Family Business Review, 18*(4), 283–303.*

Vera, C., & Dean, M. (2005). An examination of the challenges daughters face in family business succession. *Family Business Review, 18*(4), 321–45.*

Wennberg, K. (2005). Entrepreneurship research through databases: Measurement and design issues. *New England Journal of Entrepreneurship, 8*(2), 9–18.

Wennberg, K., Wiklund, J., DeTienne, D.R., & Cardon, M.S. (2010). Reconceptualizing entrepreneurial exit: Divergent exit routes and their drivers. *Journal of Business Venturing, 25*(4), 361–75.

Wennberg, K., Wiklund, J., Hellerstedt, K., & Nordqvist, M. (2011). Implications of intra-family and external ownership transfer of family firms: Short-term and long-term performance differences. *Strategic Entrepreneurship Journal, 5*(4), 352–72.

Westhead, P. (2003). Succession decision-making outcomes reported by private family companies. *International Small Business Journal, 21*(4), 369–401.*

Wortman, M. (1994). Theoretical foundations for family-owned business: A conceptual and research-based paradigm. *Family Business Review, 7*(1), 3–27.*

Wright, M., Thompson, S., & Robbie, K. (1992). Venture capital and management-led, leveraged buy-outs: A European perspective. *Journal of Business Venturing, 7*(1), 47–71. *

Yan, J., & Sorenson, R. (2006). The effect of Confucian values on succession in family business. *Family Business Review, 19*(3), 235–50.*

Yu, A., Lumpkin, G.T., Sorenson, R.L., & Brigham, K.H. (2012). The landscape of family business outcomes: A summary and numerical taxonomy of dependent variables. *Family Business Review, 25*(1), 33–57.

Zahra, S., Hayton, J., & Salvato, C. (2004). Entrepreneurship in family vs. non-family firms: A resource-based analysis of the effect of organizational culture. *Entrepreneurship Theory and Practice, 28*(4), 363–81.*

Note: The asterisk (*) identifies those papers that have been considered in the cluster analysis.

Appendix 1: Description of the cluster analysis

"Cluster analysis consists in a group of multivariate techniques whose primary purpose is to group objects based on the characteristics they possesses" (Hair et al., 2010: 508).[1] The primary goal of these techniques is to partition a set of objects into groups, based on the similarity of the objects for a set of specified characteristics. In our analysis, those characteristics denote 15 different dimensions of the studies identified, related to:

i.   level of analysis (four variables, adopted from Handler & Kram 1988)
ii. phase of succession (four variables, adopted from Le Breton-Miller et al. 2004)
iii. the family-or firm-members involved (seven variables, adopted from Sharma 2004)

We used a hierarchical cluster analysis to classify the 117 articles through 15 dummy variables. Clustering methods generally group objects by their similarity on all variables considered simultaneously (Bailey, 1975).[2] Each object, in our case each paper, must be in one, and in only one, group since cluster analysis is based on exhaustiveness and mutual exclusiveness. The cluster method chosen is the average linkage between groups considering the Jaccard similarity measure for binary data. The problem of how to cut the cluster must be solved subjectively (Bailey, 1975). There is no objective method of cutting. Following this procedure revealed the following hierarchical structure of studies:

1.   environmental studies
2.1.   firm-level studies (pre-succession)
2.2.   individual/interpersonal studies
2.2.1.   post-succession studies (individual/interpersonal studies)
2.2.2.1. managing succession (individual/interpersonal studies)
2.2.2.2. multilevel studies
2.2.2.3. pre-succession (individual/interpersonal studies)
2.2.2.4. planning succession (individual/interpersonal studies)

The highest distance between the clusters regards those studies that refer to the environmental dimension (1.), looking at factors that are external to the organization. Those studies focus on several topics; some refer to economic models, others focus on financial considerations. The cluster analysis also reveals a second group of articles that put particular attention to the firm-level dimension (2.1.). This group of articles contains two categories of studies: those that make general considerations about the succession moving from a firm perspective and studies presenting corporate governance aspects.

The largest cluster of articles refers to studies focusing on the individual and interpersonal level (2.2.1. and 2.2.2.) – totaling close to 80 percent of all studies investigated. In order to better understand and analyze the contribution of those articles, we reduced the distance between these clusters. This yielded five new groups; four clearly recognize the different phases of the succession process: pre-succession (2.2.2.3.), planning succession (2.2.2.4.), managing succession (2.2.2.1), post-succession (2.2.1); and a fifth one that we denote as multilevel studies (2.2.2.2.). This last category has attended to relations between one or several focal agents and external contingencies involved in the succession process.

In order to simplify the presentation of our findings and make a more clear classification of the papers, we maintain the content that we obtain from the cluster analysis, using a more linear classification as follows:

1.   environmental studies
2.   firm-level studies
3.   individual/interpersonal studies
3.1 pre-succession
3.2 planning succession
3.3 managing succession
3.4 post-succession
4.   multilevel studies

Notes

1.   Hair, J., Anderson, R., Tatham, R., Black, W., 2010. Multivariate data analysis: A global perspective. Prentice Hall, Englewood Cliffs, NJ.
2.   Bailey, K.D., 1975. Cluster analysis. Sociological Methodology (1974), 1–54.

Appendix 2:   The evolution of succession studies 1975–2009

The three figures here present the evolution of the succession studies considered in this review in the period 1975–2009 through three different lenses: the journal (figure 8A.1), the approach (figure 8A.2), and the level of analysis according to our cluster analysis (figure 8A.3).

Figure 8A.1 presents the attention given to succession related issues in the six journals that present the highest number of studies about succession. *Family Business Review* (FBR) presents after 1995–1999 a decreasing interest on succession that is compensated by the journals mainly referring to the entrepreneurial perspective, such as *Entrepreneurship Theory and Practice* (ETP), *Journal of Business Venturing* (JBV), and *International Small Business Journal* (ISBJ). This interest drops significantly in 2005–2009.

Figure 8A.2 presents the approach adopted by succession researchers during this time period. We recognize a first exploratory interest satisfied through case studies that favored the development of theoretical models. Multivariate techniques of analysis were introduced later, following the development of the qualitative literature and the early analysis done through descriptive statistics. In the first decade of 2000, we see a decreasing contribution given by theoretical studies that appears to be conpensated by a common path traced by case studies and multivariate analyses. At the same time, we recognize in the development of the field and the editorial lines of the journals a reduced interest in practitioners' considerations.

Figure 8A.3 and Table 8A.1 present the evolution of the succession research through the classification we have obtained from the cluster analysis presented in Appendix 1. The dotted lines represent the four perspectives of individual and interpersonal studies. The evolution presents some interesting insights. It is clear that the development of a succession passes through the necessity of managing the process, moving to the consideration of the importance of the pianification. In the late 90s, researchers focused attention on the pre- and post-succession phases, reinforcing the necessity of considering succession

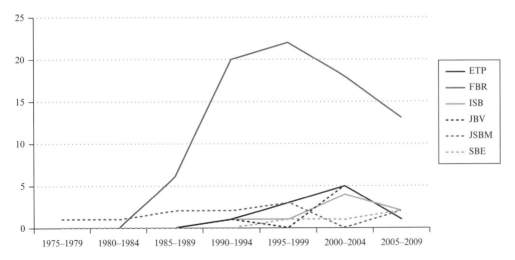

Figure 8A.1   Top six journals for succession studies in 1975–2009

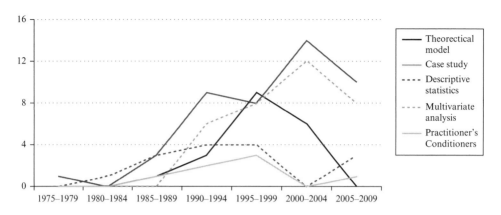

Figure 8A.2   Approaches to succession in the literature

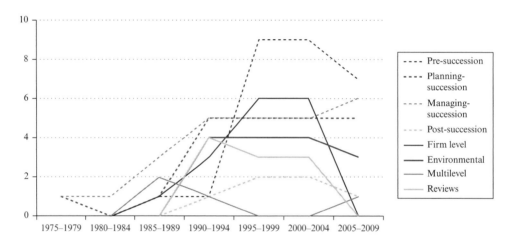

Figure 8A.3   Evolution of the succession literature according to the level of analysis

as a long and critical process. In the same period, we recognize also the introduction of other levels of analysis such as firm- and enviromental-levels. The drop in interest from 2005–2009 suggests the importance of exploring new paths of analysis that could provide new empirical results supported by solid theories and valid managerial implications.

Table 8A.1   Evolution of the succession literature according to the level of analysis

	1975–1979	1980–1984	1985–1989	1990–1994	1995–1999	2000–2004	2005–2009
Individual/Interpersonal level	2	1	5	12	20	21	19
– pre-succession – attitudes and willingness	0	0	1	1	6	3	1
– pre-succession – national/ethnical context	0	0	0	0	2	4	2
– pre-succession – predecessor/ successor	0	0	0	0	1	2	4
– planning-succession – contingencies	0	0	1	0	3	0	4
– planning-succession – general	1	0	0	2	0	3	1
– planning-succession – relations	0	0	0	3	1	2	0
– managing-succession – "co-habitation"	1	1	1	2	3	2	0
– managing-succession – family relations	0	0	0	2	2	1	2
– managing-succession – internal and external transfer	0	0	1	1	0	1	4
– managing-succession – process	0	0	1	0	1	1	0
– post-succession	0	0	0	1	1	2	1
Firm level	0	0	1	3	5	6	0
– corporate governance	0	0	1	1	2	4	0
– preliminary considerations	0	0	0	2	3	2	0
Environmental level	0	0	0	4	3	4	3
– buy-in/-out	0	0	0	1	0	0	1
– economic models	0	0	0	0	1	0	1
– fiscal dimension	0	0	0	1	1	2	1
– national/ethnical aspects	0	0	0	2	1	2	0
Multi level	0	0	2	1	2	0	1

9.   A second look and commentary on the landscape of family business

Franz W. Kellermanns and Laura J. Stanley

A commentary on a numerical taxonomy of family business outcomes

As family firm research has grown both in numbers (e.g., Debicki, Matherne, Kellermanns, & Chrisman, 2009; Wright & Kellermanns, 2011) and quality of outlets (e.g., Gómez-Mejía, Haynes, Núñez-Nickel, Jacobson, & Moyano-Fuentes, 2007; Ling & Kellermans, 2010; Schulze, Lubatkin, Dino, & Buchholtz, 2001), it is not surprising that family firm performance has become an important topic in family firm research. Indeed, understanding and measuring family business outcomes in general will be central to the future development and credibility of family firm research as a field. Examining these outcomes may provide insight into the uniqueness of family firms. As family firm researchers strive to define the boundaries of the field of family business, identifying those outcomes that differentiate family from non-family firms (e.g., socio-emotional wealth; Gómez-Mejía et al., 2007) becomes increasingly important.

Thus, the paper by Yu, Lumpkin, Brigham, and Sorenson (2012) is a timely piece that constitutes the first systematic investigation of family business outcomes.* Through detailed analysis, they identify seven different outcome domains in family firm research. Specifically, their study identifies business Performance, Strategy, Social and Economic Impact, Governance, Succession, Family Business Roles, and Family Dynamics as the key dependent variables in family firm research. In fact, they conducted an additional study in which they asked 30 prolific researchers to identify variables that deserve more research attention or that are currently missing from investigation.

In this chapter, we will comment on family business outcomes along three broad dimensions. First, we will discuss traditional macro-outcomes, represented by the clusters of business Performance and Succession identified by Yu et al. (2012). These outcomes include both financial performance and succession, as without these two factors the viability of the family would be jeopardized. Second, we will focus on intermediate business-related outcomes, characterized by the clusters of Governance, Strategy, and Social and Economic Impact identified by Yu et al. (2012). These factors tend to either facilitate or hinder the aforementioned macro-level outcomes. Lastly, we will focus on softer outcomes that stress the family side in family business research, characterized by

---

*   "A Map of the Landscape of Family Business"(also referred to as the Landscape Map) can be found on the page just inside the cover of this book and in the Yu, Lumpkin, Sorenson, and Brigham (2012) article published in *Family Business Review*. Following the Landscape Map, the "Outcome Categories by Chapter Table" (also referred to as the Outcome Categories Table) is provided. This table shows all chapters that contain content about the outcome categories that appear in this chapter.

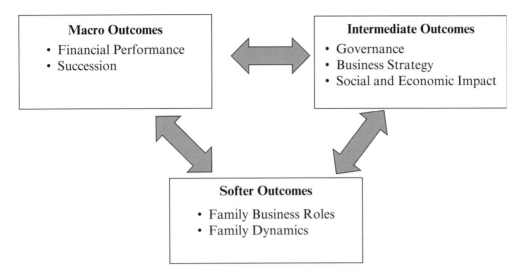

Macro Outcomes
- Financial Performance
- Succession

Intermediate Outcomes
- Governance
- Business Strategy
- Social and Economic Impact

Softer Outcomes
- Family Business Roles
- Family Dynamics

Figure 9.1   Interrelationships among the outcome groups

the Family Business Roles and Family Dynamics clusters identified by Yu et al. (2012). These aspects, aside from the succession outcome, focus on unique features to the family firm that set this type of organization apart from non-family businesses. The three broad-level outcomes are represented in Figure 9.1. It is important to note that these outcome classes have the ability to influence each other, as characterized by the reciprocal arrows in the figure. Below, we provide an overview of research in each of the outcome classes and provide examples of research in each class. We also comment about research that might be conducted in each class. The chapter concludes with suggestions for research and practice as well as additional future research opportunities.

Macro-level outcomes

Much of the strategic management and entrepreneurship research emphasizes perform-ance. Because family firm research emerged from the entrepreneurship domain, which in turn originated from strategic management research, family firm financial performance is at the heart of family business research. In this outcome class, a significant amount of research has focused on comparing the financial performance of family and non-family firms. Undoubtedly, research that emphasizes the uniqueness of family firms and clari-fies the boundaries of family business research is necessary in order to move the field forward. We will first comment on family versus non-family firm performance before we discuss succession as a second macro-level outcome.

In the realm of family firm research, many studies suggest that financial performance of family firms is worse than non-family firms (Chandler, 1977; Claessens, Djankov, Fan, & Lang, 2002; Miller, Le Breton-Miller, Lester, & Cannella, 2007; Schulze et al., 2001), mostly due to governance issues, which we will discuss in further detail in the next section of the chapter. Other studies have suggested the opposite. Specifically, these studies indi-cate that the family context may help achieve unique performance advantages (Andres,

2008; Eddleston & Kellermanns, 2007; Habbershon, Williams, & MacMillan, 2003; Sirmon & Hitt, 2003). Thankfully, this debate has been clarified in a meta-analysis by van Essen, Carney, Gedajlovic, Heugens, and van Osterhout (2011), which synthesized all published and unpublished papers on the topic. Their findings suggest that in publically traded firms, family firms outperform non-family firms (r=.007, K=123). They further show that this performance can be explained by the founder effect (this has been also suggested in prior research, e.g., Villalonga & Amit, 2006). The founder effect suggests that first generation firms (founder-run firms) achieve performance premiums, while later generation family firms do not perform as well as their non-family counterparts. Van Essen et al.'s (2011) findings point toward two important areas of further research. First, as suggested by Van Essen et al. (2011), the reasons for the underperformance of successor firms need to be investigated in more detail. Second, and equally important, these findings need to be validated for non-publically traded firms.

Family firms constitute between 60 and 90 percent of all firms across countries (e.g., Astrachan & Shanker, 2003; Chrisman, Chua, & Kellermanns, 2009). The majority of these firms are not publically traded. Thus, while it is useful to establish performance differences in publically traded firms, this research still ignores the majority of firms in existence. While there are also a substantial number of large, non-public family firms, future research needs to focus on performance differences *among* smaller family firms as well as *between* smaller family and non-family firms. Indeed, in these smaller family firms, positive effects of stewardship (e.g., Eddleston & Kellermanns, 2007) or negative effects of nepotism (e.g., Schulze et al., 2001) are much more likely to directly affect financial performance outcomes.

Studying private family firms poses additional problems. Obtaining objective data for small family firms is virtually impossible due to the private nature of many family firms. Accordingly, family firm researchers need to be aware of the challenges. While there is no panacea in terms of measuring the performance variable, multiple useful approaches can be taken. Specifically, we suggest assessing performance with multiple self-reported performance indicators (for operationalization see Eddleston & Kellermanns, 2007; Eddleston, Kellermanns, & Sarathy, 2008), while demonstrating consistency with a subset of multiple respondents per family firm (Eddleston et al., 2008; James, Demaree, & Wolf, 1993). As a matter of fact, objective and subjective performance assessments seem to correlate well in family firms (Ling & Kellermans, 2010).

Furthermore, growth of the family firm should be considered a useful and valuable dependent variable. A focus on growth would eliminate firms that are operated only to maintain a minimum income level and where succession is not a focus. In order for the business to provide income to the family across generations and to accommodate a poten- tially exponentially growing number of family members, family firms are under a "growth imperative" (Poza, 1989; Poza, Hanlon, & Kishida, 2004). Thus, investigating factors that will facilitate growth and allow for successful succession is necessary. However, not all firm growth is comparable. The type of growth (e.g., sales versus employment) needs to fit the research context and question to ensure that the drawn conclusions are valid (e.g., Shepherd & Wiklund, 2009; Wiklund, Pazelt, & Shepherd, 2009).

Succession research is another core research stream in the family firm literature and has attracted a significant amount of attention (see Debicki et al., 2009). While a full review of succession literature is beyond the scope of this chapter (for a recent review, see De Massis, Chua, & Chrisman, 2008), we would like to comment on a few essential areas of future succession research. Obtaining data from both former family firm CEOs and current family firm CEOs would ensure high data quality (for an exemplarly design, see Sharma, Chrisman, & Chua, 2003). Such an approach would reduce bias, as findings suggest that successors and incumbents often have significantly different perceptions about the succession process (Poza, Alfred, & Maheshawi, 1997). Ideally, the data would be collected during and after the actual succession process. Furthermore, future research should address the process and performance implications associated with succession within the family as well as succession from family to non-family members.

Intermediate outcomes

Yu et al. (2012) have identified a number of intermediate outcomes. These outcomes are potentially key antecedents of the aforementioned macro-outcomes. Grounded in strategy and entrepreneurship research, the tendency to link independent variables to performance variables is understandable. However, family firm research is still evolving and a theory of the family firm is in its infancy (e.g., Chrisman, Chua, & Steier, 2003; Chrisman, Steier, & Chua, 2008). Therefore, research that links constructs directly to performance may omit key mediators or contingency variables. Accordingly, family firm researchers should focus on more intermediate outcomes such as the social and economic impact (e.g., entrepreneurial behavior, learning), governance (e.g., human resources, decision-making), or business strategy (e.g., internationalization behavior, financial structure) in order to provide a more complete picture of that which makes family firms unique.

However, these intermediate outcomes do not exist in a vacuum, rather they need to be understood within the context of the family firm's history and the family members' cognition (i.e., the way they process and store knowledge as influenced by their membership in the family firm). Indeed, while the entrepreneurship literature has identified the importance of cognition pertaining to organizational processes (e.g., Baron, 2008), this literature remains widely untapped in family firm research (for exceptions see Morris, Allen, Kuratko, & Brannon, 2010; Stanley, 2010). For example, entrepreneurship research suggests that entrepreneurs are more likely to exhibit cognitive biases and to rely on past experiences when interpreting new information (Minniti & Bygrave, 1999; Walsh, 1995). Building on this evidence, researchers might determine how cognition affects decision-makers in family firms.

Recent work by Stanley (2010) suggests that early cognitive experiences may lead family firms toward path dependency. For example, family firms are often reluctant to change the culture or business models that were instituted by the founder. While this persistence can have a very positive effect, it can also constrain the family firm's ability to make decisions. Such path dependency may explain how a founder's shadow can persist beyond the first generation of the family firm and how it has the potential to explain performance differences between family and non-family firms that occur in later generations. Experiences of family firm founders in the venture creation process may affect family firm behavior even decades after the founder exits the business. Early "imprinting" of the business can create a powerful organizational culture for the family business. When starting a new business, family firm founders must endure not only a heavy cognitive load, but also intense emotional experiences. Evidence from the emotions literature suggests that cognition and emotion are reciprocal in nature such that cognition shapes emotions, and emotions strongly influence cognition through the way in which information is processed and stored into memory (Forgas, 1995; 2000; Isen, 2002). Interestingly, Morris et al. (2010) found that family founders and non-family founders differ in their affective states and decision-making. Stanley (2010) suggests that these differences in cognition are due to different patterns of emotions during the venture creation process. Indeed, family founders tend to experience more positive emotions than non-family firm founders (Morris et al., 2010; Stanley, 2010), which is likely to lead to a bonding with the business and desire for longevity and sustainability of the family firm. Accordingly, these divergent emotional experiences could be key distinguishing factors in the developmental paths of family and non-family firms.

As empirically demonstrated (Morris et al., 2010), early emotional experiences may influence family founders' cognition and behavior during early stages of the founding process. However, these experiences may also have more long-term effects, as suggested above. Early events in an organization's history often explain strategic choices and organizational outcomes well into the future (i.e., path dependence, Sydow, Schreyögg, & Koch, 2009) During venture creation, important decisions are made, but more importantly, the thought processes and subsequent actions associated with those decisions are likely to set the tone for future decisions and actions. Over time, perceptual biases and preferences often become locked-in in the culture and cultural routines, and may even dominate the development of organizational strategies, mental models, routines, and actions (Sydow et al., 2009). In this way, the family founder's early emotional experiences become imprinted on the firm, solidifying the firm's dominant decision processes and practices. Because family and non-family founders experience new venture creation differently (Morris et al., 2010; Stanley, 2010), family firms follow strategic paths that are fundamentally different from those of non-family firms. Due to family firms' reliance on the founder (e.g., Kelly, Athanassiou, & Crittenden, 2000), these differences may persist well into the future.

Furthermore, cognition may provide further insights into the occurrence of conflict (e.g., Kellermanns, Floyd, Pearson, & Spencer, 2008), which is central to family firm performance (Kellermanns & Eddleston, 2004; 2007). Another place in family firms where the relationship between cognition and emotion is very apparent is the occurrence of altruism in family firms. Indeed, cognition may help to better explain the types of altruism experienced in family firms (e.g., Eddleston & Kellermanns, 2007; Lubatkin, Ling, & Schulze, 2007; Schulze et al., 2001). This is critical, as altruism has been shown to affect various processes in family firms (e.g., Eddleston & Kellermanns, 2007; Schulze et al., 2001). These processes (e.g., reductive of negative conflict in family firms), in turn, affect the macro-performance outcomes described above.

Agency theory, which generally describes the relationship between the owner (principal) and managers (agents), and entrepreneurial behavior must also be addressed as these two topics have attracted a significant amount of attention in family firm research and are part of the identified clusters by Yu et al. (2012). The investigation of agency problems in family firms by Schulze et al. (2001) represented a significant breakthrough in family firm research, as it challenged general agency wisdom and extended existing theory. Prior to this study, it was assumed that there were no agency costs as the interest of the family members should be aligned with each other. However, Schulze et al. (2001) show that this is not necessarily the case in family firms, and that agency cost also exists in family businesses. Indeed, a later study by Chrisman, Chua, Kellermanns, and Chang (2007) showed that family firm performance can be enhanced if family members are subjected to governance mechanism, often applied only to non-family members, e.g., monitoring. This finding is notable, as family firm research has been criticized for borrowing from management theories but not giving back to these theories. Not surprisingly, agency theory has strongly influenced the family firm literature (Chrisman, Kellermanns, Chan, & Liano, 2010). However, although the topic of agency problems in family firms has received significant attention, much more research is needed. For example, we do not know how or which family and firm attributes influence the utilization of certain agency mechanisms.

Similarly, entrepreneurial behavior in family firms has attracted a significant amount of attention (e.g., Kellermanns & Eddleston, 2006; Naldi, Nordqvist, Sjoberg, & Wiklund, 2007; Short, Payne, Brigham, Lumpkin, & Broberg, 2009). This outcome variable is of particular interest, as it is considered controversial in family firm research. While a significant amount of research has characterized family firms as risk averse, some evidence suggests that family firms are more than willing to take risks, which calls for a new paradigm in family firm research (Uhlaner, Kellermanns, Eddleston, & Hoy, 2012). For example, Gómez-Mejía and colleagues (2007) showed that family firms are willing to risk all to maintain control of the organization in times of great distress. Here, the generation the business is in may serve as an additional explanatory factor. Specifically, recent research showed that the impact on strategic planning and succession planning on growth varies by the generation of the family firm (Eddleston, Kellermanns, Floyd, Crittenden, & Crittenden, forthcoming). Future research should address this ongoing debate.

Family-related outcomes

As a third outcome class, family-related outcomes need to be considered. The entire premise of family firm research is that family firms are distinct from non-family businesses due to the unique influence of the family on the business (e.g., Eddleston & Kellermanns, 2004). While the elements that constitute a family firm are important (e.g., family management, family ownership, trans-generational succession intention), the family-related outcomes are of utmost significance, as we will outline below. Research has long maintained that the family, management, and ownership domains overlap (Tagiuri & Davis, 1996), and that tension exists between the family and the business system (Sundaramurthy & Kreiner, 2008). These findings suggest that if negative effects that occur in the family (e.g., conflict) spill over into the family business, both the macro and intermediate outcomes discussed above can be affected. Overall, two contrasting views persist. Some research indicates that the family realm exerts a disturbing influence on the business system and that the family element should be eliminated through professionalization (Gedajlovic, Lubatkin, & Schulze, 2004; Schulze et al., 2001). Other research stresses the positive effects of the family by emphasizing the positive attributes the family can provide. For example, stewardship behavior (Eddleston & Kellermanns, 2007), long-term orientation (Zellweger, 2007) or socio-emotional wealth (Gómez-Mejía et al., 2007) can all lead to positive (macro) performance outcomes. The development of family firm social capital may provide a way to reconcile these two perspectives (for an example see Arregle, Hitt, Sirmon, & Very, 2007) in future research.

For this chapter, however, we would like to give particular attention to the construct of socio-emotional wealth, as this construct is unique to the realm of family business and remains widely unexplored (for exceptions, see Berrone, Cruz, Gómez-Mejía, & Larraza-Kintana, 2010; Cruz, Gómez-Mejía, & Becerra, 2010; Gómez-Mejía et al., 2007; Stockmans, Lybaert, & Voordeckers, 2010). Socio-emotional wealth "refers to non-financial aspects of the firm that meet the family's affective needs" (Gómez-Mejía et al., 2007, p. 106).

Socio-emotional wealth is derived from the non-financial benefits associated with authority, status, social capital, or the desire to transfer the organization to the next generation. These considerations may both consciously or unconsciously affect family firm behavior (see our discussion of the importance of cognition above). For example, Berrone and colleagues (Berrone et al., 2010) show that family firms pollute less than non-family firms due to their desire to maintain socio-emotional wealth. Thus, understanding how socio-emotional wealth is generated and the outcomes it affects, (e.g., family firms pollute less than non-family firms) is important to understanding family firm behavior and subsequent economic performance.

Another family-based outcome that should be mentioned is the identification of the family with the business. "Through identification, the organization becomes an extension of the employee's self and embodies the perception of 'oneness' an employee feels with an organization" (Ashforth & Mael, 1996 as paraphrased in Zellweger, Eddleston, & Kellermanns, 2010, p. 57). Family firm identification represents a connection between the family and the business system, and has recently been highlighted as an important building block in the effort to understand family firm behavior and performance (Sundaramurthy & Kreiner, 2008; Zellweger et al., 2010). Future research should more closely investigate the antecedents of family firm identification, and the relationship between family firm identification and firm performance.

Discussion

The clusters of family business outcomes identified by Yu et al. (2012) are not mutually exclusive, and provide evidence that the family and the business are highly intertwined in family firms. Thus, their clusters indirectly stress that both family and business-related outcomes need to be considered in order to fully understand family business performance.

In this chapter, we examined three types of outcomes in family firms that future research should address. Specifically, we examined macro-level outcomes, intermediate outcomes, and family outcomes. These three outcome classes are not mutually exclusive and can reinforce each other. Thus, it is necessary to understand the full spectrum of family outcomes and their relationships with each other.

While our commentary highlights some important areas of future research based on the clusters provided by Yu et al. (2012), the clusters themselves highlight areas for future research. There is a noticeable void in the cluster map at the intersection of long-term and business systems. This void points to two important gaps in family firm research.

First, no studies have investigated family business financial performance over a longer time horizon via longitudinal design. Indeed, even in the more established field of strategy, performance studies with lags longer than three to five years are virtually nonexistent. Second, this void may explain why we have a limited understanding of why public non-family firms outperform second- and later-generation family firms. Future research should focus on this previously neglected outcome category.

The possible reinforcing interplay between the outcome variables highlights the need for an improved methodology. While it may be impossible to develop a construct of family business performance that encompasses financial and non-financial aspects, the development of both financial and non-financial family firm specific constructs seems warranted. For example, the development of a familiness construct would be desirable (for a theoretical discussion, see Habbershon & Williams, 1999; Habbershon et al., 2003). Similarly, the development of a construct that directly captures socio-emotional wealth would be highly beneficial (for a discussion of the construct, see Berrone et al., 2010; Gómez-Mejía et al., 2007).

Also, the use of non-financial performance indicators needs further investigation. For example, Mahto, Davis, Pearce, and Robinson (2010) suggest that satisfaction with family firm performance should be considered as an outcome, since profit maximization is not the only desired goal in family firms. The authors found that satisfaction with performance is predicted by intermediate constructs including family harmony, family identification, and family commitment. However, satisfaction as an outcome variable poses problems. If family firms' goals and performance expectations vary (e.g., a life-style business vs. a multi-generational firm that needs to provide employment or income for multiple family members), satisfaction measures are not truly comparable. Thus, a measure that compares the family firm's economic performance on a multitude of performance indicators with a family firm's focal competitors (e.g., Eddleston et al., 2008) should be considered as a viable alternative, particularly as it correlates highly with objective performance (Ling & Kellermans, 2010). However, it must be acknowledged that both measures fail to assess the non-economic performance directly.

This chapter also has implications for practice. As previously mentioned many outcome variables work together synergistically and need to be understood as a web of complex relationships that explain economic and non-economic performance. Accordingly, both family business owners and consultants need to understand that focusing solely on family or business goals is insufficient. As each family business's goals may be different in terms of financial and non-financial performance, family firms must develop individual-level balanced scorecards (Kaplan & Norton, 1996) that reflect the needs and desires of the family. This is necessary in order to maximize the total value of the organization, which in family firms is composed of both emotional and economic value (Astrachan & Jaskiewicz, 2008; Zellweger & Astrachan, 2008). Thus, due to the interrelationships between the three performance outcome classes discussed in this chapter, these balanced scorecards should be encompassing and include multiple elements out of each outcome group. However, while this approach can be very useful to practitioners, such score-cards are not an ideal outcome measure for academic studies due to their highly idiosyncratic nature (Richard, Devinney, Yip, & Johnson, 2009).

Indeed, family firms should establish both financial and non-financial priorities. This may not be easy, since different generations may hold different attitudes regarding the organization's desired goals (Gersick, Davis, Hampton, & Lansberg, 1997). Accordingly, it is important for family members to achieve strategic consensus (Kellermanns, Walter, Floyd, Lechner, & Shaw, 2011; Kellermanns, Walter, Lechner, & Floyd, 2005) on the priorities and employ conflict management strategies when necessary (Sorenson, 1999). In the process of achieving consensus, it is crucial to consider the multi-temporal nature of the priorities and goals on which the family agrees. The desire to employ many family members can dictate a growth imperative (Poza, 1989) very early in the family firm's life-cycle (Hoy & Sharma, 2010). At the same time, all family-related outcomes and aspirations notwithstanding, the viability of the business needs to be ensured first, as without business survival, the family-related goals will never be accomplished.

Lastly, this commentary barely scratches the surface of the potential economic and non-economic outcome variables that family firm research can and should address. A recent review article by Richard et al. (2009) provides a general overview of performance measures utilized in premier journal outlets and suggests a wide variety of operationalizations. The authors conclude their article with a call for more research that addresses performance measures. They also call for more discipline-specific performance measures. We would like to echo the call for more family-firm literature and suggest that it address performance outcomes specific to family firms, e.g., socio-emotional wealth in (Gómez-Mejía et al. (2007); Zellweger, Kellermanns, Chrisman, & Chua, in press). We hope that this chapter contributes to this effort.

References

Andres, C. (2008). Large shareholders add firm performance: An empirical examination of founding-family ownership. *Journal of Corporate Finance*, *14*, 431–45.

Arregle, J.L., Hitt, M.A., Sirmon, D.G., & Very, P. (2007). The development of organizational social capital: Attributes of family firms. *Journal of Management Studies*, *44*, 72–95.

Ashforth, B.E., & Mael, F.A. (1996). Organizational identity and strategy as a context for the individual, *Advances in Strategic Management*, *13*, 17–62.

Astrachan, J., & Jaskiewicz, P. (2008). Emotional returns and emotional costs in privately-held family businesses: Advancing traditional business valuation. *Family Business Review*, *21*(2), 139–50.

Astrachan, J., & Shanker, M. (2003). Family businesses' contribution to the U.S. economy: A closer look. *Family Business Review*, *16*(3), 211–19.

Baron, R. (2008). The role of affect in the entrepreneurial process. *Academy of Management Review*, *33*(2), 328–40.

Berrone, P., Cruz, C.C., Gómez-Mejía, L.R., & Larraza-Kintana, M. (2010). Socioemotional wealth and corporate response to institutional pressures: Do family-controlled firms pollute less? *Administrative Science Quarterly*, *55*(1), 82–113.

Chandler, A.D. (1977). *The visible hand: The managerial revolution in American business*. Cambridge, MA: Belknap Press.

Chrisman, J.J., Chua, J.H., & Kellermanns, F.W. (2009). Priorities, resource stocks, and performance in family and non-family firms. *Entrepreneurship Theory and Practice*, *33*(3), 739–60.

Chrisman, J.J., Chua, J.H., Kellermanns, F.W., & Chang, E.P. (2007). Are family managers agents or stewards? An exploratory study in privately-held family firms. *Journal of Business Research*, *60*, 1030–8.

Chrisman, J.J., Chua, J.H., & Steier, L.P. (2003). An introduction to theories of family business. *Journal of Business Venturing*, *18*, 441–8.

Chrisman, J.J., Kellermanns, F.W., Chan, K.C., & Liano, K. (2010). Intellectual foundations of current research in family business: An identification and review of 25 influential articles. *Family Business Review*, 23(1), 9–26.

Chrisman, J.J., Steier, L.P., & Chua, J.H. (2008). Toward a theoretical basis for understanding the dynamics of strategic performance in family firms. *Entrepreneurship Theory and Practice*, 32(6), 935–47.

Claessens, S., Djankov, S., Fan, J., & Lang, L. (2002). Disentangling the incentive and entrenchment effects of large shareholdings. *Journal of Finance*, 57, 2741–71.

Cruz, C.C., Gómez-Mejía, L.R., & Becerra, M. (2010). Perceptions of benevolence and the design of agency contracts: CEO-TMT relationships in family firms. *Academy of Management Journal*, 53(1), 69–89.

De Massis, A., Chua, J.H., & Chrisman, J. J. (2008). Factors preventing intra-family succession. *Family Business Review*, 21(2),183–99.

Debicki, B.J., Matherne, C.F., Kellermanns, F.W., & Chrisman, J.J. (2009). Family business research in the new millennium: An overview of the who, the where, the what, and the why. *Family Business Review*, 22(2), 151–66.

Eddleston, K.A., & Kellermanns, F.W. (2004). Strategy process in family firms: An investigation of the unique psychodynamic effects on organizational performance. Unpublished manuscript, presented at the *Strategic Management Society 2004 conference*, San Juan, PR.

Eddleston, K.A., & Kellermanns, F.W. (2007). Destructive and productive family relationships: A stewardship theory perspective. *Journal of Business Venturing*, 22(4), 545–65.

Eddleston, K.A., Kellermanns, F.W., Floyd, S.W., Crittenden, V.L., & Crittenden, W.F. (forthcoming). Planning for growth: Life stage differences in family firms. Manuscript submitted for publication.

Eddleston, K.A., Kellermanns, F.W., & Sarathy, R. (2008). Resource configuration in family firms: Linking resources, strategic planning and technological opportunities to performance. *Journal of Management Studies*, 45(1), 26–50.

Forgas, J.P. (1995). Mood and judgment: The affect infusion model. *Psychological Bulletin*, 117(1), 39–66.

Forgas, J.P. (2000). *Feeling and thinking: Affective influences on social cognition*. New York: Cambridge University Press.

Gedajlovic, E., Lubatkin, M., & Schulze, W.S. (2004). Crossing the threshold from founder management to professional management: A governance perspective. *Journal of Management Studies*, 41(5), 899–912.

Gersick, K.E., Davis, J.A., Hampton, M.M., & Lansberg, I. (1997). *Generation to generation: Life cycles of the family business*. Boston, MA: Harvard Business School Press.

Gómez-Mejía, L.R., Haynes, K.T., Núñez-Nickel, M., Jacobson, K.J.L., & Moyano-Fuentes, H. (2007). Socioemotional wealth and business risk in family-controlled firms: Evidence from Spanish olive oil mills. *Administrative Science Quarterly*, 52(1), 106–37.

Habbershon, T.G., & Williams, M. (1999). A resource-based framework for assessing the strategic advantage of family firms. *Family Business Review*, 12, 1–25.

Habbershon, T.G., Williams, M., & MacMillan, I.C. (2003). A unified systems perspective of family firm performance. *Journal of Business Venturing*, 18, 451–65.

Hoy, F., & Sharma, P. (2010). *Entrepreneurial family firms*. Upper Saddle River, NJ: Pearson Prentice Hall.

Isen, A.M. (2002). Missing in action in the AIM: Positive affect's facilitation of cognitive flexibility, innovation, and problem solving. *Psychological Inquiry*, 13, 57–65.

James, L.R., Demaree, R.G., & Wolf, G. (1993). rwg: An assessement of within-group inter-rater agreement. *Journal of Applied Psychology*, 78, 306–39.

Kaplan, R.S., & Norton, D.P. (1996). *The balanced scorecard: Translating strategy into action*. Boston, MA: Harvard Business School Press.

Kellermanns, F.W., & Eddleston, K.A. (2004). Feuding families: When conflict does a family firm good. *Entrepreneurship Theory and Practice*, 28(3), 209–28.

Kellermanns, F.W., & Eddleston, K.A. (2006). Corporate entrepreneurship in family firms: A family perspective. *Entrepreneurship Theory and Practice*, 30(6), 809–30.

Kellermanns, F.W., & Eddleston, K.A. (2007). Family perspective on when conflict benefits family firm performance. *Journal of Business Research: Special Issue on Family Firms, 60*, 1048–57.

Kellermanns, F.W., Floyd, S., Pearson, A., & Spencer, B. (2008). The interactive effects of shared mental models and constructive confrontation on decision quality. *Journal of Organizational Behavior, 29*, 119–37.

Kellermanns, F.W., Walter, J., Floyd, S.W., Lechner, C., & Shaw, J. (2011). To agree or not to agree? A meta-analytical review of the relationship between strategic consensus and organizational performance. *Journal of Business Research, 64*(2), 126–33.

Kellermanns, F.W., Walter, J., Lechner, C., & Floyd, S.W. (2005). The lack of consensus about strategic consensus: Advancing theory and research. *Journal of Management, 31*(5), 719–37.

Kelly, L.M., Athanassiou, N., & Crittenden, W.F. (2000). Founder centrality and strategic behavior in the family-owned firm. *Entrepreneurship Theory and Practice, 25*(2), 27–42.

Ling, Y., & Kellermans, F. (2010). The effects of family firm specific sources of TMT diversity: The moderating role of information exchange frequency. *Journal of Management Studies, 47*(2), 322–44.

Lubatkin, M.H., Ling, Y., & Schulze, W.S. (2007). An organizational justice-based view of self-control and agency costs in family firms. *Journal of Management Studies, 44*(6), 955–71.

Mahto, R.V., Davis, P.S., Pearce, J.A., & Robinson, R.B. (2010). Satisfaction with firm performance in family firms. *Entrepreneurship Theory and Practice, 34*(5), 985–1001.

Miller, D., Le Breton-Miller, I., Lester, R.H., & Cannella, A.A. (2007). Are family firms really superior performers? *Journal of Corporate Finance, 13*, 829–58.

Minniti, M., & Bygrave, W.D. (1999). The microfoundations of entrepreneurship. *Entrepreneurship Theory and Practice, 23*(4), 41–52.

Morris, M.H., Allen, J.A., Kuratko, D.F., & Brannon, D. (2010). Experiencing family business creation: Differences betwen founders, non-family managers and founders of non-family firms. *Entrepreneurship Theory and Practice, 34*(6), 1057–84.

Naldi, L., Nordqvist, M., Sjoberg, K., & Wiklund, J. (2007). Entrepreneurial orientation, risk taking, and performance in family firms. *Family Business Review, 20*(1), 33–47.

Poza, E.J. (1989). *Smart growth: Critical choices for business continuity and prosperity.* San Francisco, CA: Jossey-Bass, Inc.

Poza, E.J., Alfred, T., & Maheshawi, A. (1997). Stakeholder perceptions of culture and management practices in family and family firms – A preliminary report. *Family Business Review, 10*(2), 135–55.

Poza, E.J., Hanlon, S., & Kishida, R. (2004). Does the family business interaction factor represent a resource or a cost. *Family Business Review, 17*(2), 99–118.

Richard, P.J., Devinney, T.M., Yip, G.S., & Johnson, G. (2009). Measuring organizational performance: Toward methodological best practices. *Journal of Management, 35*(3), 718–804.

Schulze, W.S., Lubatkin, M.H., Dino, R.N., & Buchholtz, A.K. (2001). Agency relationships in family firms: Theory and evidence. *Organization Science, 12*(2), 99–116.

Sharma, P., Chrisman, J.J., & Chua, J.H. (2003). Predictors of satisfaction with the succession process in family firms. *Journal of Business Venturing, 18*, 667–87.

Shepherd, D., & Wiklund, J. (2009). Are we comparing apples with apples or apples with oranges? Appropriateness of knowledge accumulation across growth studies. *Entrepreneurship Theory and Practice, 33*(1),105–23.

Short, J.C., Payne, G.T., Brigham, K.H., Lumpkin, G.T., & Broberg, J.C. (2009). Family firms and entrepreneurial orientation in publicly traded firms: A comparative analysis of the S&P 500. *Family Business Review, 22*(1), 9–24.

Sirmon, D.G., & Hitt, M.A. (2003). Managing resources: Linking unique resources, management, and wealth creation in family firms. *Entrepreneurship Theory and Practice, 27*(4), 339–58.

Sorenson, R.L. (1999). Conflict management strategies used in successful family businesses. *Family Business Review, 12*(4), 325–39.

Stanley, L. (2010). Emotions and family business creation: An extension and implications. *Entrepreneurship Theory & Practice, 34*(6), 1085–92.

Stockmans, A., Lybaert, N., & Voordeckers, W. (2010). Socioemotional weath and earnings management in private family firms. *Family Business Review, 23*(3), 280–94.

Sundaramurthy, C., & Kreiner, G.E. (2008). Governing by managing identity boundaries: The case of family businesses. *Entrepreneurship Theory & Practice*, *32*(3), 415–36.

Sydow, J., Schreyögg, G., & Koch, J. (2009). Organizational path dependence: Opening the black box. *Academy of Management Review*, *34*, 689–709.

Tagiuri, R., & Davis, J.A. (1996). Bivalent attributes of the family firm. *Family Business Review*, *9*(2), 199–208.

Uhlaner, L.M., Kellermanns, F.W., Eddleston, K.A., & Hoy, F. (2012). The entrepreneuring family: Is it time for a new paradigm? *Small Business Economics Journal*, *38*(1), 1–11.

Van Essen, M., Carney, M., Gedajlovic, E.R., & Heugens, P.P. M.A.R. (2011). Do U.S. publically-listed family firms differ? Does it matter? A meta-analysis. *Working Paper Utrecht University*, retrieved from http://papers.ssrn.com/sol3/papers.cfm?abstract_id=1837517.

Villalonga, B., & Amit, R. (2006). How do family ownership, control and management affect firm value? *Journal of Financial Economics*, *80*, 385–417.

Walsh, J.P. (1995). Managerial and organizational cognition: Notes from a trip down memory lane. *Organization Science*, *6*(3), 280–321.

Wiklund, J., Pazelt, H., & Shepherd, D.A. (2009). Building an integrative model of small business growth. *Small Business Economics*, *32*(4), 351–73.

Wright, M., & Kellermanns, F.W. (2011). What can family firm research learn from management and entrepreneurship? *Journal of Family Business Strategy*, *2*(4), 187–98.

Yu, A., Lumpkin, G.T., Brigham, K.H., & Sorenson, R.L. (2012). The landscape of family business outcomes: A summary and numerical taxonomy of dependent variables. *Family Business Review*, *25*(1), 33–57.

Zellweger, T.M (2007). Time horizon, costs of equity capital and generic investment strategies of firms. *Family Business Review*, *20*(1), 1–15.

Zellweger, T.M., & Astrachan, J. (2008). On the emotional value of owning a firm. *Family Business Review*, *21*(4), 347–63.

Zellweger, T.M., Eddleston, K.A., & Kellermanns, F.W. (2010). Exploring the concept of familiness: Introducing family firm identity. *Journal of Family Business Strategy*, *1*(1), 54–63.

Zellweger, T.M., Kellermanns, F.W., Chrisman, J.J., & Chua, J.H. (2012). Family control and family firm valuation by family CEOs: The importance of intentions for transgenerational control. *Organization Science*, *23*(3), 851–68.

Appendix A

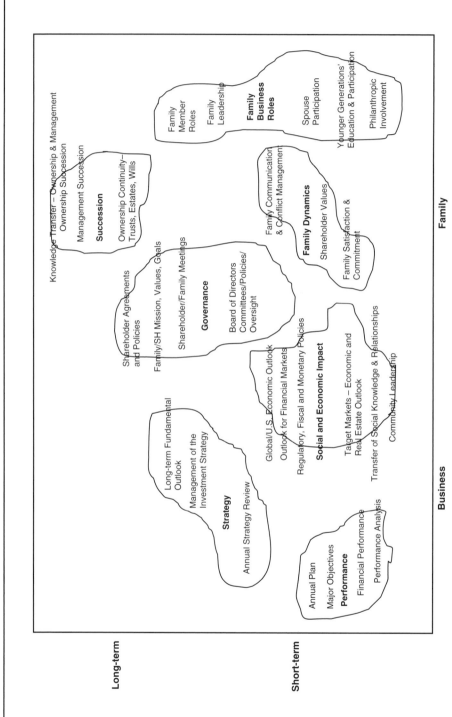

Figure A.1   The McNeely Landscape Map

Appendix B

Empirical studies from which the outcome variables were derived for the Yu, Lumpkin, Sorenson, and Brigham (2012) paper

Abetti, P.A., & Phan, P.H. (2004). Zobele chemical industries: The evolution of a family company from flypaper to globalization (1919–2001). *Journal of Business Venturing*, *19*(4), 589–600.

Aldrich, H.E., & Cliff, J.E. (2003). The pervasive effects of family on entrepreneurship: Toward a family embeddedness perspective. *Journal of Business Venturing*, *18*(5), 573–96.

Allouche, J., Amann, B., Jaussaud, J., & Kurashina, T. (2008). The impact of family control on the performance and financial characteristics of family versus nonfamily businesses in Japan: A matched-pair investigation. *Family Business Review*, *21*(4), 315–29.

Anderson, A.R., Jack, S.L., & Dodd, S.D. (2005). The role of family members in entrepreneurial networks: Beyond the boundaries of the family firm. *Family Business Review*, *18*(2), 135–54.

Anderson, R.C., & Reeb, D.M. (2004). Board composition: Balancing family influence in S&P 500 firms. *Administrative Science Quarterly*, *49*(2), 209–37.

Andersson, T., Carlsen, J., & Getz, D. (2002). Family business goals in the tourism and hospitality sector: Case studies and cross-case analysis from Australia, Canada, and Sweden. *Family Business Review*, *15*(2), 89–106.

Anonymous. (2003). Family businesses dominate: International Family Enterprise Research Academy (IFERA). *Family Business Review*, *16*(4), 235–40.

Aronoff, C. (2004). Self-perpetuation family organization built on values: Necessary condition for long-term family business survival. *Family Business Review*, *17*(1), 55–9.

Astrachan, J.H., & Jaskiewicz, P. (2008). Emotional returns and emotional costs in privately held family businesses: Advancing traditional business valuation. *Family Business Review*, *21*(2), 139–49.

Astrachan, J.H., Klein, S.B., & Smyrnios, K.X. (2004). The F-PEC scale of family influence: A proposal for solving the family business definition problem. *Family Business Review*, *15*(1), 45–58.

Astrachan, J.H., & McConaughy, D.L. (2001). Venture capitalists and closely held IPOs: Lessons for family-controlled firms. *Family Business Review*, *14*(4), 295–312.

Astrachan, J.H., & Shanker, M.C. (2003). Family businesses' contribution to the US economy: A closer look. *Family Business Review*, *16*(3), 211–19.

Au, K., & Kwan, H.K. (2009). Start-up capital and Chinese entrepreneurs: The role of family. *Entrepreneurship Theory and Practice*, *33*(4), 889908.

Barnett, T., Eddleston, K., & Kellermanns, F.W. (2009). The effects of family versus career role salience on the performance of family and nonfamily firms. *Family Business Review*, *22*(1), 39–52.

Bartholomeusz, S., & Tanewski, G.A. (2006). The relationship between family firms and corporate governance. *Journal of Small Business Management*, *44*(2), 245–67.

Basco, R., & Pérez Rodríguez, M.J. (2009). Studying the family enterprise holistically. *Family Business Review*, *22*(1), 82–95.

Bird, B., Welsch, H., Astrachan, J.H., & Pistrui, D. (2004). Family business research: The evolution of an academic field. *Family Business Review*, *15*(4), 337–50.

Birley, S. (2001). Owner-manager attitudes to family and business issues: A 16 country study. *Entrepreneurship Theory and Practice*, *26*(2), 63–76.

Birley, S. (2002). Attitudes of owner-managers' children towards family and business issues. *Entrepreneurship Theory and Practice*, *26*(3), 5–20.

Björnberg, Å., & Nicholson, N. (2007). The family climate scales – Development of a new measure for use in family business research. *Family Business Review, 20*(3), 229–46.

Blanco-Mazagatos, V., De Quevedo-Puente, E., & Castrillo, L.A. (2007). The trade-off between financial resources and agency costs in the family business: An exploratory study. *Family Business Review, 20*(3), 199–213.

Blumentritt, T.P. (2006). The relationship between boards and planning in family businesses. *Family Business Review, 19*(1), 65–72.

Blumentritt, T.P., Keyt, A.D., & Astrachan, J.H. (2007). Creating an environment for successful nonfamily CEOs: An exploratory study of good principals. *Family Business Review, 20*(4), 321–35.

Boyd, J., Upton, N., & Wircenski, M. (1999). Mentoring in family firms: A reflective analysis of senior executives' perceptions. *Family Business Review, 12*(4), 299–309.

Braun, M., & Sharma, A. (2007). Should the CEO also be chair of the board? An empirical examination of family-controlled public firms. *Family Business Review, 20*(2), 111–26.

Brown, R.B., & Coverley, R. (1999). Succession planning in family businesses: A study from East Anglia, UK. *Journal of Small Business Management, 37*(1), 93–7.

Brun de Pontet, S., Wrosch, C., & Gagne, M. (2007). An exploration of the generational differences in levels of control held among family businesses approaching succession. *Family Business Review, 20*(4), 337–54.

Brush, C.G., Edelman, L.F., & Manolova, T.S. (2008). The effects of initial location, aspirations, and resources on likelihood of first sale in nascent firms. *Journal of Small Business Management, 46*(2), 159–82.

Bruton, G.D., Khavul, S., & Wood, E. (2009). Informal family business in Africa. *Entrepreneurship Theory and Practice, 33*(6), 1219–38.

Busenitz, L.W., West, G.P., III, Shepherd, D., Nelson, T., Chandler, G.N., & Zacharakis, A. (2003). Entrepreneurship research in emergence: Past trends and future directions. *Journal of Management, 29*(3), 285–308.

Cadieux, L. (2007). Succession in small and medium-sized family businesses: Toward a typology of predecessor roles during and after instatement of the successor. *Family Business Review, 20*(2), 95–109.

Cadieux, L., Lorrain, J., & Hugron, P. (2002). Succession in women-owned family businesses: A case study. *Family Business Review, 15*(1), 17–30.

Carlock, R.S., & Aronoff, C.E. (2001). *Strategic planning for the family business: Parallel planning to unite the family and business*. Palgrave Macmillan.

Carlson, D.S., Upton, N., & Seaman, S. (2006). The impact of human resource practices and compensation design on performance: An analysis of family-owned SMEs. *Journal of Small Business Management, 44*(4), 531–43.

Carney, M. (2005). Corporate governance and competitive advantage in family-controlled firms. *Entrepreneurship Theory and Practice, 29*(3), 249–65.

Carney, M., & Gedajlovic, E. (2002). The coupling of ownership and control and the allocation of financial resources: Evidence from Hong Kong. *Journal of Management Studies, 39*(1), 123–46.

Carr, C. (2005). Are German, Japanese and Anglo-Saxon strategic decision styles still divergent in the context of globalization? *Journal of Management Studies, 42*(6), 1155–88.

Carrasco-Hernandez, A., & Sánchez-Marín, G. (2007). The determinants of employee compensation in family firms: Empirical evidence. *Family Business Review, 20*(3), 215–28.

Cater, J.J., III, & Justis, R.T. (2009). The development of successors from followers to leaders in small family firms an exploratory study. *Family Business Review, 22*(2), 109–24.

Cater, J.J., III, & Schwab, A. (2008). Turnaround strategies in established small family firms. *Family Business Review, 21*(1), 31–50.

Chang, E.P.C., Chrisman, J.J., Chua, J.H., & Kellermanns, F.W. (2008). Regional economy as a determinant of the prevalence of family firms in the United States: A preliminary report. *Entrepreneurship Theory and Practice, 32*(3), 559–73.

Chang, E.P.C., Memili, E., Chrisman, J.J., Kellermanns, F.W., & Chua, J.H. (2009). Family social capital, venture preparedness, and start-up decisions: A study of Hispanic entrepreneurs in New England. *Family Business Review, 22*(3), 279–92.

Chen, H., & Hsu, W. (2009). Family ownership, board independence, and R&D investment. *Family Business Review*, 22(4), 347–62.

Chittoor, R., & Das, R. (2007). Professionalization of management and succession performance – A vital linkage. *Family Business Review*, 20(1), 65–79.

Chrisman, J.J., Chua, J.H., & Litz, R.A. (2004). Comparing the agency costs of family and non-family firms: Conceptual issues and exploratory evidence. *Entrepreneurship Theory and Practice*, 28(4), 335–54.

Chrisman, J.J., Chua, J.H., & Sharma, P. (2004). Important attributes of successors in family businesses: An exploratory study. *Family Business Review*, 11(1), 19–34.

Chrisman, J.J., Chua, J.H., & Steier, L.P. (2002). The influence of national culture and family involvement on entrepreneurial perceptions and performance at the state level. *Entrepreneurship Theory and Practice*, 26(4), 113–30.

Chrisman, J.J., Chua, J.H., & Kellermanns, F. (2009). Priorities, resource stocks, and performance in family and nonfamily firms. *Entrepreneurship Theory and Practice*, 33(3), 739–60.

Chua, J.H., Chrisman, J.J., & Chang, E.P. (2004). Are family firms born or made? An exploratory investigation. *Family Business Review*, 17(1), 37–54.

Chua, J.H., Chrisman, J.J., & Sharma, P. (1999). Defining the family business by behavior. *Entrepreneurship Theory and Practice*, 23(4), 19–40.

Chua, J.H., Chrisman, J.J., & Sharma, P. (2003). Succession and nonsuccession concerns of family firms and agency relationship with nonfamily managers. *Family Business Review*, 16(2), 89–107.

Chua, J.H., Chrisman, J.J., & Steier, L.P. (2003). Extending the theoretical horizons of family business research. *Entrepreneurship Theory and Practice*, 27(4), 331–8.

Chung, C. (2001). Markets, culture and institutions: The emergence of large business groups in Taiwan, 1950s–1970s. *Journal of Management Studies*, 38(5), 719–45.

Chung, C., & Luo, X. (2008). Human agents, contexts, and institutional change: The decline of family in the leadership of business groups. *Organization Science*, 19(1), 124–42.

Claver, E., Rienda, L., & Quer, D. (2009). Family firms' international commitment: The influence of family-related factors. *Family Business Review*, 22(2), 125–35.

Cole, P.M., & Johnson, K. (2007). An exploration of successful copreneurial relationships postdivorce. *Family Business Review*, 20(3), 185–98.

Coleman, S., & Carsky, M. (1999). Sources of capital for small family-owned businesses evidence from the national survey of small business finances. *Family Business Review*, 12(1), 73–84.

Colquitt, J.A., & Zapata-Phelan, C.P. (2007). Trends in theory building and theory testing: A five-decade study of the academy of management journal. *Academy of Management Journal*, 50(6), 1281–303.

Cooper, M.J., Upton, N., & Seaman, S. (2005). Customer relationship management: A comparative analysis of family and nonfamily business practices. *Journal of Small Business Management*, 43(3), 242–56.

Craig, J.B., & Dibrell, C. (2006). The natural environment, innovation, and firm performance: A comparative study. *Family Business Review*, 19(4), 275–88.

Craig, J.B., Dibrell, C., & Davis, P.S. (2008). Leveraging family-based brand identity to enhance firm competitiveness and performance in family businesses. *Journal of Small Business Management*, 46(3), 351–71.

Craig, J.B., & Moores, K. (2005). Balanced scorecards to drive the strategic planning of family firms. *Family Business Review*, 18(2), 105–22.

Craig, J.B., & Moores, K. (2006). A 10-year longitudinal investigation of strategy, systems, and environment on innovation in family firms. *Family Business Review*, 19(1), 1–10.

Curimbaba, F. (2002). The dynamics of women's roles as family business managers. *Family Business Review*, 15(3), 239–52.

Dalkey, N.C., Brown, B.B., & Cochran, S. (1969). *The Delphi Method: An Experimental Study of Group Opinion*. RAND Corporation.

Danes, S.M., Loy, J.T., & Stafford, K. (2008). Business planning practices of family-owned firms within a quality framework. *Journal of Small Business Management*, 46(3), 395–421.

Danes, S.M., & Olson, P.D. (2003). Women's role involvement in family businesses, business tensions, and business success. *Family Business Review*, 16(1), 53–68.

Danes, S.M., Rueter, M.A., Kwon, H., & Doherty, W. (2002). Family FIRO model: An application to family business. *Family Business Review*, *15*(1), 31–43.

Danes, S.M., Stafford, K., Haynes, G., & Amarapurkar, S.S. (2009). Family capital of family firms bridging human, social, and financial capital. *Family Business Review*, *22*(3), 199–215.

Danes, S.M., Zuiker, V., Kean, R., & Arbuthnot, J. (1999). Predictors of family business tensions and goal achievement. *Family Business Review*, *12*(3), 241–252.

Davis, G.F., & Marquis, C. (2005). Prospects for organization theory in the early twenty-first century: Institutional fields and mechanisms. *Organization Science*, *16*(4), 332–43.

Davis, M.S. (1971). That's interesting! Toward a phenomenology of sociology and a sociology of phenomenology. *Philosophy of the Social Sciences*, *1*(4), 309–44.

Davis, P.S., & Harveston, P.D. (1998). The influence of family on the family business succession process: A multi-generational perspective. *Entrepreneurship Theory and Practice*, *22*(3), 31–54.

Davis, P.S., & Harveston, P.D. (2000). Internationalization and organizational growth: The impact of internet usage and technology involvement among entrepreneur-led family businesses. *Family Business Review*, *13*(2), 107–20.

Davis, P.S., & Harveston, P.D. (2001). The phenomenon of substantive conflict in the family firm: A cross-generational study. *Journal of Small Business Management*, *39*(1), 14–30.

Davis, P.S., & Harveston, P.D. (2004). In the founder's shadow: Conflict in the family firm. *Family Business Review*, *12*(4), 311–23.

De Kok, J.M., Uhlaner, L.M., & Thurik, A.R. (2006). Professional HRM practices in family owned-managed enterprises. *Journal of Small Business Management*, *44*(3), 441–60.

Denison, D., Lief, C., & Ward, J.L. (2004). Culture in family-owned enterprises: Recognizing and leveraging unique strengths. *Family Business Review*, *17*(1), 61–70.

DeNoble, A., Ehrlich, S., & Singh, G. (2007). Toward the development of a family business self-efficacy scale: A resource-based perspective. *Family Business Review*, *20*(2), 127–40.

Dieleman, M., & Sachs, W.M. (2008). Coevolution of institutions and corporations in emerging economies: How the slim group morphed into an institution of Suharto's crony regime. *Journal of Management Studies*, *45*(7), 1274–1300.

Distelberg, B.J., & Blow, A. (2011). Variations in family system boundaries. *Family Business Review*, *24*(1), 28–46.

Drozdow, N. (1998). What is continuity? *Family Business Review*, *11*(4), 337–47.

Dumas, C. (1998). Women's pathways to participation and leadership in the family-owned firm. *Family Business Review*, *11*(3), 219–28.

Dunn, B. (1999). The family factor: The impact of family relationship dynamics on business-owning families during transitions. *Family Business Review*, *12*(1), 41–57.

Dyck, B. (2002). Passing the baton: The importance of sequence, timing, technique and communication in executive succession. *Journal of Business Venturing*, *17*(2), 143.

Dyer, W.G., Jr. (2003). The family: The missing variable in organizational research. *Entrepreneurship Theory and Practice*, *27*(4), 401–16.

Dyer, W.G., Jr., & Dyer, W.J. (2009). Putting the family into family business research. *Family Business Review*, *22*(3), 216–19.

Dyer, W.G., Jr., & Mortensen, S.P. (2005). Entrepreneurship and family business in a hostile environment: The case of Lithuania. *Family Business Review*, *18*(3), 247–58.

Dyer, W.G., Jr., & Sánchez, M. (1998). Current state of family business theory and practice as reflected in *Family Business Review* 1988–1997. *Family Business Review*, *11*(4), 287–95.

Dyer, W.G., Jr., & Whitten, D.A. (2006). Family firms and social responsibility: Preliminary evidence from the S&P 500. *Entrepreneurship Theory and Practice*, *30*(6), 785–802.

Eddleston, K.A., & Kellermanns, F.W. (2007). Destructive and productive family relationships: A stewardship theory perspective. *Journal of Business Venturing*, *22*(4), 545–65.

Eddleston, K.A., Kellermanns, F.W., & Sarathy, R. (2008). Resource configuration in family firms: Linking resources, strategic planning and technological opportunities to performance. *Journal of Management Studies*, *45*(1), 26–50.

Eddleston, K.A., Otondo, R.F., & Kellermanns, F.W. (2008). Conflict, participative decision-making, and generational ownership dispersion: A multilevel analysis. *Journal of Small Business Management*, *46*(3), 456–84.

Edwards, P., & Ram, M. (2006). Surviving on the margins of the economy: Working relationships in small, Low-Wage firms. *Journal of Management Studies*, *43*(4), 895–916.

Ehrhardt, O., & Nowak, E. (2003). The effect of IPOs on German family-owned firms: Governance changes, ownership structure, and performance. *Journal of Small Business Management*, *41*(2), 222–32.

Emory, C.W., & Cooper, D.R. (1991). *Business research methods*. Homewood, IL.: Richard D. Irwin.

Ensley, M. (2006). Family businesses can out-compete: As long as they are willing to question the chosen path. *Entrepreneurship Theory and Practice*, *30*(6), 747–54.

Ensley, M.D., & Pearson, A.W. (2005). An exploratory comparison of the behavioral dynamics of top management teams in family and nonfamily new ventures: Cohesion, conflict, potency, and consensus. *Entrepreneurship Theory and Practice*, *29*(3), 267–84.

Erikson, T., Sørheim, R., & Reitan, B. (2003). Family angels vs. other informal investors. *Family Business Review*, *16*(3), 163–71.

Fahed-Sreih, J., & Djoundourian, S. (2006). Determinants of longevity and success in Lebanese family businesses: An exploratory study. *Family Business Review*, *19*(3), 225–34.

Feltham, T.S., Feltham, G., & Barnett, J.J. (2005). The dependence of family businesses on a single decision-maker. *Journal of Small Business Management*, *43*(1), 1–15.

Fernández, Z., & Nieto, M.J. (2005). Internationalization strategy of small and medium-sized family businesses: Some influential factors. *Family Business Review*, *18*(1), 77–89.

Fiegener, M.K., Brown, B.M., Dreux, D., & Dennis, W. (2000). CEO stakes and board composition in small private firms. *Entrepreneurship Theory and Practice*, *24*(4), 5–24.

Filbeck, G., & Lee, S. (2000). Financial management techniques in family businesses. *Family Business Review*, *13*(3), 201–16.

Fitzgerald, M.A., & Muske, G. (2002). Copreneurs: An exploration and comparison to other family businesses. *Family Business Review*, *15*(1), 1–16.

Flören, R.H. (1998). The significance of family business in the Netherlands. *Family Business Review*, *11*(2), 121–34.

Foreman, P., & Whetten, D.A. (2002). Members' identification with multiple-identity organizations. *Organization Science*, *13*(6), 618–35.

Galbraith, C.S. (2003). Divorce and the financial performance of small family businesses: An exploratory study. *Journal of Small Business Management*, *41*(3), 296–309.

Gallo, M.Á. (1998). Ethics in personal behavior in family business. *Family Business Review*, *11*(4), 325–35.

Gallo, M.Á., Tàpies, J., & Cappuyns, K. (2004). Comparison of family and nonfamily business: Financial logic and personal preferences. *Family Business Review*, *17*(4), 303–18.

Gallo, M.Á., & Vilaseca, A. (1998). A financial perspective on structure, conduct, and performance in the family firm: An empirical study. *Family Business Review*, *11*(1), 35–47.

García-Álvarez, E., & López-Sintas, J. (2001). A taxonomy of founders based on values: The root of family business heterogeneity. *Family Business Review*, *14*(3), 209–30.

García-Álvarez, E., López-Sintas, J., & Gonzalvo, P.S. (2002). Socialization patterns of successors in first- to second-generation family businesses. *Family Business Review*, *15*(3), 189–203.

Gersick, K.E., Davis, J.A., Hampton, M.M., & Lansberg, I. (1997). *Generation to generation: Life cycles of the family business*. Boston, MA: Harvard Business School Press.

Getz, D., & Petersen, T. (2004). Identifying industry-specific barriers to inheritance in small family businesses. *Family Business Review*, *17*(3), 259–76.

Gilding, M. (2004). Family business and family change: Individual autonomy, democratization, and the new family business institutions. *Family Business Review*, *13*(3), 239–50.

Gómez-Mejía, L.R., Haynes, K.T., Núñez-Nickel, M., Jacobson, K.J., & Moyano-Fuentes, J. (2007). Socioemotional wealth and business risks in family-controlled firms: Evidence from Spanish olive oil mills. *Administrative Science Quarterly*, *52*(1), 106–37.

Gómez-Mejía, L.R., Larraza-Kintana, M., & Makri, M. (2003). The determinants of executive compensation in family-controlled public corporations. *Academy of Management Journal*, *46*(2), 226–37.

Gómez-Mejía, L.R., Núñez-Nickel, M., & Gutierrez, I. (2001). The role of family ties in agency contracts. *Academy of Management Journal, 44*(1), 81–95.

Graves, C., & Thomas, J. (2006). Internationalization of Australian family businesses: A managerial capabilities perspective. *Family Business Review, 19*(3), 207–24.

Graves, C., & Thomas, J. (2008). Determinants of the internationalization pathways of family firms: An examination of family influence. *Family Business Review, 21*(2), 151–67.

Gubitta, P., & Gianecchini, M. (2004). Governance and flexibility in family-owned SMEs. *Family Business Review, 15*(4), 277–97.

Gudmundson, D., Hartman, E.A., & Tower, C.B. (1999). Strategic orientation: Differences between family and nonfamily firms. *Family Business Review, 12*(1), 27–39.

Gulbrandsen, T. (2005). Flexibility in Norwegian family-owned enterprises. *Family Business Review, 18*(1), 57–76.

Habbershon, T.G., & Williams, M.L. (1999). A resource-based framework for assessing the strategic advantages of family firms. *Family Business Review, 12*(1), 1–22.

Haberman, H., & Danes, S.M. (2007). Father-daughter and father-son family business management transfer comparison: Family FIRO model application. *Family Business Review, 20*(2), 163–84.

Hair, J.F., Jr., Black, W.C., Babin, B.J., Anderson, R.E., & Tatham, R.L. (2006). *Multivariate Data Analysis* (6th ed.). Upper Saddle River, NJ: Pearson Prentice Hall.

Hall, A., Melin, L., & Nordqvist, M. (2004). Entrepreneurship as radical change in the family business: Exploring the role of cultural patterns. *Family Business Review, 14*(3), 193–208.

Hall, A., & Nordqvist, M. (2008). Professional management in family businesses: Toward an extended understanding. *Family Business Review, 21*(1), 51–69.

Handler, W.C. (2004). Methodological issues and considerations in studying family businesses. *Family Business Review, 2*(3), 257–76.

Hanks, S.H., Watson, C.J., Jansen, E., & Chandler, G.N. (1994). Tightening the life-cycle construct: A taxonomic study of growth stage configurations in high-technology organizations. *Entrepreneurship Theory and Practice, 18*(2), 5–29.

Hatum, A., & Pettigrew, A. (2004). Adaptation under environmental turmoil: Organizational flexibility in family-owned firms. *Family Business Review, 17*(3), 237–58.

Haynes, D.C., Avery, R.J., & Hunts, H.J. (1999). The decision to outsource child care in households engaged in a family business. *Family Business Review, 12*(3), 269–81.

Haynes, G.W., Walker, R., Rowe, B.R., & Hong, G. (1999). The intermingling of business and family finances in family-owned businesses. *Family Business Review, 12*(3), 225–39.

Heck, R.K., & Trent, E.S. (2004). The prevalence of family business from a household sample. *Family Business Review, 12*(3), 209–19.

Hienerth, C., & Kessler, A. (2006). Measuring success in family businesses: The concept of configurational fit. *Family Business Review, 19*(2), 115–34.

Howorth, C., & Ali, Z.A. (2004). Family business succession in Portugal: An examination of case studies in the furniture industry. *Family Business Review, 14*(3), 231–44.

Howorth, C., Westhead, P., & Wright, M. (2004). Buyouts, information asymmetry and the family management dyad. *Journal of Business Venturing, 19*(4), 509–34.

Hoy, F., & Sharma, P. (2010). *Entrepreneurial Family Firms*. Upper Saddle River, NJ: Pearson Prentice Hall.

Ibrahim, A., Soufani, K., & Lam, J. (2001). A study of succession in a family firm. *Family Business Review, 14*(3), 245–58.

James, A.E., Jennings, J.E., & Breitkreuz, R.S. (2012). Worlds apart? Rebridging the distance between family science and family business research. *Family Business Review, 25*(1), 87–108.

Jaskiewicz, P., González, V.M., Menéndez, S., & Schiereck, D. (2005). Long-run IPO performance analysis of German and Spanish family-owned businesses. *Family Business Review, 18*(3), 179–202.

Jean, L.S., & Tan, F. (2001). Growth of Chinese family enterprises in Singapore. *Family Business Review, 14*(1), 49–74.

Jones, C.D., Makri, M., & Gómez-Mejía, L.R. (2008). Affiliate directors and perceived risk bearing in publicly traded, family-controlled firms: The case of diversification. *Entrepreneurship Theory and Practice*, *32*(6), 1007–26.

Jorissen, A., Laveren, E., Martens, R., & Reheul, A. (2005). Real versus sample-based differences in comparative family business research. *Family Business Review*, *18*(3), 229–46.

Karofsky, P., Millen, R., Yilmaz, M.R., Smyrnios, K.X., Tanewski, G.A., & Romano, C.A. (2001). Work-family conflict and emotional well-being in American family businesses. *Family Business Review*, *14*(4), 313–24.

Karra, N., Tracey, P., & Phillips, N. (2006). Altruism and agency in the family firm: Exploring the role of family, kinship, and ethnicity. *Entrepreneurship Theory and Practice*, *30*(6), 861–77.

Kayser, G., & Wallau, F. (2002). Industrial family businesses in Germany – Situation and future. *Family Business Review*, *15*(2), 111–15.

Kellermanns, F.W., & Eddleston, K.A. (2006). Corporate entrepreneurship in family firms: A family perspective. *Entrepreneurship Theory and Practice*, *30*(6), 809–30.

Kellermanns, F.W., Eddleston, K.A., Barnett, T., & Pearson, A. (2008). An exploratory study of family member characteristics and involvement: Effects on entrepreneurial behavior in the family firm. *Family Business Review*, *21*(1), 1–14.

Kelly, L.M., Athanassiou, N., & Crittenden, W.F. (2000). Founder centrality and strategic behavior in the family-owned firm. *Entrepreneurship Theory and Practice*, *25*(2), 27–42.

Kenyon-Rouvinez, D. (2001). Patterns in serial business families: Theory building through global case study research. *Family Business Review*, *14*(3), 175–91.

Ketchen, D.J., Jr., & Shook, C.L. (1996). The application of cluster analysis in strategic management research: An analysis and critique. *Strategic Management Journal*, *17*(6), 441–58.

Ketchen, D.J., Jr., Thomas, J.B., & McDaniel, R.R., Jr. (1996). Process, content and context: Synergistic effects on organizational performance. *Journal of Management*, *22*(2), 231–57.

Khanna, T., & Rivkin, J.W. (2006). Interorganizational ties and business group boundaries: Evidence from an emerging economy. *Organization Science*, *17*(3), 333–52.

Kim, H., & DeVaney, S.A. (2003). The expectation of partial retirement among family business owners. *Family Business Review*, *16*(3), 199–210.

King, S. (2003). Organizational performance and conceptual capability: The relationship between organizational performance and successors' capability in a family-owned firm. *Family Business Review*, *16*(3), 173–82.

King, S.W., Solomon, G.T., & Fernald, L.W., Jr. (2001). Issues in growing a family business: A strategic human resource model. *Journal of Small Business Management*, *39*(1), 3–13.

Klein, S.B. (2000). Family businesses in Germany: Significance and structure. *Family Business Review*, *13*(3), 157–81.

Klein, S.B., Astrachan, J.H., & Smyrnios, K.X. (2005). The F-PEC scale of family influence: Construction, validation, and further implication for theory. *Entrepreneurship Theory and Practice*, *29*(3), 321–39.

Koiranen, M. (2002). Over 100 years of age but still entrepreneurially active in business: Exploring the values and family characteristics of old Finnish family firms. *Family Business Review*, *15*(3), 175–87.

Kotey, B., & Folker, C. (2007). Employee training in SMEs: Effect of size and firm type – Family and nonfamily. *Journal of Small Business Management*, *45*(2), 214–38.

Kruskal, J., & Wish, M. (1978). *Multidimensional Scaling, in Sage University paper series on quantitative applications in the social sciences*. Beverly Hills, CA: Sage Publications.

Kuhn, T.S. (1970). *The Structure of Scientific Revolutions*. Chicago: Chicago University Press.

LaChapelle, K., & Barnes, L.B. (2004). The trust catalyst in family-owned businesses. *Family Business Review*, *11*(1), 1–17.

Lambrecht, J. (2005). Multigenerational transition in family businesses: A new explanatory model. *Family Business Review*, *18*(4), 267–82.

Lambrecht, J., & Lievens, J. (2008). Pruning the family tree: An unexplored path to family business continuity and family harmony. *Family Business Review*, *21*(4), 295–313.

Lee, J. (2006). Impact of family relationships on attitudes of the second generation in family business. *Family Business Review*, *19*(3), 175–91.

Lee, J. (2006). Family firm performance: Further evidence. *Family Business Review*, *19*(2), 103–14.

Lee, M., & Rogoff, E.G. (1996). Research note: Comparison of small businesses with family participation versus small businesses without family participation: An investigation of differences in goals, attitudes, and family/business conflict. *Family Business Review*, *9*(4), 423–37.

Lee, T. (1998). *Using Qualitative Methods in Organizational Research*. Beverly Hills, CA: Sage Publications.

Leon-Guerrero, A.Y., McCann, J.E., III, & Haley, J.D., Jr. (2004). A study of practice utilization in family businesses. *Family Business Review*, *11*(2), 107–20.

Levie, J., & Lerner, M. (2009). Resource mobilization and performance in family and nonfamily businesses in the United Kingdom. *Family Business Review*, *22*(1), 25–38.

Littunen, H. (2003). Management capabilities and environmental characteristics in the critical operational phase of entrepreneurship – A comparison of Finnish family and nonfamily firms. *Family Business Review*, *16*(3), 183–97.

Littunen, H., & Hyrsky, K. (2000). The early entrepreneurial stage in Finnish family and nonfamily firms. *Family Business Review*, *13*(1), 41–53.

Litz, R.A., & Kleysen, R.F. (2004). Your old men shall dream dreams, your young men shall see visions: Toward a theory of family firm innovation with help from the Brubeck family. *Family Business Review*, *14*(4), 335–52.

Litz, R.A., Pearson, A.W., & Litchfield, S. (2012). Charting the future of family business research perspectives from the field. *Family Business Review*, *25*(1), 16–32.

Livingston, L. (2007). Control sales in family firms. *Family Business Review*, 20(1), 49–64.

López-Gracia, J., & Sánchez-Andújar, S. (2007). Financial structure of the family business: Evidence from a group of small Spanish firms. *Family Business Review*, *20*(4), 269–87.

Lumpkin, G.T., Brigham, K.H., & Moss, T.W. (2010). Long-term orientation: Implications for the entrepreneurial orientation and performance of family businesses. *Entrepreneurship and Regional Development*, *22*(3–4), 241–64.

Lumpkin, G.T., Martin, W., & Vaughn, M. (2008). Family orientation: Individual-level influences on family firm outcomes. *Family Business Review*, *21*(2), 127–38.

Luo, X., & Chung, C. (2005). Keeping it all in the family: The role of particularistic relationships in business group performance during institutional transition. *Administrative Science Quarterly*, *50*(3), 404–39.

Mahérault, L. (2000). The influence of going public on investment policy: An empirical study of French family-owned businesses. *Family Business Review*, *13*(1), 71–9.

Mahérault, L. (2004). Is there any specific equity route for small and medium-sized family businesses? The French experience. *Family Business Review*, *17*(3), 221–35.

Manikutty, S. (2004). Family business groups in India: A resource-based view of the emerging trends. *Family Business Review*, *13*(4), 279–92.

Marshall, J.P., Sorenson, R., Brigham, K., Wieling, E., Reifman, A., & Wampler, R.S. (2006). The paradox for the family firm CEO: Owner age relationship to succession-related processes and plans. *Journal of Business Venturing*, *21*(3), 348–68.

Martínez, J.I., Stöhr, B.S., & Quiroga, B.F. (2007). Family ownership and firm performance: Evidence from public companies in Chile. *Family Business Review*, *20*(2), 83–94.

Mazzola, P., & Marchisio, G. (2002). The role of going public in family businesses' long-lasting growth: A study of Italian IPOs. *Family Business Review*, *15*(2), 133–48.

Mazzola, P., Marchisio, G., & Astrachan, J. (2008). Strategic planning in family business: A powerful developmental tool for the next generation. *Family Business Review*, *21*(3), 239–58.

McCain, K.W. (1990). Mapping authors in intellectual space: A technical overview. *Journal of the American Society for Information Science*, *41*(6), 433–43.

McCann, J.E., III, Leon-Guerrero, A.Y., & Haley, J.D., Jr. (2001). Strategic goals and practices of innovative family businesses. *Journal of Small Business Management*, *39*(1), 50–9.

McConaughy, D.L. (2004). Family CEOs vs. nonfamily CEOs in the family-controlled firm: An examination of the level and sensitivity of pay to performance. *Family Business Review*, *13*(2), 121–31.

McConaughy, D.L., Matthews, C.H., & Fialko, A.S. (2001). Founding family controlled firms: Performance, risk, and value. *Journal of Small Business Management*, *39*(1), 31–49.

McConaughy, D.L., & Phillips, G.M. (1999). Founders versus descendants: The profitability, efficiency, growth characteristics and financing in large, public, founding-family-controlled firms. *Family Business Review, 12*(2), 123–31.

McKelvey, B. (1978). Organizational systematics: Taxonomic lessons from biology. *Management Science, 24*(13), 1428–40.

McKelvey, B., & Wauchope, R. (1982). *Organizational Systematics – Taxonomy, Evolution, Classification.* Univ. of California Press.

Mickelson, R.E., & Worley, C. (2003). Acquiring a family firm: A case study. *Family Business Review, 16*(4), 251–68.

Miller, D. (2003). Lost in time: Intergenerational succession, change, and failure in family business. *Journal of Business Venturing, 18*(4), 513–31.

Miller, D., & Le Breton-Miller, I. (2006). Family governance and firm performance: Agency, stewardship, and capabilities. *Family Business Review, 19*(1), 73–87.

Miller, D., Le Breton-Miller, I., & Scholnick, B. (2008). Stewardship vs. stagnation: An empirical comparison of small family and non-family businesses. *Journal of Management Studies, 45*(1), 51–78.

Miller, N.J., Fitzgerald, M.A., Winter, M., & Paul, J. (2004). Exploring the overlap of family and business demands: Household and family business managers' adjustment strategies. *Family Business Review, 12*(3), 253–68.

Miller, N.J., McLeod, H., & Young Ob, K. (2002). Managing family businesses in small communities. *Journal of Small Business Management, 39*(1), 73–87.

Milligan, G.W. (1980). An examination of the effect of six types of error perturbation on fifteen clustering algorithms. Psychometrika, 45(3), 325–42.

Mishra, C.S., & McConaughy, D.L. (1999). Founding family control and capital structure: The risk of loss of control and the aversion to debt. *Entrepreneurship Theory and Practice, 23*(4), 53–64.

Moores, K. (2009). Paradigms and theory building in the domain of business families. *Family Business Review, 22*(2), 167–80.

Moores, K., & Mula, J. (2004). The salience of market, bureaucratic, and clan controls in the management of family firm transitions: Some tentative Australian evidence. *Family Business Review, 13*(2), 91–106.

Morris, R. (1994). Computerized content analysis in management research: A demonstration of advantages & limitations. *Journal of Management, 20*(4), 903–31.

Murphy, D.L. (2005). Understanding the complexities of private family firms: An empirical investigation. *Family Business Review, 18*(2), 123–33.

Murphy, D.L., & Murphy, J.E. (2001). Protecting the limited liability feature of your family business: Evidence from the US court system. *Family Business Review, 14*(4), 325–34.

Murray, B. (2004). The succession transition process: A longitudinal perspective. *Family Business Review, 16*(1), 17–33.

Muske, G., & Fitzgerald, M.A. (2006). A panel study of copreneurs in business: Who enters, continues, and exits? *Family Business Review, 19*(3), 193–205.

Mustakallio, M., Autio, E., & Zahra, S.A. (2002). Relational and contractual governance in family firms: Effects on strategic decision making. *Family Business Review, 15*(3), 205–22.

Nag, R., Hambrick, D.C., & Chen, M. (2007). What is strategic management, really? Inductive derivation of a consensus definition of the field. *Strategic Management Journal, 28*(9), 935–55.

Naldi, L., Nordqvist, M., Sjöberg, K., & Wiklund, J. (2007). Entrepreneurial orientation, risk taking, and performance in family firms. *Family Business Review, 20*(1), 33–47.

Nam, Y., & Herbert, J.I. (1999). Characteristics and key success factors in family business: The case of Korean immigrant businesses in Metro-Atlanta. *Family Business Review, 12*(4), 341–52.

Niehm, L.S., Swinney, J., & Miller, N.J. (2008). Community social responsibility and its consequences for family business performance. *Journal of Small Business Management, 46*(3), 331–50.

Niemelä, T. (2004). Interfirm cooperation capability in the context of networking family firms: The role of power. *Family Business Review, 17*(4), 319–30.

Okoroafo, S.C. (2004). Internationalization of family businesses: Evidence from Northwest Ohio, USA. *Family Business Review*, *12*(2), 147–58.

Olson, P.D., Zuiker, V.S., Danes, S.M., Stafford, K., Heck, R.K., & Duncan, K.A. (2003). The impact of the family and the business on family business sustainability. *Journal of Business Venturing*, *18*(5), 639–66.

Oswald, S.L., Muse, L.A., & Rutherford, M.W. (2008). The influence of large stake family control on performance: Is it agency or entrenchment? *Journal of Small Business Management*, *47*(1), 116–35.

Perricone, P.J., Earle, J.R., & Taplin, I.M. (2001). Patterns of succession and continuity in family-owned businesses: Study of an ethnic community. *Family Business Review*, *14*(2), 105–21.

Pieper, T.M., Klein, S.B., & Jaskiewicz, P. (2008). The impact of goal alignment on board existence and top management team composition: Evidence from family-influenced businesses. *Journal of Small Business Management*, *46*(3), 372–94.

Pistrui, D., Huang, W., Oksoy, D., Jing, Z., & Welsch, H. (2001). Entrepreneurship in China: Characteristics, attributes, and family forces shaping the emerging private sector. *Family Business Review*, *14*(2), 141–52.

Pistrui, D., Welsch, H.P., Wintermantel, O., Liao, J., & Pohl, H. (2000). Entrepreneurial orientation and family forces in the new Germany: Similarities and differences between East and West German entrepreneurs. *Family Business Review*, *13*(3), 251–63.

Poutziouris, P.Z. (2004). The views of family companies on venture capital: Empirical evidence from the UK small to medium-size enterprising economy. *Family Business Review*, *14*(3), 277–91.

Poza, E.J., Hanlon, S., & Kishida, R. (2004). Does the family business interaction factor represent a resource or a cost? *Family Business Review*, *17*(2), 99–118.

Poza, E.J., & Messer, T. (2004). Spousal leadership and continuity in the family firm. *Family Business Review*, *14*(1), 25–36.

Prencipe, A., Markarian, G., & Pozza, L. (2008). Earnings management in family firms: Evidence from R&D cost capitalization in Italy. *Family Business Review*, *21*(1), 71–88.

Priem, R.L., Love, L.G., & Shaffer, M.A. (2002). Executives' perceptions of uncertainty sources: A numerical taxonomy and underlying dimensions. *Journal of Management*, *28*(6), 725–46.

Randøy, T., & Goel, S. (2003). Ownership structure, founder leadership, and performance in Norwegian SMEs: Implications for financing entrepreneurial opportunities. *Journal of Business Venturing*, *18*(5), 619–37.

Reger, R.K., & Palmer, T.B. (1996). Managerial categorization of competitors: Using old maps to navigate new environments. *Organization Science*, *7*(1), 22–39.

Rodriguez, P., Tuggle, C.S., & Hackett, S.M. (2009). An exploratory study of how potential "family and household capital" impacts new venture start-up rates. *Family Business Review*, *22*(3), 259–72.

Romano, C. (2001). Capital structure decision making: A model for family business. *Journal of Business Venturing*, *16*(3), 285.

Rowe, B.R., & Hong, G. (2000). The role of wives in family businesses: The paid and unpaid work of women. *Family Business Review*, *13*(1), 1–13.

Royer, S., Simons, R., Boyd, B., & Rafferty, A. (2008). Promoting family: A contingency model of family business succession. *Family Business Review*, *21*(1), 15–30.

Rutherford, M.W., Muse, L.A., & Oswald, S.L. (2006). A new perspective on the developmental model for family business. *Family Business Review*, *19*(4), 317–33.

Sacristán-Navarro, M., & Gómez-Ansón, S. (2007). Family ownership and pyramids in the Spanish market. *Family Business Review*, *20*(3), 247–65.

Salvato, C., & Melin, L. (2008). Creating value across generations in Family-Controlled businesses: The role of family social capital. *Family Business Review*, *21*(3), 259–76.

Sanchez Soldressen, L., Fiorito, S., & Yan, H. (1998). An exploration into home-based businesses: Data from textile artists. *Journal of Small Business Management*, *36*(2), 33–44.

Santiago, A.L. (2000). Succession experiences in Philippine family businesses. *Family Business Review*, *13*(1), 15–35.

SAS Institute. (1990). *SAS Users Guide: Statistics* (6th ed.). Cary, NC: SAS Institute.

Schulze, W.S. (2003). Toward a theory of agency and altruism in family firms. *Journal of Business Venturing, 18*(4), 473–90.

Schulze, W.S., Lubatkin, M.H., & Dino, R.N. (2003). Exploring the agency consequences of ownership dispersion among the directors of private family firms. *Academy of Management Journal, 46*(2), 179–94.

Schulze, W.S., Lubatkin, M.H., Dino, R.N., & Buchholtz, A.K. (2001). Agency relationships in family firms: Theory and evidence. *Organization Science, 12*(2), 99–116.

Sciascia, S., & Mazzola, P. (2008). Family involvement in ownership and management: Exploring nonlinear effects on performance. *Family Business Review, 21*(4), 331–45.

Sekaran, U. (2002). *Research Methods for Business: A Skill-Building Approach* (4th ed.). New York: Wiley.

Shapin, S. (1995). Here and everywhere: Sociology of scientific knowledge. *Annual Review of Sociology, 21*, 289–321.

Sharma, P. (2004). An overview of the field of family business studies: Current status and directions for the future. *Family Business Review, 17*(1), 1–36.

Sharma, P., Chrisman, J.J., & Chua, J.H. (1996). *A Review and Annotated Bibliography of Family Business Studies*. London, UK: Kluwer Academic Publishers.

Sharma, P., Chrisman, J.J., & Chua, J.H. (2003). Predictors of satisfaction with the succession process in family firms. *Journal of Business Venturing, 18*(5), 667–87.

Sharma, P., Chrisman, J.J., & Chua, J.H. (2004). Succession planning as planned behavior: Some empirical results. *Family Business Review, 16*(1), 1–15.

Sharma, P., Hoy, F., Astrachan, J.H., & Koiranen, M. (2007). The practice-driven evolution of family business education. *Journal of Business Research, 60*(10), 1012–21.

Sharma, P., & Irving, P.G. (2004). Four bases of family business successor commitment: Antecedents and consequences. *Entrepreneurship Theory and Practice, 29*(1), 13–33.

Sharma, P., & Rao, A.S. (2000). Successor attributes in Indian and Canadian family firms: A comparative study. *Family Business Review, 13*(4), 313–30.

Shepherd, D.A., & Zacharakis, A. (2000). Structuring family business succession: An analysis of the future leader's decision making. *Entrepreneurship Theory and Practice, 24*(4), 25–40.

Shewchuk, R.M., O'Connor, S.J., Williams, E.S., & Savage, G.T. (2006). Beyond rankings: Using cognitive mapping to understand what health care journals represent. *Social Science & Medicine, 62*(5), 1192–204.

Short, J.C., Ketchen, D.J., Jr., Shook, C.L., & Ireland, R.D. (2010). The concept of "opportunity" in entrepreneurship research: Past accomplishments and future challenges. *Journal of Management, 36*(1), 40–65.

Short, J.C., & Palmer, T.B. (2003). Organizational performance referents: An empirical examination of their content and influences. *Organizational Behavior and Human Decision Processes, 90*(2), 209–24.

Short, J.C., Payne, G.T., Brigham, K.H., Lumpkin, G.T., & Broberg, J. C. (2009). Family firms and entrepreneurial orientation in publicly traded firms A comparative analysis of the S&P 500. *Family Business Review, 22*(1), 9–24.

Sirmon, D.G., Arregle, J., Hitt, M.A., & Webb, J.W. (2008). The role of family influence in firms' strategic responses to threat of imitation. *Entrepreneurship Theory and Practice, 32*(6), 979–98.

Smyrnios, K.X., Romano, C.A., Tanewski, G.A., Karofsky, P.I., Millen, R., & Yilmaz, M.R. (2004). Work-family conflict: A study of American and Australian family businesses. *Family Business Review, 16*(1), 35–51.

Smyrnios, K., Tanewski, G., & Romano, C. (1998). Development of a measure of the characteristics of family business. *Family Business Review, 11*(1), 49–60.

Sonfield, M.C., & Lussier, R.N. (2004). First-, second-, and third-generation family firms: A comparison. *Family Business Review, 17*(3), 189–202.

Sorenson, R.L. (1999). Conflict management strategies used by successful family businesses. *Family Business Review, 12*(4), 325–39.

Sorenson, R.L. (2000). The contribution of leadership style and practices to family and business success. *Family Business Review, 13*(3), 183–200.

Sorenson, R.L., Folker, C.A., & Brigham, K.H. (2008). The collaborative network orientation: Achieving business success through collaborative relationships. *Entrepreneurship Theory and Practice*, *32*(4), 615–34.

Sorenson, R.L., Goodpaster, K.E., Hedberg, P.R., & Yu, A. (2009). The family point of view, family social capital, and firm performance an exploratory test. *Family Business Review*, *22*(3), 239–53.

Stavrou, E.T. (1999). Succession in family businesses: Exploring the effects of demographic factors on offspring intentions to join and take over the business. *Journal of Small Business Management*, *37*(3), 43–61.

Stavrou, E.T. (2004). A four factor model: A guide to planning next generation involvement in the family firm. *Family Business Review*, *11*(2), 135–42.

Stavrou, E.T., Kleanthous, T., & Anastasiou, T. (2005). Leadership personality and firm culture during hereditary transitions in family firms: Model development and empirical investigation. *Journal of Small Business Management*, *43*(2), 187–206.

Stavrou, E.T., & Swiercz, P.M. (1998). Securing the future of the family enterprise: A model of offspring intentions to join the business. *Entrepreneurship Theory and Practice*, *23*(2), 19–40.

Steen, A., & Welch, L.S. (2006). Dancing with giants: Acquisition and survival of the family firm. *Family Business Review*, *19*(4), 289–300.

Steier, L. (2001a). Family firms, plural forms of governance, and the evolving role of trust. *Family Business Review*, *14*(4), 353–68.

Steier, L. (2001b). Next-generation entrepreneurs and succession: An exploratory study of modes and means of managing social capital. *Family Business Review*, *14*(3), 259–76.

Steier, L. (2003). Variants of agency contracts in family-financed ventures as a continuum of familial altruistic and market rationalities. *Journal of Business Venturing*, *18*(5), 597–618.

Steijvers, T., & Voordeckers, W. (2009). Private family ownership and the agency costs of debt. *Family Business Review*, *22*(4), 333–46.

Stewart, A. (2008). Who could best complement a team of family business researchers – Scholars down the hall or in another building? *Family Business Review*, *21*(4), 279–93.

Stokes, D.E. (1997). *Pasteur's Quadrant: Basic Science and Technological Innovation*. Brookings Inst Press.

Tagiuri, R., & Davis, J.A. (2004). On the goals of successful family companies. *Family Business Review*, *5*(1), 43–62.

Tan, W., & Fock, S.T. (2001). Coping with growth transitions: The case of Chinese family businesses in Singapore. *Family Business Review*, *14*(2), 123–39.

Thomas, J. (2002). Freeing the shackles of family business ownership. *Family Business Review*, *15*(4), 321–36.

Tokarczyk, J., Hansen, E., Green, M., & Down, J. (2007). A resource-based view and market orientation theory examination of the role of "familiness" in family business success. *Family Business Review*, *20*(1), 17–31.

Tsai, W., Hung, J., Kuo, Y., & Kuo, L. (2006). CEO tenure in Taiwanese family and nonfamily firms: An agency theory perspective. *Family Business Review*, *19*(1), 11–28.

Tsang, E.W. (2002a). Internationalizing the family firm: A case study of a Chinese family business. *Journal of Small Business Management*, *39*(1), 88–93.

Tsang, E.W. (2002b). Learning from overseas venturing experience: The case of Chinese family businesses. *Journal of Business Venturing*, *17*(1), 21–40.

Tsao, C., Chen, S., Lin, C., & Hyde, W. (2009). Founding-family ownership and firm performance the role of high-performance work systems. *Family Business Review*, *22*(4), 319–32.

Tsui-Auch, L.S. (2004). The professionally managed family-ruled enterprise: Ethnic Chinese business in Singapore. *Journal of Management Studies*, *41*(4), 693–723.

Uhlaner, L.M. (2005). The use of the Guttman scale in development of a family orientation index for small-to-medium-sized firms. *Family Business Review*, *18*(1), 41–56.

Upton, N., Teal, E.J., & Felan, J.T. (2002). Strategic and business planning practices of fast growth family firms. *Journal of Small Business Management*, *39*(1), 60–72.

Vallejo, M.C. (2009). Analytical model of leadership in family firms under transformational theoretical approach an exploratory study. *Family Business Review*, *22*(2), 136–50.

Van der Heyden, L., Blondel, C., & Carlock, R.S. (2005). Fair process: Striving for justice in family business. *Family Business Review*, *18*(1), 1–21.

Veliyath, R., & Ramaswamy, K. (2000). Social embeddedness, overt and covert power, and their effects on CEO pay: An empirical examination among family businesses in India. *Family Business Review*, *13*(4), 293–311.

Venkatraman, N., & Ramanujam, V. (1986). Measurement of business performance in strategy research: A comparison of approaches. *Academy of Management Review*, *11*(4), 801–14.

Venter, E., Boshoff, C., & Maas, G. (2005). The influence of successor-related factors on the succession process in small- and medium-sized family businesses. *Family Business Review*, *18*(4), 283–303.

Vera, C.F., & Dean, M.A. (2005). An examination of the challenges daughters face in family business succession. *Family Business Review*, *18*(4), 321–45.

Vilaseca, A. (2002). The shareholder role in the family business: Conflict of interests and objectives between nonemployed shareholders and top management team. *Family Business Review*, *15*(4), 299–320.

Voordeckers, W., Van Gils, A., & Van den Heuvel, J. (2007). Board composition in small and medium-sized family firms. *Journal of Small Business Management*, *45*(1), 137–56.

Wall, R.A. (1998). An empirical investigation of the production function of the family firm. *Journal of Small Business Management*, *36*(2), 24–32.

Ward, J., & Dolan, C. (2004). Defining and describing family business ownership configurations. *Family Business Review*, *11*(4), 305–10.

Welsh, D.H., & Raven, P. (2006). Family business in the Middle East: An exploratory study of retail management in Kuwait and Lebanon. *Family Business Review*, *19*(1), 29–48.

Westhead, P., & Cowling, M. (1998). Family firm research: The need for a methodological rethink. *Entrepreneurship Theory and Practice*, *23*(1), 31–56.

Westhead, P., Cowling, M., & Howorth, C. (2004). The development of family companies: Management and ownership imperatives. *Family Business Review*, *14*(4), 369–85.

Westhead, P., & Howorth, C. (2006). Ownership and management issues associated with family firm performance and company objectives. *Family Business Review*, *19*(4), 301–16.

Winter, M., Danes, S.M., Koh, S., Fredericks, K., & Paul, J.J. (2004). Tracking family businesses and their owners over time: Panel attrition, manager departure and business demise. *Journal of Business Venturing*, *19*(4), 535–59.

Wortman, M.S. (1994). Theoretical foundations for family-owned business: A conceptual and research-based paradigm. *Family Business Review*, *7*(1), 3–27.

Wu, W. (2008). Dimensions of social capital and firm competitiveness improvement: The mediating role of information sharing. *Journal of Management Studies*, *45*(1), 122–46.

Wu, Z., Chua, J.H., & Chrisman, J.J. (2007). Effects of family ownership and management on small business equity financing. *Journal of Business Venturing*, *22*(6), 875–95.

Yeung, H.W. (2000). Limits to the growth of family-owned business? The case of Chinese Transnational Corporations from Hong Kong. *Family Business Review*, *13*(1), 55–70.

Yilmazer, T., & Schrank, H. (2006). Financial intermingling in small family businesses. *Journal of Business Venturing*, *21*(5), 726–51.

Yu, A., Lumpkin, G.T., Brigham, K.H., & Sorenson, R.L. (2009, August). *A numerical taxonomy of family business outcomes: Findings and implications from studying ten years of dependent variables in family business research (1998–2007)*. Paper presented at the Annual Conference of the Academy of Management, Chicago.

Zahra, S.A. (2003). International expansion of U.S. manufacturing family businesses: The effect of ownership and involvement. *Journal of Business Venturing*, *18*(4), 495–512.

Zahra, S.A. (2005). Entrepreneurial risk taking in family firms. *Family Business Review*, *18*(1), 23–40.

Zahra, S.A., Hayton, J.C., & Salvato, C. (2004). Entrepreneurship in family vs. non-family firms: A resource-based analysis of the effect of organizational culture. *Entrepreneurship Theory and Practice*, *28*(4), 363–81.

Zahra, S.A., Hayton, J.C., Neubaum, D.O., Dibrell, C., & Craig, J. (2008). Culture of family commitment and strategic flexibility: The moderating effect of stewardship. *Entrepreneurship Theory and Practice*, *32*(6), 1035–54.

Zahra, S.A., & Sharma, P. (2004). Family business research: A strategic reflection. *Family Business Review*, *17*(4), 331–46.

Zellweger, T. (2007). Time horizon, costs of equity capital, and generic investment strategies of firms. *Family Business Review*, *20*(1), 1–15.

Appendix C

List of participants at the 2010 University of Saint Thomas Landscape of Family Business Conference

David L. Deeds – David is the Schulze Professor of Entrepreneurship at the University of Saint Thomas and Director of the Morrison Center. Prior to teaching at the University of Saint Thomas, David taught at Case Western University, Temple University, and the University of Texas in Dallas where he also served as the Academic Director of the Institute for Innovation and Entrepreneurship.

Katherine Hayes – Katherine is a member of the fifth generation of the Andersen Windows family and small business owner. Katherine also earned her MBA at the University of Saint Thomas.

Tom Hubler – Tom is an independent family business consultant who began 1980 as one of the first professional consultants for family business in the United States. Tom is a founding member and Fellow of the Family Firm Institute in Boston and currently serves as a member of the editorial board of the *Family Business Review*.

John Hughes – John has worked as an employee and independent consultant of family-owned and closely-held businesses and for more than 30 years. John has extensive experience working with businesses in the construction and real estate industry.

Sophie Bell Kelley – At the time of the conference, Sophie was the President and CEO of Adler Management, LLC—a single family office serving family businesses. Sophie earned her MBA in Marketing from the University of Minnesota, Carlson School of Management.

Sara McGinley – Sara is the Director of the University of Saint Thomas, Family Business Center. Sara earned her MA in Organization and Leadership from the University of San Francisco.

Harry G. (Paddy) McNeely, III – Paddy is a third generation family business owner and works as the CEO of his family business.

William Monson – Bill is the president of iManage, a consulting practice helping executive and owner teams manage alignment among their corporate strategies, structures, systems, and execution. Previously, Bill was the Director of the Family Business Center at the University of Saint Thomas and sat on the Board of Directors for Family Enterprise USA.

Bruce L. Paulson – Bruce is a certified public accountant and attorney with over twenty years of experience working with families of wealth. In addition, Bruce's past experience includes working with Arthur Andersen, US Bank, and US Trust Corporation.

Angela Pritchard – Angela is a fifth generation family member and works as a business manager in her family business.

Emily Pritchard – Emily is a fifth generation member of her family business. Emily earned a BA in Business Communication and Entrepreneurship from the University of Saint Thomas. Emily is the co-founder of The Social Lights, a social media and digital marketing agency that connects brands with college students.

Trina Smith – At the time of the conference, Trina was the Research Manager at the University of Saint Thomas, Family Business Center. Trina earned her PhD in Sociology from the University of Minnesota.

Joan Thompson – Joan is the Executive Vice President/CFO/Treasurer and a director of Minnesota Wire—a 42 year old second-generation family business. Joan has worked with the company in administration, finance, and HR since 1981.

Dan Vevang – At the time of the conference, Dan was the Social Media Manager at the University of Saint Thomas, Family Business Center. Dan earned an MS in Software Engineering from the University of Saint Thomas.

Peter Christian Ward – Peter is a third generation member of his family business, Ward's Balsam Lake Resort. Peter is now a partner in the family investment group and works with his father, mother, brother, and other family members. Peter earned his MBA from the University of Saint Thomas.

Ron Ward – Ron is the second generation family business owner of Ward's Balsam Lake Resort in Wisconsin and was a private practice oral and maxillofacial surgeon for over 25 years. Ron started RSW Management Inc., which he has owned and operated for the past ten years and both his sons are active employees in the business.

David Yost – David Yost is a fifth generation member of his family farm business. David graduated from the University of Minnesota with a BS in Agriculture Food Business Management. At the time of the conference he was pursuing his MBA from the University of Saint Thomas.

Michael Yost – Michael is a fifth-generation member of his family farm business. Michael is the Executive Director of the Minnesota division of American Majority, a non-profit, non-partisan, political training organization. Michael graduated from the University of Minnesota with a BS in Economics.

Mike Yost – Mike is a fourth-generation owner of his family farm. He has managed the farm for over thirty years. In 2004, he was appointed Associate Administrator of the USDA Farm Service Agency, and in 2006 he was appointed administrator of the USDA Foreign Agricultural Service.

Index

By the Grace of God

The Life of Grace Prescott

by
Della Hines Newnum

Nazarene Publishing House
Kansas City, Missouri

Copyright 2001
by Nazarene Publishing House

ISBN 083-411-8432

Printed in the United States of America

Editor: J. Wesley Eby

Cover Design: Michael Walsh

KJV (King James Version)

10   9   8   7   6   5   4   3   2   1

Contents

Della Hines Newnum is a third-generation member of the Church of the Nazarene. Her grandmother and parents were active, lifelong Nazarenes. Della and her husband, James, who have been married almost 50 years, live in Prescott Valley, Arizona. The Newnums have one daughter, two sons, eight grandchildren, and five great-grandchildren.

Della was a preschool teacher for 6½ years and a library/media technician for 17 years, before taking retirement over a decade ago. She served as NWMS president at Prescott First Church for 9 years. She has participated in three Work and Witness trips—one to Guam and two to Sun Valley Indian School.

Her previously published writings include short stories in *Standard* and an article with photograph in the former *Resource* magazine. She also had a front-page photograph on the children's publication *Wonder Time*.

Acknowledgments

I am grateful to God for the privilege of having Grace Prescott share her story with me during the last four years of her life. A great friend, she opened and shared her heart with me.

I am also grateful to Delia Berman, Grace's daughter, for her tremendous help in providing insights into family life on the mission field and by sharing precious family photographs for this book.

I would like to thank my editor, Wes Eby, for his thoughtful and perceptive suggestions that make this book more interesting and readable.

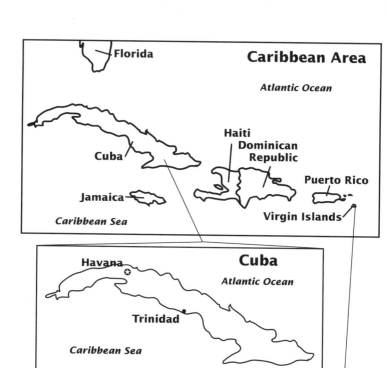

Caribbean Area

Atlantic Ocean

Florida

Cuba

Haiti
Dominican
Republic

Puerto Rico

Jamaica

Virgin Islands

Caribbean Sea

Cuba

Havana

Atlantic Ocean

Trinidad

Caribbean Sea

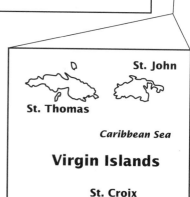

St. John

St. Thomas

Caribbean Sea

Virgin Islands

St. Croix

Frederiksted

Christiansted

Introduction

Dr. James C. Dobson—noted author, psychologist, and president of Focus on the Family—interviewed Grace Prescott for a 1983 radio program titled "A Visit with a Saint." Impressed by Grace's faith and courage, he rebroadcast the program in 1999 a few months after her death. At that time Dr. Dobson commented, "She was a saint—a woman who modeled grace under pressure . . . She went through trials that most of us will never have to endure, at least not so many of them, and yet she never wavered in her faith. She *didn't* blame God, and she just continued believing and walked with Him."*

Why would Dr. Dobson call Grace Prescott "a saint"? This book should provide the answer, for by the grace of God, she . . .

- survived spinal meningitis as a young girl
- fought a battle with asthma for many years
- gained victory over the enormous medical bills from Lyle's (her husband) surgery
- handled Deede's (her oldest daughter) bout with a ruptured appendix and peritonitis
- nursed her two oldest children during six weeks of quarantine from scarlet fever
- resided in a flea-infested house in Cuba with four children

*Grace Prescott, "A Visit with a Saint," interview by James C. Dobson, *Focus on the Family*, 1983, 1999. Used by permission.

- endured Bob's (her oldest son) near-death illness with dysentery
- learned to manage as a missionary in a country with limited provisions and equipment
- suffered with chronic back problems that eventually resulted in two operations and an allergic reaction to penicillin
- shared her children's anguish when their classmates taunted and persecuted them
- lived through the pain of separation from sending all four children to the United States for educational purposes
- grieved and accepted the tragic deaths of
  - her husband, Lyle
  - her youngest son, Woody
  - her youngest daughter, Ruth

Unquestionably, Grace was a woman of great faith and total commitment. In her Christmas letter of 1996, she wrote, "I love to read the Word and talk with my Lord. Since Lyle's departure, I have had to depend even more on the Lord for daily strength and guidance. He has never failed to meet my need. Praise His name!"

The late Dr. Earl G. Lee, her pastor for many years, wrote before his death: "Our lives have been entwined with Grace Prescott for several years. As you read *By the Grace of God*, you will feel the impact of this special lady. Mrs. Lee and I have observed Grace's life enough to see and feel her strength in Christ. 'Through many dangers, toils, and snares,' she has come victoriously"—all by the grace of God.

1

Growing Up

A redheaded girl, Dora Mae. God has given us a
fiery redhead!" With a voice indicating his
pleasure, William Yoakum* spoke to his wife just
after their second child, Grace Irene, was born.

"Yes, Will. What a darling baby!" his wife responded.

"I wonder how the Lord will use her," Preacher Yoakum pondered, talking halfway to himself
yet loud enough for Dora Mae to hear. "I just feel
somehow that God has something special for her."

This was Grace Prescott's introduction into this
world on August 11, 1910, in Woodward, Okla-
homa. Grace, the second child in a family that
would eventually grow to 12 children (four boys
and eight girls), joined the Yoakum tribe. And she
was the only redhead!

Her dad worked with his father in a drayage
business, hauling goods by horse and wagon. Also
a circuit-riding preacher, he traveled to places
where there were no churches and provided folks
the services of a minister. He became a member of
the Church of the Nazarene when it was founded

---

*A guide on page 95 provides suggested pronunciations of unfa-
miliar words in this book.

**Grace *(front left with hair bow)*
and five of her siblings.**

in 1908, and one of Grace's keepsakes was his copy
of the 1908 church *Manual.* William's mother, an
old-fashioned Methodist, was a godly influence on
her four sons and grandchildren.

During World War I a devastating influenza
epidemic swept through the Sooner state killing
many, including Grace's grandmother. Since
William became quite ill also and the doctor ad-
vised him to move to a warmer climate, the family
decided to go to California.

Mr. Yoakum purchased a brand-new Model-T
Ford with isinglass curtains that had to be installed
in rainstorms. With bedding stacked on top, canvas
water bags hanging on the radiator, a grub box tied
on the back, and other necessities attached to the

running boards, the Yoakums piled in—there were six children at the time—and headed out West.

What an adventure! There were no motels and only limited restaurants along the way. Each evening, the travelers pulled off the road, and Mother Yoakum prepared the evening meal in a big iron kettle over a campfire. Grace's father often shot rabbits with his rifle, and her mother cooked them. The huge cooking pot was even used for baking biscuits. At night the family spread bedding on the ground. Grace and her brother Frank would often lie on their backs and look up, wondering why God put so many stars in the sky.

Interstate highways were nonexistent in those days, and many roads were dirt. Whenever they got stuck, Dad Yoakum used a shovel to dig out of the sand or clay and wielded an axe to cut brush to put underneath the wheels. Then, everyone got out and pushed. After days and days of travel, they finally reached California.

Staying in the Golden State only a few months, the family moved to Arizona. In the Phoenix area, the Yoakums lived in several places, but always on a farm where they could raise cows, pigs, chickens, and much of their food. Grace's mother, a hard-working, practical woman, raised her children to know how to labor. Grace benefited from this instruction, for "hard work" paid her way through college and then carried her through life's less-than-ideal situations.

The family attended First Church of the Nazarene in Phoenix, and life evolved around church activities. Even with myriad farm chores, the Yoakums were almost always the first ones at the services and earned numerous prizes for perfect attendance. Grace loved Junior Society on Sunday evening, and she memorized the Books of the Bible, many psalms, the Beatitudes, the Ten Commandments, and other scriptures, which would provide comfort and support throughout her life.

I know that the Lord has lots of surprises planned—if *only* you will live for Him.

When Grace was nine years old, the family lived only a few blocks from their church. One evening she and her dad walked to church to hear a special speaker. During the service God spoke to her. When the altar call was given, she went forward and asked Jesus into her heart.

On their way home, father and daughter talked about the special service just attended. "You may not remember it, Grace. But your mother and I have told you about the time God healed you when you were only three years old and you almost died from spinal meningitis."

"Dad, I do remember."

"I've always felt, ever since you were born, that God has something special for you. I don't know what it is, but I know that the Lord has lots of surprises planned—if *only* you will live for Him."

How prophetic those words were!

Grace's sister Ruby, as a toddler, became ill with whooping cough and double pneumonia. The sick child was placed in a crib in the living room, and Grace became her "nurse." Even though the family gave Ruby the best medical care possible at the time, she was so weak she couldn't sit up.

One day, with Grace at her side, Ruby pulled herself up and said, "Oh, I see Jesus!" She fell back down and was gone. The death of her little sister greatly impressed Grace. From that time on, she determined that one day she would see Jesus too.

Grace, along with her crimson hair, had freckles (on which she secretly used Stillman's Freckle Cream). She did not own stylish clothes that many of her peers wore. Feeling different, she developed an inferiority complex, which she carried for years. Her bout with spinal meningitis left her with a weak back, and she had an asthmatic condition that required frequent medication.

I wonder if I'll ever be able to do anything significant for the Lord, she often thought as she considered what she perceived were handicaps and faults.

When Grace was a high school junior, she attended another Nazarene church on the east side of Phoenix. She became active in the youth group and joined them in holding street meetings downtown, inviting passersby to attend church. One Thursday night, in a cottage (home) prayer meeting, Grace made a total commitment to God and received the Holy Spirit. From that day on, she sought the Lord's will in everything she undertook.

Grace as a teenager in Phoenix

Right after high school graduation in 1932, Grace attended the district assembly. Dr. Orval J. Neese, then president of Pasadena College (now Point Loma Nazarene University), encouraged her to enroll at the school. Grace had been planning to work at F. W. Woolworth Company and finally earning some money. But, somehow, the idea of college intrigued and pursued her. She knew that her parents could not help financially and she would have to work through school. After much prayer and heart-searching, she yielded to God's will. She believed the scripture promise: "Trust in the LORD with all thine heart; and lean not unto thine own understanding. In all thy ways acknowledge him, and he shall direct thy paths" (Prov. 3:5-6, KJV). She made plans for college—by the grace of God.

2

Graduating and Marrying

Grace bought a cheap suitcase, packed her few belongings, and headed off for college. Dad Yoakum obtained a $5 ride for his daughter, and she had exactly $10 in her pocketbook. Dr. Nease arranged for Grace to enroll for only $5, leaving her $5 to live on until she could find a job. The new collegian had formed the habit of reciting Psalms 23 and 91 every night before going to sleep, and she certainly needed the comfort they brought.

With the help of Mother Ransom, the dormitory house matron, Grace landed a "good" job doing housework for a family who lived about a 45-minute uphill walk from the dormitory. Tasks included scrubbing the floors on her knees, doing the laundry on a washboard, and cooking. The lady of the house entertained often, and Grace had to prepare three-course meals and serve them to the guests. She worked there all four years of college for $6 a week, often walking to save the 10-cent bus fare. After fixing herself a cup of coffee on the radiator in her dorm room, she waited until arriving at work to eat.

Because of her asthma, the long walk to work

was so hard for Grace that she despaired of being able to continue. One day, shutting herself in her clothes closet, she prayed and begged God to heal her. She showed her faith by throwing away the asthma medication, never to use it again—just one of God's miracles that enabled Grace to continue in school.

Grace was absolutely amazed that she had captured "the most gorgeous man on campus."

At Pasadena College the plain, freckle-faced redhead met a dark-haired, handsome man named Lyle. An accomplished pianist, he sang tenor in the college quartet. Although the couple had just one date as freshmen, the next year Lyle began to court Grace in earnest. When he proposed, they decided to keep their engagement a secret until graduation. Grace was absolutely amazed that she had captured "the most gorgeous man on campus."

Lyle Eldred Prescott, the second child in a family of seven boys and one girl, was raised by a wonderful Christian mother named Delia. The family, who lived in Spring Valley in the San Diego area, were staunch members of First Church of the Nazarene and later University Avenue Church. All of the Prescott children became Christians and most of them attended Pasadena College. On Sun-

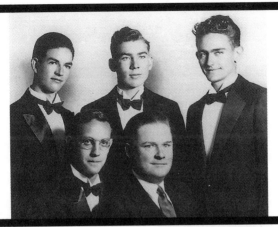

**Pasadena College quartet *(back, l. to r.)*
Lyle Prescott, Weldon Stone, Elwood Sanner.
(Front, l. to r.) Earl Schultz, Orval J. Nease.**

day, when sailors from the nearby naval base came to church, Delia invited half a dozen at a time for dinner. Grace felt blessed to be included in such a loving and generous family, and Delia became like a mother to her.

Lyle received a call to missions after hearing Mrs. Minnie Staples, a Nazarene missionary to Japan, speak at the college. During their years of education and even after graduation, Lyle and Grace helped with a Japanese church in South Pasadena. Lyle was the Sunday School superintendent; Grace taught a Sunday School class. Later they thought they might go to Japan as teachers, but this idea never materialized because of World War II.

After graduation with honors, Grace and Lyle

College graduation, 1936

scheduled a late-summer wedding. Lyle, once again, traveled, singing with the college quartet. Grace continued living in the dorm, working for $40 a month—quite a good salary in those days. She purchased a Chevy coupe for $30 for traveling to and from work. She planned the wedding while Lyle was gone, even sewing her own gown. They were married on a Saturday afternoon, August 29, 1936, at Pasadena First Church by Dr. H. Orton Wiley. That night Lyle was back at the piano, playing for camp meeting services.

The newlyweds lived in Pasadena for three years while Lyle pursued a master's degree in music. Grace had a variety of jobs. Lyle gave private piano lessons, taught music classes at Pasadena

Grace and Lyle's wedding, 1936

Academy (the high school connected to the college), and directed the academy choir.

Grace and Lyle felt they were blessed indeed when their first son, Robert Leland (Bob), was born on October 28, 1937.

Though times were difficult and finances tight, God graciously answered prayer for the young family on numerous occasions. Lyle's motto was "God will provide." He always did—by His marvelous grace.

3

Pastoring

"Oh, God, You want *me* to preach?" Lyle agonized in prayer. "I thought it was Your will that I would have a career in music."

The more Lyle sought the Lord, the more he felt a call to the ministry. After much travail and seeking the Lord, in obedience to the heavenly charge, Lyle changed his master's major from music to theology. This meant studying a year longer, but he felt assured this was God's will. Upon earning his degree, the young preacher and his spouse accepted their first pastorate at Denver Eastside Church in Colorado at the "huge" salary of $7 a week.

Here, on June 22, 1939, the Lord blessed them with a daughter and a little sister for Bobby. Though they named her Delia Elane, after Lyle's mother, she became known as Deede.

During this pastorate, both Lyle and Bobby became seriously ill with influenza. But God intervened to heal the lad when his fever became dangerously high. Another time Lyle had an emergency appendectomy and medical costs mounted. As he recovered, enough money came in to cover all costs. God, by His grace, supplied their needs with miracle after miracle.

The Prescotts at Denver Eastside Church, circa 1940.

Lyle accepted a call to the Grand Junction church on the western slope of the Rockies in Colorado. Grand Junction was a beautiful place with breathtaking landscape. A fisherman's paradise, the area fostered a love of the outdoor lifestyle that lasted a lifetime for this minister. God blessed the church and it grew.

23

Before long Deede was sitting up in her hospital bed under the oxygen tent singing "Jesus Loves Me."

Shortly before Grace was expecting her third child, three-and-a-half-year-old Deede developed appendicitis. By the time she was operated on, the appendix had ruptured. Even though the new "miracle" drug sulfa was administered, the young child developed peritonitis. She was not expected to live. As Deede lay under an oxygen tent for days, one of her nurses was Lorraine Schultz, later to become a missionary to Swaziland and Mozambique. Many interceded to God on behalf of the girl. Before long Deede was sitting up in her hospital bed under the oxygen tent singing "Jesus Loves Me." God again honored the prayers of His people, and by His grace the little girl survived.

On January 9, 1942, while in Grand Junction, the Prescott home was blessed with a second son, Elwood Lyle, who came to be called Woody. Grace put him in Deede's arms and told her that he was her baby too. From that time on a unique bond existed between this brother and sister.

In January 1944 the family moved to Omaha, Nebraska, where Lyle had accepted the call to First Church. Three weeks into this pastorate, Grace had a severe attack of tonsillitis that required surgery. The wonderful people of the church cared for their new pastor and the children while their wife and mother stayed in the hospital.

Later, when Bobby and Deede came down with scarlet fever, they were quarantined by the health department. Lyle could not return home for six weeks. He slept in the cold church basement, and Grace handed his meals out the door to him. Even though Lyle was janitor as well as pastor, God gave them a solid, God-honoring ministry there. But the call to missionary work grew even stronger.

4

Beginning the Great Adventure

Grace and Lyle had a longing to be missionaries and go abroad, referring to it as "The Great Adventure." Soon their call would be realized. At a missionary convention in a neighboring state, they talked to General Superintendent J. B. Chapman about their desire. Dr. Chapman asked them to contact C. Warren Jones, executive secretary of the mission department, about their call. Dr. Jones told them there was an opening at the Bible college in Guatemala. Lyle had the necessary qualifications, and for a time it looked as though the family would be sent there in the fall. Their college friends, Harold and Ruth Hess, were already serving as missionaries in Guatemala, and the Prescotts wanted to join them.

Back in Omaha, the Prescotts broke the news to their church and resigned. One month later, they began to travel and hold deputation services, asking for prayer as they prepared to go as missionaries. They were invited to attend the General Assembly in Minneapolis. There, the church asked them to consider serving in Puerto Rico and St. Croix in the Virgin Islands instead of Guatemala. Two small mission groups in those countries needed supervision. Though disappointed, Grace and Lyle went to their hotel room and prayed earnestly about this new offer. Believing it was God's will, they accepted and prepared for the Caribbean assignment.

The trip across the United States to Miami, where they were to fly to Puerto Rico, was reminiscent of Grace's trip with her family to California so many years before. Lyle drove an old Model T with canvas bags of water hanging on the radiator. The children took turns sitting next to him because their father knew the names of all the trees, birds, and butterflies they saw, and the ride went by quickly in his company. Along the way, they stopped occasionally so Lyle could fish the streams and creeks. They saved money by rarely eating in restaurants. Instead they bought bologna and cheese at a grocery store and made sandwiches for picnics. They arrived in southern Florida with no major problems.

The glow on the people's countenances led Deede to think that they were angels.

The Prescotts flew from Miami to Puerto Rico in a propeller plane. The time: November 1944 in the midst of World War II. The windows of the aircraft were covered to prevent anyone from spying on the United States military installations and ships in the Caribbean. When they landed at the airport,

**Bobby and Deede with dead mongooses,
thanks to their mom's accurate shooting.**

the family, children and all, underwent security
checks, including fingerprinting.

The new missionaries could not find a house to
rent in Puerto Rico for the $30 a month they had
been allotted, and the work there was not encour-
aging at all. Finally, Lyle flew to St. Croix in the Virgin Islands. After locating a suitable house, he
moved his family there. The dwelling was situated
in Frederiksted on a hill overlooking the bay and
the harbor. (Victor Borge, the famous Danish pianist, owned the house across the street.) Often
when a ship docked, Bobby and Deede ran down to

greet the sailors, who came from all over the world. Sometimes the mariners, captivated by the gregarious kids, gave them coins and trinkets.

The Prescott home had three-foot-thick stone walls. The kitchen, which was in a separate building out back, frustrated Grace, especially on days when the prepared meals had to be brought into the house through the rain. She sent to the States for a tray of baby chicks to supplement their diet. Raising chickens on St. Croix was not uneventful. She sometimes had to wield a shotgun on the mongooses that preyed on her cherished poultry. Another time the chicken coop literally blew away during a hurricane.

The Prescotts loved St. Croix and the people with their black, shiny faces. The glow on their countenances led Deede to think that they were angels. Even though the people were outgoing and re-

Grace's first WFMS (now NWMS) group in St. Croix

sponsive, the church was small. Nazarene officials decided that it was not feasible to continue the work there, or in Puerto Rico either, at that time. After one short year, the Prescott family tearfully left the dear Cruzan people, and the work was turned over to the Pilgrim Holiness denomination.

5

Settling in Cuba

"The church wants us to go to Cuba," Lyle told his beloved wife.

"Why Cuba?" Grace queried. "What about Guatemala? Can't we go there?"

"The opening in Guatemala has already been filled," Lyle explained. "As for Cuba, our church used to have work there . . . I believe about 25 years ago. They want us to reopen the field."

Grace and Lyle, taking this latest assignment as directed by the Lord, sold their furniture and flew to Havana. Lyle left Grace and their children at the Royal Palm Hotel and began to scout the island for the best place to begin.

What a challenge Grace faced! Life in a hotel with three active, mischievous children provided more thrill and frustration than this mother wanted. Mornings were spent outside the doors of the Woolworth's, waiting until it opened so the Prescott clan could have an American breakfast at the counter. For entertainment Bobby and Deede rode the hotel elevator. The first Spanish words they learned were *up* and *down* from the operator of this latest "toy." Besides the lack of activities for the children, staying in a hotel was expensive. The missionaries were anxious to find a place to live and begin their work.

While Grace and the children waited in Havana, their husband and father toured the island, looking for just the right spot. Several times he went back to Havana, ill from drinking the water.

One Friday night Lyle, his face beaming, returned to the hotel after one of his extended trips. "Grace, I've found it!" he said.

"Found what?" Grace inquired with a quizzical look.

"Our place. The place where we are to start the work." Lyle spoke with animation, his voice indicating his excitement. "I took the train clear across the island to the town of Trinidad. It's a colonial village and just happens to be the place where missionary Leona Gardner pioneered the work of the Church of the Nazarene. Once there, I became convinced that this was where God wanted the work to resume. In fact, I am so convinced that I've rented a house for us."

"Lyle, oh, Lyle. I . . . I just don't know. But . . . but if you believe this is right, then we'll go." Though Grace wondered what awaited in Trinidad, they packed their belongings. The Prescotts boarded the little coal-fired train and crossed the island, with sand and grit blowing into their eyes from the open windows. The countryside was covered with colorful bougainvillea bushes, flowers of all kinds, and royal palms. Up and down, across the rivers and around the hills, through each village, the train would no more than start than it would stop again.

The trip took a whole day. But what a wonderful way to see how the people lived and dressed. Many Cubans came up to the windows of the train with baskets of fruit and food, hawking their wares. It was an exciting day.

Shortly before arriving in Trinidad, a fellow passenger, a nicely dressed, fine-looking young man, came into the car where the Prescotts were riding. He stopped beside them.

"Are you Americans?" he asked.

"Yes, we are," Lyle responded.

"Well, I'm just a bit curious as to why a family from the United States would be traveling to Trinidad," the man remarked.

"I can satisfy your curiosity, I believe," Rev. Prescott said. "We are missionaries for the Church of the Nazarene, and we're planning to open a church in Trinidad."

"What? You're Nazarene missionaries? Why, my mother was a Nazarene missionary."

"Really? Your mother?" Both Lyle and Grace expressed great surprise at this disclosure. "Who is your mother?"

The young man answered, "Leona Gardner."

That response amazed the Prescotts just as much as the earlier revelation. They knew that Leona Gardner was among the pioneer missionaries sent to Cuba in 1902 by the Pentecostal Mission of Nashville. They had heard that Leona was a lady with a tender and caring heart, who loved the cause of holiness and Cuba. When her group united with the Church of the Nazarene in 1915, she joined also, and thereafter was known as a Nazarene. She adapted well to the country and acquired such an excellent command of Spanish that she hardly seemed like a foreigner to the Cubans. When the Cuban field was closed in 1920, she had been sent to Guatemala.

"What's your name?" Lyle finally asked, realizing they still did not know the man's name. "And how did Leona Gardner come to be your mother? I didn't know she ever married."

The links of the chain that had been broken 26 years ago were being repaired—by the grace of God.

"My name is Jorge. And as to my mother, I was abandoned as a three-month-old baby. Miss Leona Gardner, who was indeed a single lady, took me in and raised me as her own child." He went on to say that he had been educated both in Cuba and the United States, that he now lived in Havana where he worked for United States Steel, but traveled back to Trinidad often. "I truly owe everything to Miss Leona Gardner and the Church of the Nazarene," Jorge added.

What a special blessing for Grace and Lyle to meet Miss Gardner's adopted son on their way to Trinidad. The links of the chain that had been broken 26 years ago were being repaired—by the grace of God.

When the train reached Trinidad, many small, barefoot boys offered to carry the luggage for a kilo (about one cent). Jorge walked along with them toward the house that Lyle had rented. "There is still one missionary here in Trinidad who worked with Miss Leona. Her name is Grace Mendell de Santana, and she lives only two blocks from your rented house. Would you like to meet her?"

Grace Mendell de Santana

"Oh, yes, yes! We sure would!" the couple spoke as one. "But we didn't know there were any Nazarene missionaries still here," Grace commented.

"When Miss Leona left Cuba for Guatemala, Mrs. de Santana married a Cuban and remained here in Trinidad," Jorge explained.

Grace and Lyle were so excited about the news they decided to go and see her before going to their home. "This is too good to be true!" they said repeatedly.

Jorge led the way. When Grace de Santana came to the door, he introduced Grace and Lyle as Nazarene missionaries.

Mrs. de Santana broke down and wept. "For the past 26 years since Miss Leona left," the woman said between sobs, "I have prayed every day that God would bring the Nazarenes back to Cuba. And now God has answered my prayers!" Through a series of divine interventions, God had led the Prescott family to her very door.

Grace de Santana became a great blessing and help to the Prescott family as they began their work in Trinidad—just one more example of God's leading in Cuba and His marvelous grace.

6

Living and Surviving in Cuba

The de Santana home, typical of Cuban houses, was long and narrow. A hall went from the front door to the back of the dwelling. Rooms were arranged, side by side, one after the other. The hall finally opened into a patio, decorated with pots of bright flowers, often occupied by dogs, cats, and pigeons, with plenty of space for the children to play. In the kitchen a pot of beans and rice on a charcoal burner was always hot, and the family came to a large table to eat whenever they were hungry. Most families owned fighting game cocks, also kept in the patio area. What a noise they made, especially in the early morning hours!

Grace, anxious to see the house that Lyle had chosen, set off with her family trailing single file through the narrow, cobblestone streets that sloped toward the middle. Wash water and any other liquid needing disposal was poured in the street. When the rains came, everything washed down into the creeks and eventually into the sea.

The Prescott "parade" reached their rented house. Grace discovered that she could stand in the street and reach over to open the front door. Their

37

Street in Trinidad, Cuba

soon-to-be residence was so old that she could almost believe it had been built by Christopher Columbus himself. There was a large double door and tall windows with bars, but no glass or screens. Inside there was an immense, barnlike room with huge, sandstone slabs on the floor. The cracks between them were filled with dirt and—they found out later— fleas. The children soon looked like they had measles from the bites of these pesky, unwanted "varmints."

The outer wall along both sides of the house were shared with residences next door. Along each side the rooms lined up one after the other. At the rear of the house was a room with a charcoal burner for cooking. There was no running water; H_2O came from a cistern in the center of the patio and had to be carried into the house in buckets. All drinking water had to be boiled and skimmed. Ice was nonexistent.

Since the house was not furnished, the missionaries bought a table, chairs, and some "ancient" beds, the kind with flatbed coil springs that caused a reclining person to roll to the middle. Round sticks were attached to the four corners of each bed to tie on mosquito nets. Every night they could hear the hum of the malaria-carrying insects.

The "milk boy" came by every morning. He rode a donkey that had two five-gallon milk cans slung on either side in woven baskets. Since none of the homes had a doorbell, he simply gave two knocks on the door with his stick. The charcoal man, as well as other delivery people, also tapped a certain number of times to indicate who they were.

The only American family in town, the Prescotts became quite a curiosity.

The next morning Grace heard two knocks and took a pan out to meet the milk deliverer. With a long dipper he served up the milk. He was almost at the bottom of the can, and Grace noted a lot of strange things floating in it. All milk had to be strained through a cloth, boiled, and skimmed before it could be served to the children. They didn't like it very much, but it was the only milk available.

Grace learned that going to the grocery store, known as *bodegas,* was especially trying. In these little, one-room shops, large sacks of beans, rice, and lentils were stacked on the floor, and sometimes a hen would be sitting on top. Grace took a muffin pan when she wanted eggs, because she had to break them to check their freshness. Hanging from the ceiling were strings of salted and dried codfish called *bacalau.* In reality, there was really little food to be had. Since Grace didn't speak Spanish she had to take a Spanish-English dictionary along. If she couldn't find the item she wanted in the dictionary, she just looked for it in the bodega and pointed. Fresh vegetables, fish, and other perishable food items were brought into the village each day and sold at the marketplace near the center of town. It wasn't an easy way to live, but Grace and Lyle were sustained by God's grace and the feeling that God was in this great adventure.

The only American family in town, the Prescotts became quite a curiosity. Woody was the darling of their street because of his childlike sweetness. His nickname was Guiro or Guirito, which the Cuban people gave him. The locals carried him on their shoulders, and Grace was afraid he would never learn to walk. The vendors who came by often gave Bobby and Deede donkey rides. Cubans frequently peeked in the windows and asked them to "speaka English." While the children were a curiosity, they were quickly learning Spanish.

Only a few weeks after arriving in Trinidad, Lyle had to return to the States for a General Board

Guati Venegas and Lyle

meeting, so he tried to make Grace and the children as comfortable as possible before he left. The Prescotts had made friends with the Venegas family across the street, who had known Leona Gardner.

Being impressed by the former missionary, the Venegases asked Grace and Lyle to make a Nazarene out of their son, Guati. The young man had become a real help to the missionaries. When Guati heard that Lyle was leaving, he promised to take care of the family while he was gone. He took Lyle's suitcase on his shoulder, and the family watched sadly as they left to go to the train depot. It was Christmas night.

Lyle was gone seven weeks. About a week after he left, Grace and the children walked single file up the narrow street to the post office. The day was hot, and eight-year-old Bobby began to complain of a headache. Grace promised him that on the way back they would stop at the ice house to buy some ice cream. Arriving home she saw that her son's face was flushed and realized he had a high fever.

Grace remembered Mrs. de Santana's warning that the children must not eat raw fruit or drink unboiled water or milk, the primary causes of dysentery. This deadly disease killed more children in Cuba than any other illness. Boys and girls with severe dysentery usually lived only a few days. Grace *had* been careful; yet, she feared that Bobby had developed this killing malady.

After putting the children in the house, Grace ran all the way to the de Santana's and told her about Bobby. When Mrs. de Santana saw for herself how ill the lad was, she spoke with urgency, punctuating every word, "Grace, you must get the druggist to give him an injection right away." And this was done. Immediately!

By nighttime Bobby was a very sick little boy. He couldn't keep anything on his stomach, his skin was hot and burning to the touch, his eyes glassy. Grace bathed him to get his temperature down. The three Venegas sisters took turns sitting with Bobby, helping to wipe his face and bathe him.

By the afternoon of the next day, the lad's eyes were beginning to sink back into their sockets. *He's going to die*, his mother thought. *I don't know what else to do, but I know Someone who does.*

Grace went to the room where Lyle had stored big bags of charcoal so that she wouldn't run out while he was gone. As the fuel was used, the burlap sacks were folded up for reuse. Grace spread out a couple of sacks, knelt down, and began to pray earnestly.

"Lord, I don't know when Lyle will be back, and I feel so helpless," the missionary mother confessed. "Bobby's not getting any better. Please, *please*, help me."

A peace came over Grace that she found impossible to explain.

Grace reminded God about all the things she didn't like about their living conditions, and that if He really wanted them to be in Trinidad, He would have to do something. As she wept before the Lord, she really didn't pray directly for Bobby, for she felt the circumstances of his illness were beyond her control, and she threw herself on to God's mercy.

God began to remind Grace of all the times He had answered prayer by His grace. He had helped her go to school, healed her of asthma, and supplied all her needs. He reminded her of the healings of Lyle and Bobby in Denver, Deede in Grand Junction, and Bobby and Deede in Omaha. He brought a Bible verse to her mind, "Fear thou not; for I am with thee: be not dismayed; for I am thy God: I will strengthen thee; yea, I will help thee; yea, I will uphold thee with the right hand of my righteousness" (Isa. 41:10). A peace came over Grace that she found impossible to explain. And even though she had not mentioned Bobby to the Lord at all, she waited there calmly in His presence—both trusting and expecting.

When Grace walked back to her oldest child's bedside, she pulled back the mosquito netting and put her hand on his face. He was sweating but appeared to have no pulse. Hurriedly, she called Mrs. Venegas, who squeezed his jaw until he swallowed, then lifted his eyelids and peered into his eyes. She fed him some hot tea (in Cuba tea was considered a medicine and was purchased from the druggist), and perspiration drenched him as the fever went down. The crisis was over. He had lost a lot of weight. And though weak, Bobby was still alive.

God reassured Grace that He wanted them right where He had placed them. From that time on, she never doubted that they would stay in Cuba—by His grace.

Rev. Prescott finally returned to Cuba. When he heard of Bobby's illness and healing, he praised God for protecting his family. He also broke the news that Dr. Jones wanted them to move to the capital city.

In Havana the Prescotts found the same style of house they had been living in—only nicer. There was an oven with a glass front, and Grace became proficient at building a charcoal fire in it. Over a bed of coals, she was able to bake cakes and all their bread.

In those early days, the Prescott kids learned "street" Spanish from their Cuban friends. They often translated for Grace, which really helped with the shopping. Lyle, on the other hand, had not yet learned much Spanish. When the first service was held in May 1946 in the living room of their Havana home, he used a Christian man as an interpreter. But in a short time, Deede took over the job. It became imperative that the missionary learn the language, so he attended the University of Havana. He was grateful and pleased when he was able to preach in the mother tongue of the Cuban people.

Lyle and Grace completed their family on June 28, 1946, when Grace Ruth was born in the American hospital. Her birth was registered at the American embassy so she would have dual citizenship.

During the first three years in Cuba, Grace home-schooled Bob and Deede. Then this sibling pair began attending private schools. While attending the Methodist English School in Havana, they had to get up at 5 A.M., eat breakfast, and take the 6 A.M. bus to town. It was necessary to transfer twice before they reached the school, making a total of six—yes, *six*—buses a day. Since the MKs attended Spanish school in the morning and English school in the afternoon, they were fluent in both languages. When the family furloughed, the children were more advanced in their studies than American peers—except in American history and geography, which were not taught in Cuban schools, of course.

Using a correspondence course, Grace also home-schooled Woody and Ruth, as well as the two fellow missionary children, Ray and Norma Hendrix. Eventually Bob and Deede had to go to the States for schooling—Bob to Pasadena College and Deede to Pasadena Academy. The family's sadness during these times of being so far apart was real. Missionary families tend to be close-knit, because they are so far away from the homeland and have only each other. When the children go away to school, usually they can't afford to return home for holidays, which further increases the feeling of loss. Missionaries miss many golden moments in the lives of their children and grandchildren because of this separation. God gave Grace a scripture that she relied on during those times: "And all thy children shall be taught of the LORD; and great shall be the peace of thy children" (Isa. 54:13).

7

Serving and Ministering in Cuba

The first preaching outreach started in the Prescotts' living room. Lyle made wooden benches, and the neighborhood children were invited in for a Bible lesson, music, and songs, followed by Grace's homemade cookies and cake. In time the parents and adults began to come, and eventually a church was organized. This pattern was repeated successfully in many towns and villages across the island as church after church was established.

Lyle, feeling the necessity of training national pastors, started a Bible school in their home. Since this was not a satisfactory solution, he began to search for a different location for the educational institution. A 13-acre tract on a main, paved road became available for sale. The wealthy owner, the minister of agriculture for the Cuban government, had used it for a weekend retreat. The land had been planted with dozens of trees, including laurel, guava, mango, banana, avocado, and citrus. There were three buildings where the owner had raised prize chickens. The centerpiece of the "perfect" real estate was a large, spacious, Spanish-style house with tall, barred windows, double-entry doors, and a ceramic floor. Each tile was about a foot square, and four of them together formed a gorgeous rose pattern. Realizing this spacious property would be ideal for a school, and in light of the reasonable price of $13,500, Lyle asked the general church for permission to purchase it. He believed the poultry houses could be remodeled into dormitories and classrooms. After several requests, permission was finally granted. This decision proved to be a wise one.

The Prescott family moved out to the *farm*, as they called it. A sign was placed across the front that read Nazarene Mission Center. The commodious place had ample room for the children to play. Lyle made a combination chapel and Bible school out of the best of the larger-than-usual coops, and another was converted into a kitchen and dining room for students. Later, several more buildings were added—men's and women's dormitories, a home for the Bible school director, two prayer chapels converted from water cisterns, and a large tabernacle.

Thus, the Bible school in Cuba was born. The farm provided fruit, vegetables, chickens, and rabbits. The students worked the farm to pay for their studies. Yet, finances were tight, and at times little food was available for the students and workers. The Prescotts and students frequently prayed in the black beans and rice to place on the table. Their intercessions were repeatedly answered by love gifts

Entrance to the "farm"

from Nazarenes in the States. The Prescotts would receive a letter from someone saying that God had directed them to donate some money, and it was always there just when needed.

Grace began to have serious health problems. Her back had never been strong since suffering from spinal meningitis as a child. One day, she tripped over a wire in the grass while carrying cups of strong, black coffee to the students. She fell hard, wrenching her back. The pain became so intense that she finally saw an orthopedic doctor. She had pinched nerves in her back, and even though she was hospitalized for two weeks with weights on her legs, nothing would cure it except surgery. The Bible school students took care of the children.

They did the housework, cooking, and laundry while Grace recovered from the operation.

The merciless spinal pain returned accompanied by burning in her legs that Grace could only describe as "liquid fire." The doctor indicated she needed a second operation, which he performed at no charge. Although Grace had been given penicillin after the first surgery with no problem, this time she developed a severe allergic reaction to it, requiring 17 days of additional hospitalization. Though near death, she survived by the prayers of the people and the grace of God. She thanked Him, over and over and over, for giving her more years to serve Him.

On occasion the Prescotts were pelted with tomatoes and eggs, but usually most people gathered around and listened.

One unique and effective Bible school activity occurred at Christmastime. Lyle hired one of the old-fashioned streetcars with a cowcatcher on the front that traveled the streets of Havana. Huge cloth banners that promoted the Church of the Nazarene hung on each side. The students piled on this trainlike vehicle, playing accordions, maracas, castanets, tambourines, and anything else that would make music. As they went throughout the

The "Christmas streetcar"

city, they sang Christmas carols. What fun this was for the participants and observers!

Ministries often started in someone's house or on a porch or even on a street corner. And the Prescott children shared these incredible experiences with their father. Neighborhood children were attracted by the missionary kids. Lyle, an animated storyteller, would relate Bible stories with his own distinctive sound effects. Then the neighborhood youngsters would bring their parents. Deede often led the singing or interpreted for her father, so Lyle built a little stool for her to stand on. When he played the accordion or pump organ, a large crowd would gather, as Cubans love music.

Then Lyle would preach. On occasion the Prescotts were pelted with tomatoes and eggs, but usually most people gathered around and listened.

On Sundays Lyle would drop off Deede, then 12 years old, and Woody, age 9, to do a flannelgraph Bible lesson and sing songs on someone's porch. Then he'd leave 14-year-old Bobby and Grace at another place, while he went on to a third. Later he picked them all up, and they went home for lunch. No housework, homework, or anything unnecessary was done on Sunday. It was a fun day, however. Church folks came to the "farm" in the afternoon to enjoy refreshments, play games, visit with each other, and take home fruit from the many trees on the property. Sunday evenings the people went back to their own neighborhoods for church services that began around 8 P.M., the usual starting time.

Every evening the Prescott family gathered for devotions. Lyle told Bible stories in his own inimitable way. Daniel in the lions' den came along with lots of roars. Sometimes each child would be given a part to act out. This was not an optional time for the family, and everyone was expected to take a turn at praying. Once in a while the youngsters used this time not only to pray but also to tattle on each other. To their way of thinking, if you told God about another's misbehavior, you weren't an informer at all.

The young Prescott four were happy kids. They loved the church and the Cuban people. Parents and children were close, as missionary families usually are. Because they never received allowances or had a way to earn money, they usually couldn't afford to buy gifts for each other. Instead, they often gave each other coupons that were redeemed for dishwashing, shoe polishing, and other "mandated" chores.

8

Starting Camp Meeting— Cuban-Style

"Grace, why don't we have a camp meeting. You know, like the ones we used to have back in Colorado," Lyle said to his wife one day.

"That would be wonderful," Grace responded. "I believe the people here would love camp meetings as much as we used to."

"I'm confident they will, Grace. Let's do it."

The missionaries immediately made plans, and Lyle started to build a tabernacle. One night when only the framework of the building was up, he and Grace knelt down where they thought the altar would be. "Our Lord," they prayed, "let this tabernacle be the means of hundreds of Cubans coming to know You." And down through the years that prayer was answered countless times.

Camp meetings were exciting. At first the people didn't know what to expect. But once they learned, Nazarenes came by busloads, singing and rejoicing. For meals they dined on black beans and

Bible school students in front of the tabernacle

rice seasoned with garlic and onions and fried bananas—foods that the Cubans relished.

Grace wrote to friends in Colorado, telling about the tabernacle and the need for quilts. When the Prescotts went to the States on furlough, at least 50 quilts designated for Cuba awaited them. During camp meetings the people used them for bedding. The women slept on the Bible school floors and the men on tabernacle benches, each person rolled into a quilt.

Hildo Morejon, a choice young man, had been converted and miraculously healed during Lyle's visits to the tuberculosis sanitarium. Hildo's family lived on the western end of the island in rather primitive conditions. His mother was a witch doctor. When Hildo returned home, his family was amazed; they thought he would never leave the TB hospital alive. And when the Bible school opened,

Hildo enrolled. Later he became an exceptional pastor. From his family eventually came four national pastors.

Hildo married a beautiful woman, Elena, and they had two darling daughters. When Elena was pregnant with her third child, she contracted infectious hepatitis. The doctor said it would probably take her life and that of the child. Being treated in a free clinic, there were no nurses to take care of her. Spurgeon and Fae Hendrix had arrived in Cuba to take charge of the Bible school, so Fae and Grace took care of Elena and the baby. Still, both mother and infant died. Hildo, shocked and saddened, sent the two girls to live with his brother, and he moved into the Bible school dormitory with the other male students.

As preparations were made for the next camp meeting, the outpouring of the Holy Spirit was desperately needed. Everyone began to pray and fast. Early each morning Grace and Lyle met with Spurgeon and Fae to intercede for revival. As the people entreated God, they couldn't pray through about it. Their petitions seemingly rose no higher than the treetops. Louise Robinson Chapman and Fairy Chism, former missionaries to Africa who were the scheduled speakers, arrived. All plans were finalized.

When the Cuban people came, they didn't arrive singing as usual. Apparently, they were still sorrowful and depressed from Elena Morejon's death just six or seven weeks earlier. When the first service began, the jubilant rejoicing and praise was missing. Both Louise and Fairy found preaching difficult. All joined in earnest prayer about the situation.

The next day, Lyle went to see Pastor Morejon. "Hildo, God wants you to sing for the service tonight." The bereaved man, a melodic tenor, had not sung since his wife's death.

"I . . . I can't do it," the minister responded. "Especially at the . . . the camp meeting."

"But your music can lift the spirit of oppression that seems to be hovering over us," the missionary said. "I really feel that the Lord wants you to sing for His glory."

"I . . . I'll try." Hildo struggled with making a commitment. "But the Lord will have to help me."

Pentecost had come to Cuba!

"Just remember, my friend," Lyle told him, "even though Elena is gone, God is still with you. He will provide for your family. And He will help you sing again." Lyle found "His Eye Is on the Sparrow"* in the Spanish songbook and practiced with Hildo.

The service that evening was lifeless again. Then Hildo rose to sing and made it through the first stanza. When he began the refrain, "I sing because I'm happy; / I sing because I'm free," the Holy Spirit fell upon the people. They jumped to

---

*Words by Civilla D. Martin.

their feet, clapped, and threw their hands in the air. The tenor finished the chorus: "For His eye is on the sparrow, / And I know He watches me."

Soon people flocked to the altar, weeping and seeking God. The service was filled with praise and thanks to God for hearing and answering prayer. Pentecost had come to Cuba!

It was at this camp meeting that the young people in the Bible school and the national pastors testified they had been filled with the Holy Spirit. This memorable camp meeting was used by God to establish the Cuban pastors for what they would have to face in the years ahead.

9

Continuing the Great Adventure

After the unforgettable camp meeting, Lyle and Grace revealed to the Hendrixes and the other missionaries that the missions department in Kansas City had asked them to return to Puerto Rico. The Prescotts' hearts were broken at the thought of leaving Cuba. After 12 years they thought they would spend the rest of their missionary days there. (Actually because of the rise of Fidel Castro to power in Cuba, they would not have been able to remain there. Eventually all the missionaries were recalled from Cuba, and Hildo Morejon took over leadership of the work. Because of the Bible school training the Cuban national pastors had received, they were able to carry on alone.)

Lyle, Grace, Woody, and Ruth spent three years in Puerto Rico. Even though several problems and issues needed resolution, the work grew and new churches were organized.

Rev. Prescott, who loved music, wanted to play in the symphony orchestra with fellow missionary Bill Porter. The only vacant chair was in the bassoon section, so Lyle quickly learned to play this challenging instrument. A gifted musician, he was

Lyle enjoying his grand piano

able to "make music" on a carpenter's saw, glasses of water, or just two sticks, as well as the conventional instruments of piano, organ, violin, marimba, and bassoon. Lyle loved to learn. Not only did he master Spanish, but he also took classes in Italian. While Grace usually played "second fiddle" to her talented husband, she was a musician in her own right. She also played the piano and helped with the music ministry.

For their furlough in 1960, the Prescotts rented a home in Pasadena, California. The family had an enjoyable—but *busy*—year. Lyle traveled, speaking in deputation services, and worked on a manuscript for a mission book. All along, he had prayed about what God would have them do next, as he believed they had finished their work in Puerto Rico. In fact, he felt they should ask to return to the Virgin Islands, where they had served 15 years earlier. (At that time in the Caribbean area, there was Nazarene work in Haiti, Cuba, and Jamaica, but nothing else southward until the islands of Trinidad and Barbados.)

At the General Board meeting in Kansas City in January 1961, Lyle made his request, and the board agreed to consider it. On the last day of the session, General Superintendent Hugh Benner summoned Lyle and Grace to his office and informed them of the church's decision to send them back to the Virgin Islands. Lyle was overjoyed. Yet Grace was concerned that their two teenagers, Woody and Ruth, might not find adequate schooling on St. Croix. Lyle told her with assurance, "If God is in it, everything will work out."

Rev. Prescott wrote a letter to William De-Grasse, a former member of the St. Croix church, telling him of their plans. Brother DeGrasse sent a one-page reply, saying that ever since the Prescotts had left the island in 1945, he and his wife, Annesta, had prayed that God would bring them back. This dedicated couple, with little of earth's possessions, had an amazing faith that God would answer prayer. And He did!

Lyle and Grace were pleased to learn that

many Puerto Ricans had moved to St. Croix during their absence, which would offer a wonderful opportunity for evangelization. When the Prescotts arrived in the Virgin Islands, there was a joyful and heartfelt reunion. After renting a house where services could be held, they began to reestablish relationships and develop new ones.

In the meantime, all was not well with Woody and Ruth's adjustment to St. Croix. They had enrolled in Christiansted High. After the first day, they told their parents, "We're never going back to that school."

"What happened?" their mother queried.

"The students shoved and teased us," Woody said. "They even yelled, 'Yankee, go home'!"

Upon investigation, the perturbed parents learned that the children of some white Americans living and working on St. Croix had been unkind to the Cruzan students. As a result, white kids were not welcome, including Woody and Ruth. Grace and Lyle encouraged their harassed teens to continue in school, if nothing else to show that they weren't like those *other* white Americans.

The Prescotts knew how hard it would be for their children to go back, so they spent a day praying and fasting about the situation. They knew the two MKs could be a key to reach the people of the community for Christ, if they could only show the right attitude toward this rejection. Ruth played the flute and Woody the baritone, and both were already registered to play in the school band. At last, they decided to return to school.

The other students soon began to observe that these new white kids were different. Before long these two outsiders had many friends. Ruth was even elected vice president of the student body in her junior year. Later, Lyle became head of the band club, and Grace baked hundreds of cupcakes to help buy new uniforms.

When Woody finished his senior year, he went to the States to attend Pasadena College. When Ruth was ready to register for her senior year in high school, she realized she had enough credits to enroll in college too. All she needed was one English course and Spanish, which she spoke and wrote fluently. A transcript was sent to Pasadena, and she was accepted. Her astounded parents wondered how they could pay her tuition. "Let's turn the matter over to the Lord," Lyle suggested, and they rushed around to get Ruth ready to go in less than a week.

When Grace and Lyle put their daughter on a plane to California, they were indeed melancholy. Their last child had left the proverbial nest. The love, laughter, and music that Ruth had brought into their lives was gone. Lyle didn't play the piano for three days.

Later, Grace learned that she was qualified to teach third grade in the Christiansted grammar school, and this job meant Ruth's college tuition would be paid. The Lord had provided—by His marvelous grace.

All year the missionary couple saved money so their children could come home for the summer. And what a marvelous summer it was! Woody and

Ruth loved the ocean and often went lobster hunting with their dad. At the seashore the father-son-daughter trio heated a large can of water over a fire to cook the crustacean delicacies. The Prescott teens still had aquariums of tropical fish at their folks' home, and they cherished the time, once again, to care for them. They never lacked for something to do. They loved get-togethers with the people of the church. The islands truly were home to them.

At the close of the next school year when Ruth would have normally graduated from high school, she wanted to come back and receive her diploma from Christiansted High. When the Prescotts talked with the superintendent of schools, she said it wouldn't be possible. However, Ruth was invited to play with the band at the ceremony. Even though she was disappointed, she put on her red uniform with the gold tassel and joined them. When the graduates were called to receive their diplomas, Ruth was astonished and overwhelmed when her name was also called. As she walked across the platform, the students cheered and clapped.

After all the children left home, Grace and Lyle moved to a smaller house. Even though the living room was small, a number of people attended services and found the Lord. Lyle piled the furniture in the bedroom and in its place put in the benches, altar, and podium he had made. When a revival meeting was held, Lyle posted a sign in front of the house.

A woman named Lorna James, who had moved to St. Croix to work, lived next door to the DeGrasses. Though Lorna worked in a restaurant-bar and seemed to have no interest in church, her two children attended the Nazarene Sunday School regularly. When the revival began in the Prescotts' home, she must have had a hungry heart, for she attended every night. On Saturday evening she found the Lord, and her life was dramatically changed by God's grace. She went home and put the possessions of her live-in boyfriend outside the door. Lorna testified, "If I had a thousand tongues, I couldn't thank my Lord enough for digging me out of the deep, miry pit!"

Lorna could hardly read and write. She came to the parsonage every Saturday when she wasn't working (now at a place that didn't serve liquor) to learn to read the Bible. She wanted to teach a Sunday School class. Afraid that she couldn't because of her limited reading skills, Grace taught Lorna a Bible story on Saturday so she could retell it to the children on Sunday. After this enthusiastic convert finished her lesson, she visited a large, nearby public housing project and invited children to Sunday School. Each week she brought a long line of children to church. A loving person inside and out, this dedicated woman was used by God, and He blessed her efforts.

Lorna occasionally visited her home in Antigua, one of the Leeward Islands. God began to talk to her about returning there to win her family for Him. She moved to her hometown of St. John, had some benches made, placed them out on her patio, called on all her neighbors and friends, and began to hold services. Before long 30 people were converted, including almost all her family. Several

Christiansted Church of the Nazarene

years later in 1973, Louie Bustle, then a missionary in the Virgin Islands, along with a Miami pastor, held an evangelistic campaign in Antigua. Soon after, two churches were organized. In 1974 veteran missionaries Larry and Betty Faul were appointed to Antigua as the first resident missionaries. Lorna eventually became the treasurer of her church. Truly, God builds His kingdom with people, such as Lorna James, who are totally committed to Him, regardless of their education or background.

The services in the Prescott home were becoming so crowded that something had to be done. Property was expensive. With the help of a local agent, Lyle continued to look over every real estate possibility on the island. (The islands of St. Thomas, St. Croix, and St. John were purchased by the United States from Denmark in 1917 and are known as the United States Virgin Islands. The people speak English and many are of Danish ancestry or descendants of African slaves who were sent to this part of the world to work on the sugarcane plantations.)

Some land was located just off the main highway, consisting of four lots (almost an acre). But, there was a problem: no title. This property belonged to a Danish family whose members were either in the United States or Denmark. After much research and correspondence, permission was granted and a clear title was issued. This "ideal" property was purchased for the unbelievable price of only $12,500. Less than a year later the church was able to purchase an adjoining lot for $2,750. Seven years later, acres in that area were selling for $60,000.

The Alabaster fund provided the money to build the church. Lyle drew up the plans, and a builder from the States constructed it. Later a three-bedroom parsonage was built next door. Since water from wells on the island is slightly salty, a large cistern to catch the rainwater was built under the church. With another cistern nearby, the water supply was more than adequate.

A mission church was started in Frederiksted on the other side of the island. By the grace of God, the work was progressing. And Lyle and Grace were happy and fulfilled as His servants in the Virgin Islands.

10

Grieving for Lyle

The abrupt sound of the phone broke the silence of the beautiful February morning. The piercing ring compelled Grace to give the noise immediate attention. She hurried to answer it.

"There's been an accident," the person on the other end said. Grace recognized the voice as that of a Lutheran minister and close friend, who continued: "I've been asked to call you because I *knew* Lyle. Please come to the hospital in Frederiksted, but take your time. You don't need to hurry."

Hanging up the phone, Grace turned to her daughter. "Lyle's gone," she said, barely holding her emotions in check.

"What? Daddy's gone?" Ruth blurted out. "How do you know?"

"He said that he *knew* Lyle, that we did not need to hurry," Grace answered, calm on the outside but numb on the inside.

The two women, overcome with shock and anguish, drove to the hospital. As they rode through the island countryside, Grace reflected upon the past and all that had brought her to this particular moment.

Lyle had always loved the water, and fishing was his favorite form of recreation. He usually sold

Lyle, the "expert" fisherman

the fish they couldn't use themselves and put the money in his Alabaster box. Often on Monday her husband would take the day off and go fishing. He came home happy and relaxed, ready to work hard again.

Grace also thought about the reason Ruth was with them. After graduation from college, Ruth had gone to Valencia, Spain, on a student-exchange program to get a master's degree in Spanish. The father of one of her friends there passed away, and Ruth began to feel strongly she should go to St. Croix after an absence of two and a half years and see her *own* father. After a sleepless night, she wrote her parents that she was coming home. Grace and Lyle were overjoyed.

Ruth and her dad had a great time together. They practiced—she on the flute and he on the bassoon, organ, or piano—for a concert they planned to give. They fished together, and Ruth helped paint all the woodwork at the church. Bob, who had come down to take care of some business in Puerto Rico, also visited them.

Then Grace's thoughts turned to this eventful day—February 12, 1970. Along with Lyle and Ruth, she enjoyed an early breakfast and shared family devotions. Then 56-year-old Lyle had left in their Volkswagen bus to pick up a new dentist and a guest from the States who had heard that the missionary was an expert fisherman. She was ironing and Ruth, sitting nearby, was sewing when the phone call rudely and suddenly interrupted her life.

Upon arriving at the hospital, Grace and Ruth found many of the church people waiting for them. Their friends' countenances, reflecting a mix of strain and grief, conveyed the truth the wife and daughter already knew. Lyle was indeed dead!

Details of the accident were disclosed. Lyle and

his companions had first gone to the east end of the island, where they had no success. After picking up some shells and digging up some wild orchids to take home, they went to the northwest corner of the island, known for its red snapper fishing.

After preparing their lines, Lyle and the dentist walked across a black coral reef to the water's edge. No sooner than their lines were in the water, a huge wave knocked the two fishermen off their feet. A second swell, six to eight feet high, swept them out into a whirlpool. The dentist's guest ran up the hill to the coast guard station. The rescuers hurried down to the ocean and found the dentist on the shore—alive. But Lyle was floating facedown in the water. Apparently, his head had struck the coral, knocking him unconscious. Now Ruth knew why God had put it on her heart to come home and be with her dad one last time.

Two missionary couples came over from Puerto Rico to be with them. Bob flew in from Philadelphia to take care of the details. Lyle loved the Virgin Islands, so Deede asked Ruth to place a bag of Caribbean sand and shells in the casket.

At the funeral on Sunday afternoon, the church was packed with people who had known Lyle. The general church broadcast the service to missionaries around the world via shortwave radio. The next day another memorial service was held in Puerto Rico. Then on Tuesday, Grace and Ruth flew with Lyle's body to Los Angeles. Another fitting memorial service was conducted by Pastor Earl Lee at Pasadena First Church.

Groundbreaking for prayer chapel, 1972.
(L. to r.) **Dan Royer, Steve Reese, Grace Prescott,
and Ron Benefiel.**

Lyle's book, *Our 25 Years in the Caribbean,* was published in 1970, coming off the press just before his death. On the front cover is a silhouette of Lyle standing in the surf holding a fishing rod.

At the time of this tragedy, Pasadena College had been raising money for a prayer chapel. The student body president, Ron Benefiel, suggested that it be named the Lyle Prescott Memorial Prayer Chapel. When the college was relocated to Point

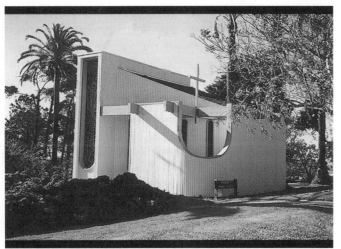
Lyle Prescott Memorial Prayer Chapel

Loma in San Diego, the prayer chapel was moved to the new campus, overlooking the Pacific Ocean.

After several days, Grace traveled to Kansas City to meet with Dr. E. S. Phillips, World Mission executive secretary. He told her no one was available at that time to replace her husband and asked her if she would be willing to return there for a time to oversee the work. She agreed.

> "My child," the Lord spoke to her spirit, "I have taken Lyle for My glory."

As Grace and Ruth flew back to St. Croix to resume the work, they observed a memorable sunset. Ruth had played "Beyond the Sunset" on her flute in one of her father's memorial services. "Mom, how beautiful!" Ruth commented. "To me this is a sign that God is confirming His will in your life."

"Amen," Grace whispered. Yet, her spirit was troubled.

Grace's life had been centered on Lyle and their children for so long that she naturally felt a tremendous void. Psalm 91 particularly bothered her. God hadn't protected Lyle as promised, and she even felt hesitant about reciting it.

"O God," Grace cried. "I don't understand. I just don't know why Lyle had to die."

"My child," the Lord spoke to her spirit, "I have taken Lyle for My glory."

"If Lyle had to leave me for Your honor and glory," the widow responded, "then I can accept it."

One morning Grace knelt at the altar in the church. "Heavenly Father, I have been a pastor's wife from the time I finished college. I really haven't worked in the secular world. I don't know how I can make a living. It seems that I don't have much of a future." As she waited before the Lord, she pled for His direction and rededicated her life to Him.

Taking her Bible, it fell open at Philippians 4:4, "Rejoice in the Lord alway: and again I say, Rejoice." *I really don't feel like rejoicing*, she thought. Then verses 6 and 7 continued, "Be careful for nothing; but in every thing by prayer and supplication with thanksgiving let your requests be made known unto God. And the peace of God, which passeth all understanding, shall keep your hearts and minds through Christ Jesus." And in verse 19 she read, "But my God shall supply all your need according to his riches in glory by Christ Jesus."

"God, thank You for Your Word," she prayed. "I know You will continue to meet my every need, that everything will work out. You've promised me that Your grace will be sufficient." She rose from the altar and left the church with a much lighter heart.

———

Louie and Ellen Bustle had been on St. Croix the year before as student volunteers, and the church folks wanted them to return to take over the work. The Bustles were asked if they would go as "associate missionaries" to pastor the church for two years when Louie's seminary year was over. They agreed, and the Cruzans were thrilled.

Grace conducted one last Vacation Bible School before leaving the islands. She and her helpers had an extraordinary two-week VBS with an average attendance of 298 children. Then Grace completed the mission records, turned them over to the Bustles, and flew to the States. It was the end of an era. She had completed 26 years as a missionary in the Caribbean—by the grace of God.

11

Serving and Ministering at Home

Grace sat in the sanctuary of Pasadena First Church, listening to the anointed preaching of Earl Lee. As he talked about the cycle of victorious living outlined in Psalm 37, she drank it in. His insightful messages shined new light on the scripture for her. She promised God that from then on she would trust, delight, commit, and then rest.

The Prescotts had joined Pasadena First in 1968, two years before Lyle's untimely death. When Grace and Ruth returned to the States, they became a part of the church, the site of Lyle and Grace's marriage 36 years earlier. Rev. Lee and his wife, Hazel, became close to Grace.

No task was too menial for this servant of the Lord.

One Sunday she talked with her pastor about her desire to become involved in the ministry of the congregation. She was not content to be just a sit-in-a-pew-and-keep-it-warm member. As the two visited, Dr. Lee looked around the sanctuary where they were standing.

"Grace, we need someone to make certain tissues at the altars are always available, that the Kleenex boxes are always full. Would you accept this ministry?"

"Certainly. I'll be glad to do this." And she did. Faithfully.

No task was too menial for this servant of the Lord. And over the next two and a half decades, Grace served the Lord in Pasadena First in myriad ways—member of the church board, sanctuary choir, and NMWS council; facilitator of a women's Bible study, which was so popular that ladies who wanted to participate were put on a waiting list; participant in Early Christians, a prayer group that met every Friday morning; and coordinator for the NMWS reading books for children, which she fulfilled by going to the kids' department during Sunday School to pass out the books.

Grace's distinctive ministry—the one for which Pasadena Nazarenes knew her best—was cooking. She prepared meals for church members who went out calling on Wednesday evenings, dinners for Sunday School classes, lunches for Bible study groups, and banquets for special occasions. She literally became the church cook.

This humble saint's contributions to the Kingdom extended beyond her local community of faith. For numerous years, she served on the Los

Angeles District NWMS Council and Laymen's Retreat Board.

But all these fulfilling ministries did not earn a living, and at age 60 Grace was not old enough to receive Social Security or a missionary pension. A friend in the church helped her obtain a job as an instructional aide in Pasadena Unified School District. It required the ability to speak Spanish, and Grace filled that qualification competently. Hired to teach children remedial reading, she kept this position for five years until her retirement.

God began to open other doors. Churches invited her to speak about the mission work, so she prepared a slide presentation and began to travel. Many times, while still teaching, she flew out of Los Angeles on Friday night, held services in some other part of the United States, and took a late Sunday night flight back home.

Word of Grace's gift soon circulated, and she began to hold missionary services and Faith Promise Conventions, even as far away as Hawaii and Alaska. Thrilled that God could use her in this way, she felt that the Lord was extending her ministry beyond Lyle's lifetime in a way never anticipated.

Grace was assigned a cottage at Casa Robles Missionary Retirement Center in California in 1976. For 22 years she enjoyed both her own cozy cottage and the fellowship of the other retired missionaries.

Not long after moving there, Grace learned that Louie and Ellen Bustle, along with Jerry and Toni Porter, were beginning Nazarene work in the Dominican Republic. They asked Grace to act as

**Grace at Casa Robles with
Dr. Louise Robinson Chapman, 1992.**

housemother to a group of college students among summer volunteers, who lived in small villages and held evangelistic services throughout the country. As a result of the efforts of all these groups, 11 churches were organized.

The next summer, at Louie Bustle's request, Grace escorted a group of 16 teens from Pasadena First Church to the Dominican Republic for six weeks. They worked hard. In spite of less-than-ideal living conditions, the teens loved the Dominicans and wanted to stay longer.

Even in retirement, Grace never lacked for ways to serve her Master. Whether in Pasadena, at Casa Robles, throughout the States, or around the world, God's will was her will—by His grace.

12

Taking Pride in Her Children

Robert (Bob) had a government career in the Department of Housing and Urban Development (HUD) as an administrator. In 1984, he left this federal agency and spent seven years helping organize and administer the new office of Nazarene Compassionate Ministries in Kansas City. He traveled extensively, organizing crises relief and self-help programs in 37 countries with money donated for humanitarian purposes. Then he was asked by HUD to return as director of the Detroit office. Later, he and his wife, Bernice, who also works for HUD, were assigned to the Washington, D.C., area.

In addition to supply pastoring for churches and holding other church leadership roles across the years, he has served as Washington District NWMS president for six years. At the 1997 General Assembly, he was elected to the NWMS General Council. Upon his retirement from HUD in May 1999, Bob returned to Nazarene Compassionate Ministries as administrative director. He is the father of three sons: Robert, Ronald, and Richard.

Delia (Deede), who attended both Pasadena Academy and Pasadena College, supported herself through school by working as a waitress, cleaning houses, and taking care of children. She remembers a sermon by Dr. W. T. Purkiser, then president of the college, titled "I Needed My Past." Looking back on her life, Deede is convinced her many experiences on the mission field in the areas of personal relationships and the ministry with her father have helped her in many aspects of life.

Deede, now retired from a successful business career, lives in Arizona with her husband, Rick Berman. They owned and operated a number of fast-food restaurants and a food-distribution business in California. After going on a mission trip to Guatemala to rebuild a Christian school destroyed by the 1976 earthquake, she returned to the United States determined to raise money to educate the disadvantaged Mayan children of that institution. She helped raise thousands of dollars to pay for the education of every child in the school. She continues this ministry with the Mayan Indians, organizing and leading several mission trips a year. She has five children: Rorie, Allen, Brad, Greg, and Chris.

Elwood (Woody) attended Pasadena College and took flying lessons on the side. He desired to be a pilot and eventually earned a commercial pilot's license. He met his future wife, Leslie, at college, and they were married in September of 1968 at Pasadena First Church. (The church gave a love

Grace with her four children, 1971.
***(L. to r.)* Bob, Deede, Woody, and Ruth.**

offering to Grace and Lyle so they could attend the ceremony, the only one of their children's weddings they were able to attend.)

Woody had a job flying commuter planes between Los Angeles International Airport and Lancaster, California. While waiting for openings with various airlines, he held other jobs, including working with public transportation in the Los Angeles area. His hobby was woodworking, and he loved helping people. He was always available to help any time of the day or night. He used his own truck to help senior adults who were moving into smaller quarters.

When Rev. Earl Lee announced that his son, Gary, was one of the hostages being held in Iran, Woody was most concerned. He obtained one of the metal bracelets that said "Gary E. Lee, State Department, Free the Hostages." Woody wore one and encouraged others to wear them until Gary was released.

━━━━━

When Ruth went to Spain as an exchange student, instead of staying six weeks she stayed two-and-a-half years. She loved being in a Spanish-speaking country again and obtained work teaching English at the Spanish Naval Academy. A tall, striking lady, she was given a contract to do modeling for the House of Balenciaga clothing line. This experience gave Ruth poise and the ability to dress with flair. After Lyle's death she returned to the States where she taught Spanish at Point Loma Nazarene University for several years. She was married in the Lyle Prescott Memorial Prayer Chapel on campus in 1977.

What a comfort Grace's children were to her!

The job most meaningful to her was for a private boarding school that served blind and mentally challenged adults. The goal of the organization was to train the occupants so they could leave the institution and live independently. Starting out as cook—Ruth was a gourmet chef—she was promoted to general manager and director of the enterprise.

When a second facility was opened, she was given the job of remodeling and redecorating the building. She developed a warm, attractive place, even though the residents were visually impaired. When asked why she expended so much energy to decorate, she replied, "Well, while they can't see, their families can. If it is attractive, families will visit more often and spend more time here." Ruth also believed that if God saw fit to heal and give her clients sight, she wanted the first thing they saw to be beautiful.

She loved her "students," and they loved her. When the residents heard her car drive up outside, they would chant "Ruth, Ruth, Ruth" until she walked in the door and greeted them.

———

What a comfort Grace's children were to her! And she took justifiable pride in their accomplishments, testimonies, and service for the Lord.

13

Experiencing More Loss

Even though Ruth appeared strong and robust, in 1979 she began to display symptoms of a cold that just would not go away, including a sore throat with swelling. She saw several doctors, but no one could diagnose her problem. Finally in April 1980, a Nazarene doctor determined that Ruth had Hodgkin's disease at the third stage. She entered City of Hope in Duarte, California, for chemotherapy. Her illness was found to be far advanced, although doctors said there would have been a 90 percent chance for a cure if diagnosed early. Ruth, a single parent with one child, Gracielinda, was only 33 years old when the disease engulfed her.

After two rounds of chemotherapy, the young mother was deathly ill, and her veins collapsed from all the injections. Grace moved in with Ruth to help take care of her and Gracielinda. Ruth was in and out of the hospital for over three years. It was an exhausting and difficult time, yet Grace survived by God's grace.

At the same time, Woody had a job driving a bus for the Los Angeles transit district. He asked for his route to be changed so he would have about

Grace with Woody at Pasadena First Church, 1975

10 minutes of turn-around time several times a day at the City of Hope. He spent this time with Ruth.

Early on the morning of August 27, 1980, Woody was driving his small truck to work on the Pasadena Freeway. A huge truck—its driver apparently asleep—struck Woody's vehicle and dragged it over 400 feet, crushing it against a wall. It exploded in flames, trapping its occupant inside. The only things left in the ashes of the horrible inferno were a metal briefcase, with Woody's driving logs and Bible inside, and Gary Lee's bracelet that he had been wearing.

The manner in which her son died was hard for Grace to bear. She had nightmares about it for a long time afterward. Deede, who had been close to Woody, had a dream about his tragic death. She saw his truck going down the freeway and catching fire. Out of a large, white cloud an arm came down and pulled Woody out of the cab and sat him up on the cloud. It was as if God was saying, "Woody didn't suffer. I took him away from all of that, and he's fine." Though this dream was comforting, Woody's death was a great blow. He had lived with Deede and her family while attending college and going to flight school, and the entire family was devastated.

Woody's memorial service, with over 1,200 attending, was held at Pasadena First Church in place of a Sunday evening service. Rev. Earl Lee passed a microphone through the congregation so anyone who wished could say something about Woody. Person after person told of a particular service Woody had rendered for them—fixing appliances, mowing lawns, repairing furniture, moving household goods, and so on. Woody had been there for people who didn't have anyone else to call on, and now they were paying him tribute. Those who met the humble man never forgot his loving and caring spirit. Woody was survived by his wife, Leslie, and three children: Clayton, Carolee, and Luke.

Grace did not blame God.

Since Ruth was fighting her own losing battle with cancer, her brother's loss was especially calamitous to her. And how difficult it became for the whole family, for they had to go from grieving for Woody to watching their beloved Ruthie grow ever weaker. She had prayed that she would not have to go through the last weeks of suffering that many cancer patients endure, and God answered

Grace with Ruth at Pasadena First Church, circa 1980.

her petition. Ruth gave Gracielinda a party on her fifth birthday in 1983, even decorating the cake and hiring a pony for the children to ride. Just nine days later, she passed away suddenly while in the hospital for treatment.

Ruth's funeral was special. Her family and friends, including all her blind students, came together to remember her and say good-bye. When the minister spoke her name, a chant arose from the students, "Ruth, Ruth, Ruth," just as they used to greet her when she drove up to the school. She had a tremendous influence on their lives, and today is still remembered for the unconditional love she gave them.

But how does a wife and mother comfort herself when she loses her husband and two youngest children in such unexpected, tragic ways? First of all, Grace did not blame God. She always said that the Lord knew what He was doing and He does not make mistakes. "It is at times like this that you lean on your faith," she testified, "and God's Word becomes your greatest comfort.

"Some years ago I was blessed by a remark made by my pastor's wife at a women's retreat," Grace continued. "While Hazel was a missionary in India, she often heard the statement, 'Don't wait until the rain comes to thatch your roof.' That comment reminded me that long ago—before my marriage, the birth of my children, and over 44 years in ministry and missionary life—I had 'thatched my roof' by settling my walk with God and turning to His Word for my strength. I have to admit that there were times of tears, sorrow, questioning, and despair over the loss of my loved ones, but His Word comforted me."

Grace's advice to anyone going through difficult times was to pray and read the Bible. "Let God give you some promises from His Word," she encouraged. "Memorize them. Quote them. Depend on them. God's Word is true."

Once again, Grace grieved and remembered and went on living—by the grace of God.

14

Going Home

The Prescott family held a reunion at Camp Pinerock, the Arizona District center in Prescott, in June 1998. Families were present from Florida, Oregon, Colorado, California, Arizona, and Washington, D.C.—85 people in all—ranging in age from 3 months to 87-year-old Grace, who attended in a wheelchair. What a wonderful time they had! On Sunday they had a service in the tabernacle with Bob speaking. The service closed by the relatives joining hands and singing together.

Camp Pinerock meant a great deal to Grace. She attended camp meeting there almost every summer for 25 years until the last couple of years when she was physically unable to climb the steps and walk to services. How fitting that the last earthly family reunion she would attend was at this beloved site.

Later that summer, when Grace became very weak and short of breath, her doctor installed a pacemaker. Unable to build up strength, the retired missionary was forced to curtail many of her activities.

When son, Bob, was the speaker at the Los Angeles District Laymen's Retreat in October, she was able to be with him. She spent Thanksgiving with Leslie (Woody's wife) and their two sons.

During the last 30 days of her life, due to declining health, Grace terminated her various ministries—facilitating the women's Bible study, cooking responsibilities, serving on the District NWMS Council and Laymen's Retreat Board. It seemed that the Lord was saying, "Grace, it's all right to cease your labors now. Time to come home, My precious child."

Early in December Bob flew to California to accompany Grace back to his home in Maryland, where she planned to stay through the Christmas holidays. Her breathing, however, became so labored that she was admitted to the hospital, where she stayed for a week. The medical team worked to reduce fluids, thin her blood, and establish a drug level that would allow her heart to function more easily. Grace was so glad to leave the hospital and return to Bob's home on December 16. She looked forward to addressing the envelopes for her annual Christmas letter.

Grace truly modeled a hope-filled and awe-filled lifestyle.

Always the "great encourager," Grace particularly enjoyed corresponding with people. She included a personal message in every Christmas greeting, and she responded to every holiday card with a thank-you note. Through the years, she wrote to countless individuals with words of en-

Grace with Deede and Bob at family reunion in 1998.

couragement, usually citing an appropriate scripture verse. She took special delight in communicating with college youth, as she remembered her days at Pasadena College and how important mail was to her at that time in her life.

Grace praised God no matter what happened, joyfully accepting the circumstances—even the hardships—of her life. Even through and in her many trials, she always gave thanks to her Lord for the amazing life He had allowed her to live. Grace truly modeled a hope-filled and awe-filled lifestyle.

Early the next morning on December 17, Grace passed away peacefully—by the grace of God. Bob and Deede mailed her Christmas letter, along with a message about her homegoing and an invitation to the memorial service. To quote from their letter, "Early this morning, she [Grace] had just risen from bed when, in an instant of transformation her heart ceased beating and her spirit took wings. Bob was at her side quickly, but she was already being welcomed to her heavenly home. The physical suffering and limitations she had quietly endured for 47 of her 88 years were over, and she entered into perfect health."

A service of celebration for Grace Irene Prescott was held at First Church of the Nazarene in Pasadena on Sunday, December 27, 1998. Many friends and family presented tributes, each one stressing the spirit of servanthood that characterized Grace's life and ministry. General Superintendent Jerry Porter gave the message. Dr. Louie Bustle, now World Mission Division director, presented the Grace Prescott Memorial Project, a fund that has been established to construct a building in Cuba in her honor.

It was Grace's prayer that those hearing the story of her life would be inspired to let God reign and rule completely in their lives. She knew from personal experience that it is the happiest and most fruitful way to live. One of her favorite hymns, "Jesus Led Me All the Way," was sung at her funeral. From her childhood to her prime-time years, she was truly led all the way—*by the grace of God.*

Pronunciation Guide

The following information is provided to assist in pronouncing unfamiliar words in the book. The suggested pronunciations, though not always precise, are close approximations of the way the terms are pronounced in English.

Antigua	an-TEE-gwuh or an-TEE-guh
bacalau	bah-kah-LAU
Balenciaga	bah-lehn-see-AH-gah
bodegas	bod-DAY-gahs
Christiansted	KRIHS-chuhn-STEHD
Croix	KROI
Cruzan	KROO-zhuhn
DeGrasse	dee-GRAS
de Santana	day sahn-TAHN-nah
Duarte	DWAHR-tee
Frederiksted	FREHD-er-ihk-STEHD
Guati	GWAH-tee
Guiro	GWEE-roh
Guirito	gwee-REE-toh
Hildo Morejon	EHL-doh moh-ray-HOHN
Jorge	HOHR-hay
Valencia	vuh-LEHN-shee-uh
Villegas	vee-YAY-gahs
Venegas	vay-NAY-gahs
Yoakum	YOH-kuhm